Beyond Garrison
Antislavery and Social Reform

Why was antebellum Massachusetts one of the few Northern states in which African American males enjoyed the right to vote? Why did it pass personal liberty laws that helped protect fugitive slaves from federal authorities in the two decades preceding the Civil War? Why did the Bay State at this time integrate its public facilities and public schools? *Beyond Garrison* finds answers to these important questions in unfamiliar and surprising places. Its protagonists are not the leading lights of American abolitionism grouped around William Lloyd Garrison but are the less well-known men and women in country towns and villages, encouraged by African American activists throughout the state. Bruce Laurie's fresh approach trains the spotlight on the politics of such antislavery advocates. Laurie demonstrates their penchant for third-party politics, with a view toward explaining the relationship between social movements based on race, class, and nationality, on the one hand, and political insurgency, on the other.

Bruce Laurie was born in Linden, New Jersey, and received his Ph.D. from the University of Pittsburgh in 1971. He did postdoctoral work at the University of Pennsylvania and has taught at Mount Holyoke College and the University of Warwick. He is currently Professor of History at the University of Massachusetts Amherst. Professor Laurie has been honored with fellowships from the Carnegie Foundation, the National Endowment for the Humanities, and the American Antiquarian Society. He has traveled to Western Europe, West Africa, the Caribbean, and Mexico, and he is a member of the Organization of American Historians and the American Historical Association. His articles and reviews have appeared in numerous collections of essays, as well as in *Labor History*, *Journal of Social History*, and *Journal of American History*. Professor Laurie is on the editorial committee of *Labor: Studies in Working-Class History of the Americas*. He is the coeditor of *Class, Sex, and the Woman Worker* (1977) and of *Labor Histories: Class, Politics, and the Working-Class Experience* (1998). He is also the author of *Working People of Philadelphia, 1800–1850* (1980), and *Artisans into Workers: Labor in Nineteenth-Century America* (1989).

Beyond Garrison

Antislavery and Social Reform

BRUCE LAURIE
University of Massachusetts Amherst

CAMBRIDGE
UNIVERSITY PRESS

CAMBRIDGE UNIVERSITY PRESS
Cambridge, New York, Melbourne, Madrid, Cape Town, Singapore, São Paulo

Cambridge University Press
40 West 20th Street, New York, NY 10011-4211, USA

www.cambridge.org
Information on this title: www.cambridge.org/9780521844086

First published 2005

Printed in the United States of America

A catalog record for this publication is available from the British Library.

Library of Congress Cataloging in Publication Data

Laurie, Bruce.
Beyond Garrison : antislavery and social reform / Bruce Laurie.
   p.   cm.
Includes bibliographical references.
ISBN 0-521-84408-8 – ISBN 0-521-60517-2 (pbk.)
1. Antislavery movements – Massachusetts – History – 19th century.
2. Abolitionists – Massachusetts – History – 19th century.   3. African American
abolitionists – Massachusetts – History – 19th century.   4. African Americans – Civil
rights – Massachusetts – History – 19th century.   5. Massachusetts – Politics and
government – 1775–1865.   6. Massachusetts – Race relations – Political aspects.
7. Social movements – Massachusetts – History – 19th century.   8. Social reformers –
Massachusetts – History – 19th century.   I. Title.
E445.M4L38   2005
326′.8′09744–dc22   2004020223

ISBN-13   978-0-521-84408-6 hardback
ISBN-10   0-521-84408-8 hardback

ISBN-13   978-0-521-60517-5 paperback
ISBN-10   0-521-60517-2 paperback

For Becca

Contents

Illustrations

Acknowledgments

This book took shape in my mind during my residency at the American Antiquarian Society in 1993–4, which was funded through a grant from the American Antiquarian Society/National Endowment for the Humanities Fellowship and the generosity of Lee R. Edwards, Dean of the College of Humanities and Fine Arts at the University of Massachusetts Amherst. Dean Edwards topped off my fellowship by allowing me to stretch a semester-long stay into a year's leave. I arrived at the American Antiquarian Society thinking about a project on the social life and politics of the "middling class," the spongy social layer of petty proprietors and small farmers poised between the established middle class and the working class. My preliminary work showed the middling sort to be a nervous and rambunctious lot with a habit of fueling third-party insurgencies in Massachusetts, and as far as I could tell at the time, elsewhere in the North as well. I already knew something of this group's political activism with tradesmen in the Working Men's parties of the Jacksonian Era but was surprised to find that its leaders – and village journalists especially – were also deeply involved in antislavery politics. I was just as surprised to learn that very few historians had paid much attention to the nitty-gritty of the political activism of abolitionist groups apart from giving us the groups' occupational breakdowns to show that workers and small employers formed the backbone of abolitionism and antislavery. I decided to concentrate on antislavery politics in Massachusetts because, frankly, I was looking for a good excuse to write about the place I have called home for more than thirty years and because antislavery was stronger there than anywhere else. I must confess that I have always found the

union of personal and professional interests to be a powerful incentive. I
was drawn in, and I have never regretted it.

I made some progress on my project at the American Antiquarian Society but had to put it on hold for three years while I served a term
as chair of my department at the University of Massachusetts Amherst.
When I got back to researching and writing in early 1998, I benefited
greatly from the help of many people. I cannot say enough about the
staff at the American Antiquarian Society. I mean no insult to any other
library or staff when I say that in my experience there is no library quite
like the society's, and not simply for its voluminous collection of materials on American history through Reconstruction. Its staff combines
uncommon courtesy and professionalism with a genuine eagerness to assist and delight in helping scholars to succeed. I especially would like to
thank Georgia B. Barnhill, Joanne D. Chaison, and Marie E. Lamoureux
for directing me to helpful sources. President Ellen S. Dunlap and Vice
President for Collections and Programs John B. Hench both offered me
the support of their offices along with a firm hand of friendship that has
endured to this day. Daria D'Arienzo, Head of Archives and Special Collections at Amherst College; Sherrill Redmond, Coordinator of Special
Collections of the Sophia Smith Collection at Smith College; and Tevis
Kimball, Curator of the Boltwood Room at Jones Library in the town of
Amherst all graciously put up with my requests for more and more mate-
rials. So did the librarians of the Massachusetts Historical Society, notably
Megan Friedel and Kim Nusco. William Thompson, Stephen T. Robinson,
and Michael Milewski of the W.E.B. DuBois Library on my campus helped
me track down graphics and retrieve obscure public documents. Deputy
Archivist John McColgan and Reference Archivist Kristen Sweet at the
Archives of the City of Boston were particularly accommodating, as
was John Harrington III, Reference Archivist at the Massachusetts State
Library in Boston. I also would like to thank, in no particular order, the
following librarians and library staff: Kate Boyle, Martha Mayo, Nancy
Richard, Cara Gilgenbach, William O. Dupuis, Margaret R. Dakin,
Marian Walker, Adam Novitt, Faith Kaufman, Brian Tabor, Karen V.
Kukil, and Peter Nelson. Special thanks go to Dr. Kathleen Nutter at
the Sophia Smith Collection, Ms. Susan J. Lisk, Executive Director of the
Porter Phelps Huntington Foundation, and Ms. Jean M. Crossman of the
Imaging Department at the University of Massachusetts Amherst.

Several historians went out of their way to help me work through this
manuscript. Professor Kevin Sweeney of Amherst College could easily
have written this book himself. Before he moved on to other subjects,

he wrote pioneering work on Massachusetts politics at the turn of the 1840s. Professor Sweeney turned over to me his files from his own graduate school project when he learned of my project. Professor Edmund B. Thomas, Jr., of Fitchburg State College in Massachusetts shared with me his extensive files on the party affiliations and votes of the representatives and senators in the Massachusetts General Court. Paul Gaffney and Jonathan Tucker shared their illuminating manuscripts on African Americans in Northampton and Amherst, respectively. Leonard L. Richards, my colleague in the History Department at UMass, offered invaluable criticism of my introduction and of Chapter 8. Eric Arnesen of the University of Illinois at Chicago helped sharpen my thinking on the questions of racial identity and the politics of race. David Montgomery, my longtime mentor, has retired from Yale but not from history or indeed friendship or constructive criticism. Having read the entire manuscript, he offered characteristically sharp and illuminating help. Marla Miller and Barry Levy, fellow historians in my department who are engaged in important work on early Massachusetts, generously compared notes with me while offering their unflagging inspiration and encouragement. David Glassberg, my department chair, provided unstinting financial support at key junctures. I have also benefited in myriad ways from the intellectual stimulation of the following people: Mary Wilson, Philip Khoury, Paula Baker, Jules Chametzky, Edward Countryman, Daniel Czitrom, Daniel Gordon, Alfred Young, Christopher Clark, Brian Ogilvie, Ronald P. Formisano, John Higginson, Robert Gross, John Bracey, Francis Couvares, Stephen Nissenbaum, Michael Hillard, Milton Cantor, Elisabeth Lasch-Quinn, David Blight, and Eric Foner.

A good number of graduate and undergraduate students, whose published and unpublished work is cited in this book, made significant contributions to this work. Over the last decade or so, Patrick Brown, Patric Whitcomb, Sara Dubow, Robert Montgomery, Glendyne Wergland, Patrick H. Crim, Hal Goldman, Kazuteru Omori, Andrew Barker, Robin Henry, Mark Santow, Dan Koprowski, and Brad Paul wrote dissertations and seminar papers on various aspects of Massachusetts politics that sharpened my thinking and greatly enriched my narrative. William F. Hartford directed me to useful sources and through his fine work on the Boston Associates helped clear a path for my own work. Andrew Gyory, Matthew H. Crocker, and Mark Voss-Hubbard, who have also gone on to do revisionist work on Massachusetts politics, showed how it is possible be loyal friends, invaluable sounding boards, and sharp critics at once. Alexander Laytin, a gifted undergraduate history major, did not flinch when I recommended that he investigate a faction of the Democratic Party for his senior thesis; he produced a first-class study that makes a real contribution to the literature. Brian Bixby, a talented doctoral candidate in my department and historian in-the-making, checked my references and footnotes.

It is difficult to be grateful enough to Cambridge University Press. In an age that has seen the craft of the book go the way of the cordwainer and handloom weaver, Cambridge stands out as an island of artful production and intellectual integrity. Senior Editor Lewis Bateman has been a great source of support and encouragement, the kind of editor every writer ought to have. Ciara McLaughlin, his editorial assistant, did splendid work, as did Senior Production Controller Eric Schwartz. Lewis also chose rigorous and dutiful outside readers who, alas, I know only as Reader A and Reader B but who can take much of the credit for whatever intellectual virtues readers find in this book. They provided particularly helpful advice on how I might better set the political context in which my story unfolds and on how I might present my thesis in light of previous work. This flattery extends to Carolyn Sherayko, who did my index. I am especially grateful to Camilla T. Knapp, Production Editor at Cambridge University Press, and to my copy editor, Susan Greenberg, who offered superb editorial assistance. Their careful and subtle reading of the manuscript greatly improved the text. I took most of their advice, along with that of the reviewers I mentioned, but assure readers that any mistakes or misconceptions in the finished work are mine, not theirs.

No acknowledgment of friends and colleagues who helped bring this book along would be complete without mention of academic venues that allowed me to try out my ideas. I benefited greatly from commentary on what became Chapter 4 at a session of the New England Seminar at the American Antiquarian Society in 1993. A meeting of the New England Historical Association in 2002, chaired by Professor Melanie Gustafson of the University of Vermont, provided stimulating commentary on my thesis about race. In between, in 1997, I read a version of my work on political reform to a meeting of the Five College History Seminar, which helped me to clarify my thesis on the fit between insurgent politics and what I call "Yankeedom," or the culture of small-town New England. That the seminar, now more than thirty years old, has become an intellectual mainstay of our Five College System is in no small measure due to the generous support of Five College Executive Director Lorna Peterson and Director of Academic Programs Nate Therien. Finally, I have long had the honor and pleasure of being affiliated with the Milan Study Group, the sponsor for more than twenty years of a biennial seminar that brings a small group of Americans specializing in the antebellum period together with their European counterparts. Founded and directed by Professor Loretta Valtz Mannucci of the University of Milan, the seminar has consistently provided equal measures of exemplary hospitality and intellectual stimulation. I have read several papers there over the years, most recently a draft in 2000 of what became Chapter 8 in this book. I was then and continue to be grateful to the seminar participants for their helpful criticism; it goes without saying that all of us owe a deep debt of gratitude to Professor Mannucci for all that she has done over the years. Her recent retirement closes an important chapter in the transatlantic discussion of American history.

I need to mention extraprofessional sources of support. On the theory that all work and no play makes one a dull historian, I have to say that I have been blessed with longtime friends not connected with the academy. I have known Ed Hack and Travis Cronshey since undergraduate days, Bob Sawicki longer, and Joe Ziepniewski longer still. I always look forward to the relief their company affords me from the rigors of the academy, all the more so when the occasion is a fly-fishing trip to Maine, Canada, or wherever. There is no substitute for their humor and fellowship, except for the love and support I derive from family. Leslie Laurie, my wife and friend, has always been there for me. She has helped me balance work, home, and leisure. Our daughter, Becca, now in her second year of college, has left our rural redoubt for the bright lights of the city. She went there with our blessing and in her own quiet way brushed aside the adage that you're not supposed to do what your parents do – and in particular what your father does. An eager student of history in her high school days, she continues to study U.S. history in college, and if she does not go on to become a historian, she will likely remain one of the rare Americans whose understanding of the present is informed by her understanding of the past. One could do a lot worse. This book is dedicated to her because of what she means to me regardless of what she chooses to become professionally. She will always be my best friend and loving daughter.

Abbreviations Used in Footnotes

Journals

AAAPSS	*Annals of the American Academy of Political and Social Science*
AHR	*American Historical Review*
ANCH	*American Nineteenth Century History*
AQ	*American Quarterly*
CWH	*Civil War History*
EIHC	*Essex Institute Historical Collections*
FS	*Feminist Studies*
HC	*Historia Contempóranea*
HJM	*Historical Journal of Massachusetts*
HSSH	*Histoire Sociale/Social History*
IESS	*International Encyclopedia of the Social Sciences*
ILWCH	*International Labor and Working-Class History*
JAH	*Journal of American History*
JNH	*Journal of Negro History*
JSH	*Journal of Social History*
LH	*Labor History*
MHR	*Massachusetts Historical Review*
NEJBS	*New England Journal of Black Studies*
NEM	*New England Magazine*
NEQ	*New England Quarterly*
NST	*Nature, Society, and Thought*
NYH	*New York History*
PAAS	*Proceedings of the American Antiquarian Society*

PH	*Pennsylvania History*
PHR	*Pacific Historical Review*
RAH	*Reviews in American History*
WMQ	*William and Mary Quarterly*

Newspapers (arranged by place)

AR	*Amherst Record*
BA	*Boston Atlas*
BB	*Boston Bee*
BC	*Boston Courier*
BDA	*Boston Daily Advertiser*
BET	*Boston Evening Transcript*
BM	*Boston Daily Mail*
BMJ	*Bostonian and Mechanics' Journal*
BMJA	*Boston Mechanic and Journal of the Useful Arts*
BP	*Boston Morning Post*
BR	*Boston Reformer*
Comm	(Boston) *The Commonwealth*
DC	(Boston) *The Chronotype*
Eman	(Boston) *Emancipator (and Republican)*
Lib	(Boston) *The Liberator*
LJNS	(Boston) *Latimer Journal and North Star*
NEA	(Boston) *New England Artisan*
PU	(Boston) *Protective Union*
FRM	(Fall River) *The Monitor*
M	(Fall River) *The Mechanic*
GAR	*Greenfield American Republic*
GGC	*Greenfield Gazette and Courier*
LA	*Lowell American*
VI	(Lowell and Boston) *Voice of Industry*
VP	(Lowell) *Voice of the People*
NAWT	*North Adams Weekly Transcript*
HG	(Northampton) *Hampshire Gazette*
HH	*Hampshire Herald*

NC   *Northampton Courier*

PS   *Pittsfield Sun*
NS   (Rochester, N.Y.) *North Star*

SR   *Springfield Republican*

MS   (Worcester) *Massachusetts Spy*
SSWR   (Worcester) *State Sentinel and Worcester Reformer*
WRTW   *Worcester Reformer and True Washingtonian*

Manuscript Collections

GFP   Garrison Family Papers, Sophia Smith Collection, Smith College, Northampton, Mass.
PPHFP   Porter Phelps Huntington Family Papers, Amherst College Archives and Special Collections, Amherst, Mass.
WSP   William Schouler Papers, Massachusetts Historical Society, Boston
WSRP   William S. Robinson Papers, Boston Public Library

FIGURE 1. Leaders of the Free Soil Party in Massachusetts. *Left to right*: Henry Wilson, Anson Burlingame, Erastus Hopkins, Nathaniel Prentiss Banks, and George S. Boutwell. (Daguerreotype. Courtesy Massachusetts Historical Society, Boston, Mass.)

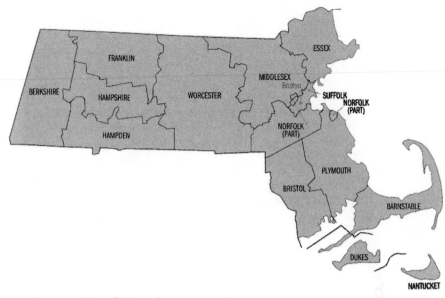

FIGURE 2. Map of Massachusetts counties.

Beyond Garrison

Antislavery and Social Reform

Introduction

Beyond Garrison is about the politicization of abolitionism in antebellum Massachusetts. It seeks to show how and why a group of abolitionists embraced political action at the turn of the 1830s and where they took the movement over the next two decades. It is not a study of William Lloyd Garrison, not directly anyway. No historian of abolitionism, least of all one writing about the Bay State, can afford to ignore Garrison, for no other abolitionist of the age had such sweeping renown. As the best-known abolitionist in the United States, Garrison was also the one American known to everyone in the Caribbean, Latin America, and Western Europe. Yet each generation of Americans, it seems, needs to rediscover Garrison. In the last half century, nearly a dozen biographies of Garrison and scores of articles on him have appeared, a vast body of work that initially treated his public life and more recently has delved into his upbringing and private affairs. We know him as well as or better than we know any other leading figure in his time.[1]

---

[1] On Garrison's personal life, see R. Jackson Wilson, *Figures of Speech: The Literary Marketplace, From Benjamin Franklin to Emily Dickinson* (New York: Knopf, 1989), pp. 117–58, and Harriet Hyman Alonso, *Growing Up Abolitionist: The Story of the Garrison Children* (Amherst: Univ. of Massachusetts Press, 2002). On his public life, see John L. Thomas, *The Liberator: William Lloyd Garrison* (Boston: Little, Brown, 1963); Walter McIntosh Merrill, *Against Wind and Tide: A Biography of William Lloyd Garrison* (Cambridge: Harvard Univ. Press, 1963); Aileen S. Kraditor, *Means and Ends in American Abolitionism: Garrison and His Critics on Strategy and Tactics, 1834–1850* (New York: Pantheon Books, 1969); James Brewer Stewart, *William Lloyd Garrison and the Challenge of Emancipation* (Arlington Heights, Ill.: H. Davidson, 1992); and Henry Mayer, *All on Fire: William Lloyd Garrison and the Abolition of Slavery* (New York: St. Martin's Press, 1998).

There is also much we do not know or do not fully appreciate, not so much about Garrison as about the larger antislavery project. This void stems in part from scholars' enduring fascination with Garrison, a fascination that has left much of the antislavery movement in his shadow. The problem goes beyond the narrow focus of biography as a genre to the tendency of some abolitionist biographers and institutional historians alike to view abolitionism from a Garrisonian perspective on the question of the strategy and tactics needed to end slavery and bring about racial equality.

Such scholars maintain that the tactic of moral suasion, an enduring signature of Garrisonianism in the antebellum years, represented a more exalted order of activity than political action did. Henry Mayer's recent and much acclaimed biography of Garrison, which traces the roots of moral suasion to the Protestant doctrine of the moral autonomy of the individual, accepts the Garrisonian dictum that the reformation of the self had to precede voting or indeed collective action in general. Mayer's perspective reverses a derisive portrait of "the great agitator" sketched by Albert Hobbs Barnes in the 1930s and famously elaborated by Stanley Elkins twenty-five years later. Those historians alternately depicted Garrison and his followers as "anarchists" and "fanatics," driven by a self-defeating "anti-institutional radicalism" that rejected the fundamental institutions of order and authority from political parties and churches down to the Constitution.[2] Barnes facetiously repeated the charge hurled at Garrison in 1836 that the abolitionist "nominated Jesus Christ to be President of the United States and the World," or, more accurately, that Garrison would have done so had he believed in the efficacy of political action.[3] For his part, Mayer sounds very much like Garrison himself, asserting that "voters first had to accept immediatism as their soul-force" before they could be trusted to do the right thing at the ballot box. Otherwise, they were mere "tools of party" and not "free moral agents," just as Garrison had maintained.[4] Mayer takes Garrison's detractors to task for having "narrowed the story of abolitionism" after 1840 by drawing attention to its political stage.[5]

---

[2] Mayer, *All on Fire*; Albert Hobbs Barnes, *The Antislavery Impulse* (New York: D. Appleton-Century, 1933); and Stanley M. Elkins, *Slavery: A Problem in American Institutional and Intellectual Life* (1959; Chicago: Univ. of Chicago Press, 1963). Also Richard Hofstadter, *The American Political Tradition and the Men Who Made It* (New York: Alfred A. Knopf, 1948), pp. 137–63.

[3] Barnes, *Antislavery Impulse*, p. 93.

[4] Mayer, *All on Fire*, pp. 263–4 and 276. Quote is on p. 263.

[5] Ibid., pp. 358–9, 274–7, 368–9, and 381–3.

This uncritical acceptance of Garrisonian moral suasion applies to Garrison's position on race as well. A principled foe of racism, Garrison found it impossible to envision emancipation or racial equality without a thoroughgoing transformation of the hearts of men and women. Political abolitionists, said Garrison's early friend Frederick Douglass, looked upon slavery as "the creature of law; we regarded it as a creature of public opinion."[6] This distinction between the morality of race and slavery and their politics forms the core of scholarly assessment of Garrison's activism. Critics see Garrison's perfectionism as a liability. It "defined goals," writes John L. Thomas, "and at the same time denied the authority of institutions through which these goals might be attained."[7] Garrison's admirers, of course, see it differently. Their version of the shift from moral suasion to political antislavery is a declension narrative, a retreat from high-minded egalitarianism to the opportunism of the Liberty Party, the first legitimate antislavery party, formed in 1840, and then of the Free Soil Party, the Liberty Party's successor, formed in 1848. A standard declensionist account argues that the Liberty Party sacrificed on the altar of electoral politics the racial idealism it inherited from Garrisonianism. The party's "sensitivity" to "Northern rights" bore the "makings of a white supremacist's antislavery, an ideology in which racism and sectionalism could easily reinforce one another." The Free Soilers strayed even farther from racial enlightenment, denouncing slavery "as a menace to white society" yet "expressing contempt for black-skinned people."[8] The point of this work is that political abolitionism was essentially racist.

The Garrisonian denigration of politics brings the current political scene to mind. We see it in the entrepreneurs and Hollywood idols who seek office, as H. Ross Perot did in 1992 and Arnold Schwarzenegger in 2003. Such individuals run not so much as antiestablishment figures but as antipoliticians with no political experience. Some observers attribute the current political climate to modern-day culture warriors and

---

[6] Douglass, quoted in ibid., p. 326.

[7] Thomas, *Liberator*, p. 232.

[8] James Brewer Stewart, *Holy Warriors: The Abolitionists and American Slavery* (New York: Hill and Wang, 1976), p. 105. Richard H. Sewell, *Ballots for Freedom: Antislavery Politics in the United States, 1837–1860* (New York: Oxford Univ. Press, 1976), pp. 95–100 and 158–60, takes a more balanced view on the Libertyites and the Free Soilers, as does Eric Foner, "Racial Attitudes of the New York Free Soilers," in Foner, *Politics and Ideology in the Age of the Civil War* (New York: Oxford Univ. Press, 1980), pp. 77–93.

identity politicians who resemble the Garrisonians, partly in their single-issue zealotry but mostly in their holier-than-thou celebration of the "cultures" of "the other" as morally pure and unerringly correct, and in their condemnation of politics as corrupt. The sociologist Todd Gitlin, for one, assails the rigidity of modern-day culture warriors, whose purity and absolutism "de-moralize the proponents of commonality, choke off the forbearance, the reciprocity, and, yes, the deal-making that are the pre-requisites of a successful democratic politics in a complicated society."[9] The civil rights activist Bayard Rustin was aware of this tendency long before Gitlin. He despaired over the slogan "the personal is political" because it substituted the politics of metaphor and symbolism for the nitty-gritty politics of civil rights and economic equality. As Rustin ruefully put it, "People who seek social change will, in the absence of real substantive victories, often seize upon stylistic substitutes."[10] This is not to suggest that political flexibility ought to be an end in itself. There is obviously much to be said for sticking to principle and for shunning compromises that are unquestionably harmful, as anyone familiar with the Constitution's infamous "three-fifths clause" presumably would concede.[11] But ruling out politics and compromise as a matter of principle is self-defeating.

This contemporary disenchantment with politics extends to historians, who in the last twenty years or so have shown more interest in the study of society and culture than in the study of politics. I will have more to say on this later. Here it is enough to observe that no aspect of the new cultural history is more important than its work on race. The advent of "whiteness studies," as the study of race is now called, has deepened the perception embedded in past work on political antislavery that racism has

---

[9] Todd Gitlin, *The Twilight of Common Dreams: Why America Is Wracked by Culture Wars* (New York: Henry Holt, 1995), p. 35. Also see pp. 126–65. Richard Rorty, *Achieving Our Country: Leftist Thought in Twentieth-Century America* (Cambridge: Harvard Univ. Press, 1998), goes a step farther in a condemnation of the left, both old and new, for their misguided idealisms headed by rejecting patriotism and incrementalism, only to call in the end for a kind of utopianism. One can regret Rorty's confusion and hackneyed treatment of the left on most issues (save patriotism) and still find merit in his impatience with the politics of identity.

[10] See John D'Emilio, *The Life and Times of Bayard Rustin* (New York: The Free Press, 2003). Quote is from Michael Anderson, "The Organizer," *New York Times Sunday Magazine*, Nov. 9, 2003, p. 13.

[11] See, for instance, Gary B. Nash, *Race and Revolution* (Madison, Wisc.: Madison House, 1990), and Leonard L. Richards, *The Slave Power: The Free North and Southern Domination, 1780–1860* (Baton Rouge: Louisiana State Univ. Press, 2000).

long pervaded American culture and politics.[12] Such an analysis makes the racial liberalism of the Garrisons of American history look rather admirable.

This book runs against the grain of the recent wisdom on antislavery and race. It argues that political action was an effective strategy consistent with moral rectitude and not a naive plunge into a smarmy world of compromise and accommodation. It does not question Garrison's sincerity on political action or race relations, only the efficaciousness of his strategy of moral suasion. Garrison's relentless agitation in the name of equal rights shook a nation that needed plenty of shaking. He tried hard to make antebellum Americans aware of the contradiction between the nation's lofty ideals enshrined in the Declaration of Independence and its disgraceful treatment of African Americans, as well as make them aware of the complicity of Northerners and their institutions – including the Protestant churches – in the maintenance of Southern slavery. But while Garrison may have awakened the conscience of some Northerners, he also led his followers into something of a moral dead end. He steadfastly insisted that the answer to the moral cleansing of individual souls was more moral cleansing, a seemingly endless pursuit of self-purification that mistook the avoidance of politics for progress even as political abolitionism eclipsed his own movement.

Many of the "other" antislavery reformers who appear in this book abhorred slavery and racial discrimination as passionately as did Garrison. Some national leaders in the Liberty Party, it is true, and many more Free Soilers, gradually traded immediate emancipation for the containment of slavery in the South, and they drew back from the racial equality that was the hallmark of Garrisonianism. Not a few of them can be described only as racists. However, their Bay State counterparts pursued a more idealist course. Elizur Wright, Chauncey Langdon Knapp, and Henry Ingersoll Bowditch were but a few of the state's Libertyites turned Free Soilers who fought against slavery and against the exclusion of blacks from public facilities. They reacted strongly to events on the national scene such as the Mexican War and the Fugitive Slave Act without losing sight of the impact of slavery and race on state politics. With the approval and

---

[12] David R. Roediger, *The Wages of Whiteness: Race and the Making of the American Working Class* (1991; New York: Verso, 1999). For a critical review of this genre, see Eric Arnesen et al., "Whiteness and the Historians' Imagination," *ILWCH* 60 (Fall 2001): 3–92.

support of African American activists they worked hard and successfully for laws that offered fugitive slaves some protection from slave catchers, gave black children access to mainline schools, and allowed African American travelers to use public transportation without the humiliation of Jim Crow accommodations. Indeed, few antislavery advocates waged a harder battle against segregation in antebellum Massachusetts than did Bowditch.

If Bowditch and his friends do not fit the image of the racist projected in whiteness literature, neither is it helpful to think of them as though they were modern liberals who believe in racial equality. Rare was the Bay Stater in and around antislavery circles who thought that blacks were the equals of whites.[13] Men like Bowditch were racists of a sort (if by that one means committed to white supremacy), but their racism was different from that of the street-corner toughs and courthouse politicians who sought to harm African Americans in the streets and in politics. My point is that there was no single perspective on race either in antebellum Massachusetts or probably anywhere else at the time; instead, there was a spectrum of opinion bound up with the larger context of racism by benign paternalism and militant colonizationism. Different states and regions were situated at different points on this spectrum, with New England located toward the paternalistic end and Massachusetts at the region's forefront.

Because they were politicians bent on winning elections and exercising political power, Free Soilers had to work out alliances with groups that did not necessarily share their main objective of abolishing slavery. This need for alliances proved to be at once controversial and troublesome. It was controversial because the single-issue men in the Free Soil Party's ranks feared that tacking more planks onto its platform risked distracting the party from ending slavery and improving the conditions of African Americans. Also, some Free Soilers were economic conservatives and as such were uneasy with demands for popular reform that welled from below. It was troublesome because the Free Soilers had to assemble a diverse coalition of groups. Some of these groups were organized into movements, as were the labor reformers, prohibitionists, and African Americans; others were only loosely associated as interests, as were the countryfolk angry at

[13] For an engaging discussion of the problem of race and racial identity, see John Stauffer, *The Black Hearts of Men: Racial Abolitionists and the Transformation of Race* (Cambridge: Harvard Univ. Press, 2002). Also see Paul Goodman, *Of One Blood: Abolitionism and the Origins of Racial Equality* (Berkeley and Los Angeles: Univ. of California Press, 1998).

Boston for its economic and political power. The politics of alliance and coalition enhanced the influence and power of Bay State Free Soilers, but it also unleashed debilitating factional discord.

The central importance of coalitions in the making of antislavery politics in Massachusetts has decisively shaped the perspective of this book. It quickly became clear to me that it made no sense to reproduce the conventional angle of vision on the reform groups radiating around antislavery from the core of the movement to its periphery. We already have a pretty good idea of how abolitionists perceived labor reformers and feminists, but we have a poorer one of how those reformers looked upon antislavery. This is especially true for groups that have received scant attention, such as African Americans, villagers, and townsfolk. Therefore I dedicate much space in this book to social movements and, in particular, to their relationships to antislavery. I thus build on the pioneering work done on Bay State politics by Ronald P. Formisano, who studied the fit between popular movements, on the one hand, and regular politics and third-party insurgencies, on the other.[14]

The politics of race (and class) is an important part of my story. Recent scholarship on "whiteness" identifies working people as the shock troops of racism. This mounting body of work, based deeply in popular culture, is necessarily inferential.[15] It assumes, for example, that workers who attended Jim Crow concerts, one of the more popular amusements for the many, accepted the racist stereotypes in such entertainment. Such an approach is understandable given the paucity of direct evidence; one searches labor papers and private correspondence in vain for commentary by ordinary workers on race. Working people were even more reticent on the topic than their social betters, forcing historians to look for other evidence. Two other sources, which inform this book, offer a different picture. One source is the social composition of antislavery societies in Massachusetts. Recent studies show, as this one does, that wage-earning workingmen and workingwomen were a significant segment of a larger social configuration consisting of middling people, that is, mechanics, small retailers, and petty professionals.[16] The question is how to interpret

---

[14] Ronald P. Formisano, *The Transformation of Political Culture: Massachusetts Parties, 1790s–1840s* (New York: Oxford Univ. Press, 1983).

[15] See also Roediger, *Wages of Whiteness*, and Noel Ignatiev, *How the Irish Became White* (New York: Routledge, 1995).

[16] Edward Magdol, *The Antislavery Rank and File: A Social Profile of the Abolitionists' Constituency* (Westport, Conn.: Greenwood Press, 1986); John B. Jentz, "The Antislavery Constituency in Jacksonian New York City," *CWH* 27 (June 1981): 101–22; and

such a finding. Because local antislavery societies expressed sympathy for slaves and for free blacks we can dismiss the possibility that such workers were the sneering racists featured in the literature. The other source on race is politics. Voting patterns for the Liberty Party and the Free Soil Party point in the same direction as the antislavery societies, if in a qualified way. Workers who voted for the Libertyites were probably closer to the abolitionist spirit than workers who were Free Soilers. The Free Soil Party drew a wider popular vote that likely included men animated by racial hatred and by the region's historic antipathy to the South, an antipathy heightened by the tightening of sectional tensions at the turn of the 1840s and into the 1850s. Nonetheless, Free Soil lawmakers in places like Lynn and Lowell had liberal voting records on race, and these politicians presumably reflected the views of their constituents. This is not to suggest a direct correspondence between the voting records of politicians and the attitudes of their electorates; nor is it to claim that workers and ordinary men who voted for antislavery politicians had race in mind when they went to the ballot box. Many of the voters may well have been venting anger at the South, or at Catholic immigrants, or at both. A voter could be, and many were, anti-Southern and anti-immigrant as well as more open-minded on race than the conventional wisdom on popular racism would have us believe.

What are we to make of this? Two forces shaped workers' views on slavery and race. One influence was religion. Libertyism and to some extent Free Soilism did best in towns with large concentrations of evangelical churches drenched in religious perfectionism. That the Quaker strongholds of Lynn and New Bedford delivered strong antislavery votes is no accident.[17] Also, it is clear that evangelicalism reached only so far. The other influence was politics. Years of agitation against the proslavery policies of the Democratic Party – especially the controversial "gag rule" – and in favor of civil rights influenced voters who were from the working

Mark Voss-Hubbard, "Slavery, Capitalism, and the Middling Sorts: The Rank and File of Political Abolitionism," *ANCH* 4 (Summer 2003): 53–76.

[17] On Lynn, see Paul G. Faler, *Mechanics and Manufacturers in the Early Industrial Revolution: Lynn, Massachusetts, 1780–1860* (Albany: State Univ. of New York Press, 1981), and on New Bedford, see Kathryn Grover, *The Fugitive's Gibraltar: Escaping Slaves and Abolitionism in New Bedford, Massachusetts* (Amherst: Univ. of Massachusetts Press, 2001). Also see John L. Brooke, *The Heart of the Commonwealth: Society and Political Culture in Worcester County Massachusetts, 1713–1861* (New York: Cambridge Univ. Press, 1989), pp. 353–88, and Formisano, *Transformation of Political Culture*, pp. 327–9. Goodman, *Of One Blood*, pp. 103–21, doubts that evangelical religion alone motivated antislavery because many activists were orthodox Protestants.

class and not simply from the fabled middle class universally described as antislavery's best friend. But politics was not a one-way street in antebellum Massachusetts any more than it is today. Antislavery agitation provoked a virulent reaction from conservative Democrats, who leaned on white supremacy harder and harder to attract voters at home and to ingratiate themselves with their friends in the South. The Democrats soon learned, however, that pro-Southern, or "doughface," politics wore thin in Massachusetts. They also learned that for all the attention showered on Garrison, his camp was far outnumbered by antislavery activists – black and white, male and female – who bent their energies toward the ballot box. Politics had meaning and significance extending beyond Garrison.

The passion of antislavery activists for political engagement flies in the face of recent work that questions the popularity of politics. In *Rude Republic: Americans and Their Politics in the Nineteenth Century,* Glenn C. Altschuler and Stuart M. Blumin tell us that Americans were not as enthusiastic about the "second party system" as "new political historians" would have us believe.[18] Never mind the cider-soaked picnics, the dazzling parades and processions, or the huge voter turnouts, warn Altschuler and Blumin, explaining that these were merely episodes on the political calendar, not part of everyday life. Besides, the participants did not turn out on their own volition; they had to be coaxed out by paid operatives who often had to pay them to participate. The criticism that this interpretation of popular politics gives a distorted picture that ignores urban centers of political power in favor of a few country towns is correct in the abstract but not for this book. *Beyond Garrison* draws heavily on the kinds of communities profiled in *Rude Republic* but has difficulty accepting that book's claims. It is facile to dismiss voter turnout of some eighty percent as the result of bribery or coercion or both. Even if participants had to be dragged or lured to the parade or the polling booth, the fact is that they showed up. They showed up because so much was at stake, if not in the posturing of political debate, then surely in the formation of policy over slavery, civil rights, and liquor licensing. Few Bay Staters were indifferent to these issues. They were engaged and even fervent, moreover, because when it came to crafting legislation politics may have been something of a private club. There politics ended; it began, however, in the streets and meeting halls filled by the myriad mass movements of the age that took shape in the shadows of the parties and gave the parties motion and

[18] Glenn C. Altschuler and Stuart M. Blumin, *Rude Republic: Americans and Their Politics in the Nineteenth Century* (Princeton, N.J.: Princeton Univ. Press, 2000).

momentum. The historian who looks for "politics" in the parties alone misses this critical dimension of politics.[19]

Beyond Garrison opens at the beginning of the abolitionist movement in the early 1830s. I ask the reader's forbearance as Chapter 1 moves over the familiar ground of the movement's origins to establish several key points about its prepolitical stage. The Bay State abolitionist movement was based in the countryside, in small rural towns and rising industrial centers; it was decidedly weaker in Boston and other urban centers inland and along the coast. It also enjoyed strong support from women, including younger women often influenced by their parents and the clergy, as well as by their employers. Moreover, the antislavery movement did not make a sudden and unexpected veer into politics; in Massachusetts, as elsewhere, activists had waded into the political arena as petitioners in the great "postal campaign" of 1835. This campaign made a huge impression on Elizur Wright and his friends in the central office of the American Anti-Slavery Society in New York City and on such movement stalwarts as William Goodell and Gerrit Smith farther upstate. In 1837 the New Yorkers experimented with the political strategy of "vote scattering," a strategy that was pursued the following year in Middlesex County, Massachusetts. Chapter 1 ends with a close look at vote scattering to give the reader a deeper appreciation for the potential and pitfalls of political abolitionism.

Chapter 2 deals with the formation of the Liberty Party in 1840 and the party's development through the next decade. It places Libertyism in the political context of the Second Party System, discussing the party's social base and the competition the Libertyites faced from Whigs and Democrats. It suggests that the insurgency benefited not only from the strength of abolitionism in Massachusetts but also from the congressional fight over gag rule, winning over some Democrats disillusioned with their party's seeming subservience to its Southern wing. The chapter also suggests that the antislaveryism of the Whigs, however weak and feeble it appeared to be from the outside, was strong enough to sustain the loyalty of country Whigs. The strength and durability of Whiggery constrained the growth of Libertyism; the growing dispute over slavery, however, nurtured it. Party lieutenants deftly exploited popular outrage over the case

---

[19] For an illuminating discussion of the impact of extrapolitical associations on modern U.S. politics, see John Micklethwait and Adrian Wooldridge, *The Right Nation: Conservative Power in America* (New York: Penguin Press, 2004). Also see their "For Conservatives, Mission Accomplished," *New York Times*, May 18, 2004, p. A 25.

of George Latimer, a fugitive slave tracked down by his master in Boston on the eve of the 1842 election. The Liberty Party elected a half dozen representatives and held the balance of power in the State House – a far cry from the conventional picture of amateurish clerics barely able to stay afloat in the stormy and unfamiliar waters of reform politics.

Chapter 3 addresses the question of party strategy. It shows the Liberty Party divided loosely into two camps: a dominant one of single-issue men determined to keep the focus on slavery, and a subordinate one of equally determined eclectic reformers willing to work with popular movements and, in particular, labor reformers. Neither group was consistent, honoring their positions in the breach when it suited their interests. Nonetheless, the single-issue faction was consistent enough and powerful enough to give the party their imprint, if not without some resistance from the reformers. Both factions, however, drew together behind antislavery and civil rights, taking their cues from the civil rights coalition formed from white abolitionists, both Garrisonians and anti-Garrisonians, and African American activists, who saw themselves as friends of Garrison but endorsed the civil rights program of the Libertyites. Liberty Party men cobbled together their civil rights program in negotiations with the Democrats following the election of 1842, demanding reforms from the Democrats in return for ceding control of the state to them. They succeeded in repealing a ban on interracial marriage as well as in enacting a personal liberty law, and they came within a few votes of ending segregation on the railways. To cite such initiatives is to say nothing new; historians have known about them since at least the 1950s.[20] My point here is to show that the political struggle over civil rights exacerbated the split between Garrisonians and Libertyites and that the laws of 1843 were the project of the Libertyites.

The work of the eclectic abolitionists is the subject of Chapter 4. Led by the former Garrisonian Elizur Wright, this group looked forward to fusing labor reform with abolitionism in politics. It sought out allies in several industrial towns and hamlets, notably Amesbury and Lowell, who in the mid-1840s spearheaded the drive for a ten-hour workday. The group publicized the ten-hour movement in its press and encouraged the party at the local level to nominate ten-hour advocates for public office. The drive for labor reform was played out vividly in Lowell, the Bay State's most celebrated industrial city. Lowell became the home of the New England

---

[20] See, for instance, Louis Ruchames, "Jim Crow Railroads in Massachusetts," *AQ* 8 (1956): 61–75, and his "Race, Marriage and Abolition in Massachusetts," *JNH* 40 (1955): 250–73.

Workingmen's Association (NEWA), the largest labor group in the Commonwealth and the first one to have women leaders. Under the direction of Sarah G. Bagley and her colleagues, the NEWA took the bold step during the Mexican War of coming out for abolitionism. When the NEWA formed a Workingmen's ticket in 1846, the stage was set in Lowell for a spirited dialogue between Workingmen, running on a ten-hour platform, and Libertyites, reaffirming their stand for single-issue antislavery. The groups coalesced in 1847 when a vestige of the Workingmen endorsed the Libertyites only to see the Liberty Party collapse before the next election.

The stature of political antislavery soared in 1848 when the Free Soil Party emerged from the ruins of the Libertyites. The rise of the Free Soil Party is charted in Chapter 5. Free Soil leadership brought together a large group of former Libertyites and Conscience Whigs, as well as some erstwhile Garrisonians and a few former Democrats – such men as Henry Wilson, Richard Henry Dana, Jr., and Charles Sumner who were long associated with antislavery. Free Soil leaders were linked to a tangle of popular movements and interests by social reformers such as William S. Robinson and Whiting Griswold who became secondary leaders in the party. Robinson, the Lowell journalist who graduated from the temperance movement to labor reform, shared local party leadership with temperance crusaders and advocates of political reform from the towns, as well as with a small group of African Americans. The voice of the "townies" carried more weight in 1850 when Wilson and his fellows forged an alliance with country Democrats led by the Greenfield lawyer Whiting Griswold. Together they formed the Coalition government that ran the Commonwealth for the next two years.

Chapters 6, 7, and 8 spotlight three aspects of Free Soil politics – first labor, then political reform, and finally race – by taking a close look at voting in the State House and at the constitutional convention of 1853. Several political patterns are revealed. One is that laborism proved to be weak in politics even though workers were among the most tightly organized dissidents in the Commonwealth and had the support of Free Soil leaders, including Wilson and Robinson. Labor reform was thwarted again and again, not only by urban Whigs, who had fought off ten-hour drives in the workshops since the late 1820s, but also by conservative Free Soilers, who hailed mainly from country districts. Indeed, the bulwark of the opposition beyond urban Whiggery consisted of rural lawmakers – Whigs and Democrats as well as Free Soilers – divided by party but united behind an emerging culture of what I call "Yankeedom," a culture that celebrated the New England town and its civic institutions as the defining feature of the region. In a second pattern, economic and political populism, a mainstay of country politics, eclipsed laborism in the give-and-take of Coalition horse trading. Country politicians were thwarted by urban Whigs and Free Soilers when they tried to put across a reapportionment scheme that shifted power from Boston and the cities to the rural districts. Urban and country Whigs, however, then crippled a secret ballot law, a measure very popular in the factory districts with Yankee workers seeking protection from the political influence of Whiggish agents and overseers.

Nevertheless, country politicos found willing partners among Yankee workers on nativism and its companion program of liquor licensing, the third and perhaps sharpest pattern cut by the Coalition. Country "drys" from all parties (with the notable exception of some Democrats looking to court Irish voters) had faced resistance from Whig regulars on liquor regulation ever since the infamous "fifteen-gallon law" of 1838 badly divided Whiggery, delivering the state to the Democrats in 1839. But in 1852 the drys helped urban Free Soilers pass a stiff prohibition law that unleashed a liquor panic in the rural towns. Where the parties stood on antiforeignism before the nativist landslide of 1854 is unclear because of the absence of roll call votes on several nativist bills. But prohibition was scarcely the only nativist arrow in the quiver of Free Soil, for the party was responsible for the most proscriptive laws on the books before the Know-Nothing legislature of 1855. Indeed, nativism was arguably Free Soilism's most important legacy.

Free Soilers suffered one embarrassment after the next on civil rights and antislavery. Not long after making the pact that created the Coalition in 1850 they antagonized and then alienated their Democratic partners by nominating Charles Sumner for the six-year seat in the U.S. Senate. Sumner was simply unacceptable to the Democracy's pro-Southern leaders, who held the line against the nomination through the winter and spring of 1851. The bruising fight over Sumner, with its unmistakable subtext of racism, emboldened Democratic resistance to civil rights. In the first formal Coalition legislatures of 1851 and 1852, Democrats joined with conservative Whigs to defeat both a resolution assailing slavery and a stronger personal liberty bill; in 1853 essentially the same alliance scuttled measures giving blacks the right to bear arms as militiamen. The party of antislavery was more effective on nativism.

Chapter 9 demonstrates how the forces of laborism, nativism, and race that were reflected in Free Soilism informed succeeding third parties in the

Commonwealth. Neither the Know-Nothings, who swept the state in the election of 1854, nor the Republicans, who took the governor's chair for the first time in 1858, proved particularly responsive to the favorite reforms of Bay State workers. The Know-Nothings failed to pass a ten-hour bill or a secret ballot measure; Republicans did not even entertain either measure. The labor movement, which had brought such issues to the fore, had petered out, relieving popular pressure on the Republicans. Besides, the new party had nativist fish to fry, much like its immediate predecessor. As is well known, the Know-Nothings had passed a shopping list of reforms in the populis spirit and, surprisingly, had amassed an impressive record on civil rights, a record that surpassed the Free Soilers' performance. Their personal liberty law, for instance, went far beyond what the Free Soilers had proposed. The Know-Nothings pushed the nativist agenda, implicit in Whiggery and obvious in Free Soilism, to higher levels.

Republicans either rolled up the nativist banner or waved it with gusto, depending on which historians one reads. One group sees nativism as insignificant in the making of the new party, a distant second to antislavery; another sees nativism as central, far more important than antislavery.[21] Without getting into the details of that debate, it is enough to say here that the evidence points in two directions. First, nativism was undeniably one of the pillars of the Republican Party, partly because the issue was so deeply embedded in the Bay State's Protestantism and serial anti-Democratic political organizations. In addition, working-class districts – Lowell, Salisbury, and so forth – that had sent Free Soilers to the State House voted nativist after the Know-Nothings faded in other precincts around the state. The Republicans were simply responding to a major component of their electoral base when they restricted the political rights of immigrants, among their other nativist policies.[22] In fact, there was no hard-and-fast division between Republicans who were nativist and those who were antislavery; more often than not, nativists supported antislavery and vice versa. Second, nativism scarcely took shape in a political vacuum. The political fluidity at the local level attending the collapse of Whiggery coincided with the national debate over slavery. From the outbreak of

[21] Dale Baum, *The Civil War Party System: The Case of Massachusetts, 1848–1876* (Chapel Hill: Univ. of North Carolina Press, 1984), on the one hand, and William E. Gienapp, *The Origins of the Republican Party, 1852–1856* (New York: Oxford Univ. Press, 1987), on the other.

[22] John R. Mulkern, *The Know-Nothing Party in Massachusetts: The Rise and Fall of a People's Movement* (Boston: Northeastern Univ. Press, 1990).

the Mexican War in 1846 to the coming of the Fugitive Slave Act in 1850 and of the Kansas-Nebraska Act in 1854, antislavery sentiment rose and fell. After 1856, however, the drama in Kansas riveted the nation's attention on the question of slavery, gradually and decisively sweeping nativism to the political margin. Nonetheless, it is difficult to see how Republicanism could have succeeded in the Bay State before about 1858 without deferring to the antiforeign sentiments in its ranks.

Political nativism lasted longer in Massachusetts than in any other state. It was last seen on ballots in 1857, but it did not really die. Instead, it was driven underground by antislavery and sectional discord, lurking just below the surface as an instinct without discrete partisan political expression. No one understood the stubbornness of Yankee nativism better than did Republican politicians, who knew they had to come up with a suitable substitute for the proscriptive legislation of the Know-Nothings, something that would resonate in the old towns and in the factory centers, the party's nearly bifurcated rural-urban base. The Republican Party added a protective tariff plank to its platform in the late 1850s, mimicking other parties in the North and borrowing the old Whig formula that had worked so well in the Lowells of the Commonwealth. It is doubtful that the tariff had much appeal in the country – in Yankeedom. Possibly that is one reason why Republicans emphasized the ideology of free labor, a grand vision developed in the 1840s that defined the good society as one that provided opportunities for ordinary men to climb the social ladder on their own merits.[23] Such a vision had considerable appeal. But it would not do justice to the cultural and political heritage of the Bay State to deny the galvanic power of anti-Southernism, an ethos nearly as old as the Commonwealth itself and one that became emphatically more magnetic as the 1850s drew to a close. Its resonance with Yankeedom gave anti-Southernism great and arguably unparalleled currency in world of Republicanism, bringing together Yankee city and country town and bridging the pro– and anti–civil rights factions in the party.[24]

How typical was antislavery politics in Massachusetts? How many other Republican organizations reflected the position of their Bay State colleagues on the questions of civil rights and nativism? Is this a case

---

[23] Eric Foner, *Free Soil, Free Labor, Free Men: The Ideology of the Republican Party before the Civil War* (New York: Oxford Univ. Press, 1970).

[24] Formisano, *The Birth of Mass Political Parties: Michigan, 1827–1861* (Princeton, N.J.: Princeton Univ. Press, 1971), pp. 263–4 and 277–81, and William F. Hartford, *Money, Morals, and Politics: Massachusetts in the Age of the Boston Associates* (Boston: Northeastern Univ. Press, 2001), pp. 91–2.

of "Massachusetts exceptionalism," as noted by one reviewer of the manuscript for this book? *Beyond Garrison* ends with a discussion of Massachusetts and the nation, placing the state in the larger context of antislavery politics as Northerners donned the blue uniforms of their region to settle the issue of slavery once and for all.

I

"An Experiment of Immense Consequence"

From Moral Suasion to Politics

Elizur Wright, Jr., was a complicated man. A devout evangelical Protestant from a long line of Connecticut ministers, Wright trained for the ministry in the 1820s, only to become an outspoken atheist who, in the 1840s, pronounced Christianity a "total failure." Although an early convert to abolitionism, loyal to William Lloyd Garrison, he turned to political abolitionism and against Garrison's policies of apolitical moral suasion and anarchistic nonresistance. A loving husband and tender father, Wright was an intrepid reformer who appeared to have no private life. He was a well-known activist with friends in and around the abolitionist movement, but he made enemies out of friends because of his impatience and tactlessness. Theodore Dwight Weld, a mentor of Wright's in the early 1830s, found him insufferable by the end of the decade.[1] Weld was correct. Wright went through life torching bridge after bridge between himself and his friends and patrons, but he never seemed to doubt that another bridge was down the road. Possibly, he was too intense and resourceful to worry about scorched friendships and ruined relationships. The point, however, is not to put Elizur Wright on the couch. He commands our attention because his career in the abolitionist movement during the 1830s allows us to explore the movement's geographic configuration

---

[1] TDW to JGB, May 23, 1837, in Dwight L. Dumond, ed., *The Letters of James Gillespie Birney, 1831–1857*, 2 vols. (New York: D. Appleton-Century, 1938), 1: 381–3, and TDW to Gerrit Smith, Oct. 23, 1839, in Gilbert H. Barnes and Dwight L. Dumond, eds., *The Letters of Theodore Dwight Weld, Angelina Grimké Weld, and Sarah Grimké, 1822–1844*, 2 vols. (New York: D. Appleton-Century, 1934), 2: 809–12.

FIGURE 3. Elizur Wright in old age and youth. (Philip Green Wright and Elizabeth Q. Wright, *Elizur Wright: The Father of Life Insurance* [Chicago: Univ. of Chicago Press, 1937], p. 138.)

and social base, and its transition from moral crusade to political party.[2]

Wright's early years fit the pattern of scores of men and women of the Yankee Diaspora.[3] Wright was born in 1804 to Elizur and Clarissa Richards Wright in the farming village of South Canaan in the remote northwestern corner of Connecticut. His father, a farmer and school teacher, as well as a deacon in the local Congregational church, was lured to the Western Reserve in 1810 by the opportunity to join a community organized by a fellow cleric offering large tracts of land on the cheap to trusted Christians. Settling in the village of Tallmadge, the elder Wright worked the land and taught school, just as he had in Connecticut, establishing a bible school and also helping found Western Reserve College. He sent his son to Yale in 1822, where the young student

[2] On Wright, see Lawrence B. Goodheart, *Abolitionist, Actuary, Atheist: Elizur Wright and the Reform Impulse* (Kent, Ohio: Kent State Univ. Press, 1990). Also Philip G. Wright and Elizabeth Q. Wright, *Elizur Wright: The Father of Life Insurance* (Chicago: Univ. of Chicago Press, 1937), and Jane H. Pease and William H. Pease, "The Political Gadfly: Elizur Wright," in Pease and Pease, *Bound with Them in Chains: A Biographical History of the Antislavery Movement* (Westport, Conn.: Greenwood Press, 1972), pp. 218–44.

[3] See Peter R. Knights, *Yankee Destinies: The Lives of Ordinary Nineteenth-Century Bostonians* (Chapel Hill: Univ. of North Carolina Press, 1991).

encountered Nathaniel William Taylor, the reform Protestant whose anti-Calvinist doctrines of free agency and self-perfection propelled a whole generation of youthful men and women into combat against drink and slavery. Wright would eventually follow along but not before teaching school in New England in the mid-1820s and then returning to Ohio in the late 1820s, first to work for the American Tract Society and then for Western Reserve as a professor of mathematics and natural philosophy. He was already an abolitionist of the colonizationist school by the time he arrived at Western Reserve. Also an avid reader, in the early 1830s Wright claimed to have been converted to immediatism by Garrison's influential pamphlet "Thoughts on African Colonization." He was himself soon writing anticolonizationist polemics for the local press and fighting with the colonizationist administration of the school, burnishing a reputation as a nuisance and political embarrassment.[4] The denouement came in August 1833 when he brought down the wrath of the administration by walking arm-in-arm with a black man at the commencement ceremony. When told that he was fired, Wright snapped that he had already decided to leave.[5] It was the first time he got the sack for flaunting his politics; it would not be the last.

Wright's anticolonizationist polemics got him known in the East, where abolitionists were just beginning to organize. Garrison was among those who took notice. He wrote in 1832 that he had followed Wright's essays in the Ohio press "with a delight bordering on enthusiasm" and then agreed to publish Wright's work in the newly formed *Liberator*.[6] Such early celebrity in the tiny abolitionist circle could not have been more timely. It explains why in fall 1833 Garrison and Arthur and Lewis Tappan turned to Wright when they launched the American Anti-Slavery Society (AASS) in Philadelphia following preliminary meetings in New York City, where Wright would live for the next six years. Thus Wright was present at the creation of the American abolitionist movement in 1833, a movement he would help shape and then, when he bolted at the end of decade, reshape. His official position as secretary of domestic correspondence masked an impossible calendar of responsibilities, from directing the growing staff of field agents to answering

---

[4] Goodheart, *Abolitionist, Actuary, Atheist*, pp. 3–60. For samples of Wright's early abolitionist writing, see *Lib*, Jan. 5, 1833, Mar. 20, 1833, and June 1–15 passim, 1833.

[5] Goodheart, *Abolitionist, Actuary, Atheist*, pp. 53–60. Also see EW to TDW., Sept. 5, 1833, in Barnes and Dumond, *Letters of Theodore Dwight Weld*, 1: 116–17.

[6] Quoted in Goodheart, *Abolitionist, Actuary, Atheist*, p. 55. Also see *Lib*, Jan. 5 and Feb. 23, 1833.

correspondence and churning out the movement's famously prodigious literature.[7] He was excited, not deterred, by the blistering work load; he told Weld the following summer that he was writing "about 200 letters with *my own hand* to auxiliaries and friends.... Have written 30 to day."[8]

Shortly after the formation of the AASS an elated but wary Wright wrote Weld that the "National Society is now *organized*, the question is whether it shall *live*. The infant is sound in its limbs, but its breathing is the problem."[9] Wright and his associates in New York expected their newborn to grow up in the city. After all, their movement was born in Philadelphia, administered in New York, and centered in Boston, the home of its leading voice and signature organ. Their grand plan, an urban strategy to "abolitionize" Northern cities, was badly in need of someone with organizational savvy to take command from the central office. Wright, convinced that Weld would trade his tenacious independence for the excitement of the job, worked hard but in vain to lure the minister from his redoubt in upstate New York. Weld bluntly put an end to the issue in April 1836. "I am Backwoodsman," wrote the self-effacing Yankee. "Let me keep about my own business and stay in my own place."[10] After that Wright had to relent, but he could not resist reprimanding his favorite field agent for being "egotistical" and putting his own idiosyncrasies ahead of the cause. Though he failed to land Weld, by that spring Wright had come around to Weld's view that rural areas and small towns provided more fertile organizing ground than did the city. Wright ordered field staff in an AASS petition campaign to "take hold of the country – the yeomanry of the *country towns*, leaving the cities to themselves for the present."[11] This new strategy soon prevailed. For the rest of the 1830s and into the 1840s, abolitionists bent their energies to organizing what they came to call "the

---

[7] See Leonard L. Richards, *"Gentlemen of Property and Standing": Anti-Abolitionist Mobs in Jacksonian America* (New York: Oxford Univ. Press, 1970), pp. 50–1, 71–3, and 162–3. Also see Goodheart, *Abolitionist, Actuary, Atheist*, pp. 61–2.

[8] EW to TDW, Aug. 14, 1834, in Barnes and Dumond, *Letters of Theodore Dwight Weld*, 1: 166.

[9] EW to TDW, Dec. 31, 1833, ibid., 1: 121.

[10] Quoted in Mark Perry, *Lift Up Thy Voice: The Grimké Family's Journey from Slaveholders to Civil Rights Leaders* (New York: Viking, 2001), p. 136. See also, TDW to Lewis Tappan, Apr. 5, 1836, in Barnes and Dumond, *Letters of Theodore Dwight Weld*, 1: 286–9.

[11] Quoted in Goodheart, *Abolitionist, Actuary, Atheist*, p. 79. Also see American Anti-Slavery Society, *Second Annual Report* (New York: Dorr and Butterfield, 1835), p. 48. Hereafter AASS, *Annual Report*.

country," by which they meant just about anywhere outside metropolitan areas.

Two factors influenced abolitionists like Wright to adopt Weld's position on their movement's future. One factor was the rash of horrifying riots targeting abolitionists that gripped Northern cities in the mid-1830s. Egged on by well-dressed men, mobs of ordinary men terrorized abolitionists in the nation's leading urban centers. Starting in New York in fall 1833, a menacing crowd of over a thousand threatened the inaugural meeting of the AASS in the downtown, only to be thwarted when officials changed the venue at the last minute. The society was not as lucky the next year. Spread by negrophobic journalists and politicians, wild and fantastic rumors of an abolitionist plot to encourage racial amalgamation ignited the worst race riot to its time. Marauding gangs went on a three-day rampage in New York during the second week in July 1834, razing some sixty buildings and a half dozen churches, vandalizing the homes and offices of movement leaders, and roughing up African Americans in what proved to be a rehearsal for the bloody antidraft riots in 1863. On the advice of friends, Lewis Tappan left for the country on July 9, just hours before the mob sacked his Rose Street house. A day later the mob could be found in the Five Points area, trashing the chapels of abolitionist ministers, reserving its special fury for those places of worship suspected of having integrated pews.[12] The violence spread from New York to other cities a year later, culminating in the well-known mobbing of Garrison in Boston.[13] In the earlier New York riot, the mob almost got to Wright as well. Alarmed by the threat to Tappan, Wright sprinted from Manhattan to his Brooklyn home and his ailing wife, who had just given birth, barring the door and keeping an ax at hand.[14] He had thought that the mayhem would benefit the movement, that although "the great men of the city are not with us, hundreds of the smaller ones are coming to the standard."[15]

---

[12] Richards, *"Gentlemen of Property and Standing,"* pp. 113–22. Also see Jack Tager, *Boston Riots: Three Centuries of Social Violence* (Boston: Northeastern Univ. Press, 2001).

[13] Tager, *Boston Riots*, pp. 88–93. Also see Henry Mayer, *All on Fire: William Lloyd Garrison and the Abolition of Slavery* (New York: St. Martin's Press, 1998), pp. 188–210, and John L. Thomas, *The Liberator: William Lloyd Garrison* (Boston: Little, Brown, 1963), pp. 178–208.

[14] Lewis Tappan to TDW, July 10, 1834, in Barnes and Dumond, *Letters of Theodore Dwight Weld*, 1: 153–60. Also, Linda Kerber, "Abolitionists and Amalgamators: The New York City Race Riots of 1834," *NYH* 48 (1967): 28–39.

[15] Quoted in Goodheart, *Abolitionist, Actuary, Atheist*, p. 77. AASS, *Third Annual Report*, (1836), pp. 62 and 87.

It took another year of mob violence to convince him that the sons of toil in the city were no friendlier to the movement than their betters. Small wonder that abolitionists reconsidered converting the metropolis.

The other factor influencing abolitionist strategy had to do with the location of the movement. Wright and his fellows were urbanites by choice, not by birth. They migrated to the cities from the villages and small towns of their birth in rural New York and New England. Many abolitionists have been profiled by modern biographers and historians who have left the impression that the city was the base of their movement.[16] This is misleading. Abolitionist leaders were urbanites; their followers were townsfolk and countryfolk, as the geographic distribution of abolitionist societies in Massachusetts makes clear. Boston, the "Hub City," had no equal when it came to the concentration of political and economic power, a fact that had irritated "the country" since the time of the Shaysites and continued to grate on countryfolk into the antebellum years. The Hub was no such thing, however, when it came to abolitionists on the ground. The Commonwealth boasted some two hundred fifty societies with a total of about sixteen thousand members in 1838, just as the movement stalled in the wake of the 1837 panic and ensuing seven-year depression. Suffolk County, the home of Boston, had seven societies, three of which, with a total of five hundred followers, were in the city itself. Many other counties with a fraction of Boston's seventy thousand residents, however, had several times the number of societies and just as many members. Essex County immediately to its north, had the largest number of societies (41), followed by Middlesex County (35), and then by Worcester County (32), in the "heart of the Commonwealth." Next came Plymouth, Bristol, and Norfolk counties in the southeastern region of the state, with seventeen to nineteen societies each, followed by the western counties of Franklin and Hampshire, with fifteen and nineteen societies, respectively. Furthermore, the westernmost county, Berkshire, had as many societies as Boston had but only a fraction of the city's population.

Even more revealing are the membership figures for select towns in "the country." The Essex County village of Andover and the Plymouth County village of Abington had just as many societies as Boston and just as many members (500 each). Not far away, the bustling shoemaking town of Lynn boasted as many societies as Boston and even more members (600); its neighboring shoe town of Haverhill had three societies with

---

[16] For instance, Thomas, *Liberator*; Mayer, *All on Fire*; and James Brewer Stewart, *William Lloyd Garrison and the Challenge of Emancipation* (Arlington, Ill: H. Davidson, 1992).

some two hundred members. The cotton textile center of Lowell had three societies with four hundred fifty members, and Fall River, its rival in the southeast, had two societies with just as many followers. Nor were such figures aberrations. The tiny textile hamlet of Amesbury in Middlesex County, had no fewer than four societies with about three hundred fifty members.[17] Thus the radical abolitionist Thomas Wentworth Higginson was only partly correct when he proclaimed, "Radicalism went with the smell of leather" – a reference to the strength of abolitionism in places like Lynn – for abolitionism also followed the scent of cotton textiles, and of country corn as well.[18]

Bay State abolitionism had a distinctive social composition within this geographic context. If the movement had taken on the social coloration initially envisioned by Lewis Tappan and Wright, not only would it have been centered in the city, it would have been a coalition of the wealthy and of the solid middle class affiliated with the evangelical church. However, by the mid-1830s, as he started to lose faith with the clergy, Wright began to speak a social language laced with sharp criticism of the rich, a language that would eventually express his labor radicalism in the 1840s.[19] In the mid-1830s, however, Wright sounded more like a Locofoco Democrat (the sobriquet for economic radicals), but with a moralistic inflection. Perhaps he was mimicking William Goodell, who like Wright had grown up in rural Connecticut and wound up in New York in the mid-1830s. A former merchant turned journalist, and a lifelong Calvinist, Goodell used his *Emancipationist* to assail moral laxity and aristocracy, both of which he attributed to the excessive acquisitiveness brought on by the market revolution. He may well have influenced Wright, who shared a two-family house with him in Brooklyn.[20] Or Wright may have begun to acquire his new social vocabulary through clashes with wealthy lads at Yale who demeaned him as a swamp Yankee; possibly it thickened through his more recent encounters with the antiabolitionist brawlers in New York. Wright did not need anyone to tell him that the city's nabobs

[17] Computed from AASS, *Fifth Annual Report* (1838), pp. 132–7.
[18] Thomas Wentworth Higginson, *Cheerful Yesterdays* (Boston: Houghton Mifflin, 1898), p. 115.
[19] Goodheart, *Abolitionist, Actuary, Atheist*, pp. 85–97.
[20] Paul Goodman, *Of One Blood: Abolitionism and the Origins of Racial Equality* (Berkeley and Los Angeles: Univ. of California Press, 1998), pp. 69–80. See also William Goodell, *The Democracy of Christianity; or, An analysis of the Bible and its doctrines in relation to the principle of democracy*, 2 vols. (New York: Cady and Burgess, 1849–82), and Goodell, *Slavery and Anti-Slavery: A History of the Great Struggle in both Hemispheres . . .* (1852; New York: Negro Universities Press, 1968).

TABLE 1.1. *Abolitionists in Lynn and Worcester, 1830s*

	Lynn		Worcester	
	N	%	N	%
Unskilled & Menial Service	1	0.8	1	2.1
Semiskilled & Service	2	1.6	2	4.2
Proprietor-Manager-Official	20	15.9	12	25
Skilled	88	69.8	24	50
Commerce & Sales	4	3.2	2	4.2
Semiprofessional	2	1.0	1	2.1
Professional	2	1.0	–	
Farmers	2	1.6	6	2.5
Misc.	6	4.8	–	

Compiled from the subscriber lists of the Worcester Anti-Slavery Society Constitution, 1838–9, and from the minute books of the Lynn Anti-Slavery Society, 1832–9, and "linked to occupational data," pp. 45–6.
Source: Computed by Edward Magdol, *The Antislavery Rank and File: A Social Profile of the Abolitionists' Constituency* (Westport, Conn.: Greenwood Press, 1986), p. 47, Table 4-1.

had a huge stake in Southern slavery and bore a murderous animus for slavery's critics. Thus, in 1836 Wright used his annual report to the AASS to announce what amounted to a new departure in his thinking, skewering the "merchants, politicians, and aristocrats of our principal cities, who are most corrupted by our southern trade and companionship, and their humble imitators in our more inland towns." It was these "purse-proud aristocrats" who had set the rabble, the "penniless profligates," on Wright and his friends. Abolitionists now had to look elsewhere for support, namely, to the "uncorrupt yeomanry" and the "clear-headed, free laborers and mechanics of the North." These social groups, he emphasized, formed the "fair field" of the "middle ground."[21]

Wright's middle ground of ordinary people formed the core of abolitionism in the Bay State during the 1830s, as indicated by Table 1.1, which shows the occupations of abolitionists in Lynn and Worcester.[22] Although author of this table claimed that it reflects the "proletarian"

[21] AASS, *Third Annual Report* (1836), pp. 62ff.
[22] Table from Edward Magdol, *The Antislavery Rank and File: A Social Profile of the Abolitionists' Constituency* (Westport, Conn.: Greenwood Press, 1986), p. 47. Also see John Jentz, "The Antislavery Constituency in Jacksonian New York City," *CWH* 27 (June 1981): 101–22. Goodman, *Of One Blood*, pp. 161–72, comes at the question of labor and antislavery from the perspective of working-class leaders.

base of the movement, the term is anachronistic today if by it he meant factory hands. There were few factory workers in Lynn or in Worcester, which was a major producer of metal and metal goods. "Skilled" laborers in both places worked in small shops or at home as outworkers, not in factories.[23] Furthermore, many such laborers were closely tied to the land, either as part-time farmers themselves or as the farmers' offspring. Much like their counterparts in Lowell, they frequently left their work benches for family farmsteads, especially in late summer to help with the harvest.[24] The men among them kept one foot in the old world of agriculture and one foot in the world of industry, practicing what modern historians call bi-employment by doing wage work and farming.[25] The time when proletarians, strictly speaking, would figure in the antislavery movement in appreciable numbers was still a decade away. In the 1830s the movement's members are more accurately and more broadly described as plebeians – ordinary people who earned their livings literally "by the sweat of their brow," that is, by manual labor.

Another aspect of the occupational mix noted in Table 1.1 that needs amplification is the relatively large representation of proprietors. In both towns, such men constituted the second largest occupational group. In Lynn they were largely petty entrepreneurs in the shoemaking industry; in Worcester they were a mix of master craftsmen in a broad range of trades.

---

[23] Alan Dawley, *Class and Community: The Industrial Revolution in Lynn* (Cambridge: Harvard Univ. Press, 1976), pp. 2–96, and Paul G. Faler, *Mechanics and Manufacturers in the Early Industrial Revolution: Lynn, Massachusetts, 1780–1860* (Albany: State Univ. of New York Press, 1981), pp. 8–27. On Worcester, see Joshua S. Chasan, "Civilizing Worcester: The Creation of an Institutional and Cultural Order, Worcester, Massachusetts, 1848–1876" (Ph.D. diss., Univ. of Pittsburgh, 1974), and John L. Brooke, *The Heart of the Commonwealth: Society and Political Culture in Worcester County Massachusetts, 1713–1861* (New York: Cambridge Univ. Press, 1989), pp. 269–309. For a useful discussion of the social structure of rural towns and industrializing cities, see Robert S. Doherty, *Society and Power: Five New England Towns, 1800–1860* (Amherst: Univ. of Massachusetts Press, 1977).

[24] Thomas Dublin, *Women at Work: The Transformation of Work and Community in Lowell, 1826–1860* (New York: Columbia Univ. Press, 1979), pp. 22–57.

[25] Daniel Vickers, *Farmers and Fishermen: Two Centuries of Work in Essex County, Massachusetts, 1630–1850* (Chapel Hill: Univ. of North Carolina Press, 1994); Bruce Laurie, "'We are not afraid to work': Master Mechanics and the Market Revolution in the Antebellum North," in Burton J. Bledstein and and Robert D. Johnston, eds., *The Middling Sorts: Explorations in the History of the Middle Class* (New York: Routledge, 2001), pp. 50–68; and Mark Voss-Hubbard, *Beyond Party: Cultures of Antipartisanship in Northern Politics before the Civil War* (Baltimore: Johns Hopkins Univ. Press, 2002), pp. 17–37.

This generation of abolitionists stood poised between, landless day workers and the old commercial elite, roughly approximating Wright's "middle
ground."

What accounts for this social configuration? What drew the occupants
of Wright's middle ground to the moral high ground of abolitionism?
Historians have approached this problem from three broad perspectives –
religion, social identity, and politics. The religious approach is a thread
of academic continuity running from Gilbert H. Barnes's seminal study
in the 1930s through the work of Dwight L. Dumond in the 1950s and
continuing into the present in the writing of a number of historians, most
notably those engaged in bringing women into abolitionism.[26] Although
each work in the religious group has its own emphasis, the larger body
identifies the origins of and sustenance for abolitionism in the new Protestantism forged in the brimstone of the later stage of the Second Great
Awakening. Not all historians who consider religion in the movement see
it that way. David Donald argued in the 1950s that Calvinism, not the
new Arminianism, was the preferred confession of antislavery activists;[27]
more recently, the late Paul Goodman found religious heterodoxy among
abolitionists, stressing the presence of orthodox Calvinists.[28] Donald, of
course, is more properly associated with the social identity school of abolitionist historiography for his highly provocative prosopographic analysis
of abolitionist leaders. In it, he argued that the movement reflected the
angst of older families in rural regions of the North and New England especially, who latched onto abolitionism as a replacement for their moral
authority lost in the early stages of rampant commercialism.[29] Donald
came under attack from critics for focusing on leaders and speculating
about the upbringing of his subjects. He was also revised by scholars
from within his own social identity school who argued that abolitionists

[26] Gilbert H. Barnes, *The Anti-Slavery Impulse, 1830–1844* (1933; New York: Harcourt,
Brace, 1964); Dwight L. Dumond, *Antislavery: The Crusade for Freedom in Amer-
ica* (Ann Arbor: Univ. of Michigan Press, 1961); Julie Roy Jeffrey, *The Great Silent
Army of Abolitionism: Ordinary Women in the Antislavery Movement* (Chapel Hill:
Univ. of North Carolina Press, 1998); and Debra B. Van Broekhoven, *The Devotion
of These Women: Rhode Island Women in the Antislavery Network* (Amherst: Univ. of
Massachusetts Press, 2002).
[27] David Herbert Donald, "Toward a Reconsideration of the Abolitionists," in Donald,
Lincoln Reconsidered: Essays on the Civil War Era (New York: Alfred A. Knopf, 1956),
pp. 19–36.
[28] Goodman, *Of One Blood*, esp. pp. 103–21.
[29] Donald, "Toward a Reconsideration of the Abolitionists." This interpretation heavily influenced Stanley M. Elkins, *Slavery: A Problem in American Institutional and Intellectual
Life* (1959; Chicago: Univ. of Chicago Press, 1963), pp. 140–206.

and antislavery activists came from more prosperous families or more dynamic sectors of the economy than his genteel Yankees.[30]

Scholars in the political school of abolitionism share very little with each other except an emphasis on the importance of politics.[31] It is enough to observe here that two political historians of antislavery who do see things similarly are Leonard L. Richards and William W. Freehling. Both emphasize the split in the Democratic Party over the politics of slavery, beginning with the question of gag rule in the mid-1830s and running through the 1840s into the 1850s. This intraparty split, one may infer, reached down to the grass roots in Northeastern communities, turning ordinary men not only against the South but also against slavery.[32] The likelihood is, however, that national politics did not become a formative force until the late 1830s and was so only episodically thereafter.

The dispute among the three approaches to the study of abolitionism is not only over angles of vision. It runs deeper to the more basic question of how we know what we know. Social historians, and some historians of voting behavior as well, generally assume that to know who people were is to know why they did what they did. This assumption has led these scholars to associate evangelical religion with abolitionism, a plausible inference, to be sure, but one that does not get us far enough. We need to look at what people did, not simply at who they were, in order to gain a better idea of why middling people – both men and women – formed the foundation of abolitionism in its early years. This is not to dismiss the role of popular religion in the making of abolitionism; indeed, there is no doubt that it was a decisive force early on. But it does suggest that it was not enough to be a Congregationalist or Baptist if the local minister or leading family in town was indifferent to or opposed to emancipation. A look at what such town leaders and authority figures did on the ground offers helpful insight into the meaning of lived experience.

---

[30] See, for instance, Richards, *"Gentlemen of Property and Standing,"* pp. 131–55, and James B. Stewart, *Holy Warriors: The Abolitionists and American Slavery* (New York: Hill and Wang, 1976), pp. 37–8.

[31] I refer here to the polarity over Civil War causation between those who emphasize the importance of slavery or nativism in the break-up of the Second Party System. I have chosen to defer discussion of this debate until Chapter 9.

[32] Leonard L. Richards, *The Slave Power: The Free North and Southern Domination, 1780–1860* (Baton Rouge: Louisiana State Univ. Press, 2000), and William W. Freehling, *The Road to Disunion: Secessionists at Bay, 1776–1854* (New York: Oxford Univ. Press, 1990), esp. pp. 308–36 and 345–52, and Freehling, *The Reintegration of American History: Slavery and the Civil War* (New York: Oxford Univ. Press, 1994), pp. 198–200 and 213–14.

FIGURE 4. Elizabeth Whiting Phelps Huntington. (Porter Phelps Huntington Family Papers. Courtesy Amherst College Archives and Special Collections. Amherst College, Amherst, Mass.)

The Porter Phelps Huntington family in the Hampshire County village of Hadley suggests that the most important authority figures for many abolitionists in the country were parents – mothers in particular.[33] A founding family of Hadley in the eighteenth century, the Huntingtons epitomized Early National gentry in the region except for their religion. They were renegade Congregationalists who became Unitarians (of all things). Their riverfront farm of some six hundred acres, with its mix of slave and free labor in colonial times, yielded a comfortable livelihood until the 1820s when the family began to slip into social decline. The

---

[33] See Donald, "Toward a Reconsideration of the Abolitionists."

family was then headed by the Reverend Dan Huntington and his wife, Elizabeth Whiting Phelps Huntington, who followed her husband into Unitarianism.[34] Elizabeth also had a mind of her own. A dour and brooding woman obsessed with the salvation of her eleven surviving children, she was in the 1830s a colonizationist who seems to have subscribed to the *Liberator* and to have once tried – without much success – to persuade Garrison that colonizationists were as honorable as immediatists and had something to contribute to the movement. As she innocently wrote in a draft letter to Garrison in 1834, "Many [colonizationists] sustain high characters... both as to learning and abilities; besides an eminent... piety.... Would it not be better to let them labor and bid them your speed? In this wise work, is there not room for all the benevolent to act, without fear of interfering with one another, at least without incurring censure[?]"[35] She was more successful with her sons, at least three of whom were closely identified with antislavery or abolitionism, first as Garrisonians and then as Libertyites and Free Soilers, and all of whom, like their mother, eventually repudiated colonization.[36]

Though it is not clear if Elizabeth Huntington joined an abolitionist society, Mary White, her counterpart in the Worcester County town of Boylston, certainly did. The White family were prosperous country merchants living with their ten children in a "mansion house" in the town center; fittingly, Mary's husband, Aaron, was known as "The Squire." He tended the store; she tended to reform, helping to establish the Boylston Female Anti-Slavery Society in 1835. Like Elizabeth Huntington, Mary passed on her zeal to her children, who accompanied her to abolitionist lectures and sewing bees, and helped her to carry antislavery petitions door-to-door around town.[37] Though Mary White and scores of local abolitionists like her undoubtedly drew strength from the movement's

---

[34] On Elizabeth Whiting Phelps Huntington, see boxes 12–14, PPHFP, Amherst College Archives.

[35] Ibid., EWPH to WLG, box 12, folder 20.

[36] They were Charles Phelps Huntington (1802–68) William Pitkin Huntington (1804–85), and Frederic Dan Huntington (1819–1904). For samples of her sons' thinking, see ibid., William Pitkin Huntington to EWPH, Feb. 11, 1839, b.19, f.5. Charles is treated in Chapter 3.

[37] Mary Fuhrer, *Letters from the "Old Home Place": Anxieties and Aspirations in Rural New England, 1836–1843* (Boylston, Mass.: Old Pot Publications, 1997), esp. pp. 1–35 and 47–63. Also, Fuhrer, "'We all have something to do in the cause of freeing the slave': The Abolition Work of Mary White" (paper prepared for the Dublin Seminar, Deerfield, Mass., June 15–17, 2001). I would like to thank Mary Fuhrer for sharing this work with me.

FIGURE 5. Mary White. (Courtesy of the Boylston Historical Society and Museum, Boylston, Mass.)

myriad activities and events, their abolitionist sympathies began as family affairs.

Beyond the immediate influence of the family, local clergy also proved to be a source of abolitionism, possibly the most important one in the tight-knit towns of rural New England. Indeed, next to prominent families like the Huntingtons and the Whites, clergymen were the most powerful figures in "the country." They were especially forceful if they themselves came from such families, as in the example of the Huntingtons. The influence of the men of the cloth explains why some villages and country towns spawned outsized abolitionist organizations. In such cases, local abolitionist societies were congregations under a different name. Mary White, for instance, did not form the Boylston Anti-Slavery Society wholly on her own; she enjoyed the support and encouragement of Harriet Sanford, the wife of the local minister, and of the minister himself.[38] Nor was this pattern limited to rural towns or to Congregationalists, Unitarians, and Quakers.[39] In Lowell, the Methodist minister Orange Scott's kinetic pulpit was a favorite venue for abolitionist speakers and Scott himself was an unofficial correspondent for the *Liberator* until his break with Garrison in the late 1830s over political action.[40] He also organized the first of the city's several abolitionist societies, which drew on his congregation of eight hundred worshippers whom he described as *"right* almost to an individual" on antislavery."[41]

That abolitionist sentiment in Lowell issued from the pulpit and not from the counting house is not surprising. The owners of the city's mills, after all, were synonymous in the mid-1830s with the conservatism of the newly formed Whig Party. No elite in the region had a greater stake in slavery, and few defended it more strongly in the 1830s. In response to surging abolitionism in summer 1835, Whig politicians called the infamous meeting at Faneuil Hall to condemn meddling in Southern affairs and uphold their commercial ties with the planters. The regional compact between the sections sealed in the Constitution, said party solon Harrison Gray Otis in a thinly veiled defense of slavery, "binds every man's conscience by all that is sacred in good faith, and sound in good policy."[42]

It would be a mistake, however, to assume that the Boston Associates, the owners of the largest textile mills in the state, reflected the opinion of employers in general, or even of those involved in the production of

---

[38] Fuhrer, "'We all have something to do in the cause of freeing the slave.'"

[39] See Ronald P. Formisano, *The Transformation of Political Culture: Massachusetts Parties, 1790s–1840s* (New York: Oxford Univ. Press, 1983), esp. pp. 217–21 and 289–301, and Brooke, *Heart of the Commonwealth*, pp. 353–68. See also John R. McKivigan, "'Vote as You Pray and Party as You Vote': Church-Oriented Abolitionism and Antislavery Politics," in Alan M. Kraut, ed., *Crusaders and Compromisers: Essays on the Relationship of the Antislavery Struggle to the Antebellum Party System* (Westport, Conn.: Greenwood Press, 1983), pp. 179–203.

[40] On Scott, see Donald G. Matthews, "Orange Scott: The Methodist Evangelical as Revolutionary," in Martin B. Duberman, ed., *The Antislavery Vanguard: New Essays on the Abolitionists* (Princeton, N.J.: Princeton Univ. Press, 1965), pp. 71–101. Also Thomas, *Liberator*, pp. 261–3, and Amy Swerdlow, "Abolitionism's Conservative Sisters: The Ladies' New York City Anti-Slavery Societies, 1834–1840," in Jean Fagan Yellin and John Van Horne, eds., *The Abolitionist Sisterhood: Women's Political Culture in Antebellum America* (Ithaca, N.Y.: Cornell Univ. Press, 1994), pp. 31–44, esp. n. 10.

[41] *Lib*, Feb. 4, 1837. For additional coverage on abolitionism in Lowell by Scott and others see ibid., Jan. 23, 1836, May 19, 1837, and Aug. 18, 1837. Also see Magdol, *Antislavery Rank and File*, pp. 70–3.

[42] Quoted in Mayer, *All on Fire*, p. 198. Also see William F. Hartford, *Money, Morals, and Politics: Massachusetts in the Age of the Boston Associates* (Boston: Northeastern Univ. Press, 2001), pp. 91–118.

cotton cloth. Proprietors living above the store – many of them associated with the popular sects – were no friends to the South or to slavery. Such "lesser men" and even grandees in smaller factory towns beyond the orbit of the Boston Associates were involved in the movement, some of them as leaders of local abolitionist societies. In Fall River, Nathaniel B. Borden of the legendary clan of textile entrepreneurs, balanced his activism in the local evangelical church with the running of his mill. A tireless movement sentinel with many other uniforms, Borden served briefly in Congress and longer in one of the town's antislavery societies; in 1839 it was re- ported that his "hands"came up with a donation of eleven dollars for the cause, presumably at their boss's behest.[43] In nearby New Bedford, as in any place in the region with a community of Quakers, observant en- trepreneurs organized or headed abolitionist groups.[44] Lynn's version of the abolitionist entrepreneur was Nathan Breed, head of a Quaker family whose business interests included the largest shoe factory in town.[45]

If Elizur Wright's abolitionist "baby" had a fairly easy birth and an un- complicated childhood, its adolescence in the late 1830s proved to be tu- multuous. Infighting erupted and fueled the factionalism that ultimately sundered the movement. Of course, such squabbling was hardly unique to abolitionism. Popular movements in the United States – from temper- ance to labor and civil rights – have had to deal with differences over strategy and tactics, some successfully, some not. A historian of popular insurgencies attributes factionalism to the pace of a movement's devel- opment, arguing that movements that grow slowly and deliberately have a better chance of success because of their ability to digest change and acclimate recruits to larger goals and objectives.[46] Abolitionism soared in the Bay State, adding about fifty local societies a year from 1833 to

---

43 On Borden, see Mary H. Blewett, *Constant Turmoil: The Politics of Industrial Life in Nineteenth-Century New England* (Amherst: Univ. of Massachusetts Press, 2000), pp. 41, and 55–6. Also MASS, *Eighth Annual Report* (1839), p. xlix.

44 Kathryn Grover, *The Fugitive's Gibraltar: Escaping Slaves and Abolitionism in New Bed- ford, Massachusetts* (Amherst: Univ. of Massachusetts Press, 2001). For recent work on the well-known association between Quakers and abolitionism and women's rights, see Nancy A. Hewitt, "Feminist Friends: Agrarian Quakers and the Emergence of Women's Rights in America," *FS* 12 (Spring 1986): 27–49, and Keith Melder, "Abby Kelley and the Process of Liberation," in Yellin and Van Horne, *Abolitionist Sisterhood*, pp. 231–48.

45 Faler, *Mechanics and Manufacturers*, pp. 69–71, and Dawley, *Class and Community*, pp. 29–30.

46 Lawrence Goodwyn, *Democratic Promise: The Populist Movement in America* (New York: Oxford Univ. Press, 1976).

1838, or about one a week. Though such an impressive pace may have encouraged discord, other factors unquestionably figured in, beginning with the movement's grounding in popular religion. Protestantism, by nature schismatic, was a pervasive part of American life. Every community had at least one Protestant church. One could, of course, join myriad popular movements in antebellum America, with the possible exception of temperance or Sabbatarianism, and avoid entanglement with the church. But that was largely impossible for abolitionists simply because, at this stage, abolitionism *was* the church, and the church was everywhere. The movement's appeal to women likewise aroused controversy. Female abolitionists were charged with violating conventions of femininity in both the larger public sphere and the intimate setting of the home and family. It did not matter that the majority of these women vehemently denied the charges, just as they denied having sympathy for early-day feminism.[47] It was the perception that mattered.

Then there were nettlesome personalities, none looming larger than Garrison. When he spoke, people had to listen, even if they preferred not to. He was a towering figure with a gift for words and for getting them out into the public sphere. When he proclaimed on launching his *Liberator*, "I will be heard!" he meant it – and he was. Few movements ever had a more effective propagandist. Even a book like this one, which seeks to bring about a better appreciation of the movement's secondary leaders like Wright and to demonstrate the importance of political abolitionism, must reckon with Garrison, especially with the Garrison of the 1830s when he fomented the factionalism of religion, women's rights, and politics.

The trouble began in the mid-1830s, as nearly every Garrison biographer has shown, with Garrison's infatuation with radical perfection and his subsequent support for women's rights.[48] Henry B. Stanton was among the first to express alarm at Garrison's plunge into religious extremism, which was marked by Garrison's searing and unrelenting assaults on conservative clerics. Garrison upset observant laymen like Stanton, who had met Wright in the early 1830s while a student at Lane Theological Seminary and became an early field agent in Ohio for Wright. In 1836, Stanton left for New York to help with the AASS's petition campaign,

---

[47] Jeffrey, *Great Silent Army of Abolitionism*. Also see Nancy Hewitt, *Women's Activism and Social Change: Rochester, New York, 1822–1872* (Ithaca, N.Y.: Cornell Univ. Press, 1987), and Swerdlow, "Abolitionism's Conservative Sisters."

[48] Thomas, *Liberator*, pp. 208–35, and Mayer, *All on Fire*, pp. 213–39.

FIGURE 6. Henry B. Stanton. (Elizabeth Cady Stanton, *Eighty Years and More* [1815–97] [London: T. Fisher Unwin, 1898], bet. pp. 70 and 71.)

joining the society's agency committee and then taking a seat on its executive board, its chief decision-making body.[49] Stanton was part of an
inner circle that included Wright, the Reverend Joshua Leavitt, and James

---

[49] On Stanton, see Arthur Henry Rice, "Henry Brewster Stanton as a Political Abolitionist"
(M.A. thesis, Columbia Teachers College, 1968), and Dumas Malone et al., eds., *Dictionary of American Biography*, 20 vols. (New York. C. Scribner's Sons, 1928–36), 17:
525–6.

Birney, who interpreted petitioning as evidence that political action short of third partyism could work because some mainstream politicos, and Whigs especially, responded to popular pressure tactfully applied.

Tact, however, was not Garrison's strong suit, not from the beginning of the movement and certainly not in spring 1837 when clergymen, riled up by the feminism of the touring Grimké sisters, lashed out at abolitionists in the church. At a June 1837 meeting of the "Association of Massachusetts Clergymen" (the leading Congregational body in the state), the agitated divines ordered every Congregational minister to read a "pastoral letter" assailing interference in the affairs of the church by abolitionists and feminists. The letter told congregants in no uncertain terms that their ministers were the agents "of God ordained of God to be your *teacher,*" with sole authority to set clerical agendas, so that it was a "violation of [the] sacred... to encourage a stranger" to address extraneous and unauthorized matters. Women's "unostentatious prayers" were welcome, the letter went on, but when a woman "assumes the place and tone of man as a pubic reformer her character becomes unnatural." All reformers – men and women – were warned to stick to "private efforts" for their "spiritual good."[50] For his part, Garrison could not let this implied threat of excommunication pass – he scoffed at it as "popery" and orchestrated a larger attack from his movement surrogates in a bold confrontation with the Protestant establishment.

Garrison's audacity in the "pastoral letter" affair only begins to account for the sectarian backlash that would complicate his movement. The religious question carried a particularly potent charge because it was inextricably bound up in the question of gender, just as the conservatives had implied. Women entered the movement via the portals of the popular sects and Quakerism, which identified slavery as a "sin" in violation of the words of the Lord, a sin that demanded both atonement and eradication.[51] Such biblical terminology suffused the pronouncements of local abolitionist groups in towns and villages across the Bay State. The Uxbridge Female Anti-Slavery Society invoked in its constitution and by-laws "scriptural" injunctions against slavery as the foundation of their group.[52] Their coreligionists in neighboring Andover spoke of their

---

[50] The most recent coverage of this familiar episode is in Mayer, *All on Fire*, pp. 234–6. Quotes are on p. 234.

[51] Jeffrey, *Great Silent Army of Abolitionism*, pp. 134–70. Also see Debra Gold Hansen, *Strained Sisterhood: Gender and Class in the Boston Female Anti-Slavery Society* (Amherst: Univ. of Massachusetts Press, 1993).

[52] *Lib*, Mar. 19, 1836.

"God-like work" and "duty" to rescue the slaves from the "sin against god."[53] Those in Fitchburg likewise believed that they had enlisted in a crusade against "sin" and for the restoration of families shattered by godless planters.[54] The abuse of slave families was uppermost too in the mind of Mary Ann L. Gage, a former resident of South Reading who lived in Concord, Ohio. In 1836, Gage wrote to Garrison recalling her days as a founding member of the South Reading antislavery society. An enthusiastic evangelical, she told her readers what they already knew, namely, that slavery was "man-stealing" and a "sin" that defamed the "sanctity of the marriage relation."[55]

Such single-minded religiosity did not rule out social tensions. In Fall River, for instance, a group of women factory operatives, possibly daughters of the "middling sort," announced that they were leaving the mainstream antislavery society "in this village." According to a missive redolent with labor metaphors, they wanted a more hands-on approach to their abolition work than they thought possible under their local society's more socially prominent leaders, who preferred reading groups and discussions. "We were not doing all that was required at our hands; we felt that we must become *working women* in the cause of those who toil without wages, and suffer without redress," wrote the secessionists. They decided not to "rest in peace upon our pillows, while we neglect to perform our *whole* duty toward those sufferers," but to make "articles bearing representations of slavery with appropriate anti-slavery mottos" and sell them without neglecting the more traditional activities of "reading . . . and holding anti-slavery discussions" sponsored by the established leadership.[56]

This small but revealing disagreement in Fall River discloses class stress rooted in social difference, not in class consciousness, at least not in the minds of these working-class activists. The secessionists believed that they were locked in an unfortunate disagreement over means to a shared end. They expressed themselves in the same evangelical language as their opponents, insisting that when all was said and done "christian women" in the region would pull together to celebrate the "day" when the "black man would stand erect by the side of his white brother, and the black woman

---

[53] Ibid., Aug. 27, 1836.
[54] Ibid., Feb. 25, 1837.
[55] Ibid., Sept. 27, 1836.
[56] Ibid. For an impressive treatment of such daughters in nearby Rhode Island, see Van Broekhoven, *Devotion of These Women.*

would [be] restored to women's rights and privileges."[57] The potent force of religion had trumped class.

Religion also trumped class when it came to individual women. "A Woman" abolitionist in 1838 took issue with a hostile male observer who had said that women's place was in church, not at the barricades, a common complaint against female activists.[58] If this were true, asked "Woman," how could women answer the call of God? She drew precisely the opposite conclusion from scripture, retorting that it "may serve the purposes of man's selfishness better for women to be the first, but if the commands of the Savior are to be obeyed, it becomes needful...to 'call no man master but work out her own salvation' *in her own way.*" She took offense at being attacked for "leading armies to victory." Besides, she added, it was not clear to her that the military was the "appropriate sphere of *man,*" or that men were much of a model at all, if all they had to offer was "becoming a wealth-seeker, a bigot, an ambitious statesman, or an intriguing politician." In closing she asked, "Is society forever to remain as it is now?" "Woman" thought not, because "Christianity has more to do for the world and for woman than it has yet accomplished."[59] It was left to another correspondent, or "S.B." as she called herself, to pursue the feminist logic implied in the letter from "Woman." A resident of Lowell irked by the refusal of a minister to open his church to the Grimké sisters, "S.B." confessed that she was an "ultra" on women's rights. But "such has been the opposition to female effort and influence manifested towards me, in contending for the rights of the poor slave, that I have often had to quit for a season...and contend for my own and the rights of my sex." Confident that she represented the "feeling of

---

[57] A few months later, the Fall River Ladies's Anti-Slavery Society, and probably the working-class secessionists, published an address explaining why wage workers like themselves were better off than slaves. Their labor was compensated and thus a "source of happiness." It went on: "Daughters, can you realize the feelings of those who daily behold their parents driven to the unpaid labor of the field...by the driver's whip; and who, when their parents are sick, may not administer to their comfort? You may serve from your wages a daily pittance with the sweet and hallowed thought 'this shall purchase comforts for my sick mother; this shall alleviate the distress of my father.' And when your daily task is performed, your feet carry you lightly to your homes, with the evidences of your filial affection. Do you know that for the daughters of *slavery* there are no pleasure like these?" See *Lib*, Dec. 17, 1836. For a more militant disquisition on the virtues of "free labor," see the letter of "A Free Woman of Amesbury," ibid., Aug. 18, 1837.

[58] Jeffrey, *Great Silent Army of Abolitionism*, pp. 86–93.

[59] *Lib*, Nov. 30, 1838.

many of my sisters," she signed off "Your affectionate and sincere sister in Christ."[60]

Few abolitionists outside of Garrison's group had much sympathy for the feminism of "S.B." Indeed, Garrison's conspicuous support for such women is one reason why his following shrank by the end of the 1830s.[61] His critics in the New York office included Stanton, who doubted feminism in principle before his 1840 marriage to Elizabeth Cady, and Wright who opposed it for tactical reasons. Wright once betrayed his own caution on the "woman question" when, in 1838, he wrote that the "tom turkeys," ought to do "the gobbling." But his real objection was political. He believed that the issue of women's rights deflected attention from abolitionism and discredited emancipation among the broader public, calling it abolitionism's "tin kettle."[62] It was Garrison's religious extremism, however, that estranged Garrison from Wright's clique in New York.

Henry Stanton was one of the first New Yorkers to assess the perils of Garrison's anticlerical pugnacity. A shrewd political observer and clever tactician, Stanton envisioned the antislavery movement as an agglomeration of groups with different valances, not as an amorphous mass of the righteous. Like all coalitions, it had to be nurtured and maintained. That is why he was so troubled by the pastoral letter affair. In late summer 1837 he was sent to Massachusetts by his associates in the central office to assay the damage firsthand. In September country congregations were still smoldering from Garrison's salvos when Stanton wrote to James Birney in strict confidence that the movement was endangered. Garrison had widened the fissure between "conservatives" and "ultras" and because most of the conservatives in New England were estranged. Such conservatives within the movement, Stanton added ominously, were so influential that they could "sway half the Abolitionists" in the region with a single sermon. He recommended the "calming influence" of the *Emancipator,* now in the sober hands of Leavitt, to settle Yankee tempers, along with pushing Birney to become corresponding secretary so

[60] Ibid., Mar. 30, 1838. Also, July 13, 1838.
[61] Richard Curry and Lawrence Goodheart, "The Complexities of Factionalism: The Letters of Elizur Wright, Jr., on the Abolitionist Schism, 1837–1840," *CWH* 29 (Sept. 1983): 243–59; Aileen Kraditor, *Means and Ends in American Abolitionism: Garrison and His Critics on Strategy and Tactics, 1834–1850* (1969; Chicago: Ivan R. Dee, 1989), esp. pp. 3–77 and Gerda Lerner, *The Grimké Sisters from South Carolina* (New York: Schoken Books, 1971), pp. 243–68.
[62] EW to Amos Phelps, July 11 and Aug. 17 1838, in Curry and Goodheart, "Complexities of Factionalism," pp. 255–6. Also, Goodheart, *Abolitionist, Actuary, Atheist,* p. 105.

that the New Yorkers could take better advantage of his gifts.[63] Stanton's blandishments won over Birney, who eagerly joined Stanton's inner circle and quickly did its bidding by telling Lewis Tappan that he, too, was deeply "disappointed" by Garrison and doubted that Garrison could be "reduced to moderation." Birney concluded, "His departure from us" could well be "the best thing."[64]

Stanton, ever the office politician, confronted an additional personnel problem in the summer of 1837 – Elizur Wright. Stanton was deeply conflicted about the intrepid Yankee. He wrote Birney, in confidence, that he greatly admired Wright's dauntless devotion, tireless dedication, and "transcendent talents," as well as his "steadfast labor." No one worked harder for the cause day in and day out, putting endless hours into the drudgery of correspondence and bearing the pressure of editorial work, not to mention coping with the difficulty of managing a far-flung field staff. But the overwrought Wright was also becoming a liability, "not popular with a certain class of men" in the movement for whom middle-class decorum mattered and who "we must have with us." Such "respectables" were put off by Wright's brusqueness and his indifference to them; Wright did not "desire" their acceptance and, as far as Stanton could see, "will never have it either." They were also troubled by the *"tone and dress"* of his correspondence and annual reports, which is to say their pique was not strictly personal. It was becoming political, for Wright embodied what Stanton called "Anti Slavery Locofocoism, whose spirit and developments [sic] prevent many good men from joining our ranks."[65]

Stanton's assessment of Wright rings true in part. He accurately captured the corresponding secretary's overwrought work ethic, social stiffness, and devil-may-care attitude. Possibly, he also grasped the conservatives' critique of Wright's politics, though it should be kept in mind that Stanton was seeking to lure Birney to the New York office as a counterweight to Wright and thus had an interest in painting as dark and dire a portrait of him as possible. The fact is, however, that Wright's politics in summer and fall 1837 were not fixed or well formulated. Nor can they be easily summarized. Wright was in a transition from the heartfelt evangelical Protestantism he absorbed at home and then at Yale (and shared with the movement's mainstream) to a kind of economic radicalism, which he

[63] HBS to JB, Sept. 1, 1837, in Dumond, *Letters of James Gillespie Birney*, 1: 420–4.
[64] JB to LT, Sept. 14, 1837, in ibid., pp. 424–5. Quote on p. 425.
[65] HBS to JB, Aug. 7, 1837, in ibid., pp. 404–12.

would more fully express in the mid-1840s. In the second half of the 1830s, he was still aligned closely with the religious emotionalism of the Second Great Awakening. He was only beginning to think more seriously about the social dimensions of abolitionism when he wrote his annual reports in 1836 and 1837.[66] It was the references in them to the conservatism of the clergy and the urban middle class that mainstream clerics found so offensive.

Thus when Wright feuded with Garrison in summer 1837, it was not over political radicalism but over Garrison's anticlericism and feminism. Aware of Stanton's growing concern about the "great agitator" and possibly encouraged by it, Wright was nonetheless uneasy with the prospect of rejecting Garrison, his idol, the man who had brought him into the antislavery movement and who had become something of a patron. He expressed his concerns in early September 1837 to the Reverend Amos Phelps, an old friend from Yale days and a reliable ally in the movement. "The man [Garrison] has done more for the slave than I can ever hope to do. I love him, too, like a brother. But," he continued in painful dismay and obvious disillusionment, "I believe his non-combattism and his perfectionism" threaten the cause, adding that Garrison's feminism was a diversion and his fight with the clergy a calamity. Garrison should have known better, he told Phelps, than to pick a fight with the pastorate, a fight that he could never win.[67] Two weeks later, Wright turned on his mentor directly in a letter laced with rage and fury over Garrison's views on "government and religious perfection," which amounted to nothing less than "downright fanaticism," just as his harshest critics had charged. Garrison was "wrong, wrong, wrong" to have aroused the clergy and ought to be "cashiered" – an extraordinary indictment and a measure of just how poisonous their relationship had become.[68] Wright was still in a stew two weeks later, fuming to Garrison, "Bah! I am sick of these outrages on God's *common sense.*"[69] He cooled off long enough to say that he hoped the editor would "nobly refuse to build an anti-slavery sect on the ruins of the theological," but in fact he had no such hopes at all. Even though the formal break would not come for two years – when Wright

[66] See, for instance, EW to TDW, Apr. 21, 1836, and Sept. 22, 1836, in Barnes and Dumond, *Letters of Theodore Dwight Weld*, 1: 291–2 and 337–9. Also see Goodheart, *Abolitionist, Actuary, Atheist*, pp. 77–8 and 80–2.

[67] EW to AP, Sept. 5, 1837, in Curry and Goodheart, "Complexities of Factionalism," p. 250.

[68] EW to WLG, Sept. 16, 1837, in ibid., p. 251.

[69] Ibid., pp. 251–2.

broke ranks and bolted to the anti-Garrisonian Massachusetts Abolition Society and then joined the Liberty Party – Wright had already effectively parted ways with Garrison and his policies.

Wright and his allies had reached several conclusions by fall 1837. They would refrain from antagonizing the clergy over economic and social policy but would not spare Garrison. They would substitute political action for moral suasion, alienating many more activists than the Garrisonians at first but forging ahead anyway believing that the success of the petition campaign held greater promise. Wright took notice as his field agents collected tens of thousands of signatures in 1836, so many that in his 1837 annual report he called for "increasing floods of petitions." He could hardly contain himself when ordered to strengthen coordination among county societies to reach "active individuals" in every town in the North.[70] This traditional form of politicking, centered as it was on Wright's "middle ground" in "the country," succeeded beyond anyone's expectation. Perhaps more than any other experience, petitioning transformed Wright and his fellows from moral suasionists into political abolitionists. Wright was speaking for them in 1837 when he wrote in his annual report that slavery originated in spiritual depravity and sin but was "politically created," "politically sustained,"and could "only be broken politically."[71] Wright and his allies had three choices – petitioning, nonpartisan questioning of office seekers, and third partyism. They were already involved in the first but were not quite prepared for the third because men like Stanton were Whigs who optimistically believed that their party would respond to popular pressure. Nonpartisan questioning, in which candidates were polled and if responsive were endorsed, won by default.

By the late 1830s the tactic of vote scattering often accompanied the questioning of candidates. In vote scattering, if the candidates did not respond favorably to their questions, abolitionist leaders instructed their followers to vote for anyone else – a friend, a favorite son, and so on – and thereby bring the regulars around. The origins of vote scattering are obscure. William Goodell said it was borrowed from the British, a

---

[70] On petitioning, see Deborah Bingham Van Broekhoven, "'Let Your Names Be Enrolled': Method and Ideology in Women's Antislavery Petitioning," in Yellin and Van Horne, *Abolitionist Sisterhood*, pp. 179–99, and Susan Zaeske, *Signatures of Citizenship: Petitioning, Antislavery, and Women's Political Identity* (Chapel Hill: Univ. of North Carolina Press, 2003). Also AASS, *Third Annual Report* (1836), esp. p. 84, and Fourth *Annual Report* (1837), esp. p. 26. Quote in Goodheart, *Abolitionist, Actuary, Atheist*, p. 78.

[71] AASS, *Fourth Annual Report* (1837), pp. 113–14.

plausible explanation given the history of transatlantic appropriations by American abolitionists.[72] Goodell and his fellow New Yorker Beriah Green may have discussed this strategy in 1837, and unquestionably used it in 1838.[73] Whatever its beginnings, vote scattering was the talk of Wright's inner ring by early 1838, and by spring it was official policy of the American Anti-Slavery Society. In early summer Birney, Stanton, and Wright, now joint corresponding secretaries, wrote a letter, published two months later in Leavitt's *Emancipator,* explaining how to implement the new policy. They noted that the last annual meeting of the AASS had resolved to oppose forming a third party, a point the authors continually stressed, on the ground that it would "neutralize our influence." They also pointed out that the association proposed to reward its friends and punish its enemies (anticipating the policy of the American Federation of Labor in the early twentieth century). Members were urged to "interrogate candidates for office "on the subject of Slavery" and to "vote, irrespective of party, for those only who will advocate the principle of Universal Liberty." In elections where neither party responded favorably abolitionists "should either not vote at all, or scatter their votes as circumstances may render advisable."[74] Other movement organs and succeeding editions of the *Emancipator* built morale and passed on electioneering tips from members of the executive committee. Readers were reminded that political insurgency had a recent and honorable history in New York, as the Anti-Masonic movement indicated.[75] They were also told how to implement the policy, from how to form interrogation committees at the local, county, and state levels to how to frame questions to ask the candidates.[76] The fewer and more "simple" the questions, the better, noted a piece in the *Emancipator* that included three questions concerning an end to the slave trade in Washington, D.C., the abolition of slavery in the territories, and a bar to the admission of any more slave states to the Union.[77]

[72] *Eman,* Sept. 20, 1838. Also a letter signed "A Friend of Man," ibid., Aug. 30, 1838.
[73] Lee Benson, *The Concept of Jacksonian Democracy: New York as a Test Case* (New York: Atheneum, 1965), pp. 110–12, suggests that "questioning," if not vote scattering, began in New York State in 1837. See also Milton C. Sernett, *Abolition's Axe: Beriah Green, Oneida Institute, and the Black Freedom Struggle* (Syracuse, N.Y.: Syracuse Univ. Press, 1986), pp. 109–19, and Sernett, *North Star Country: Upstate New York and the Crusade for African American Freedom* (Syracuse, N.Y.: Syracuse Univ. Press, 2002), pp. 104–6.
[74] *Eman,* Sept. 20, 1838. On Leavitt, see Hugh Davis, *Joshua Leavitt, Evangelical Abolitionist* (Baton Rouge: Louisiana State Univ. Press, 1990).
[75] *Eman,* Sept. 20 through Oct. 18, 1838.
[76] Ibid., Sept. 20, 1838.
[77] Ibid.

Although Wright and his friends promoted vote scattering generally, they believed it was likely to be most effective in states that had majority rule, that is, that required candidates to get an absolute majority of the votes cast in order to win. The faithful could exercise the balance of power in such states and thus strongly influence party policy. Massachusetts was a good candidate because it was a bastion of abolitionism and one of the few states that had majority rule. So in fall 1838 the abolitionist gaze was on the Bay State. An anonymous columnist in the *Liberator* called the vote scattering compaign in the Fourth Congressional District in Massachusetts "an experiment of immense consequence."[78] Even Garrison, aware that he was being upstaged by political abolitionists, and none too comfortable about it, went along, dropping his objection to voting. He covered the election closely in his *Liberator*, publishing reports from the field by such movement stalwarts as Stanton, Phelps, and John Greenleaf Whittier, along with letters from lesser lights affiliated with local antislavery societies.[79] He promoted vote scattering before election day in editorials that explained how to cast ballots in districts pursuing the new political strategy.[80] In mid-December, following a run-off election, he saluted the "integrity displayed by our friends" in the Fourth, predicting that "their example will inspire our abolitionist brethren throughout the country to do likewise.[81] Six weeks later, Garrison applauded the "unswerving integrity political friends of bleeding humanity," in the Fourth who turned out in great enough numbers to force still another runoff.[82]

Garrison had another reason to sound supportive. That the Fourth included Middlesex County – one of the banner abolitionist counties in the state and arguably in the nation – made it a promising testing ground for the new strategy. The election more closely resembled a saga, however, for the initial poll was followed by three runoffs stretching from December to the following March. No one had ever seen anything like it; few would forget what they saw.

Stanton arrived in Middlesex sometime in the fall to help the county organization with the campaign. He found an impressive movement at the county level, tightly organized in cities and towns and so eager to get going that it had jumped the gun. Months before the official start of the

[78] *Lib*, Jan. 18, 1839
[79] Ibid., Nov. 9, 16, and 23, 1838; Dec. 21, 1838, and Jan. 18, 1839.
[80] Ibid., Nov. 2, 1838.
[81] Ibid., Dec. 21, 1838.
[82] Ibid., Feb. 8, 1839.

campaign the Middlesex County Anti-Slavery Society had already prepared its questionnaire for the candidates – the Whig nominee Nathan
Brooks of Concord and the Democratic incumbent William Parmenter of
East Cambridge.[83] Brooks was a lawyer turned insurance executive, with
a name among the party's temperance advocates, and a political veteran of
several terms in the state's House and Senate. When faced with the abolitionists' questionnaire, however, he simply refused to answer; he thought
that his wife's close association with local abolitionists would suffice for
him to secure the antislavery vote, as the antislavery activist Henry Wilson
later charged.[84] It did not. A local wag and irate abolitionist who interpreted Brooks's silence to mean that the candidate favored "letting slavery alone" recommended letting "*him* alone."[85] Another called Brooks a
"*colonizationist*," the curse of the era for abolitionists.[86] Parmenter did
respond to the abolitionists' questionnaire, but his answers were so vague
and evasive that the county committee pronounced him unfit for consideration, and recommended vote scattering.[87] Through early November the
committee used the press, town meetings, and countywide gatherings to
publicize its strategy.[88] About three hundred abolitionists scattered their
votes, somewhat fewer than expected but a large enough number to prevent either candidate from polling the required majority, forcing another
election in late December.[89] The committee redoubled its efforts for the
new poll, with still more rallies and local meetings that brought out more
women as well as more men.[90] This time they more than doubled the
number of scatters to over six hundred fifty, just about half of the estimated abolitionist vote in the county, which forced still another run
off.[91]

By the beginning of the new year the Massachusetts race had grabbed
national attention. Nathaniel P. Rogers watched events unfold from
nearby New Hampshire, and James Birney reported that his colleagues

[83] Ibid., Aug. 13, 1838. Louis Ruchames, ed., *The Letters of William Lloyd Garrison, 1805–
1879*, 6 vols. (Cambridge: Harvard Univ. Press, 1971–81), 2: 447, n. 12.

[84] Henry Wilson, *The Rise and Fall of the Slave Power in America*, 3 vols. (Boston: James
R. Osgood, 1872–7) 1: 546.

[85] *Lib*, Nov. 2, 1838.

[86] Ibid., Nov. 9, 1838.

[87] Ibid., Nov. 2, 1838.

[88] Ibid., Nov. 2, 9, and 23, 1838.

[89] Ibid., Nov. 16 and 23, 1838.

[90] *Lib*, Nov. 23, 1838.

[91] Ibid., Dec. 21, 1838.

in the New York office were clamoring for news as the third runoff approached.[92] Henry Stanton, on site, dashed from meeting to meeting trying to offset a potentially damaging intervention by Democratic stalwart Benjamin Hallett, Jr. A rising star in his party, Hallett represented its new urban strategy of appealing to the masses by raising the specter of prohibition and by resorting to race baiting, his party's most potent weapon against abolitionism.[93] Hallett scared up more votes for Parmenter, but not enough to put the Democratic candidate over the top, thanks to a hundred-vote increase in the number of scatters. With the persistent effectiveness of scattering some antislavery men were convinced that they had at last broken the grip of partisanship on the electorate, only to see party loyalty undo their work in the third and last runoff.[94] In March, a Whig whom Stanton had taken to be a friend publicly repudiated the scattering campaign. His defection, coupled perhaps with the fears aroused by Hallett's hysterical populism, cut the number of scatters by over two hundred and narrowly threw the election to Parmenter and the Democrats.[95]

The election's conclusion greatly relieved a nervous Garrison. The Bay State's leading abolitionist, says his most recent biographer, did not necessarily oppose political engagement, only political action divorced from moral conviction. Good politics – indeed, its only acceptable form – had to be rooted in "good conscience," and voters had to go to the polls as "free moral agents, not as the tools of party."[96] Garrison found partisan activity especially objectionable because the "tyrant party" overrode conscience, because it required compromise, and because it threatened his policy of making abolitionism *the* issue, or what he and his opponents alike called the "one idea." While it would be foolish to dispute Garrison's distrust of politics over the long haul, it is equally misleading to find consistency in a man who was terribly inconsistent and who was not only responsive to events but also more than a little opportunistic when his own interests were at stake. Garrison's mind, in other words, did not slam shut like a bear trap, in part because Garrison could not afford for it to do so, notably when he seemed to be outflanked by events.

---

[92] Ibid., Jan. 18, 1839.
[93] Ibid., Feb. 8, 1839.
[94] Ibid., Mar. 22 and 29, 1839.
[95] Ibid., Apr. 5 and 12, 1839.
[96] Quoted in Mayer, *All on Fire*, p. 264.

There were times when he actively encouraged political engagement, even as he denied doing so, and times when he accepted it, at least episodically, for lack of an alternative.[97]

Garrison's response to the abolitionist electioneering of 1838–9 in the Fourth is a signal case of his situational ethics. The tactic of vote scattering, it is important to recall, caught on at the local level in Garrison's own backyard. He had nothing to do with it, and rightly felt caught in the middle between Henry Stanton's New Yorkers and the Middlesex County Anti-Slavery Society. Garrison had no choice early on but to play along. In December, following the first runoff, he predicted that the vote scattering would force one or more of the regular parties to nominate abolitionists for office.[98] A month later, following the second runoff, he elaborated this point, publishing an unsigned column that reflected his position that vote scattering would obviate the need for a third party.[99] But the defeat two months later ended any talk of politics. The "immense" experiment had suddenly shrunk in stature, meriting only passing mention in the *Liberator*. Perhaps he secretly hoped for defeat all along, for shortly before the last runoff he lamely confided to his brother-in-law that the Democrats would probably win because "Bro. Stanton was premature in stirring up the political waters in that District."[100]

Wright had no such reservations. Whereas the vote scattering campaign of 1838–9 failed to seat an abolitionist in Congress, it did reveal the possibility of directing abolitionist sentiment into political channels. Wright and his allies thus tried to seize the moment, starting with the January meeting of the Massachusetts Anti-Slavery Society (MASS), which incidentally took place in the midst of the campaign in the Fourth. They dispatched Stanton to the meeting with a resolution that would have made political activity (of an unspecified sort) incumbent upon all members. This proposal set the stage for the now famous confrontation between Stanton and Garrison, who successfully rallied his forces against

---

[97] This line of argumentation closely follows Kraditor, *Means and Ends in American Abolitionism*, who claims that Garrison was not opposed to politics per se. Garrison endorsed petitioning and even vote scattering but not partisan involvement, because it threatened to restrict his movement's following. While it is certain that Garrison recognized fine distinctions between partisan politics and pressure group tactics, I do not find him to be as consistent as Kraditor maintains. He was, if anything, inconsistent and not a little opportunistic.

[98] *Lib*, Dec. 21, 1838.

[99] Ibid., Jan. 18, 1839.

[100] WLG to George W. Benson, Mar. 19, 1839, in Ruchames, *Letters of William Lloyd Garrison*, 2: 442–7. Quote on p. 444.

the measure.[101] Defeated at the convention, the political abolitionists met a few weeks later in Boston to form the Massachusetts Abolition Society, a rival to Garrison's MASS, and quickly recruited Wright to be an officer and editor of their organ, the *Massachusetts Abolitionist*.[102] The seeds of political abolitionism, sown in petitioning and watered by vote scattering, had sprouted. The "new organization," as political abolitionism would be called, had an enthusiastic cultivator in Wright, who told an intimate that his "plan was not to enter the field to cut up the weeds – the isms – but to hoe the corn and till it well, and let the weeds look out for themselves."[103]

Wright was much too optimistic. He inadvertently complicated matters when he turned his "new org" organ into a platform for his pet grievances, assailing the clergy, taunting advocates of women's rights, and pressing for a third party. His hard-hitting editorials angered his sponsors, who asked him to leave in May 1840.[104] The timing was fortuitous. His allies, notably the New Yorkers Alvan Stewart and Myron Holley, tried repeatedly to organize an abolitionist party through the fall and winter of 1839 and 1840, but encountered stiff resistance from Garrisonians and even from political abolitionists who continued to favor political action short of third partyism. It took four raucous meetings and herculean organizing before they inaugurated the Liberty Party in April 1840, a month before Wright was fired.[105]

The appearance of the Liberty Party was signal moment in the history of abolitionism. No one knew in 1840 where it would lead. Garrisonians condemned Wright and his allies as a ruinous and misguided force, and some historians have not been much kinder. One scholar finds them to have been an unimpressive band of "conservatives" and second-raters with a litany of personal weaknesses and liabilities. James Birney, the former Alabama slave owner who became an abolitionist and the party's first nominee for president, retained "the oligarchic planter's hauteur"; Henry Stanton was suspect for his "transparent ambition and reputation for mendacity"; Amos Phelps was "hot tempered" and "too preoccupied with petty grievances to offer much direction and inspiration." As

---

[101] Mayer, *All on Fire*, pp. 254–8, and Thomas, *Liberator*, pp. 266–9.
[102] Goodheart, *Abolitionist, Actuary, Atheist*, pp. 106–8.
[103] Quoted in ibid., p. 107.
[104] Ibid., pp. 111–12.
[105] Mayer, *All on Fire*, pp. 261–84. Also Sernett, *North Star Country*, pp. 104–28; Elizur Wright, Jr., *Myron Holley; And What He Did for Liberty and True Religion* (Boston: Elizur Wright, 1882); and Sewell, *Ballots for Freedom*, pp. 43–73 and 88–106.

for Wright, "his administrative talents far exceeded his literary gifts."[106]
One could add that nothing exceeded his intemperance and lack of tact.
What was a fledging movement to do with such a collection of misfits
and losers, and the likes of Garrison to contend with? This scholar asserted that in "disassociating themselves from [Garrison's] vision, they
condemned themselves to obscurity and allowed Garrison...to put his
stamp upon the age."[107] This assessment is half right. No "new org"
abolitionist came close to challenging Garrison's stature as the nation's
foremost abolitionist. The new movement, however, would become anything but obscure in the Bay State, where it would become a critical political force that broadened the foundation of antislavery, blended civil
rights into the larger struggle, and prepared the ground for its political
successors.

[106] Mayer, *All on Fire*, p. 268.
[107] Ibid., p. 284. For a similar interpretation of the relative merits of Garrisonianism and
    Libertyism without such a negative view of its leaders, see Stewart, *Holy Warriors*,
    pp. 95–6 and 97–105.

2

"Evil . . . from a Very Small Party"

The Rise of the Liberty Party

Massachusetts was one of the most innovative states in antebellum America. Its storied entrepreneurs in the textile industry organized the first mills to integrate the weaving of cloth with the spinning of thread; more obscure but no less visionary mechanics in the metal trades made armaments and precision equipment that were the envy of the world.[1] Catholics founded one of their first major colleges there; social reformers pioneered the first asylums for the blind and mentally troubled; and writers launched the first American Renaissance. It was one of the few states in which African American men enjoyed the right to vote, and it was one of the first states to recognize married women's property rights.[2] But the Bay State's appetite for experimentation extended only so far, stopping at the ballot box. Between 1834 and 1850, voters gave the Whigs a commanding majority in the state legislature, or the General Court, as it was formally known, and elected the party's candidate for governor every year but two. Massachusetts was something of a one-party state.

---

[1] On Massachusetts textiles, see Caroline F. Ware, *The Early New England Cotton Textile Manufacture: A Study of Industrial Beginnings* (Boston: Houghton Mifflin, 1931), and Laurence F. Gross, *The Course of Industrial Decline: The Boott Cotton Mills of Lowell Massachusetts, 1835–1955* (Baltimore: Johns Hopkins Univ. Press, 1993). On the badly understudied metal and arms industries, see Bruce K. Tull, "Springfield Armory as Industrial Policy: Interchangeable Parts and the Precision Corridor" (Ph.D. diss., Univ. of Massachusetts Amherst, 2001).

[2] See Richard H. Chused, "Married Women's Property Law, 1800–1850," *Georgetown Law Journal* 71 (June 1983): 1359–1425. Also see Glendyne R. Wergland, "Women, Men, Property, and Inheritance: Gendered Testamentary Customs in Western Massachusetts, 1800–1860" (Ph.D. diss., Univ. of Massachusetts Amherst, 2001), esp. pp. 6–40.

The Democracy, Whiggery's main opposition, might have been more competitive were it not for its chronic factionalism. The party had a small but powerful urban wing based in Boston and headed by David Henshaw. Closely tied to the national party, the Henshawites, or "hunkers," as they were known, mirrored the laissez-faire politics that had become the national party's trademark but stood for little other than support for the South and patronage for one another. Democracy's rural wing in the state was several times larger than the hunkers. It was led by Marcus Morton, who paired economic radicalism with an antislavery ethos born of anti-Southernism and often laced with racism. Such Locofocos were found on the geographic periphery of the state, with patchy strongholds in the southeast outside of Cape Cod and broad support in the westernmost county of Berskshire.[3] They gave the Democracy its reputation as a party of farmers, a reputation borne out in part by the fact that in the early 1840s over half of its delegation in the state's House were farmers (as against about 40% of the Whigs).[4]

Famously insular and parochial, and suspicious of concentrated power, Locofoco Democrats would have preferred to work their fields in ignorance of events in the nation's capital. The increasingly boisterous controversy over slavery, however, could not help but reach rural America, arousing even the most localistic farmers and townsfolk. The signal event was the struggle over gag rule, in which Southern Democrats responded to the American Anti-Slavery Society's "petition campaign" by demanding that petitions dealing with slavery be tabled. Northern Democrats initially went along out of partisan loyalty but such fealty soon irritated them and their constituents. Gag rule looked more and more to Yankee Democrats like a violation of free speech, a restraint that did not go down well with men whose party stood for the personal liberty of small government. It also evoked the anti-Southern feeling of rural and small town New England. As the historian William Freehling has observed,

---

[3] Ronald P. Formisano, *The Transformation of Political Culture: Massachusetts Parties, 1790s–1840s* (New York: Oxford Univ. Press, 1983), pp. 268–320; William F. Hartford, *Money, Morals, and Politics: Massachusetts in the Age of the Boston Associates* (Boston: Northeastern Univ. Press, 2001), pp. 130–1, 182–3, and 204–5; and Jonathan Earle, "Marcus Morton and the Dilemma of Antislavery in Jacksonian Massachusetts, 1817–1849," *MHR* 2 (2002): 61–88.

[4] Compiled from House of Representatives, Journal of the House of Representatives, 1842, mss. Massachusetts State Archives, Boston, Mass. The actual percentages are Democrats 55% and Whigs 41%, a surprisingly high percentage overall given that Massachusetts was the most industrial state in the Union. Nonetheless, the disparity between the parties is still striking.

"[C]ontests over gagging congressional slavery debates epitomized why Yankees previously hostile to abolitionists became furious over the slave power."[5] Many Northern Democrats were furious enough to vote against renewing the "gag" in 1840, even though they otherwise tended to stick with their party.[6] Their stand against what was being dubbed "the slave power" initially played well in their home districts, enhancing the Democracy's stature on farms and in villages at the turn of the 1840s but also making its rural wing vulnerable to the blandishments of rival parties with antislavery credentials.

Whig hegemony rested in part on ideological and economic forces. Party rhetoric reflected a blend of evangelical Protestantism and secular corporatism, with an overlay of industrial paternalism and regional pride. Evangelicalism could be a source of contention and division, as it was in 1838 when drys based in the country pushed through a tough liquor licensing bill that split the party so badly that the Democrats won the governorship for the first time.[7] Evangelicalism also accounts for the nativism in country Whiggery, a force that not only propelled the drive for prohibition but also put the party on record for sabbatarian laws and mandatory bible reading in public schools among other implicitly anti-Catholic policies.[8] This same evangelical sensibility sustained antislavery sentiment in country Whiggery. Quieter and decidedly less conspicuous than Garrisonianism, Whiggish antislavery was nonetheless a significant tendency that gave the party credibility in such antislavery strongholds as Worcester and Middlesex counties.[9] Party potentates in Boston and in the industrial outposts of the Boston Associates generally opposed the

[5] See William W. Freehling, *The Road to Disunion: Sectionalists at Bay, 1776–1854* (New York: Oxford Univ. Press, 1990), pp. 308–36 and 345–52, and Leonard L. Richards, *The Slave Power: The Free North and Southern Domination, 1780–1860* (Baton Rouge: Louisiana State Univ. Press, 2000), pp. 81–2, 132–3, 156–7, and 173–8.

[6] Richards, *Slave Power*, pp. 138–9.

[7] Formisano, *Transformation of Political Culture*, pp. 227–37. Also Ian R. Tyrell, *Sobering Up: From Temperance to Prohibition in Antebellum America, 1800–1860* (Westport, Conn.: Greenwood Press, 1979), pp. 94–5 and 237–9.

[8] Formisano, *Transformation of Political Culture*, pp. 297–301.

[9] Leonard L. Richards, *The Life and Times of Congressman John Quincy Adams* (New York: Oxford Univ. Press, 1986), pp. 90–5; Hartford, *Money, Morals, and Politics*, pp. 94–118; Arthur B. Darling, *Political Change in Massachusetts, 1824–1848: A Study of Liberal Movements in Politics* (New Haven, Conn.: Yale Univ. Press, 1925), pp. 344–5; Kinley J. Brauer, *Cotton Vesus Conscience: Massachusetts Whigs and Southwestern Expansion, 1843–1848* (Lexington: Univ. of Kentucky Press, 1967); and Michael F. Holt, *The Rise and Fall of the American Whig Party: Jacksonian Politics and the Onset of the Civil War* (New York: Oxford Univ. Press, 1999), esp. pp. 178–81 and passim.

moralistic policies of country Whiggery. As a rule, party and faith formed something of a seamless whole.[10]

The secular companion to Yankee Protestantism was a corporate vision of a stratified social order composed of ranks arranged hierarchically and mutually interdependent. Whiggish corporatism assumed that everyone had a place within the social order, from the merchant and industrialist down to the yeoman farmer, village mechanic, and casual laborer, along with their spouses and children. It placed the accent on obligations and responsibilities individuals, groups, and classes owed to one another, rather than on individual rights government was obliged to protect.[11] The proper role of government, much like that of the paternalistic employer, was protection from harm. No form of protection mattered more to Whigs than did protectionism, that is, tariff schedules. Indeed, Whiggery's investment in the tariff and in workplace paternalism were inversely related, so that the rhetoric of tariff politics strengthened as paternal provisions weakened. Whig politicians promoted protectionism itself as a labor program, or what they were fond of calling their "high wage" policy.[12] It went with the reminder that Democrats stood for free trade, which meant wage reductions and unemployment for workers and ruin for all.[13] "Two dollars a day and roast beef," was the Whigs' robust appeal to labor.[14]

Whig hegemony also depended on the reciprocity of patronage and paternalistic arrangements that helped bind the classes to one another and, by extension, to the Bay State's dominant party. Patronage in this context extended beyond courthouse politics in which party leaders rewarded lieutenants and lesser functionaries with jobs and plied voters with money, liquor, or whatever. Both parties relied on such conventional incentives.[15] Patronage also involved more opaque rewards, one of which

[10] Formisano, *Transformation of Political Culture*, pp. 268–301. Also Daniel Walker Howe, *The Political Culture of the American Whigs* (Chicago: Univ. of Chicago Press, 1979), and Holt, *Rise and Fall of the American Whig Party*, pp. 300–1 and 185–7.

[11] Formisano, *Transformation of Political Culture*, pp. 268–301.

[12] *MS*, Oct. 30, 1846, and *BA*, Nov. 11 and 13, 1848, Nov. 2, 1852, and May 4, 1853. For a different view of the tariff, see James L. Huston, "A Political Response to Industrialism: The Republican Embrace of Protectionist Labor Doctrines," *JAH* 70 (June 1983): 35–57. Also see Jonathan A. Glickstein, *American Exceptionalism, American Anxiety: Wages, Competition, and Degraded Labor in the United States* (Charlottesville: Univ. of Virginia Press, 2002), esp. pp. 191–7 for a subtle interpretation of tariff politics.

[13] *Comm*, June 8, 1853.

[14] Charles Cowley, *Illustrated History of Lowell* (revd. ed.; Boston: Lee and Shepard, 1868), p. 158.

[15] See, for instance, Stephen W. Nissenbaum, "The Firing of Nathaniel Hawthorne," *EIHC* 114 (1978): 57–86, and Formisano, *Transformation of Political Culture*, pp. 307–10.

was clearly inadvertent in that it was not contrived explicitly to encourage partisanship. It derived instead from prosaic economic intercourse, from relations between employer and employee, buyer and seller, and so on. The expanding web of market exchange in Jacksonian America meant that everyone but the most remote subsistence farmer became enmeshed in commerce. Workers on the rolls of Whig, and sometimes of Democratic, factory owners, for instance, understood that political fealty was an asset and often a condition of employment. This tacit feature of labor contracts proved particularly important in Massachusetts because of the power and authority wielded by the Boston Associates, the tightly spun tangle of families that controlled thousands of jobs in the textile and metallurgical industries and ran the Whig Party. Before conditions deteriorated at the turn of the 1840s such employers and their agents rarely had to tell employees how to vote; everyone involved assumed that voting Whig was part of the job.[16] It was called "influence." And influence remained unchallenged until discontent in the early 1850s over the length of the workday confronted managerial authority.

Whiggish influence reached beyond the state's industrial enclaves. Its orbit extended to the local economy of smaller towns and villages in which craftsmen counted the elite as prized customers because they paid promptly and in cash, avoiding the long delays and payment in kind that typified the old barter economy.[17] Village swells and worthies needed local tradesmen for everything from supplying clothing and household furnishings to constructing buildings and maintaining carriages and other means of transportation. They favored tradesmen who were known to be resourceful and were reliable enough to respond at a moment's notice to fix a shattered window or a broken wagon wheel. The Worcester cabinetmaker Lansford Wood (1806–44) typified such tradesmen. Wood was a versatile man whose multiple sources of income included rent from his small farm and fees from leasing his horse and cart.[18] He made fine furniture in his shop for the Salisburys, the Lincolns, and other mainstays of

---

[16] See Chapter 6.

[17] Christopher Clark, *The Roots of Rural Capitalism: Western Massachusetts, 1780–1860* (Ithaca, N.Y.: Cornell Univ. Press, 1990), and Daniel Vickers, *Farmers and Fisherman: Two Centuries of Work in Essex County, Massachusetts, 1630–1850* (Chapel Hill: Univ. of North Carolina Press, 1994).

[18] Lansford Wood, Account Book, 1833–1841, ms., American Antiquarian Society, Worcester, Mass. Hereafter AAS. On the incomes of middling sorts, see Bruce Laurie, "'We are not afraid to work': Master Mechanics and the Market Revolution in the Antebellum North," in Burton J. Bledstein and Robert D. Johnston, eds., *The Middling Sorts: Explorations in the History of the Middle Class* (New York: Routledge, 2001), pp. 50–68.

the town's Whig elite. He doubled as their handyman, painting railings and repairing gas mains as readily as he made furniture. He was also their political ally, for by the mid-1840s Wood was one of a number of mechanics on the Whig Party's town committee, a body that fused together the economic relationships and common political interests of manufacturers and tradesmen.[19]

The patronage of the press was more explicitly political, and it was distinctly partisan. No political party was complete without a party organ. Since parties cut across class lines and had to bring together members from different cultural and interest groups, a single party organ did not have the necessary reach, especially in the more cosmopolitan cities and larger towns. Each party required multiple organs, geared to different audiences. Given the advent of mass politics, this meant the paper had to have a popular touch designed for the mechanics and tradesmen who divided their loyalties between both parties.

In Boston, Whiggery's plebeian paper was the *Boston Courier*, founded by Joseph Tinker Buckingham, who had arrived in the city at the turn of the century. He traveled to Boston from the western part of the state via remote, rural Connecticut and started several papers and journals, only to see them fail, one by one. Buckingham had better financial luck following the War of 1812, and then he achieved some political celebrity as a supporter of the Middling Interest, a populist insurgency in the mid-1820s.[20] His journalistic gifts caught the attention of the political upstart Daniel Webster, attracted by Buckingham's youthful bearing and popular touch. Webster helped put together a consortium of small businessmen to back what became Buckingham's *Boston Courier*, which evolved into the most important voice of popular Whiggery in the city. But because of Buckingham's tough-minded independence the *Courier* was not consistently partisan.[21] More troublesome still was his ornery dislike of the South, a popular perspective among ordinary people but one not shared by the state's textile manufacturers dependent on Southern cotton for

---

[19] *SSWR*, May 3, 1844.

[20] On the Middling Interest, see Matthew H. Crocker, *The Magic of the Many: Josiah Quincy and the Rise of Mass Politics in Boston, 1800–1830* (Amherst: Univ. of Massachusetts Press, 1999), pp. 62–5 and 70–98. Also see Formisano, *Transformation of Political Culture*, pp. 181–7.

[21] Joseph Tinker Buckingham, *Personal Memoirs and Recollections of Editorial Life*, 2 vols. (Boston: Ticknor, Reed, and Fields, 1852). Also see Gary J. Kornblith, "From Artisans to Businessmen: Master Mechanics in New England, 1790–1850" (Ph.D. diss., Princeton Univ., 1983), pp. 291–349.

FIGURE 7. Joseph Tinker Buckingham. (Joseph Tinker Buckingham, *Personal Memoirs and Recollections of Editorial Life*, 2 vols. [Boston: Ticknor, Reed, and Fields, 1852], frontispiece.)

their factories and on the votes of Southern Whigs in Congress for tariff protection. Buckingham's impatience with Whiggery's romance with the South opened a highly publicized breach in the late 1840s. No one who had followed Buckingham's career was surprised. He had had several skirmishes with his patrons over the years, not over slavery but over class loyalty.[22]

---

[22] Kornblith, "Becoming Joseph T. Buckingham," in Howard B. Rock et al., eds., *American Artisans: Crafting Social Identity, 1780–1860* (Baltimore: John Hopkins Univ. Press, 1995), pp. 123–34.

One of Buckingham's run-ins with Boston's power elite is worth recounting for what it reveals about social tensions among skilled laborers, master mechanics, and merchant capitalists. In March 1832, following the formation of the New England Association of Farmers, Mechanics, and Other Working Men, shipbuilding tradesmen in Boston resolved to meet with master craftsmen "for the purpose of adopting a uniform system . . . to govern the hours of labor, and if possible, to unite the interests of the employer and the employed."[23] Some of these workers had been in the same position in 1825 when about five hundred house carpenters walked off their jobs in the nation's first major strike for a ten-hour workday. The house carpenters' work stoppage began in late March or early April with great hoopla but soon petered out and by mid-summer collapsed in the face of opposition from the master craftsmen who employed them. The decisive power, however, was that of the merchant capitalists who financed building construction and hired the master craftsmen to recruit labor and direct the work. At a meeting shortly after the strike began the merchants denounced the journeymen's pernicious "associations and combinations," and threatened to blacklist recalcitrant masters and journeymen.[24]

The 1832 strike rehearsed the previous one even though it ran from early spring to late summer. Journeymen again aroused the merchants, who once more clubbed together and talked about another firing spree. This time, however, the beleaguered workmen drew support from beyond their trades. Buckingham planted a reporter in the merchants' meeting, and then published the story. "Spectator" asserted that the shipwrights' and caulkers' grievances were just and "ought to be remedied." As he saw it, the dispute exposed the arrogance of the merchants and shipowners and their irritating habit of "imposing their own terms." The reporter ridiculed their hypocrisy, jealousy of power, and "selfishness which blinds the intellect and hardens the heart," and he closed with a common man's interpretation of the uses of organization and the lessons of the city's Revolutionary tradition: "The spirit of association has extended itself to the industrious employments, and it is too late to repress it. Merchants were regarded as a degraded class by the Federal aristocracy. They raised

[23] John R. Commons et al., eds., *Documentary History of American Industrial Society*, 10 vols. (1958; Cleveland: A. H. Clark, 1910–11), 6: 81–6. Quote on p. 82. David R. Roediger and Philip S. Foner, *Our Own Time: A History of Labor and the Working Day* (Westport, Conn.: Greenwood Press, 1989), pp. 24–5, and Kornblith, "Artisans to Businessmen," pp. 501–2.

[24] Commons, *Documentary History*, 6: 81–2.

themselves by *association*. The laboring class will accomplish what the merchants had done ... *by association*."[25]

Buckingham's stealthy journalism caused a huge uproar. Within a few days he was confronted by enraged merchants demanding to know the identity of "Spectator" and demanding that Buckingham apologize for his paper's underhandedness. The feisty journalist flatly refused, retorting that *he* was owed the apology for having been attacked publicly instead of consulted at a private meeting. Besides, he told the merchants, he agreed completely with Spectator's views and saw no reason for a retraction.[26]

Though this episode bore the imprint of Buckingham's steadfast independence, it also reveals something more general about the complexity of a man's identity, the forces that competed for his loyalty, and the strength of Whiggery. Buckingham was an old-fashioned master craftsman, loyal to his fellow tradesmen and responsible for his employees. Other master mechanics looked to him for leadership, electing him head of the Massachusetts Charitable Mechanic Association (MCMA), their most important organization.[27] He served the MCMA for years in various capacities but also looked out for the interests of his own employees, who thought so well of him that they once agreed to a pay moratorium to spare him a certain sentence of imprisonment for debt.[28] Buckingham was also a political agent in the pay of a party that was deferential to Southerners he personally found loathsome and nakedly antagonistic to organized labor. He complained about Massachusetts elites yet served them nearly all his editorial life, breaking ranks with them at just about the time he would have retired anyway. That the Whigs could count on such a man testifies to their political strength – and to what a fledgling party like the Liberty men were up against.

The Liberty Party at first more closely resembled a burlesque than a serious political contender. Its founders, Alvan Stewart and Myron Holley, both from upstate New York, had faced contempt and ridicule at the meetings they called in fall and winter 1839–40 to organize a party. Not until April 1840 did they prevail, and then only by fewer than a dozen votes out of some seventy-five cast. Even in the Bay State, where the strength

---

[25] *BC*, June 2, 1832.
[26] Ibid., June 7, 1832.
[27] Joseph Tinker Buckingham, comp., *Annals of the Massachusetts Charitable Mechanic Association* (Boston: Crocker and Brewster, 1853).
[28] See Laurie, "'We are not afraid to work.'"

of third party sentiment was second only to that in New York, politically minded abolitionists remained skittish. Over half the subscribers
to Wright's *Massachusetts Abolitionist* canceled their subscriptions in
protest against his editorials for a new party.[29] Wright's firing was followed by the Bay State party's initial nominating convention, which suffered from bad judgment and bad luck. Its first nominee for governor
refused the call, and its choice for lieutenant governor died suddenly during the summer, forcing operatives to quickly put together a new ticket.[30]

Bay State Libertyites gradually found firmer political ground. Though
party activists thought of themselves as the moral voice of the people,
uncorrupted by "party," they inexorably copied the structures of political
orthodoxy.[31] A state central committee directed and coordinated party
affairs, communicating to cadre directly and through the official organ
of Reverend Joshua Leavitt's *Emancipator*. This structure left an organizational void between the state committee and the ordinary voter despite
repeated urgings from state leaders for tighter and deeper organization
down to school districts.[32] To fill it, a hierarchy of town and county committees was set up in 1843, along with a host of ad hoc groups that shot
up in the election season of late summer and early fall.[33] By election time
1844, the Libertyites had party infrastructure that reached down to the
precinct level in virtually every city and town, along with an active press,
including such local and regional sheets as the *Hampshire Herald, Middlesex Standard*, and *Amesbury Transcript*, to complement the *Emancipator*, joined a year later by Elizur Wright's *Chronotype*. The appearance
of Wright's paper followed a reorganization program ordered by the
state committee and carried out by Henry B. Stanton, who had opened
a law practice in Boston and worked for the party ever since. Stanton
firmed up operations by giving county and district committees greater

---

[29] Lawrence B. Goodheart, *Abolitionist, Actuary, Atheist: Elizur Wright and the Reform
Impulse* (Kent, Ohio: Kent State Univ. Press, 1990), pp. 111–12.

[30] See Ralph Harlow, *Gerrit Smith, Philanthropist and Reformer* (New York: Holt, 1939),
pp. 147–8.

[31] On the antipartyism of political insurgents, see Mark Voss-Hubbard, *Beyond Party:
Cultures of Antipartisanship in Northern Politics before the Civil War* (Baltimore: Johns
Hopkins Univ. Press, 2002), pp. 9–10 and 440–7, and Holt, *American Whig Party*,
pp. 30–2, 270–3, and 345ff.

[32] *Eman*, Aug. 25 and Dec. 8, 1842. Also Reinhard O. Johnson, "The Liberty Party in
Massachusetts, 1840–1848," *CWH* 28 (Sept. 1982), esp. pp. 242–3. For different perspectives on the Libertyites, see Alan M. Kraut, ed., *Crusaders and Compromisers: Essays
on the Relationship of the Antislavery Struggle to the Antebellum Party System* (Westport,
Conn.: Greenwood Press, 1983).

[33] *Eman*, Mar. 3 and July 20, 1843. Also Oct. 16, 1844.

FIGURE 8. John Greenleaf Whittier. (John Greenleaf Whittier, *Poetical Works*, 4 vols. [Boston: Houghton Mifflin, 1892], 3: frontispiece.)

authority and improving coordination up and down the line.[34] His party had evolved into a political contender. The journalist and poet cum operative John Greenleaf Whittier told a county convention shortly after the reforms of 1843 took hold that the "Liberty party is no longer an experiment. It is vigorous reality, exerting . . . a powerful influence."[35]

Rising luminaries like Whittier took their party work seriously. The Amesbury poet doubled as a journalist and local leader (he was never much of a speaker and left stumping to others). He also sought the support and involvement of fellow writers and intellectuals of the American

[34] Johnson, "Liberty Party in Massachusetts," pp. 243–4, and *Eman*, Mar. 4, 1846 and Feb. 3, 1847.
[35] John Greenleaf Whittier to the District Convention, Jan. 15, 1844, in John B. Pickard, ed., *The Letters of John Greenleaf Whittier*, 3 vols. (Cambridge: Harvard Univ. Press, 1975), 1: 624.

Renaissance, whom he knew only by reputation. In the mid-1840s, seeking to engage the Sage of Concord in party affairs, he began a sporadic correspondence with Ralph Waldo Emerson. Both men were scheduled to appear at a party rally in Middlesex County to protest the impending annexation of Texas. Unable to attend, Whittier assured Emerson that while he welcomed Emerson's "manly voice" in "an honest effort to rally all who really love freedom . . . against the encroachment of her eternal foe," it was time for a stronger commitment. "Let me say to thee," he wrote in his best Quakerese, "and through thee to the convention, that mere words, able addresses and dignified resolutions on your part, unless followed up by an absolute consecration of yourselves to the great work of universal liberty will avail nothing."[36] Emerson may not have deserved such a scolding, for he attended the gathering and saw to it that Whittier's letter was published (belatedly, it turned out); he nonetheless remained coldly aloof. Whittier had no better luck with Henry Wadsworth Longfellow. Just about a year earlier, on the eve of the 1844 elections, Whittier tried to recruit his fellow poet to consider running for Congress, adding that Longfellow's recent book of verse "on Slavery have been of great and important service to the Liberty movement." Longfellow thanked Whittier for the compliment but firmly declined the invitation "because I do not feel myself qualified for the duties of such an office, and because I do not belong to the Liberty Party. Though I am a strong anti-Slavery man, I am not a member of any society, and fight under no single banner."[37] So much for the intellectuals.

Libertyism never did establish a following among the literati in Cambridge or Concord. Nor did it find much of an audience in the Commonwealth's eastern ports, county seats, industrial cities, or farming communities. Such frontline industrial cities as Worcester, Lowell, and Lynn matched the party's vote of 5 to 10 percent in the state as a whole. The type of industry did not matter, for these single-industry cities specialized in different products – metal goods, textiles, and shoes, respectively – but proved equally tepid.[38] All such places, with the notable exception of Lynn, continued to be reliably Whig through 1847 or so. Libertyism ran no better in Democratic farming communities. It fared best in the towns and industrial villages of "the country." Its candidates in Essex County, for instance, gathered up to a third of the vote, over three times

[36] Ibid., JGW to RWE, Sept. 20, 1845, pp. 662–6. Quote on p. 663.

[37] Ibid., JGW to HWL, Sept. 4, 1844, pp. 646–7.

[38] For an interpretation of the influence of industry type an voting, see John L. Brooke, *The Heart of the Commonwealth: Society and Political Culture in Worcester County, Massachusetts, 1713–1861* (New York: Cambridge Univ. Press, 1989), pp. 368–88.

the statewide average; in Whittier's Amesbury, a woolen mill village with resident ownership, Liberty office seekers got 46 percent of the vote in 1844. The party did equally well in the industrial equivalents of Amesbury throughout the country.[39] In the Worcester County hamlet of Dudley, the home of Dudley Manufacturing Company, the Libertyites effectively displaced the Whigs.[40]

Who were the people who supported the Liberty Party? According to the most thorough study, in Amesbury they were master craftsmen and skilled workers in the traditional handicrafts of shoemaking, hatmaking, and so on, and in the newer trade of carriage building, who together accounted for two-thirds of the party activists. Factory hands employed in the local woolen mill made up another 16 percent, with the rest scattered among farmers, professionals, and small retailers.[41] The northern Worcester County factory town of Lancaster had a similar political configuration, according to a report compiled by a local Whig in 1844 for the Worcester grandee Stephen Salisbury. It showed that the Whigs claimed a solid majority of 60 percent of the vote, followed by the Democrats' 24 percent, and the Libertyites' 9 percent (the remainder went to a category called "doubtful"). Whig and Democratic votes had distinctive political geographies, with the former centered in the town's commercial core and the latter in its rural periphery, reproducing the larger pattern of political geography in miniature. Whigs also dominated the factory district, drawing the same proportion (58 percent) of the vote as in the town as a whole. The Libertyites, however, won 20 percent of the factory vote in Lancaster, or over twice their proportion statewide; indeed, the mill neighborhood accounted for half the Libertyites' vote, compared to 17 percent for the Whigs and 10 percent for the Democrats.[42]

Liberty operatives were keenly aware of their followers. Journalists printed occasional pieces supportive of labor and advertised the occupations of their candidates in factory towns.[43] It would be a mistake, however, to describe the party's base as working class; the term "working class" is still somewhat premature for small industrial towns in the 1840s, as it was for the leading factory towns in the 1830s. The Lowells of the Commonwealth were increasingly centers for factory workers with no

---

39 Mark Voss-Hubbard, "Slavery, Capitalism, and the Middling Sorts: The Rank and File of Political Abolitionism," *ANCH* 4 (Summer 2003): 5–6.

40 Formisano, *Transformation of Political Culture*, p. 287.

41 Voss-Hubbard, "Slavery, Capitalism, and the Middling Sorts," pp. 56–7.

42 Formisano, *Transformation of Political Culture*, p. 287–8.

43 *Eman*, Feb. 1 and June 19, 1844, and Apr. 1, 1846. Johnson, "Liberty Party in Massachusetts," pp. 255–6.

means of support other than their wages; the workers were proletarian-
ized – and they were Whigs. In the industrial villages, however, the old
pattern of bi-employment and intermittent stints in the mills still prevailed though attenuated and compromised by advancing industrialism.
Mill workers were joined in equal numbers by the children and close relatives of the village craftsmen and master mechanics of Main Street. Together they formed the political expression of Wright's "middle ground,"
or what one modern theorist calls a "popular bloc."[44]

Liberty Party leaders divided roughly into two camps over political
strategy. Some favored a single-issue agenda, others a more eclectic one.
The single-issue men far outnumbered their rivals and controlled the party
machinery. They favored aligning the party with the evangelical church,
following Stanton's cautious strategy in the late 1830s. Their great cause
was "one idea" abolitionism, that is, restricting party policy to ending
slavery or slavery's expansion, and they resisted the efforts of party rivals
to adopt reforms promoted by labor activists, political dissidents, and
other insurgents either loosely allied with antislavery or not allied at all.
This policy drew great intellectual strength from the slogan "the absolute and unconditional divorce of the Government from slavery," which
Salmon P. Chase, the party stalwart in Ohio, coined in 1843. Contrary
to the Garrisonians, the slogan pointed to a federal government that was
empowered to abolish slavery and duty bound to act wherever it could –
in the territories, in Washington, D.C., in interstate trade, and so on.[45]
The national party after 1843 added additional planks – one on smaller
government – but even these usually reflected the "one idea" policy. For
instance, one such plank opposed the use of slaves on public works in
the South.[46] At the state level, and in Massachusetts especially, the "one
idea" policy proved more difficult to sustain, largely because its advocates
closely identified themselves with allied crusades such as temperance. In
the Bay State, key Liberty Party leaders actively cultivated the drys, aware
no doubt that a good many supported abolitionism and were only loosely
tethered to the Whigs. That is why, in summer 1841, Whittier proposed to
Wright that the party nominate for governor the Reverend John Pierpont,

---

[44] See Ernesto Laclau, *Politics and Ideology in Marxist Theory: Capitalism, Fascism, Populism* (London: NLB, 1977), pp. 143–98.

[45] Eric Foner, *Free Soil, Free Labor, Free Men: The Ideology of the Republican Party before
the Civil War* (New York: Oxford Univ. Press, 1970), pp. 78–81. Also James Brewer
Stewart, "Abolitionists, Insurgents, and Third Parties: Sectionalism and Partisan Politics
in Northern Whiggery, 1836–1844," in Kraut, *Crusaders and Compromisers*, pp. 27–43.

[46] Alan M. Kraut, "Partisanship and Principles: The Liberty Party and Antebellum Culture,"
in Kraut, *Crusaders and Compromisers*, p. 85.

the Boston divine and temperance stalwart.[47] It was a shrewd proposal but unlikely to yield votes in the political fields. Most abolitionists supported temperance, but far fewer temperance advocates supported abolitionism. It was simply too radical.

Thus, Libertyism established much stronger ties to the evangelical church and to the abolitionist movement itself. Local antislavery societies affiliated with the Massachusetts Abolition Society served as party adjuncts, raising money through fundraisers and fancy fairs.[48] Mary White, the Boylston activist who had been a Garrisonian in the 1830s, made an easy transition to Libertyism. She reported steady support for the "Abolition Ticket" in her village, telling her diary in the mid-1840s that the Reverend Mr. Sanford regularly discussed abolitionist politics from his pulpit and at society meetings. "Mr. Sanford preached ... a call to repentance," she wrote, "on the importance of choosing good rulers and putting away slavery from our mindset." An evening meeting, she went on, was "mainly of politics. May the Lord direct the electing of this nation that slavery and oppression ... may cease."[49]

As White's diary entries suggest, activist ministers sustained Libertyism in the towns and villages of the country.[50] Whittier certainly thought so. "Our active men are mostly deacons," he told his brother, explaining that this alliance of pulpit and party was not uncomplicated. It did get complicated once, when local ministers scheduled a revival that conflicted with local elections in town meeting and kept the faithful in church, helping the opposition. "In other words," wrote the poet, "if the Devil can't get the Church, he will take the State, rather than nothing."[51] But normally the clergy helped the party, providing voters as well as the cardinal tenet of the "one idea" policy, that slavery was unchristian – that it was sin.[52]

---

[47] JGW to EW, July 21, 1841, in Pickard, *Letters of John Greenleaf Whittier*, 1: 508–9

[48] Julie Roy Jeffrey, *The Great Silent Army of Abolitionism: Ordinary Women in the Antislavery Movement* (Chapel Hill: Univ. of North Carolina Press, 1998), pp. 164–8, and *Eman*, Feb. 3, 1842, Aug. 25, 1842, and June 6, 1847.

[49] Quoted in Fuhrer, "'We all have something to do in the cause of freeing the slave': The Abolition Work of Mary White" (paper prepared for the Dublin Seminar, Deerfield, Mass., June 15–17, 2001), p. 13. Also JGW to Elizabeth Neall, Aug. 28, 1841, in Pickard, *Letters of John Greenleaf Whittier*, 1: 520.

[50] Henry Mayer, *All on Fire: William Lloyd Garrison and the Abolition of Slavery* (New York: St. Martin's Press, 1998), pp. 368–9, and John R. McKivigan, "'Vote as You Pray and Pray as You Vote': Church-Oriented Abolitionism and Antislavery Politics," in Kraut, *Crusaders and Compromisers*, pp. 179–203.

[51] JGW to MFW, Feb. 7, 1843, in Pickard, *Letters of John Greenleaf Whittier*, 1: 585.

[52] The best modern treatment of this traditional theme is Jeffrey, *Great Silent Army of Abolitionism*.

FIGURE 9. Rev. Joshua Leavitt. (Portraits of American Abolitionists. Massachusetts Historical Society. Courtesy of the Massachusetts Historical Society, Boston, Mass.)

Single-issue abolitionism did not rest on moral principle alone. It was bolstered in the early 1840s by an economic argument put forth by the Reverend Joshua Leavitt, a Congregational minister and a former lawyer turned journalist and political activist.[53] Leavitt helped change the focus of abolitionism not only by breaking with Garrison over politics but also

---

[53] Hugh Davis, *Joshua Leavitt, Evangelical Abolitionist* (Baton Rouge: Louisiana State Univ. Press, 1990). Also see Alan Kraut, "Liberty Party in Antebellum Culture," in Kraut, *Crusaders and Compromisers*, pp. 85–6.

by developing a line of reasoning that shifted attention from the plight of the slave in the South to the state of the economy in the North. In his famous speech "The Financial Power of Slavery," published in 1841 and then widely distributed as a pamphlet, Leavitt argued that the South was an economic burden directly responsible for the hard times at the turn of the 1830s and for the slowing down of the Northern economy even in better times. Southerners squandered investment capital borrowed from Yankee financiers, thwarting recovery from the worst downturn to its time and depriving the North of revenue that would end the depression and sustain growth.[54] Leavitt used his *Emancipator* to popularize this regional interpretation of economic growth, as well as to promote such causes as cheap postage, free trade, and abstinence from drink. He also took an occasional swipe at greed and avarice, for he was too iconoclastic to accept unbridled capitalism.[55] He was nonetheless a free labor advocate, imbued with the individualistic strain of mainstream abolitionism and pretty much of a single-issue abolitionist impatient with party men working to enlarge the platform. He asserted in 1843 that "until we remove ... slavery it matters little what our opinions are on political economy."[56] Leavitt clung to this position through the decade, often assailing his opponents as misguided radicals who would dilute antislavery.[57]

Leavitt thus put forth an economic interpretation of slavery with a regional twist that retained the moral indignation that had long fueled abolitionism. Largely on the strength of its appeal to Yankees imbued with an anti-Southern ethos, his position would form the intellectual foundation of the Republican Party. William Goodell, Wright's former friend in his New York days, was more in tune with the perspective of eclectic abolitionism. Goodell was a fervent moralist who, conversant with scripture, used biblical injunctions for radical purposes. In his *Democracy of Christianity*, Goodell invoked the moral economy of the ancient Hebrews and primitive Christians against which to measure modern social and economic relationships. He treated the nineteenth century as a "Mammon age," replete with an arrogant aristocracy that bred economic inequality along with contempt for manual labor. He concluded that abolitionism

---

[54] Joshua Leavitt, *The Financial Power of Slavery* (New York: Leavitt, 1841). Also see Leavitt, *Memorial of Joshua Leavitt, praying that, in revision of the tariff laws, the principle of discrimination may be inserted* ... (Washington, D.C.: Allen, 1842).

[55] *Eman*, Apr. 1, 1844, Mar. 12, 1845, and Apr. 21, 1847.

[56] Ibid., Apr. 20, 1843.

[57] For instance, ibid., July 21, 1847.

would fail if it continued to rely upon morality and conscience. It had to expand its platform with programs appealing to mechanics and working people that would reduce inequality and improve social conditions.[58]

It is impossible to know who read Goodell or how much his policies influenced party activists. We do know that his perspective was well represented in the factory districts. In Fall River the Reverend Asa Bronson was minister of the First Baptist Church, head of the local antislavery society, and founding member of the Liberty Party. Bronson denounced local textile manufacturers as he spoke up for their operatives – alas too loudly for the Borden family, who had him purged from his pulpit.[59] John Orvis, a sometimes newspaper editor, spent part of the 1840s in Lowell, where to promote Fourierism he helped edit the *Voice of Industry* and then the ephemeral *New Era of Industry*.[60] Daniel F. Morrill, a fellow Fourierist and a founder of the Liberty Association in Amesbury, was another labor partisan drawn to newspaper work. In 1847, Morrill became editor of the *Essex Transcript*, the most important party organ in the northeastern corner of the Commonwealth.[61]

The Liberty Party also attracted more celebrated men. Henry Ingersoll Bowditch, a public health physician and Harvard graduate from a leading Boston family, was one.[62] Another was the lawyer Samuel Edmund Sewall. Sewall, descended from one of the Commonwealth's most prominent mercantile families and a graduate of Harvard College's class of 1821, was one of Garrison's early funders. A founding member of the New England Anti-Slavery Society and major patron of the *Liberator*, he was there to calm the "great agitator" when he was mobbed in 1835 but later became a thorn in Garrison's side as a Libertyite. Although Sewall would be known as a friend of fugitive slaves and a leading advocate of women's rights, he

---

[58] On Goodell, see Paul Goodman, *Of One Blood: Abolitionism and the Origins of Racial Equality* (Berkeley and Los Angeles: Univ. of California Press, 1998), pp. 63–80.

[59] On Bronson, see Edward Magdol, "A Window on the Abolitionist Constituency: Anti-slavery Petitions, 1836–1839," in Kraut, *Crusaders and Compromisers*," pp. 50–1. Teresa Anne Murphy, *Ten Hours' Labor: Religion, Reform, and Gender in Early New England* (Ithaca, N.Y.: Cornell Univ. Press, 1992), pp. 149, 169, and 171–3. Also Asa Bronson, *An Address on the Anniversary of the Fire ... Pursuant to the Request from the Ladies' Mechanic Association* (Fall River: N.p., 1844).

[60] On Orvis, see *DC*, June 16, 1848. Also see Carl J. Guarani, *The Utopian Alternative: Fourierism in Nineteenth-Century America* (Ithaca, N.Y.: Cornell Univ. Press, 1991), pp. 303–5, 310–11, and 393–4.

[61] On Morrill, see Voss-Hubbard, "Slavery, Capitalism, and the Middling Sorts," pp. 20–1.

[62] Vincent Y. Bowditch, *Life and Correspondence of Henry Ingersoll Bowditch*, 2 vols. (Boston: Houghton Mifflin, 1902).

FIGURE 10. Henry Ingersoll Bowditch. (Vincent Y. Bowditch, *Life and Correspondence of Henry Ingersoll Bowditch*, 2 vols. [Boston: Houghton Mifflin, 1902], frontispiece.)

was at the same time the new party's most recognizable name in Boston and in the state at large.[63]

The most outspoken advocate of eclectic Libertyism was Elizur Wright, another former Garrisonian and Liberty Party founder in the Commonwealth. Wright's was not the radicalism of instant conversion, for it could be traced partly to the influence of Goodell and mostly to his experiences at home and abroad in the first half of the 1840s. The sacking Wright suffered as editor of the *Massachusetts Abolitionist* in spring 1840 left him without steady work and with no prospects; as he ruefully put it, he

---

[63] George T. Garrison Family Scrapbook, 3 vols., GFP: 2. Also see John L. Thomas, *The Liberator: William Lloyd Garrison* (Boston: Little Brown, 1963), pp. 125–7 and 204–5.

FIGURE 11. Samuel Edmund Sewall. (Portraits of American Abolitionists. Massachusetts Historical Society. Courtesy of the Massachusetts Historical Society, Boston, Mass.)

had "to cut" his "own fodder in my own way."[64] This metaphor proved apt. Wright patched together a mean income from intermittent work in publishing and a subsistence from working a small plot of rented land in Dorchester. He was so hard-pressed to support his growing family that he hawked his own translation of Fontaine's *Fables*, eventually deciding to promote the book in person to Europeans. He set sail in March 1844 for an eight-month tour on stipend from Leavitt, landing first in Ireland

[64] Quoted in Goodheart, *Abolitionist, Actuary, Atheist*, p. 114.

and then moving on to England. As a recent biographer observes, Wright was "strongly affected" by the poverty of the Irish peasant and English factory worker.[65] He was also moved, perhaps more strongly and profoundly, by the agitation of labor reformers in the English Midlands. At Coventry Wright heard the Irish Repealer Daniel O'Connell deliver an impassioned speech on the immiserization of migrant laborers toiling in the "harvest fields for the most scanty wages.... I did not look to see if there were streamlets on other faces," he wrote in his column for Leavitt's *Emancipator*. "I noticed afterwards there had been some on mine."[66] He later met Joseph Sturge among other abolitionists and Chartists working for suffrage reform, Corn Law repeal, and related causes, and he took special notice of the efforts of patricians and middle-class reformers stumping for a legally prescribed ten-hour day. These were heady experiences for a middle-aged man who had broken with the movement that had consumed his prodigious energy in the 1830s, losing any number of friends and associates along the way, and had risked his all on a political party with a hazy future. Now he took his inspiration from British labor reformers. In the 1830s Wright had expressed a preference for working with the great middling interest of mechanics, workers, and yeomen, not because of their presumed class interests, but because these groups were untainted by the corruptions of the rich and the poor; they were needy but also more virtuous. Wright had seldom taken notice of their economic interests, and when he did, workers had reason to wish he had not, for he denounced unions in the heyday of "workieism" in the 1830s as monopolies that interfered with the immutable laws of the free market.[67] No longer. If Wright learned anything during his tour of England and Ireland, it was that workers had legitimate economic needs and that people like him could help them out. He also developed an appreciation for Chartism and other forms of primitive socialism on the Continent.[68] The Elizur Wright who returned to Boston in 1844 had become a man of some political sophistication. The trip had honed his ideology but left his personality as rough and rude as ever.

Wright ended for good the free laborist phase of his life in the mid-1840s. As others have observed, he continued to be something of an American exceptionalist convinced that conditions in the United States

[65] Ibid., p. 122.
[66] *Eman*, Apr. 24, 1844. Also, ibid., May 1 and July 10, 1844.
[67] Goodheart, *Abolitionist, Actuary, Atheist*, p. 130.
[68] DC, July 22, 1846 and Nov. 11, 1847.

made it possible to avoid the extremes in wealth and the chronic class strife characteristic of the Old World.[69] In fact, he remained committed to reconciling differences between capital and labor through state-sponsored banks and workshops modeled after those set up by French radicals, and through privately owned consumer cooperatives promoted by the Protective Union movement. Wright's was not a lonely voice. John Orvis, Wright's associate in abolition and labor reform, told the readers of the *New Era of Industry* in 1846 that he proposed to liberate workers from "commercial and industrial feudalism," not through struggle or violence but through "harmoniz[ing] social relations by means of land reform, cooperation, and abolitionism."[70] Such lofty aspirations should not be confused with the objectives of free laborists. To associate Wright, Orvis, and other labor reformers with such a convention is to flatten out and ultimately misconstrue their thought. While they promoted more ethical and humane economic structures marked by cooperative social relations, underpinned by what David Montgomery has called the "community-of-interest ideal," they were not synonymous with the middle-class reformers skeptical of competitive capitalism but not skeptical enough to come up with a substitute. Many of Wright's associates were leading bourgeois radicals in the 1860s, and a decade later, not a few repudiated their past, ending public life as laissez-faire Democrats or Liberal Republicans. That said, it is essential to keep their political careers in mind. In the 1840s and into the 1850s they were youngish and middle-aged men of modest means and dissident politics, not silver-haired reformers disillusioned with the course of Reconstruction, wary of a militant labor movement that rejected them, and critical of the community of interest ideal, not to mention increasingly sympathetic to railroad and other business interests that had courted them for the better part of a decade. They had lost faith in labor reform.[71] Earlier on, however, in the 1840s, they hewed to a political perspective more cautious than the working-class

---

[69] Goodheart, *Abolitionist, Actuary, Atheist*, pp. 130–1, and Jonathan Glickstein, "'Poverty is not slavery': American Abolitionists and the Competitive Labor Market," in Lewis Perry and Michael Perman, eds., *Antislavery Reconsidered: New Perspectives on the Abolitionists* (Baton Rouge: Louisiana State Univ. Press, 1979), pp. 195–218.

[70] *DC*, June 16, 1848. Orvis was joined in this project by such Fourierists with abolitionist sympathies as Morrill. See Voss-Hubbard, "Slavery, Capitalism, and the Middling Sorts," pp. 21–2.

[71] David Montgomery, *Beyond Equality: Labor and the Radical Republicans, 1862–1872* (New York: Alfred A. Knopf, 1967), pp. 335–86, and Bruce Laurie, "The 'Fair Field' of the 'Middle Ground': Abolitionism, Labor Reform, and the Making of an Antislavery Bloc in Antebellum Massachusetts," in Eric Arnesen et al., eds., *Labor Histories: Class,*

radicalism of the 1830s if consistent with it, and still critical of competitive capitalism.

For his part Wright was extremely touchy about being associated with middle-class reformers and often went out of his way to assert his independence, all the more so if he wound up in league with them. He made this point emphatically on the question of free trade, a hobbyhorse of Locofoco Democrats. Wright explained again and again that his endorsement of free trade did not make him a Democrat or a friend of their business patrons. He favored free trade because protectionism was both an unfair tax on ordinary people and a misguided industrial policy that inevitably concentrated capital into fewer hands. Tariffs protected capital, not labor.[72] As Wright saw it, laissez-faire was mistaken as tariff policy and no better as social policy precisely because it left the weak at the mercy of the strong. It was up to government to "see that the republic takes no damage. It is its business to look particularly after the weak."[73]

Who were the "weak"? Wright and his allies thought the weak to be working people – free laborers – as well as slaves. The fact that in the 1840s abolitionists like Wright could oppose slavery and speak up for labor not as individuals but as part of a popular movement indicates how far abolitionism had departed from the apolitical, single-issue orientation of its Garrisonian origins. This point merits some amplification, for the 1840s was not the first time that abolitionists considered the plight of labor, or that labor advocates considered the plight of the slave; the dialogue began a decade earlier. Garrison himself addressed labor reform in the first edition of his *Liberator* in January 1831. Motivated no doubt by the stirrings of trade unionists in and around Boston, the editor came out squarely against agitating the class question. It was wrong, he wrote, to "inflame the minds of our working classes against the more opulent, and to persuade them that they are...oppressed by a wealthy aristocracy." This was not "reform" so much as dangerous and mindless agitation that in seeking to cure "one evil threatens to inflict a thousand others."[74] He pursued his point at the end of the month in a lengthier editorial that exposed the core of his Whiggish and free laborist perspective on economic and social affairs. Class distinctions, wrote Garrison, inhered in

---

Politics, and the Working-Class Experience (Urbana: Univ. of Illinois Press, 1998), pp. 45–70.

[72] DC, Mar. 13, 1846, July 15 and 17, 1847, and Feb. 24, 1848. Also, ibid., Mar. 19 and Apr. 16, 1846.

[73] Ibid., Aug. 13, 1846.

[74] *Lib*, Jan. 1, 1831.

the "nature of things," but class conflict did not because the interests of
the "laboring classes" and the "wealthy" were congruent and harmonious. Where, he asked, was the evidence for callous exploitation of the
poor by the rich? Answering his own question, he asserted that he had
found no such thing either in "commercial enterprises, which whiten the
ocean with canvas and give employment to a useful and numerous class
of men, [at work] in manufacturing establishments, which multiply labor
and cheapen the necessities of the poor," or "[in] the luxuries of their
tables, or the adornments of their dwellings, for which they must pay in
proportion to their extravagance."[75] Not long afterward Garrison saw
the industrial revolution close up during a tour of Lynn, the shoemaking center where the same Quaker entrepreneurs who ran the shops and
mills were local leaders in his movement. "*The whole country,*" wrote
Garrison of his fellow abolitionists, "*stands on a better footing for their
labors.*"[76] Small wonder that Garrison overlooked the grievances of the
town's increasingly militant working people or that he ignored the complaints of workers in his own city. As his modern biographers tell us, he
reflected the free laborist doctrine that identified self-possession as the
highest form of freedom – the condition that Northern workers long enjoyed and that Southern slaves had yet to achieve. Garrisonians argued
that it was preposterous for workers to deny that they were free or for
their advocates to speak of workers as "wage slaves." There was only one
kind of slavery, and it was in the South.[77]

Working-class abolitionists affiliated with the labor movement in the
1830s were thin on the ground. They gravitated to labor organizations
in the region, the most important of which was the New England Association of Farmers, Mechanics, and Other Working Men. Formed in
late 1831, the New England Association quickly gained a solid footing in
factory towns where a ten-hour workday was the absorbing question.[78]
Its reform-minded leaders used the stump and their press to elevate the
horizons of the membership, publishing abolitionist tracts and describing

---

[75] Ibid., Jan. 29, 1831. Also, ibid., Jan. 9, 1836.

[76] Ibid., Apr. 21, 1831.

[77] Foner, *Free Soil, Free Labor, Free Men,* remains the most rounded treatment of free laborism. Also see Jonathan A. Glickstein, *Concepts of Free Labor in Antebellum America*
(New Haven, Conn.: Yale Univ. Press, 1991), esp. pp. 83–92, and Louis S. Gerteis, *Morality and Utility in American Antislavery Reform* (Chapel Hill: Univ. of North Carolina
Press, 1987).

[78] See John R. Commons et al., *History of Labour in the United States,* 4 vols. (New York:
Macmillan, 1918–35), 1: 158–62 and 298–301; Roediger and Foner, *Our Own Time,*
pp. 1–79; and Murphy, *Ten Hours' Labor,* pp. 32–56.

workers as "friends of the colored people."[79] Some of them, moreover, appealed to Garrison for help. In an early number of the *Liberator*, "W." asserted an "intimate connexion" between the "Working Men's Party" and Garrison's New England Anti-Slavery Society that was rooted in mutual repugnance to slavery and inequality. Such injustices, "W." argued, stemmed from the "ignorance" of the many imposed by the few, from the "indolence of the enslaved and the oppressed," and from the "perpetuation" of the idea that the "working classes" are dependent on the "wealthy, educated, and exalted." Both movements also shared common objectives: abolitionists drummed up support for slaves "by awakening the moral sense of those who now enjoy the fruits of their labors, to the injustice and wickedness of thus robbing their fellow men of the products of their . . . toil"; labor reformers tried to make workers more aware of their own rights, and the rich more aware of their obligations to the poor.[80]

"W." left it to his colleagues to bring the movements together. The mobbing of Garrison in the streets of Boston evoked an outpouring of sympathy from self-described workingmen and from labor advocates wary of Garrison but troubled by what they interpreted as an assault on freedom of expression – and from the upper classes, no less.[81] Quick to disassociate himself from the editor, if not from his movement, "Democrat" had no difficulty at all defending Garrison's right to speak out. He was even less reticent in pointing out collusion, a conspiracy really, between "the Southern Slave-master and northern Aristocrat" against slave and workingman. Troubled by such strident rhetoric but clearly thankful for the support, Garrison reprinted "Democrat's" missive from the labor press.[82] He also published another letter in a similar vein from the same source written by "A Working Man" alarmed by the threat to "FREE DISCUSSION" posed by a "restless spirit of Aristocracy." "Working Man" wanted a mass meeting to clear the good name of honest laborers unfairly maligned as "'disorganizers,' 'mobocrats,' and 'desperados,' and the like, by the very men who *instigated* and *participated* in that outrage." As they took a stand for the "principles of 76," the speakers would "wipe out the foul calumny and place it where it belongs – on the heads of their traducers."[83]

---

[79] *NEA*, Aug. 25, 1833. See also ibid., Sept. 20, 1832 and Oct. 10, 1833.
[80] *Lib*, Jan. 29, 1831.
[81] Ibid. Also, ibid., Oct. 31 and Nov. 14, 1835. See *BR*, Oct. 28 and Dec. 8, 1835, for the originals of Garrison's reprints.
[82] *Lib*, Nov. 14, 1835.
[83] Ibid., Oct. 31, 1835.

"Working Man" never did get his meeting as far as we can tell. For his part, Garrison was unquestionably gratified by the concern and support he received from labor advocates in a moment of crisis, but he was reluctant to pursue the overtures of the labor activists. Nor would he change his position when labor reformers reopened the dialogue in the mid-1840s.[84] In that decade, as they had in the 1830s, the labor and abolitionist movements "talked past one another," as the historian Eric Foner has argued.[85] But in the 1840s the movements also drew closer together at the local level, if not in the higher echelons of the Liberty Party, and for two reasons. First, antislavery sentiment and abolitionism itself enjoyed much greater support among the ranks of labor; for the first time, the labor movement – and not just its leaders – took a stand against slavery where it was, not simply against its territorial expansion. Second, Garrisonianism was not the only abolitionist movement in the field. It had a rival in the Libertyites, a rival that was much larger in number and included activists like Wright eager to adopt labor reform. When working people spoke to Libertyite abolitionists, they spoke with one another, not past one another. It would take a few years, however, for the labor movement to develop before it could cultivate ties to the Libertyites. For the moment, the new party pursued voters, and not the votes of workers as such.

The Liberty Party had striking success in Massachusetts. It survived longer than any other insurgency and just about equaled the raw vote, if not the percentage, of the Anti-Masons in the early 1830s, the most successful third party to its time. As can be seen in Table 2.1, its (gubernatorial) vote climbed steadily in numerical terms until 1844, then stabilized at around 9,000, before reaching its apogee of nearly 10,000 and about 10 percent of the vote in 1846. The party's strength exceeded its numbers because elections gradually became more competitive. In the 1830s, National Republicans and Whigs drew between 53 percent and 65 percent of the vote, dipping below 50 percent twice. From 1840 to 1847, by contrast, Whigs exceeded 55 percent only once and typically ranged between 47 percent and 56 percent of the vote. In addition, as we have already seen, candidates had to garner a majority of the vote cast in order to win. These factors greatly enhanced the Liberty Party's influence; three times – 1842,

[84] Ibid., Mar. 27 and July 10, 1846. Also ibid., Mar. 26 and Oct. 1, 1847.
[85] Eric Foner, "Abolitionism and the Labor Movement in Antebellum America," in Foner, *Politics and Ideology in the Age of the Civil War* (New York: Oxford Univ. Press, 1980), pp. 57–76. Quote is on p. 61.

TABLE 2.1. *Liberty Party Vote in Massachusetts, 1840–1847*

Year	Number of votes[a]	Percentage
1840	1,081	(0.8)
1841	3,488	(3.1)
1842	6,382	(5.4)
1843	8,901	(7.3)
1844	9,635	(7.2)
1845	8,316[b]	(7.9)
1846	9,997	(9.8)
1847	9,193	(8.7)

[a] Gubernatorial vote only.
[b] This poll saw a major decline in the vote across the board.

Source: Adapted from Formisano, *Transformation of Political Culture*, Appendix 2, p. 351.

1843, and 1845 – the Libertyites prevented any candidate from getting the required majority, forcing the state legislature to name the governor; in 1842 they threw the gubernatorial election to the Democrats, only the second time Jacksonians won the governor's chair between 1832 and 1850. The party also had some success in local and state contests, though it is difficult to know precisely how much because returns were sometimes incomplete and party identities sometimes indeterminate. In 1840 the Libertyites elected a handful of local officials in scattered communities across the state, and in 1842 the party celebrated a banner year, with a record increase in its vote that not only determined the gubernatorial race and a few congressional elections but also placed at least six representatives in the State House.[86]

Not everyone appreciated the majority rule that gave third parties in the state such an advantage. Some party regulars periodically growled that it was unfair and argued instead for plurality rule, then prevalent across the nation. They cited the 1842 election as reason for reform, only to see the Judiciary Committee of the Massachusetts House of Representatives report that change was "inexpedient."[87] Defenders of the status quo either feared that such a change would unleash more drastic measures or believed that the Libertyites "will soon die away, if left alone," as one of

[86] Johnson, "Liberty Party in Massachusetts," pp. 250–1. The six towns included Middlefield, Hampshire County; Easton, Bristol County; and Barnstable, Barnstable County.
[87] *BC*, Mar. 24, 1843.

them put it, with the recent example of the Anti-Masons. That historical parallel infuriated Representative Fowle of Boston, who took the floor of the House in March 1843 to denounce the Judiciary Committee's report as naive and wrongheaded. Fowle intoned that Anti-Masonry was a "comparatively mild delusion. The seat of the disorder was here in the midst of us; but slavery is beyond our reach, and all we have hitherto done by agitating the subject at the North, is to make each other mad, and spread the monomania." "[T]he evil," he said, "proceeds from a very small party; and the two great parties . . . may, by uniting for their common safety, prevent the third party . . . from ever playing the same game again." Fowle predicted that fellow regulars would live to regret their refusal to thwart the "pretended foes of slavery, who will have a hearty laugh at their simplicity."[88]

It was the election of 1842 that angered Fowle. The Liberty vote increased threefold between 1840 and 1841 and nearly doubled between 1841 and 1842. The early increase owed largely to deeper and stronger organization following the party's chaotic start. Over the next two years the disorganized ranks regrouped into local committees and formal nominating conventions. The party also fielded stronger tickets for state executive offices, nominating Samuel E. Sewall, the former Garrisonian and well-known lawyer, for the 1842 contest.[89] Whigs entered the election nervously eyeing what they began to call the "party of the flank," warning voters that a vote for the Libertyites was a vote for the Locofocos.[90] Their concerns proved well-founded, partly because of the higher profile of the new party but also because of a protracted commotion over a fugitive slave that intensified during the election season and dragged on for another six months. By the time the celebrated Latimer case had run its course in summer 1843, the Libertyites had grown into something rather more than a nuisance.

Fugitive slave cases in the historical literature are virtually synonymous with the dramatic episodes of the late 1840s and early 1850s in Boston involving William and Ellen Craft, Shadrach Minkins, and Anthony Burns.[91] In fact, there were fugitive slave cases in the country

[88] Ibid.

[89] Darling, *Political Changes in Massachusetts*, pp. 297–81.

[90] Ibid., p. 292.

[91] For instance, Gary M. Collison, *Shadrach Minkins: From Fugitive Slave to Citizen* (Cambridge: Harvard Univ. Press, 1997), and Albert Von Frank, *The Trials of Anthony Burns: Freedom and Slavery in Emerson's Boston* (Cambridge: Harvard Univ. Press, 1998).

starting in the late 1830s. In the Worcester County village of Holden in 1839, a thirteen-year-old slave girl named Anne fled Olivia Eames, her owner. Born in Massachusetts, Eames had lived in Louisiana and then returned to her place of birth with Anne in tow. When Anne sought refuge at the Holden Anti-Slavery Society, Eames sued society president Samuel Stratton for conspiracy to take her property, but she lost in court.[92] Four years later Northampton was inflamed by a maddeningly complicated case involving Catherine Linda, the slave servant of W. B. Hodgson, a Georgian on vacation in the region. When Linda allegedly told local abolitionists that she wished to be free, the Northampton activist Erasmus Darwin Hudson sought to obtain a writ of habeas corpus in court. Although this legal drama ended when Linda told a judge that she was not interested in freedom, it was soon replaced by another one, when her owner sued Hudson for seizing his property. As Hudson paced in a jail cell, local Libertyites exploited the episode, baiting village Whigs into an exchange of words that left them looking self-interested and small-minded. Such episodes, said one Whig, made the locals look bad and harmed the tourist business to boot. Besides, added the Whiggish *Northampton Gazette* in an editorial that only enhanced the abolitionist credentials of the Libertyites, needless encounters with slave owners did nothing for the cause. "If slavery is ever abolished," it feebly added, "it must be done by the slaveholders themselves."[93]

Libertyites and a growing proportion of the electorate saw the issue differently. The Amesbury activist John Greenleaf Whittier began his 1845 essay "The Black Man" with an anecdote about John Fountain, a free black who had been jailed in Virginia on suspicion of helping slaves escape. Released from custody in return for a promise to leave the state, Fountain still had to flee a mob, leaving behind his wife and children in slavery. He went on a speaking tour to raise funds to buy their freedom, a tour that ran through Lowell where he took a break to thank the poet for his help. The visit prompted Whittier to reflect on the political meaning of slave catching. "It is in this way," he wrote, "that the terrible reality of slavery is brought home to the people of this section of the country. Occasionally a fugitive from oppression seeks shelter among us, and reveals the horrors

---

[92] On the Eames case, see Holden Anti-Slavery Society, *Report of the Holden Slave Case* (Worcester: Colton and Howland, 1839).

[93] *HG*, Sept. 16, 1845. Also *NC*, Aug. 9 and 16, 1845. Quote is Patric Whitcomb, "'A Party of Principle': The Northampton Liberty Party and Antislavery Politics" (seminar paper, Univ. of Massachusetts Amherst, 1999), p. 23. Also, *HH*, Aug. 12 and 19, Sept. 16, and Nov. 10, 1845, and Jan. 13, 1846.

of his house of bondage. . . . As a result, we no longer regard slavery in the abstract."[94]

Whittier had a point. Abolitionists and antiabolitionists in Worcester County debated the meaning of the Eames case long after it was settled. Four years after Anne was freed, a putative "Lover of Liberty" told the readers of a county sheet that the former slave had misspent her freedom. Removed from her mistress, she was taken in by a "respectable family of Friends," but she became so "troublesome and unmanageable" that she was sent to another one, which also gave up and passed her on to a black family. "Liberty" charged that the father of Anne's child was paying a mere "pittance" for her board and that meddlesome abolitionists were "the primary cause of her present situation." "We hope and trust," he concluded, that her abolitionist friends "will take care that the she not suffer, nor the town be obliged" to support her and her child.[95] This dark version of Anne's story irked her defenders, including a self-described "Real Lover of Liberty" who retorted that the rendition written by "Liberty" was not only mean-spirited, but it was also wrong. Stories like Anne's collapsed the distinction between local and national events and played into the hands of Libertyism.[96]

No fugitive slave episode bore more political weight than the Latimers'. In fall 1842, George Latimer, a light-skinned black man, fled with his wife from their Norfolk, Virginia, owner James Gray by hiding in the hold of a ship bound for the North. The vessel eventually arrived in Boston via Baltimore and Philadelphia. Latimer tried to blend in among the African Americans living in the city's black quarter known as the Hill, but he was spotted by one of Gray's agents, who had him arrested on October 21 on a trumped-up charge of larceny, and then alerted Gray. When Gray showed up at the federal court in Boston for an article of removal, as required by the 1793 Fugitive Slave Law, Judge Joseph Story ordered Latimer detained until his owner produced evidence of title. But instead of returning to court, Gray agreed to allow local abolitionists to buy Latimer out of slavery for four hundred dollars.[97]

[94] John Greenleaf Whittier, *The Stranger in Lowell* (Boston: Waite, Pierce, 1845), p. 49.

[95] *MS*, Mar. 16, 1842.

[96] Ibid.

[97] Massachusetts House of Representatives, House Doc. No. 41, "Fugitives from Slavery" (1843). Also *Proceedings of the Citizens of the Borough of Norfolk, on the Boston Outrage, in the Case of the Runaway Slave George Latimer* (Norfolk: Broughton and Son, 1843); *LJNS*, Nov. 11, 1842ff; and Collison, *Shadrach Minkins*, pp. 55, 71, 87–8, and 120. It is not clear if Mrs. Latimer's freedom was included. She drops from view.

Poised between the Holden and Northampton incidents, the Latimer episode had an impact that dwarfed that of the others. In Boston, it crystallized the feud between Garrisonians and Libertyites, as each side organized separately and fought for the spotlight. Two Latimer Committees quickly emerged – one formed by Garrisonians and the other by Libertyites – which ran on parallel tracks but also collided head on. The Garrisonian committee, organized at an October 23 meeting headed by the African Americans William Cooper Nell, Charles Remond, and the Reverend J. T. Raymond, proved relatively ineffective. Its fundraising stumbled, and its attempts to enlist legal counsel for Latimer turned into an embarrassment because the Liberty leader Samuel Sewall had already taken the case. It was Sewall who negotiated Latimer's release, using funds raised by his party's Latimer Committee headed by Henry I. Bowditch, William F. Channing, and Frederick Cabot with the help of Nathaniel Colver. The committee also sponsored meetings and demonstrations, and doubled as the editorial board of the *Latimer Journal and North Star,* a hard-hitting if short-lived propaganda sheet. The committee's work annoyed Garrison and his closest associates, notably Maria Chapman Weston, who denounced Sewall's bargain with Gray as financial "compensation" for slavery.[98] This poisonous spirit infected public meetings called to build a united front in the name of liberating poor Latimer. Bowditch did his best to bring harmony to a late-October meeting by placing Garrisonians on the podium, only to watch the gathering plunge into tumult when Wendell Phillips rose to "CURSE...the Constitution."[99] The histrionics resumed at another joint meeting on November 19 to celebrate Latimer's release when the Garrisonians voted down a motion to place Nathaniel Colver on the business committee, electing Weston in his place. A red-faced Colver stormed out, and Leavitt denounced the "proscriptive spirit" borne of an "OLD GRUDGE." Bowditch openly fretted in despair, then listened in horror to gratuitous assaults on his party by Garrison loyalists Phillips and Stephen Foster.[100]

The Garrisonians' vendetta became bloodier as the November 1842 election approached. Garrison had never forgiven the political abolitionists for their betrayal several years earlier, and he eagerly seized the opportunity to get back at them. In an election-eve editorial, he dismissed the

---

[98] *Lib*, Nov. 25, 1842. Also ibid., Dec. 2, 1842 and Jan. 6, 1843.

[99] Patrick H. Crim, "'The Ballot Boxes Are Our Arms!': The Latimer Fugitive Slave Case and the Liberty Party in Massachusetts" (seminar paper, Univ. of Massachusetts Amherst, 1999), esp. pp. 9–10. Quote is on p. 9.

[100] Bowditch, *Life and Correspondence of Henry Ingersoll Bowditch*, 1: 133–6.

Whig candidate John Davis as a surrogate for Henry Clay, and Marcus
Morton as a shill for "Martin Van Buren, or John C. Calhoun." He described Sewall as a "meritorious man" but a terribly misguided one doing
the bidding of those "who are waging a war of extermination against
the American Anti-Slavery Society," a preposterous charge based on his
obsessions. "We recommend to voting abolitionists to scatter their votes
in all such cases," went his vindictive advice aimed at hitting the Libertyites where it hurt most.[101] As it turned out, very few abolitionists took
Garrison's advice. A puny one hundred eighty of them scattered their
votes, leaving the great orator a bit humbled and without much to say
except that the electorate had been "led astray."[102]

While the Libertyites bore Garrisonian anger with some magnanimity,
they also reaped a political dividend from the Latimer affair, parlaying
the tumult into votes in the 1842 election. The six thousand votes for
Liberty candidates caused a deadlock in the gubernatorial race and left
one hundred seats in the House, sixteen in the Senate, and six for the U.S.
Congress hanging for want of a majority. When the runoffs concluded in
late December, the Libertyites captured six seats in the House and held the
balance of power since the chamber was evenly weighted between Whigs
and Democrats and both needed Liberty support to elect a speaker, fill
the contested seats in the Senate, and name the next governor.[103] The
complicated horse-trading that followed suggests that the party of the
"flank" had moved into the center of politics. The Liberty men made a
serious if unsuccessful bid for the bloc of sixteen Senate seats (which went
to the Democrats) and lost the governorship (to the Democrats as well)
but wound up holding the trump card for speaker. They held out through
four ballots before throwing the speakership to H. A. Collins, a Whig
from the abolitionist wing of his party, in return for favorable action on
civil rights bills.[104]

It is difficult to know if the Liberty vote represented first-time voters
or cross-overs from the established parties. Probably most were refugees
from the regulars, more so the Whigs than the Democrats. The rural wing
of Whiggery was always suspicious of the urban leadership because of the
leaders' indifference to moral reform. Rural Whigs also became increasingly restive over the leaders' seeming indifference to the audaciousness

[101] *Lib*, Nov. 11, 1842.
[102] Ibid., Jan. 17, 1843.
[103] *Eman*, Dec. 14, 1842.
[104] Ibid. Also, ibid., Jan. 12 and 19, 1843; *MS*, Jan. 18, 1843; and Darling, *Political Change
in Massachusetts*, pp. 248–9.

of Slave Power as reflected in the Latimer case and in the growing controversy over the annexation of Texas.[105] The advent of Libertyism offered such country dissidents a political alternative they did not have in 1838. Those who did bolt after 1840 over slavery represented the provincial and more plebeian counterpart of the "Conscience Whigs," the urban and upper-class antislavery men who would leave the party in 1847–8 over the Texas question. Such country abolitionists showed their urban cousins a way out of Whiggery.

As for Democrats turned Libertyites, some may have left their party earlier over gag rule. They were probably a minority within a minority, however, because the Yankee Democracy had enough of an antislavery edge to prevent a bolt of much significance.[106] The disaffection of Democratic voters seems to have had less to do with national politics or indeed with the local ramifications of antislavery politics than with the deepening of the market economy and growing materialism within the context of localism. Both trends were more easily associated with Whigs than with Democrats because of the former's undeniable link with the Boston Associates, the largest and most urbane employers in the Commonwealth, who embodied the industrial revolution. Such Whiggish industrialists had little regard for the local economies of the village, for the shop trades of Main Street that set the slower, more deliberate pace of economic life.[107] Quite the contrary, they built their own towns literally from the ground up, first Waltham, then Lowell, Lawrence, and Holyoke, but could not help but be seen as a more general threat to traditional ways.[108]

---

[105] See Crim, "'The Ballot Boxes Are Our Arms!'" and Whitcomb, "A Party of Principle."

[106] Richards, *Slave Power*, pp. 132 and 138, shows that New England Democrats beat a retreat from supporting the rule between 1836 and 1840. Also see Earle, "Marcus Morton and the Dilemma of Antislavery."

[107] Voss-Hubbard, "Slavery, Capitalism, and the Middling Sorts," pursues this line of reasoning quite effectively. Jonathan Prude, *The Coming of Industrial Order: Town and Factory Life in Rural Massachusetts, 1810–1880* (New York: Cambridge Univ. Press, 1983), pp. 158–80, demonstrates fissures and tensions *within* rural industrial towns between local manufacturers and townsfolk connected to the artisanal/agricultural economy over a variety of political issues, including taxation, water rights, and roads, and also banking.

[108] Any number of works on the Boston Associates make this basic point, starting with Ware, *New England Cotton Manufacture*, and continuing on through Thomas H. O'Connor, *Lords of the Loom: The Cotton Whigs and the Coming of the Civil War* (New York: Charles Scribner's Sons, 1968), and Thomas Dublin, *Women at Work: The Transformation of Work and Community in Lowell, Massachusetts, 1826–1860* (New York: Columbia Univ. Press, 1979).

When Elizur Wright and his friends in the Liberty Party pitched their program of economic radicalism to working people in the country, they were not inventing dissent. They were seeking to build ties with their counterparts at the local level. What made local abolitionists so effective in the towns of the country is that nearly all were homegrown or relatively long-time residents, not outsiders. Such a pedigree gave them legitimacy. Their perspective was no more of a foreign import than they themselves were. It reflected broader apprehensions over the intensification of industrialism and the acquisitiveness that came in its wake. In politics, their voice remained localized – heard clearly in the banter at the general store and post office but weakly at best among the single-issue abolitionists in control of the Liberty Party's statewide apparatus, who paid only lip service to economic grievances. Such leaders made their party more hospitable to Democratic voters with antislavery instincts than to those with economic grievances.

Thus Bay State voters in the 1840s took the Liberty Party more seriously than most modern historians recognize. One school of thought sees the party as a "surrogate religious denomination," a reluctant actor stymied by the pietism of its evangelical origins.[109] A second and more recent school treats the Libertyites as reform politicians not much different from others in the reform tradition. A still more recent interpretation, which tries to synthesize these positions, winds up endorsing the traditional view of a party constrained by piestistic anti-institutionalism.[110] The problem with this work is that it tries to force the Libertyites into a single mold. They are better thought of as a coalition of single-issue and eclectic abolitionists and antislavery advocates, with the latter as junior

---

[109] For instance, Richard O. Curry, ed., *The American Abolitionists: Reformers or Fanatics?* (New York: Holt, Rinehart and Winston, 1965); Ronald Walters, *The Antislavery Appeal: American Abolitionism after 1830* (Baltimore: Johns Hopkins Univ. Press, 1976), esp. p. 16; Lewis Perry, *Radical Abolitionism: Anarchy and the Government of God in Antislavey Thought* (Ithaca, N.Y.: Cornell Univ. Press, 1973), pp. 170–87. Also see Aileen Kraditor, "The Liberty and Free Soil Parties," in Arthur Schlesinger, Jr., ed., *History of U.S. Political Parties*, 4 vols. (New York: Chelsea House, 1973); 1: 741–881; and Kraditor, *Means and Ends in American Abolitionism*, pp. 140–77. Also see Brooke, *Heart of the Commonwealth*, pp. 353–83, even though his analytical categories are unique.

[110] Richard H. Sewell, *Ballots for Freedom: Antislavery Politics in the United States, 1837–1860* (New York: Oxford Univ. Press, 1976), pp. 43–79. Also see Paul Kleppner, *The Third Electoral System: Parties, Voters, and Political Cultures* (Chapel Hill: Univ. of North Carolina Press, 1979), pp. 65–6. This literature is reviewed quite ably in Kraut, *Crusaders and Compromisers*, pp. 1–22.

partners. More than this, they were not preoccupied with the national question of slavery, as nearly all historians assume. Though attentive to the national scene, they also figured prominently in the politics of civil rights and labor reform in Massachusetts, as the next two chapters will show.

3

"Our Colored Friends"

Libertyism and the Politics of Race

In spring 1839 when he became editor of the *Massachusetts Abolitionist*, the organ of the anti-Garrisonian faction that would form the Liberty Party, Elizur Wright made an overture to African Americans his first order of business. Eager for their support but aware of their loyalty to Garrison and his policies, Wright pointed out that Garrison himself had previously come out for sympathetic politicians; in fact, Garrison had criticized African Americans in 1834 for failing to vote for an antislavery office seeker. "Can our colored friends," asked Wright with a more than a hint of his signature sarcasm, "allow us the liberty of differing from him as much as he differs from himself!"[1] Although African Americans may have been amused by the barb, few seem to have heeded the invitation to join the new party. Through the mid-1840s most African Americans remained skeptical of politics and loyal to Garrisonian nonresistance. The Liberty Party, however, became a leading force for civil rights in politics in Massachusetts. The impetus came partly from Liberty leaders like Wright and partly from two groups outside of formal party circles. One group consisted of white Garrisonians, who applied moral pressure; the other consisted of a growing group of African American activists associated with Garrison but increasingly impressed with the promise of reform politics. Both groups, together with some Liberty men, formed what can arguably be described as the nation's first civil rights movement.

The story of civil rights in antebellum Massachusetts is necessarily intertwined with the question of race. And race, in the current

---

[1] Quoted in Lawrence B. Goodheart, *Abolitionist, Actuary, Atheist: Elizur Wright and the Reform Impulse* (Kent, Ohio: Kent State Univ. Press, 1990), p. 107.

historiographical climate, has become synonymous with the idea of "whiteness," a concept invented over a decade ago by David R. Roediger in his magisterial book *The Wages of Whiteness*. Roediger argues that whiteness trumped alternative markers of identity – ethnicity, region, and so on – and that it originated not with politicians or elites but with the working class. Northern workers embraced white supremacy as psychological compensation for the social subordination and loss of autonomy imposed upon them by the early industrial revolution. Such workers projected their anxieties onto blacks, whose putatively libertine ways gave symbolic expression to a world lost in the smoke of the factory. They expressed their chauvinism in the vulgar language of popular racism and in such popular amusements as blackface minstrelsy with its crude jokes and stock figures redolent of racism.[2] This simple but powerful formulation fully deserves what a recent observer aptly calls "charismatic history," for it launched the field of whiteness studies.[3] Indeed, historians as well as social scientists have since applied Roediger's concept of whiteness to everyone they study from the Famine Irish to East European Jewish immigrants.[4] Most recently, whiteness has been adapted to New England in the period under study here. In *Disowning Slavery*, the historian Joanne Pope Melish places whiteness at the core of "New England nationalism," an emergent outlook that sought to cleanse the region of African Americans through a range of policies from warning out to colonization, that is, expelling blacks from their communities or sending them to Africa, respectively.[5]

This formulation does not square with antebellum Massachusetts. To see a uniformity of whiteness, a single conception of race, is to simplify a more complex landscape. Roediger himself recognized the possibility of a countertendency to whiteness by referring to workers in the abolitionist camp imbued with the moralistic egalitarianism of the popular religious sects. But such workers were stymied because of what he calls

[2] David R. Roediger, *The Wages of Whiteness: Race and the Making of the American Working Class* (1991; New York: Verso Press, 1999), esp. pp. 95–131. Also see Jean H. Baker, *Affairs of Party: The Political Culture of Northern Democrats in the Mid-Nineteenth Century* (Ithaca, N.Y.: Cornell Univ. Press 1983), and Eric Lott, *Love and Theft: Blackface Minstrelsy and the American Working Class* (New York: Oxford Univ. Press, 1993).

[3] David Brody, "Charismatic History: Pros and Cons," *ILWCH* 60 (Fall 2001): 43–7.

[4] Noel Ignatiev, *How the Irish Became White* (New York: Routledge, 1995), and Karen Brodkin, *How Jews Became White Folks and What that Says about Race in America* (New Brunswick, N.J.: Rutgers Univ. Press, 1998).

[5] Joanne Pope Melish, *Disowning Slavery: Gradual Emancipation and "Race" in New England, 1780–1860* (Ithaca, N.Y.: Cornell Univ. Press, 1998).

"the rhetorical framework of white slavery," which obliged them to identify with slaves, a step that proved next to impossible because of their
own ingrained racism and reluctance to admit their social subordination.[6]
Though Roediger has since recognized the possibility of multiple forms
of racial awareness, some of them politically benign, his original concep-
tualization of whiteness has proved remarkably durable.[7] Moreover, this
work is self-consciously cultural, linguistic, or psychological, and often all
three at once. This is why scholars of whiteness have been more at home
in cultural studies programs than in history departments. Historians have
been critical of such scholars for failing to marshal enough evidence and
for relying on questionable explanatory tools borrowed from social psy-
chology.[8]

Whiteness studies, as a rule, also overlook the realm of politics and
the exercise of political power. Power inheres in social relations of all
descriptions – especially in race relations – and is best handled through
the study of politics. Political analysis allows us to explore not only how
blacks and whites used race in public discussion but also how far they were
prepared to go in pursuit of their objectives. To illustrate this point, it is fair
to say that nineteenth-century Americans never had a chance "to vote" on
what historians of whiteness describe as culture – a minstrel show, to cite a
resonant example. Historians of whiteness assume minstrelsy was popular
solely on the basis of its existence and attendance. Few of them can tell
us what the audience was thinking and how strongly it felt, or indeed if
there was an "it" – a single group – at all. Political analysis gets around
these problems by allowing for a more precise picture and by opening the
possibility of drawing sharper distinctions among perspectives. We can
better understand forms of racism, in other words, if we understand the
political contours of the larger category of race. This point is implicit in
Alexander Saxton's *The Rise and Fall of the White Republic*, which refers
to "hard" and "soft" expressions of racism, that is, different conceptions
of difference based on race.[9]

---

[6] Roediger, *Wages of Whiteness*, pp. 86–7.
[7] David R. Roediger, *Colored White: Transcending the Racial Past* (Berkeley and Los
    Angeles: Univ. of California Press, 2002).
[8] Though a number of critics have made this point, one of the more forceful arguments
    in this spirit is Eric Arnesen, "Whiteness and the Historians' Imagination," *ILWCH* 60
    (Fall 2001): 3–42.
[9] Alexander Saxton, *The Rise and Fall of the White Republic: Class Politics and Mass
    Culture in Nineteenth-Century America* (New York: Verso, 1990), pp. 148–50, 259–62,
    and 281–2.

Race is treated here as a spectrum, not as a binary opposition. It is seen as an outlook with a range of views from paternalism at one end and exclusionism at the other, with degrees of segregation located between these extremes. It is also seen as a political force, not in the abstract but in the way race consciousness has been defined by George Fredrickson, namely, as an outlook allied to a political program.[10] Exclusionism was a blatantly racist perspective that assumed that African Americans were inherently inferior, possibly dangerous, and unquestionably beyond redemption. Exclusionists supported a policy of social proscription that would segregate blacks or remove them entirely. It really did not matter that removal – as in African colonization – was a practical impossibility. Exclusionsists did not take colonization literally; they saw it as a metaphor for one's stand on race. It is important to add that exclusionism was not confined to the Democratic Party, contrary to what much recent historiography would have us believe.[11] Democrats strongly favored proscriptive policies but so did conservative Whigs, so that exclusionism crossed party lines. Nor were all exclusionists fire-breathing race baiters with a visceral hatred for blacks; some were genteel sorts who saw blacks as a pitiful race that would be better off in Africa.[12] Segregationists were prepared to live with blacks but only if the blacks were confined to their own neighborhoods, labor markets, and social organizations. Paternalists went a step further, accepting integration of public accommodations and frequently forging personal bonds verging on friendship with African Americans on an individual basis.[13]

Race relations in Massachusetts, and perhaps in the region at large, generally leaned toward the paternalistic end of the spectrum in the period under investigation. This is not to suggest that all white Bay Staters in contact with African Americans were paternalists; most preferred segregation and some preferred exclusionism. Nor does it mean that blacks favored paternalism over equality. It means simply that to some extent

[10] George M. Fredrickson, *A Short History of Racism* (Princeton, N.J.: Princeton Univ. Press, 2002), esp. pp. 1–13.

[11] For instance, Baker, *Affairs of Party*, pp. 212–58; Ignatiev, *How the Irish Became White*; and Roediger, *Wages of Whiteness*, esp. pp. 141–3.

[12] Historians are divided on this question of Whiggish racism. See Leon F. Litwack, *North of Slavery: The Negro in the Free States, 1790–1860* (Chicago: Univ. of Chicago Press, 1961), esp. pp. 88–93, and Leonard L. Richards, *The Slave Power: The Free North and Southern Domination, 1780–1860* (Baton Rouge: Louisiana State Univ. Press, 2001), pp. 116–20.

[13] See John Stauffer, *The Black Hearts of Men: Radical Abolitionists and the Transformation of Race* (Cambridge: Harvard Univ. Press, 2002).

paternalism set the tone in law as well as in social relations, without erasing other forms, and that for want of a realistic alternative blacks tended to comply even as they struggled for equal rights. Their struggle, moreover, was necessarily political, not simply cultural, and it was politics that strongly influenced the larger racial climate. Paternalists, after all, were political actors, as were segregationists and exclusionists, and the battles among them in the political arena proved decisive. Who was in charge in a given community or place mattered to African Americans. They – or at least a select few – had an easier time of it in places with enlightened leaders – and a tougher time in places where paternalists were weaker than or outnumbered or checked by racists or exclusionists.

Paternalism in the Bay State was rooted in the religious culture and peculiar demography of its Yankee past, a past that included a form of slavery circumscribed by climatic conditions and shaped by settlement patterns. The harsh climate, unforgiving soil, and short growing season made plantation slavery an impossibility in New England; family or domestic slavery predominated in the region and in Massachusetts especially, home of the largest number of slaves (some 4,000) through the 1750s when it was surpassed by Connecticut.[14] To put this another way, in the formulation of the historian M. I. Finley, New England was a society with slaves and not a slave society.[15] The limited scope of the region's slavery had larger social and ideological ramifications. Since blacks were relatively few and not central to the economy, Yankee slavery did not depend on the support, either active or tacit, of poor whites, as it did in Virginia and, indeed, throughout the South. Nor did divines and intellectuals in New England have to develop a racial defense of slavery as did their counterparts in the antebellum South – or much of a defense at all compared to the other slave societies in the hemisphere.[16]

---

[14] Ira Berlin, *Many Thousands Gone: The First Two Centuries of Slavery in North America* (Cambridge: Harvard Univ. Press, 1998), pp. 47–63 and Table 1, pp. 369–70, and Berlin, *Generations of Captivity: A History of African-American Slaves* (Cambridge: Harvard Univ. Press, 2003), pp 30–1; L. J. Green, *The Negro in Colonial New England* (New York: Columbia Univ. Press, 1942); R. C. Twombly and R. H. Moore, "Black Puritan: The Negro in Seventeenth-Century New England," *WMQ* 24 (1967): 224–42; and William D. Piersen, *Black Yankees: The Development of an Afro-American Subculture in Eighteenth-Century New England* (Amherst: Univ. of Massachusetts Press, 1988).

[15] M. I. Finley, "Slavery," *IESS* 14 (1968): 307–13.

[16] Carl N. Degler, *Neither Black nor White: Race Relations in Brazil and the United States* (Madison: Univ. of Wisconsin Press, 1971), pp. 25–92; Edmund S. Morgan, *American Slavery, American Freedom: The Ordeal of Colonial Virginia* (New York: W.W. Norton 1975), esp. pp. 215–38; and Peter Kolchin, *Unfree Labor: American Slavery and Russian Serfdom* (Cambridge: Harvard Univ. Press, 1978), pp. 157–91.

When early New Englanders did defend slavery they did not draw upon the Romans, or the harsher Greeks, or such early church fathers as Paul.[17] They instead looked back to the ancient Hebrews, as the historian Betty Wood has persuasively argued, and that legacy had two important implications. First, the Hebraic form of servitude, with its time constraints and notions of residual "rights," defined slaves as property but also recognized them as persons in limbo between slave and citizen. In colonial New England, as among the ancient Jews, slaves fell "somewhere between the indentured servant and chattel slave."[18] They enjoyed privileges unknown to the slaves farther South, including access to the courts and control of property. Some African American slaves were freed because of their military service during the American Revolution; many more were freed because of a series of legal cases they themselves brought before the courts in the early 1780s.[19] Thus climate and demography combined to make slavery in New England less harsh and arguably more lenient than in the South.

Second, leniency was sanctioned by Puritan notions of "Christian usage." This doctrine invested masters with responsibility for the spiritual and material welfare of their servants. Good masters fed and clothed their slaves well and also taught them – or had them taught – to read and write.[20] They also took some responsibility for former slaves following emancipation, sometimes even finding them work. This ethic persisted long after emancipation, as local elites, typically associated with the Federalists and then with the Whigs and Free Soilers, sometimes extended a paternal hand to individual blacks. Such a practice helps explain why race relations in New England were never as rude or harsh as in other parts of the North and why, as we will see, a small black elite – sponsored in part by white patrons – took shape before the Civil War.

Charles Porter Huntington was an exemplar of genteel exclusionism. The eldest son of Dan and Elizabeth Whiting Phelps Huntington in Hadley, he established a law firm in Northampton following his graduation in 1822 from Harvard College.[21] Invited in 1830 by the leading citizens of Northampton to deliver a Fourth of July address, Huntington

[17] Peter Garnsey, *Ideas of Slavery from Aristotle to Augustine* (Cambridge, Eng.: Cambridge Univ. Press, 1996), and Jennifer A. Glancy, *Slavery in Early Christianity* (Oxford, Eng.: Oxford Univ. Press, 2002).

[18] Betty Wood, *The Origins of American Slavery: Freedom and Bondage in the English Colonies* (New York: Hill and Wang, 1998), pp. 104–7. Quote is on p. 105.

[19] James M. Rosenthal, "Free Soil in Berkshire County, 1781," *NEQ* 10 (1937): 781–5, and Melish, *Disowning Slavery*, pp. 64–5 and 95–6.

[20] Wood, *Origins of American Slavery*, pp. 104–7.

[21] On Huntington, see "Porter-Phelps-Huntington Family Finding Aid," PPHFP.

FIGURE 12. Charles Porter Huntington. (Porter Phelps Huntington Family Papers. Courtesy Amherst College Archives and Special Collections. Amherst College, Amherst, Mass.)

penned an erudite and searching speech that showed he was very much his mother's son on the question of the colonization. Following an admirable analysis of the sources of the Revolution, the young lawyer turned to the anomaly of slavery in the midst of the republic. He counted two million slaves in the South and (mistakenly) reckoned there were half a million free people of color in the North, "more free blacks than there are people in Massachusetts. Free are they called?" he asked rhetorically. "Is that creature free whom the laws of society, if not the laws of the land, pronounce an outlaw ... whose color is a blot upon his character? [who cannot walk with us or eat with us?] who is too degraded for a menial in our dwellings? Such freedom" was, he said, "worse than Southern slavery." But the South was not solely responsible for this "curse" because the North was complicit in the slave traffic and could not "cast the sin" at Southern feet. What to do? he asked. The "one way of escape" from the "deadly evil" of slavery was "restoring these oppressed people to the land of their ancestors. Experience has shown that removal is their & our last hope."[22] Colonization was a favor, not a punishment.

Huntington's younger brother, William Pitkin Huntington, also observed family tradition by joining his father as a Unitarian minister and by espousing his mother's colonizationism.[23] William moved to Illinois in the late 1830s where he at once sought out the local colonization society, which was headed by Porter Clay, older brother of the more famous Henry. The clergyman found Porter to be unimpressive – "somewhat broken by recent affliction" and in "no ways brilliant." As for the colonization cause, Huntington was beginning to waffle, confessing to his mother that "the appeal to *my* charity would be much stronger, were it sustained by those who are the ostensible objects of it, for it is notorious, that the mass of free blacks are opposed to African Colonization."[24] We do not know if William repudiated colonization, though it is likely that he did; we do know that Charles Huntington had second thoughts in the 1840s when he developed characteristically paternalistic bonds with local African Americans and ran for office on the Free Soil ticket. We also know that Frederic Dan, their youngest brother, became a firebrand abolitionist in Boston in the 1840s. Even their mother changed her mind.[25] Garrison was not the only refugee from a belief in colonization.

Nor, if a telling drama in the life of Edward Dickinson of neighboring Amherst is any guide, were all racial paternalists abolitionists. Dickinson, the father of the reclusive poet Emily, was one of the wealthiest men in the western Massachusetts college town and easily its most influential figure. He was a hidebound Whig who had a Yankee's contempt for slavery but also a conservative's dislike of abolitionists. He nonetheless found himself

---

[22] Ibid., "Lecture, July 5, 1830," b. 17, f. 18. Brackets in original.
[23] PPHFP, Finding Aid, p. 60.
[24] WPH to EPHW, Feb. 11, 1839, ibid., b. 19, f. 5.
[25] On Arria Sargent Huntington and Frederic Dan Huntington, see ibid., Finding Aid, pp. 23 and 36–7, respectively. On the family's self-image, see Arria Sargent Huntington, *Under a Colonial Roof-Tree: Fireside Chronicles of Early New England* (Syracuse, N.Y.: Woolcott and West, 1890), and Theodore Gregson Huntington, "Sketches of family life in Hadley," PPHFP, box 21.

FIGURE 13. Edward Dickinson. (Photograph by A. Marshall, Boston, Mass. By permission of Jones Library, Inc. Amherst, Mass.)

in the middle of a bizarre racial episode in 1840–1 with no choice but to act the part of the patrician.[26]

Cities and towns in the Commonwealth dealt with the poor and dependent in the middle of the nineteenth century by indenturing them to

---

[26] Alfred Habegger, *My Wars Are Laid Away in Books: The Life of Emily Dickinson* (New York: Modern Library, 2002), p. 293.

families willing to support them, presumably on a modest subsidy.[27] The town thus saved some money, and families that took in the poor gained cheap labor. Whether the system degenerated at times into a form of quasi-slavery or whether it ensnared African Americans more than whites is not known. What is known is that Mason and Susan Shaw, former residents of Amherst, acquired two African American servants through indenture, a seventeen-year-old woman from officials in Boston and a ten-year-old girl, Angeline Palmer, from officials in Amherst. In late May 1840, Susan Shaw, who had been staying at the home of her married daughter in Belchertown, allowed Angeline (and the other servant) to visit Angeline's grandmother in Amherst before leaving for their new home in Georgia. A day or so before, Angeline overheard Mrs. Shaw read aloud (probably to her daughter) a letter from her husband indicating that he intended to sell the young servant into slavery while in the South and then claim that she had fled when the family returned to Amherst without her. While in Amherst, Angeline got word of the plot to her half brother, Lewis Frazer, who with two friends, Henry Jackson and William Jennings, appealed to the Board of Selectmen. The board refused to act, noting that the Shaws had regularly traveled to the South and back without incident and implying that Frazer was being alarmist.[28]

Frazer and his friends then hatched a plot of their own. On May 26, Mrs. Shaw arranged to have her servants returned by stagecoach to her daughter's place in Belchertown to get ready to leave for the South. Shortly after they arrived, Frazer showed up in a wagon with Jackson and Jennings. He bolted into the house, wrestled Angeline from the Shaws, and fled with her. The three men tore through Belchertown into north Amherst to place Angeline at a safe house. She was then spirited off to Colrain, a remote hill town in Franklin County, where she lived for a time before returning to Amherst. Her half brother and his accomplices went into hiding for several months, only to be charged with assault and abduction by a grand jury when they resurfaced.[29]

Jackson, Frazer's friend and a longtime Amherst resident, had known the Dickinsons for years. He had worked for Edward's father in some capacity and then served as a wagoner and messenger for Edward and

[27] Barry Levy, "Poor Children and the Labor Market in Colonial Massachusetts," *PH* 64 (Summer 1997): 287–307.

[28] *NC*, Dec. 2, 1840.

[29] Ibid. Also, *AR*, Jan. 29, 1902, and James Avery Smith, *The History of the Black Population of Amherst, Massachusetts, 1728–1870* (Boston: New England Historic Genealogical Society, 1999), pp. 26–30.

FIGURE 14. Henry Jackson. (Photograph by C. R. Kentfield, Amherst, Mass. By permission of Jones Library, Inc. Amherst, Mass.)

other local businessmen.[30] It was probably Jackson who prevailed on Edward Dickinson to serve as counsel when the case reached district court. Edward got the men off but was powerless when they flatly refused the tell the judge where Angeline was hiding.[31] Their reticence got them a three-month sentence in what would today be called a "minimum security installation," for they were free during the day and allowed to accept donations of food from local supporters. According to one account, their release in June was "met by congratulations of all classes, coupled with commendations of their display of pluck in taking Angeline from possible harm to a safe place."[32] As for Edward Dickinson, the episode did nothing

[30] *AR*, Jan. 29, 1902.
[31] *HG*, Mar. 31, 1841.
[32] Daniel Lombardo, *A Hedge Away: The Other Side of the Dickinson's Amherst* (Northampton, Mass.: Daily Hampshire Gazette, 1997), p. 247.

to soften his political conservatism but quite a bit for his reputation as a village paternalist.

Though paternalists accepted the dominant racial discourse that defined blacks as socially and intellectually inferior to whites, they also believed that black men were both human beings and citizens and were entitled to basic civil rights short of full citizenship. It did not occur to paternalists to dispute the right of black men to vote, a right that black males had long enjoyed and exercised in Massachusetts even as it was being rolled back in nearly every other Northern state.[33] Paternalists also assumed that a select few blacks could improve themselves – intellectually, morally, and economically – if they had the right educational experiences and economic opportunities. Hardly any encouraged full social equality for blacks, but many did object to the segregation of public accommodations, because of principle or because they associated it with the South. Paternalists also responded to pressure to expand the public space carved out for blacks by earlier generations of whites. They disagreed with one another over how much space was appropriate, not over whether African Americans were entitled to any space at all.[34]

The paternalism of antislavery approached the race question from a dual perspective of rights and responsibilities or obligations. This may surprise modern readers who tend to think of these approaches as mutually exclusive, that a rights approach implies egalitarianism and a paternalistic approach implies hierarchy.[35] This is why modern liberals favor rights, and modern conservatives obligations. Such a distinction unquestionably applied to other social relationships in antebellum Massachusetts, the best

[33] Alexander Keyssar, *The Right to Vote: The Contested History of Democracy in America* (New York: Basic Books, 2000), pp. 54–9, and Litwack, *North of Slavery*, esp. pp. 74–88.

[34] I am suggesting here that modern egalitarianism was barely evident in this period. Or put another way, it was too uncommon to be considered as a category of belief on race. For an engaging sketch of such a figure, see the portrait of the lowly shoemaker Martin Stowell in Albert Von Frank, *The Trials of Anthony Burns: Freedom and Slavery in Emerson's Boston* (Cambridge: Harvard Univ. Press, 1998), pp. 23–6, 63–70, and ff. Some would also describe the young Thomas Wentworth Higginson and Gerrit Smith in that way for a period. See Higginson, *Cheerful Yesterdays* (Boston: Houghton Mifflin, 1898), and Higginson, *Contemporaries* (Boston: Houghton Mifflin, 1899); Tilden G. Edelstein, *Strange Enthusiasm: A Life of Thomas Wentworth Higginson* (New Haven, Conn.: Yale Univ. Press, 1968); and Stauffer, *Black Hearts of Men*.

[35] Some conservative elites, notably those of Revolutionary Massachusetts, fused these principles, as did Free Soilers, as we shall see. For a fine treatment of Revolutionary Whiggery and of its successor Jeffersonian Federalism, see David Hackett Fischer, *The Revolution of American Conservatism: The Federalist Party in the Era of Jeffersonian Democracy* (New York: Harper and Row, 1965), and Fischer, *Paul Revere's Ride* (New York: Oxford Univ. Press, 1994).

example being the debate over gender and women's rights. This debate, which began in the late 1830s over the right of women to participate fully in the abolitionist movement, crystallized in the late 1840s when a formal feminist movement took shape, as reflected in conventions of feminists held at Seneca Falls in 1848 and at Worcester two years later.[36] The battle was joined in 1853 when a small but vocal group of women petitioned the convention assembled to amend the Massachusetts constitution to allow women to vote on ratification. One deligate, William B. Greene, a Worcester County farmer and self-described Democrat, saw women's suffrage as a simple matter of extending individual rights. He argued that "people," not just men, are endowed with the "natural right" to the franchise, that women are "*people*," and thus that "the women of Massachusetts have a natural right to vote." Probably a Quaker, Greene maintained that enlightened religion bolstered his case because "people" are "the ones upon whom shines the intellectual light which lighteth every man that cometh into the world" and that women, who "are capable of receiving that intellectual light," are "rational creatures, human beings, enjoying all the faculties which belong to human beings."[37] Thus, natural rights and proper religion made women humans and also citizens.[38]

Though Greene had some allies, he aroused defenders of patriarchy from all parties who brought slightly different opinions to bear but who shifted the debate at the core of paternalism from the discourse of rights to the discourse of obligations or responsibilites. Abijah P. Marvin, a Worcester County clergyman and Free Soiler, flatly denied that women had a natural right to vote; even if they did, "it would be of no use," and possibly "dangerous," because "it would lead uncivilized man to exert his brute power, to keep women in a state of subjugation."[39] Women's "great sphere" was in the home. It was an error to think of women outside the realm of the family or as individuals. Stressing a point raised again and again by social conservatives, generally in response to demands for the expansion of rights, Marvin asserted that societies and by extension polities

[36] Judith Wellman, *The Road to Seneca Falls: Elizabeth Cady Stanton and the First Women's Rights Convention* (Urbana: Univ. of Illinois Press, 2004).

[37] *Official Report of Debates and Proceedings in the State Convention, Assembled May 4th 1853, to Revise and Amend the Constitution*, 3 vols. (Boston: White and Potter, 1853), 2: 726–8. Quote is on p. 726. Hereafter *Constitutional Convention*.

[38] For the resolution of the debate as far as the petitioners were concerned, see ibid., and esp. pp. 753–55, as well as Mrs. W. S. Robinsion, ed., *"Warrington" Pen-Portraits: A Collection of Personal and Political Reminiscences from 1848 to 1876, from the Writings of William S. Robinson* (Boston: Mrs. William S. Robinson, 1877), p. 116 n. 2.

[39] *Constitutional Convention*, 2: 749.

are founded "upon families" and not upon "individuals," as among the ancient Jews. "What," he asked, is the "connection [of the family] with the state?" "[In] those representative bodies where the laws are made," each family had a vote. "But it does not follow that each individual in the family has a right to be a representative, or to vote for one." The question was, who was "best qualified"? The answer was in the social division of labor, that is,

[between] labor in the house at home, and labor out of doors; between influences exercised within the family and without the family; between taking care of the family within the house, and providing for it, taking care of its interests by thought, labor and other exertions in the field, the shop, the store, and the assembly.

This distinction between "duties" was ordained by "God" and could never be "altered or repealed . . . ignored or tampered with, without causing great confusion and mischief."[40] The strictures of patriarchy, however, did not leave women or even children without a voice. They mattered precisely because they were "more virtuous and . . . nearer to . . . God than men"; they therefore enjoyed what Marvin called "virtual representation," a hoary term rarely heard since the Revolution. When husbands and fathers voted, they necessarily reflected the views of their wives and children. It was their duty to represent the family.

This polarity between the discourse of rights and the discourse of duties did not carry over to the paternalism of race relations. The same abolitionists who spoke of the importance of treating blacks as citizens also spoke of blacks in the most patronizing and condescending terms. The New England Anti-Slavery Society was only six months old when in June 1832 Garrison was already directing homilies at African Americans. "Be industrious," he told African Americans. "Let no hour pass unemployed. Labor diligently in your business and show to all around that you are not 'idle.'" He added, at his righteous best, "Be virtuous. Use no bad language."[41] The first meeting of the New England Anti-Slavery Society likewise had no trouble vowing to "improve the character and condition of the free people of color" and to "obtain for them equal civil and political rights and privileges with the whites."[42] Nor was this language limited to paternalistic whites. Samson Harris Moody, a self-described *"colored man,"* openly mused that the aftermath of slavery

---

[40] Ibid. Quotes are on pp. 747 and 748.
[41] *Lib*, June 23, 1832.
[42] Board of Managers of the New England Anti-Slavery Society, *First Annual Report* (New York: Dorr and Butterfield, 1833), p. 13. Hereafter NEASS.

could be fraught with peril as well as promise. Both races would benefit from liberation, he supposed, but only if blacks were "civilized and naturalized." Whites could expect antisocial behavior to occur unless they helped prepare African Americans for freedom by providing them with education and employment.[43]

Better employment was precisely what paternalists had in mind.[44] No one in antebellum America gave any thought to using government to prohibit discrimination in labor markets; that is a modern idea that awaited the middle of the twentieth century. Paternalists proposed privatistic solutions to the problem of African American employment. They tried without much success to establish institutes and training schools to "procure for . . . [free blacks] mechanical trades, and reputable pursuits, by which they may become highly useful to the country, and banish their general poverty."[45] They also developed close if predictably asymmetrical relationships with black clients in order to improve the clients' economic status, either seeking out black men of talent and ambition or simply coming upon them by happenstance. In either case they acquired black clients, typically by providing jobs or arranging schooling or vocational training. Garrison took on several young black apprentices, starting with Thomas Paul, Jr.;[46] Ellis Gray Loring, the abolitionist attorney, trained Robert Morris in the law;[47] and Henry Ingersoll Bowditch, the Libertyite leader, helped Lewis Hayden land the patronage position of messenger at the State House.[48] Such relationships in Boston may well have extended beyond a relatively well-off clique of abolitionists like Loring or Bowditch and to friendly employers like Garrison who had relatively little money

---

43 *Lib*, Mar. 24, 1832.

44 *Eman*, July 28, 1842. For a useful discussion of racism in labor markets from a black perspective, see George A. Levesque, *Black Boston: African-American Life and Culture in Urban America* (New York: Garland Publishing, 1994), pp. 111–28.

45 NEASS, *First Annual Report* (1833), p. 22. See also NEAAS, *Fifth Annual Report* (1838), pp. 8–9. The American Anti-Slavery Society echoed this commitment in its Declaration of Sentiments which the society adopted at its initial meeting in 1833 and then at its annual meetings through the 1830s and beyond.

46 Henry Mayer, *All on Fire: William Lloyd Garrison and the Abolition of Slavery* (New York: St. Martin's Press, 1998), pp. 116 and 207.

47 James Oliver Horton and Lois E. Horton, *Black Bostonians: Family Life and Community Struggle in the Antebellum North* (New York: Holmes and Meier, 1979), pp. 55–6.

48 Vincent Y. Bowditch, ed., *Life and Correspondence of Henry Ingersoll Bowditch*, 2 vols. (Boston: Houghton, Mifflin, 1902), 1: 205–9. Also Horton and Horton, *Black Bostonians*, pp. 54–55, and Stanley J. Robboy and Anita W. Robboy, "Lewis Hayden: From Fugitive Slave to Statesman," *NEQ* 46 (Dec. 1973): 591–613.

but were in a position to help. It is impossible to know if white employers hired black Bostonians on the waterfront because they believed in the black cause or because they needed cheap labor. What we do know is that such employers did hire blacks before the influx of the Irish in the 1850s and that blacks thought of them as "friends."[49]

Not much is known either about economic relations between white patrons and black clients in other port cities or in the country. In the port city of Salem, the West Indian–born immigrant John Remond and his wife, Nancy, established a grocery and catering business, among other services that enjoyed the support of the town's elite. The Remonds seem to have benefited measurably from such a clientele but not enough to ensure their children a quality education. When in 1835 the school authorities banned their daughters from the local high school, the Remonds took their children to Rhode Island for a seven-year exile so that they could attend private school.[50] African American men had an easier time of it in New Bedford, Salem's commercial rival on the South Shore, because New Bedford's black community of one thousand people in 1850 was several times larger (between 5 and 7.5 percent of the city) and included many tradesmen.[51] Black craftsmen in other places customarily wound up underemployed for a lack of employers willing to take them on.[52] In New Bedford, however, white Quakers had no qualms about hiring black tradesmen and ordinary workers.[53] In the country, economic life for blacks was rather harder, because African American numbers were smaller, their organizations weaker, and their allies fewer. In addition, untold numbers of blacks in Berkshire County were runaways from New York State, where slavery remained legal well into the century. Runaways stole into the Berkshires, seeking refuge in the towns of the region,

[49] See, for instance, the speech of John Swett Rock, *Lib*, Mar. 16, 1860. On Rock, see George A. Levesque, "Boston's Black Brahmin: Dr. John Swett Rock," *CWH* 26 (Dec. 1980): 326–46.

[50] Sibyl Ventress Brownlee, "'Out of the Abundance of the Heart': Sarah Ann Parker Remond's Quest for Freedom" (Ph.D. diss., Univ. of Massachusetts Amherst, 1997). The schooling episode is on pp. 60–1. Also Ruth Bogin, "Sarah Ann Parker Remond: Black Abolitionist from Salem," *EIHC* 110 (Apr. 1974): 120–50, and Nick Saluatore, *We All Got History: The Memory Books of Amos Webber* (New York: Times Books, 1996), pp. 99–121.

[51] Kathryn Grover, *The Fugitive's Gibraltar: Escaping Slaves and Abolitionism in New Bedford, Massachusetts* (Amherst: Univ. of Massachusetts Press, 2001), p. 54.

[52] Glendyne Wergland, "Women, Men, Property, and Inheritance: Gendered Testamentary Customs in Western New Massachusetts, 1800–1860" (Ph.D. diss., Univ. of Massachusetts Amherst, 2001), pp. 174–218.

[53] Grover, *Fugitive's Gibraltar*, pp. 10–11 and 281–2.

a region, incidentally, that was heavily Democratic and therefore hostile. They had to keep a low profile.[54]

This racialized system of patron-client relations at the local level illuminates the larger pattern of race relations in the Bay State. Though Massachusetts was the scene of antiblack and antiabolitionist violence between 1825 and 1855, it looked civil by comparison to New York and Pennsylvania. Stump speakers were hectored or roughed up, and their meetings sometimes disrupted, but Bay Staters, and more to the point Bostonians, never experienced anything remotely resembling the racial violence that erupted in Jacksonian New York City or Philadelphia.[55] In the putative "City of Brotherly Love," race riots persisted into the late 1840s, not simply because Philadelphia, like New York, had strong commercial ties to the South. Nor was the violence necessarily because of the relative sizes of the black populations. Boston's blacks (about 2,000) in 1850 were smaller in number than New York's (about 12,000) or Philadelphia's (about 20,000) but not significantly different as a proportion of the population.[56] The key difference was the strength of the white abolitionist movement in each city and the larger authority of white paternalists in conjunction with the rise of a civil rights movement that cut across racial lines.

Few abolitionists – "new org" and "old org" alike – believed that paternalism by itself would improve race relations, even if blacks clung to the idea that the worldly success of African American individuals would dissolve prejudice against their race as a whole. Nor did they believe that the race question could be reduced to that of the abolition of slavery. Both groups realized that the same racist etiquette that secured slavery in

---

[54] Wergland, "Women, Men, Property and Inheritance," pp. 198–201.

[55] Jack Tager, *Boston Riots: Three Centuries of Social Violence* (Boston: Northeastern Univ. Press, 2001), pp. 76–139. On Philadelphia, see Michael Feldberg, *The Philadelphia Riots of 1844: A Study of Ethnic Conflict* (Westport, Conn.: Greenwood Press, 1975); on New York, see Leonard L. Richards, *"Gentlemen of Property and Standing": Anti-Abolitionist Mobs in Jacksonian America* (New York: Oxford Univ. Press, 1970), pp. 113–22; and on the larger pattern of violence, see David Grimsted, *American Mobbing, 1828–1861: Toward Civil War* (New York: Oxford Univ. Press, 1998). Fischer, *Paul Revere's Ride*, p. 19, suggests that violence was not an acceptable way of resolving disputes in New England. Though he is referring here to a familial dispute in the late-colonial era, his point seems to have broader social and temporal application.

[56] Horton and Horton, *Black Bostonians*, p. 2. Also Leonard P. Curry, *The Free Black in Urban America, 1800–1860: In the Shadow of the Dream* (Chicago: Univ. of Chicago Press, 1981), pp. 1–14.

the South kept African Americans in subordination in the North. They worked against racial segregation, slowly and haltingly at first in the 1830s and then vigorously in the 1840s and into the 1850s as the civil rights movement evolved. This was hardly the equivalent of its modern counterpart, for there were no student groups or tightly organized mass actions. Nor was there a charismatic leader in the mold of Martin Luther King, even if Garrison did come close. Never an inspiring speaker, Garrison was a forceful if not a lyrical writer and a shrewd tactician, at least regarding civil action. He appeared inconsistent and hypocritical, however, when it came to translating demands into public policy because of his aversion to politics.[57] All of this aside, in the context of the 1840s, the activity of whites and blacks, who sometimes worked together and sometimes separately, added up to a civil rights movement that bore the stamp of paternalism.

Several convergent forces accounted for this significant dimension of abolitionism.[58] The idea of color-blind equality – that all men are brothers and therefore equal – was one such force. Such egalitarianism, rooted in evangelical Protestantism and in the equal rights tradition of the Declaration of Independence, may well have been as familiar to their antebellum forebears as it is to modern Americans. It is noteworthy, however, that early abolitionists redoubled their commitment to equality to disassociate themselves not only from the racism of society in general but also from the racist legacy of the colonization movement. That Garrison and other movement founders started out as colonizationists invested this project with special urgency.[59] For Garrison, as the historian John Thomas observed, assailing colonization became a "vendetta," an obsessive blood feud Garrison conducted through emotional pamphlets, blistering editorials, and searing lectures.[60] This was not a simple matter of atonement;

---

[57] Litwack, *North of Slavery*, pp. 243–4, pointed this out long ago.

[58] African American scholars have long been aware of the struggles of blacks for civil rights. See Benjamin Quarles, *Black Abolitionists* (New York: Oxford Univ. Press, 1969), esp. pp. 168–96. Also see Litwack, *North of Slavery*, pp. 113–52. My own view of white support for black civil rights is more optimistic than Litwack's in *North of Slavery*, pp. 214–46. In any event, recent work is more focused on white racism than on white liberalism, however flawed and limited it was.

[59] See Richards, "*Gentlemen of Property and Standing*," pp. 21–6 and 165–6 on the policy implications of anticolonizationism. The American Colonization Society still awaits a thorough treatment. For a fine start, see John David Smith, ed., *The American Colonization Society and Emigration* (New York: Garland Publishers, 1993).

[60] John L. Thomas, *The Liberator: William Lloyd Garrison* (Boston: Little, Brown, 1963), pp. 144–54. Quote is on p. 145.

strategic interests were at stake as well. Its past association with colonization was a millstone that had to be cast off if abolitionism was to broaden its appeal to whites and especially to blacks. Fighting against racism was a way of promoting abolitionism.[61]

Personal experience also encouraged racial toleration and activism for racial equality. Gerrit Smith believed that if he had had the opportunity to get to know African Americans personally he would never have succumbed to racism for so long.[62] The Libertyite leader Henry Ingersoll Bowditch experienced what Smith had in mind.[63] Bowditch met Frederick Douglass for the first time in 1842 at a Marlboro Chapel rally to protest the detention of the fugitive slave George Latimer. Determined to come to grips with his own doubts about racial equality, Bowditch decided to treat Douglass as an equal, inviting him to his home for dinner, "[just] as I would have invited a white friend. It is useless to deny," he confided to his journal, "that I did not like the thought of walking with him in open midday up Washington Street. I *hoped* I would not meet any of my acquaintances" for fear of social censure. But as luck would have it, when the two men turned onto Washington Street, they ran into a young acquaintance of Bowditch's whose facial expression revealed her disapproval and but strengthened his resolve. "It was . . . somewhat like a cold sponge bath, – that Washington Street walk by the side of a black man, – rather terrible at the outset but wonderfully warming and refreshing afterwards! I had literally jumped 'in medias res.'" This defining moment not only endeared Bowditch to Douglass, who remembered it years later; it also marked the beginning of Bowditch's civil rights activity.[64]

A related if somewhat more ambiguous source of abolitionism's racial liberalism had to do with a growing sense of regional identity, which I shall refer to as "Yankeedom" or "the country," the term townsfolk

---

[61] James Brewer Stewart, *William Lloyd Garrison and the Challenge of Emancipation* (Arlington Heights, Ill: H. Davidson, 1992), pp. 60–2.

[62] AASS, *Fifth Annual Report* (1838), pp. 30–6. For a more extended treatment of the question of male friendship across the race line, see Stauffer, *Black Hearts of Men*.

[63] Dumas Malone et al., eds. *Dictionary of American Biography*, 20 vols. (New York: C. Scribner's Sons, 1928–36), 2: 137–8.

[64] Bowditch, *Life and Correspondence of Henry Ingersoll Bowditch*, 1: 137–8, and William S. McFeely, *Frederick Douglass* (New York: Simon and Schuster, 1991), p. 93. For more on this, see Litwack, *North of Slavery*, pp. 222–3. Also Theodore Dwight Weld was also fond of recounting stories of his personal relationships with African Americans, though outside of New England. See Gilbert H. Barnes and Dwight L. Dumond, ed., *The Letters of Theodore Dwight Weld, Anglina Grimké Weld, and Sarah Grimké*, 2 vols. (New York: D. Appleton-Century, 1934), 2: 679.

used to refer to their area. New Englanders, of course, had developed a regional consciousness before the 1830s; it spread and deepened appreciably, however, as the antebellum era wore on. This sense of Yankeeness was a fluid and malleable construct that meant different things to different people beyond its obvious association with the Pilgrim and Puritan past. In the minds of some Whiggish political activists it gradually became synonymous with growing hatred of the South, an increasingly strident anti-Southernism that drew strength from the unpopular War of 1812, the political embarrassment suffered by favorite son President John Quincy Adams in the election of 1828, and subsequent political squabbles over the tariff, western expansion, and other issues that reflected and excited regional feelings. No aspect of this proved stronger than the belief that Southerners had eclipsed Yankees in the halls of government, that "they" were running the country. For some Yankees, anti-Southern feeling stopped at regional chauvinism; for others like Joseph Buckingham it evolved into antislavery sentiment, if not abolitionism.[65]

The abolitionist version of Yankeedom bore particular cultural and racial implications. It became strongly associated with the notion of a unique social and moral order rooted in the rough economic equality and political integrity of village New England. Timothy Dwight had called it the *"village manner"* in his posthumous *Travels in New-England and New-York* (1821–2), by which he meant a form of cultural cohesion and togetherness that produced a sense of community, higher levels of mutual sympathy, social reciprocity, and popular refinement.[66] The village manner celebrated regional customs, revered middling folk, and made a fetish of "the town," with its neighborly people of English stock who mingled on leafy town commons and worshipped together in plain white churches. Yankeedom invited two broad forms of self-comparison. In

---

[65] For the political implications of Yankee identity, see Richards, *The Slave Power*. Also see Harlow W. Sheidley, *Sectional Nationalism: Massachusetts Conservative Leaders and the Transformation of America, 1815–1836* (Boston: Northeastern Univ. Press, 1998). On its cultural formation, see Stephen W. Nissenbaum, "New England as a Region and Nation," in Edward L. Ayers et al., eds., *All Over the Map: Rethinking American Regions* (Baltimore: Johns Hopkins Univ. Press, 1996), pp. 38–61; Joseph A. Conforti, *Imagining New England: Explorations in Regional Identity from the Pilgrims to the Twentieth Century* (Chapel Hill: Univ. of North Carolina Press, 2001); and David Jaffe, *People of Wachusett: Greater New England in History and Memory* (Ithaca, N.Y.: Cornell Univ. Press, 1999).

[66] Nissenbaum, "New England as a Region," p. 48. Also see Timothy Dwight, *Travels in New-England and New-York*, 4 vols. (London: W. Baynes and Son, 1823), esp. 1: 132–43 and 4: 328–51 and 449–63.

one, Yankeedom led townsfolk to think of themselves as people of virtue, the "real people," as some would describe themselves in the 1850s, who had been defeated in state politics by wily urban elites. This expression of Yankee identity nursed the extreme parochialism that would emerge from time to time before the great nativist outburst of the mid-1850s. In the other, Yankeedom encouraged Bay Staters, and antislavery activists especially, to contrast themselves with Southerners on the question of race relations. It led them to associate racial oppression with the South and oppression's opposite, racial toleration, with the North, and more narrowly with their own region.

Thus Bay State abolitionists in the 1840s began to look upon their cultural and regional heritage as justification for coming out against slavery and for extending a paternal hand to free people of color. Henry Wilson, the Whig antislavery activist who represented Natick in the state legislature in the mid-1840s, invoked his Yankee background to justify a resolution he drafted in 1845 against the annexation of Texas. The former shoemaker told his fellow lawmakers, in "sober earnest," that he wished Washington lawmakers "to feel, to think, and to act as Massachusetts men, who have been reared under the institutions of the Pilgrim Fathers, should think, feel, and act."[67] Several years earlier, Bowditch called on Whittier to write a "few lines" in honor of poor George Latimer confined in Leverett Street Jail. "Give us, I pray you," he wrote, invoking the language of abolitionist Yankeedom, "some loud trumpet peal in behalf of New England's rights."[68]

Reality, of course, proved more complicated. Few towns lived up to the ideal, invented by country ideologues, of like-minded villagers united behind Enlightenment traditions of equal rights. Indeed, it is doubtful whether the country formed a coherent whole at all either economically or politically. It tended to split between the relatively prosperous towns in the river valleys and the poorer farming communities in the hills and uplands, known then and now as "hill towns." The former leaned toward Whiggery, the latter toward Democracy, a pattern political historians have found elsewhere as well.[69] Amherst, Deerfield, and Sunderland, in the fertile floodplain of the Connecticut River, were Whiggish strongholds

---

[67] Henry Wilson, *The Rise and Fall of the Slave Power in America*, 3 vols. (Boston: James R. Osgood, 1872–7), 1: 485.

[68] John B. Pickard, ed., *The Letters of John Greenleaf Whittier*, 3 vols. (Cambridge: Harvard Univ. Press, 1975), 1: 579, reprints part of a letter from HIB to JGW.

[69] One of the best of these works is Harry L. Watson, *Jacksonian Politics and Community Conflict: The Emergence of the Second Party System in Cumberland County, North Carolina* (Baton Rouge: Louisiana State Univ. Press, 1981). For the economic aspect

ringed by Democratic hill towns. Whig and Democratic politicians in the country differed over economic policy, but as we shall see, they drew together against the economic power and religious diversity of the city. A mean-spirited streak of nativism lurked just below the seemingly genteel surface of the country culture.

Nonetheless, the parochial hamlets whose denizens glared at outsiders sometimes showed another side when it came to African Americans. They occasionally accommodated African Americans in the spirit of paternalism. The third and fourth generations of the Huntingtons of Hadley, spanning the late antebellum and the Civil War years, were fond of telling stories about race that cast their family in the most favorable light. No one mentioned the family's colonial-era slaves. Instead, in his memoir, Theodore Gregson Huntington lionized his grandfather as an early civil rights activist, insisting that he seated himself in the "black only" pews to protest the inclusion of a Jim Crow section in a newly built church.[70] The memoir of Theodore's niece, Arria Sargeant Huntington, overlooked her grandmother's colonizationist past for the more reassuring portrait of a principled liberal who took in a young black man.[71] Though Elizabeth's act of charity seems more plausible than her father's heroism, such stories served to justify the racial liberalism that became a hallmark of Elizabeth's children. This is not to suggest a pattern of racial paternalism among the first families of country. Edward Dickinson remained a conservative Whig throughout the political turmoil of the early 1850s, resisting the trend toward deserting Whiggery for Free Soilism. Dickinson loathed slavery, but he also despised abolitionists and seems to have extended only a stingy paternal hand when it came to African Americans.[72] The difference between the Dickinsons and the Huntingtons was in their political legacies. The Huntingtons, after all, had favored colonization, and their rejection of its racist legacy may well have been a belated atonement. Other paternalists may have been motivated by crasser considerations. They forged unequal bonds with individual African Americans partly because they wanted inexpensive and tractable labor in a region where workers tended to be scarce, relatively expensive, and sometimes maddeningly independent.[73]

---

of this pattern, see Christopher Clark, *The Roots of Rural Capitalism: Western Massachusetts, 1790–1860* (Amherst: Univ. of Massachusetts Press, 1990).

[70] Theodore Gregson Huntington, "Family Sketch" ms., PPHFP, b. 21.

[71] Huntington, *Under a Colonial Roof-Tree.*

[72] Habegger, "*My Wars Are Laid Away in Books*," pp. 109–10, 183–4, 292–300, 401–2, and 560–2.

[73] Jonathan Prude, *The Coming of Industrial Order: Town and Factory Life in Rural Massachusetts, 1810–1860* (New York: Cambridge Univ. Press, 1983), pp. 133–7.

Finally, and a factor that has come to light only recently, was pressure
for civil rights exerted by blacks themselves. Perhaps because it was so
small, the African American community in Boston proved to be more cohesive and assertive than its counterparts in other port cities in northern
New England. By the mid–1840s Boston's black community had a handful
of churches that anchored a web of civic, political, and social organizations. These groups were headed by a highly visible cadre of articulate
and visible leaders, most of them men, and nearly all of them either associated with the clergy or engaged in small businesses or craft work.[74] The
more familiar of them – the Baptist ministers Leonard A. Grimes and Peter
Randolph, to name just two – would achieve celebrity in the 1850s in dramatic confrontations with state and federal authorities over enforcement
of the Fugitive Slave Act.[75] In the 1840s, however, blacks were honing their
leadership skills. William Cooper Nell, who was the son of a community
leader, caught Garrison's attention when Nell headed an abolitionist youth
group in the early 1830s. Garrison hired Nell to run errands and then took
him on as a printer's apprentice at the *Liberator*. Nell never forgot his
debt to Garrison; even as he plunged more earnestly into the politics of
integration during the 1840s and 1850s, Nell remained Garrison's loyal
friend and defender.[76] Jehial C. Beman, a Connecticut-born Methodist
minister, was older and better known than Nell and also more independent minded. A skilled organizer imbued with the ethic of social uplift,
Beman worked for better education and improved jobs and employment
prospects for his people. He did not share Nell's affection for Garrison,
embracing politics and helping form the Massachusetts Abolition Society
in 1839 before throwing in with the Liberty Party a year later.[77] Though

---

74 Horton and Horton, *Black Bostonians*, pp. 15–25. Also, James Oliver Horton, *Free Peo-
    ple of Color: Inside the African American Community* (Washington, D.C.: Smithsonian
    Institution Press, 1993). For comparison, see Theodore Hershberg, "Free Blacks in Ante-
    bellum Philadelphia: A Study of Ex-Slaves, Freeborn, and Socioeconomic Decline," *JSH*
    5 (1971–2): 183–209, and Graham Russell Hodges, *Root and Branch: African Americans
    in New York and East Jersey, 1613–1863* (Chapel Hill: Univ. of North Carolina Press,
    1999), pp. 226–70.

75 Horton and Horton, *Black Bostonians*, pp. 27–52. Also Horton, *Free People of Color*;
    Benjamin Quarles, *Black Abolitionists* (New York: Oxford Univ. Press, 1969); and Robert
    S. Levine, *Martin Delany, Frederick Douglass, and the Politics of Representative Identity*
    (Chapel Hill: Univ. of North Carolina Press, 1997).

76 On Nell, see Horton and Horton, *Black Bostonians*, pp. 57–9 and 63–4. Also see Robert
    P. Smith, "William Cooper Nell: Crusading Abolitionist," *JNH* 55 (July 1970): 182–
    99, and Elizabeth Rauh Bethel, *The Roots of African-American Identity: Memory and
    History in Antebellum Free Communities* (New York: St. Martin's Press, 1997), pp. 3–4
    and 195–6.

77 Horton and Horton, *Black Bostonians*, pp. 48–9.

FIGURE 15. William Cooper Nell. (Portraits of American Abolitionists. Massachusetts Historical Society. Courtesy of the Massachusetts Historical Society, Boston, Mass.)

Beman and Nell disagreed over tactics, both were avid integrationists who fought the Commonwealth's regime of separate accommodations in schools, transportation facilities, and other areas of public life. Not all blacks, however, shared their integrationist politics. A small but vocal group that would gain a larger audience in the 1850s advocated an early form of race pride that favored the development of autonomous institutions organized by blacks for blacks. In the 1840s, however, the integrationists went unchallenged.[78]

Such black activist men had the support and encouragement of several black women, including Susan Paul, the most visible in the 1830s. The daughter of the Baptist minister Reverend Thomas Paul who founded

[78] Ibid., pp. 73–4. On emergent black nationalism, see Patrick Rael, *Black Identity and Black Protest in the Antebellum North* (Chapel Hill: Univ. of North Carolina Press, 2002), esp. pp. 209–13, 216–17, 238–9, and 255–66, and Levine, *Martin Delany*, pp. 64–9 and 208–78.

Boston's African Baptist Church in 1805/6, Susan Paul was a leading light in the Boston Female Anti-Slavery Society. She was also an outspoken feminist by the end of the 1830s who nonetheless placed greater emphasis on the struggle against segregation.[79] So did Sarah Ann Parker Remond, the daughter of the highly entrepreneurial Salem family headed by the caterer and provisioner John Remond. Sarah Remond modeled herself after her brother Charles, a favorite of Garrison's and a leading black abolitionist in the early 1840s. She spent the greater part of the 1840s helping with the family business in Salem; then, in the 1850s, she made her mark by taking a leading part in the integrationist struggle in Boston and establishing herself on the lecture circuit before departing for Europe and what would become a lifelong exile, first in England and then in Italy.[80]

While Susan Paul and other blacks in Boston loudly denounced segregation and racial oppressions in the 1830s, their colleagues in the port cities and outlands protected their own more quietly.[81] Perhaps they feared drawing attention to themselves in a period in which white support was far from clear. Frederick Douglass described black New Bedford in the late 1830s as a close community, privately but acutely vigilant against those who imperiled fugitives in its midst; at the same time, the community was quite prepared to act if need be. He recounted the story of a free black in a dispute who threatened to turn in a runaway slave, was discovered, and was tried and convicted by a local church. The congregants would have punished him on the spot had he not dived out of a window and fled.[82]

Garrison decried the injustice of segregation and inequality in the first editions of the *Liberator*. He took special exception to a 1705 law, strengthened in 1786, which prohibited interracial marriage and punished clergymen who performed marriage ceremonies for people of different races. In 1831 and throughout the decade, Garrison railed against this marriage ban as unjust and particularly objectionable because it was a part of the

[79] Horton and Horton, *Black Bostonians*, p. 65, and Debra Gold Hansen, *Strained Sisterhood: Gender and Class in the Boston Female Anti-Slavery Society* (Amherst: Univ. of Massachusetts Press, 1993), pp. 14, 19, and 76ff.

[80] Brownlee, "Out of the Abundance of the Heart."

[81] Litwack, *North of Slavery*, pp. 105–11, and Peter P. Hinks, *To Awaken My Afflicated Brethren: David Walker and the Problem of Antebellum Slave Resistance* (University Park: Pennsylvania State Univ. Press, 1997), esp. pp. 63–115.

[82] Frederick Douglass, *My Bondage and My Freedom*, in Henry Louis Gates, Jr., ed., *Douglass Autobiographies* (New York: Library of America, 1994), pp. 357–8.

old colony's slave code.[83] The ban was patently racist, contrary to liberty and individual choice, and above all, a "disgraceful badge of servitude" unworthy of a Christian republic and anathema to Yankees.[84] Garrison also condemned discrimination against African Americans in labor markets, highlighting the exclusion of black men from trades and handicrafts. Not a single black man, he said, citing the Boston city directory for 1830, could be found engaged in the conventional crafts or trading "in any article except clothing."[85] Garrison stirred up petitioning for repeal of the marriage ban, and he worked energetically for several years to raise funds for a manual labor school to train African American young men in craft work. Lawmakers responded by nearly repealing the marriage ban in 1831, but the following year they took a firmer stand against any such action.[86] The school project stalled for lack of interest and funds. In desperation, a committee of the New England Anti-Slavery Society, which had taken over the project, turned to Alfred Noyes, the Millinarian Christian and communitarian. Noyes agreed to integrate the curriculum and its students into his academy in Canaan, New Hampshire, in return for the few thousand dollars already raised. The committee watched its plan collapse when Noyes's academy failed.[87]

The end of the 1830s brought an upsurge in civil rights activity. In 1838 a recrudescent movement for repeal of the marriage ban began with a group of white women in eastern industrial towns. In Lynn its leaders were Abby Kelley and other members of the Lynn Female Anti-Slavery Society who having attended the 1837 Anti-Slavery Convention of American Women in New York returned home determined to carry out the convention's injunction to overcome racial prejudice. Kelley and her friends represented youth in rebellion against the more cautious leadership found in local Quaker meetings and evangelical churches. By making the cause of repeal their own, these women took a stand not only against racism but also against the social conservatism of their parents and elders in their places of worship – a pattern reproduced again

---

[83] *Lib*, May 7, 1831. See also, Louis Ruchames, "Race, Marriage, and Abolition in Massachusetts," *JNH* 40 (July 1955): 250–73, and George S. Levesque, "Politicians in Petticoats: Interracial Sex and Legislative Politics in Antebellum Massachusetts," *NEJBS* 3 (1983): 40–59.

[84] *Lib*, June 11, 1831. Also ibid., Jan. 28 and Feb 11, 1832, and Feb 15, 1839.

[85] Ibid., Jan. 22, 1831, and Sept. 28, 1832.

[86] Ibid., Feb. 11 and 17, 1832. Also Ruchames, "Race, Marriage, and Abolition," pp. 251–3.

[87] NEASS, *Third Annual Report* (1835), pp. 26–7. The NEASS became the Massachusetts Anti-Slavery Society in 1835. Hereafter MASS. See also *Lib*, July 4 and 5, 1835.

and again through the 1840s.[88] In 1838 alone, working door-to-door in the towns of the country, Kelley's legions gathered about five thousand names, most of them women's.[89] Their example stimulated the Garrisonians in Boston to restart their dormant campaign for repeal the next year by calling a meeting at Marlboro Chapel to kick off an even more ambitious petition drive.[90] The campaign, which soon drew in the fledgling Libertyites as well, nearly doubled the number of signatures to nine thousand. Since nearly four thousand of the signers were men and therefore voters, politicians had to take notice.[91]

Politicians, in fact, debated repeal every year from 1839 to 1843. A dismissive report in 1839 concealed a feverish debate laced with misogynist and racist invective.[92] Cartoonists and politicians alike depicted the women seeking repeal as miscegenationists on the prowl for black lovers;[93] one Democrat said he'd rather see his daughter "die" than marry a black man.[94] Whigs were just as racist and alarmist as the Democrats despite Whiggery's reputation among modern historians for moderation.[95] As bills moved through the State House, the *Boston Daily Advertiser,* thought to be more moderate than the *Boston Atlas,* spewed racist diatribes worthy of Democratic segregationists and exclusionists. The *Advertiser* editor, Nathan Hale, expressed "surprise" at the support for such an outrageous measure.[96] He darkly predicted that permissiveness sanctioned by repeal would make Massachusetts a magnet for black men looking to marry white women; this "unnatural mixture of the two races" would lead to "degradation of the species and the shortening of the duration of life," because science showed that blacks had a shorter life span than whites.[97] What could be "more immoral," he asked, than the

---

[88] See Sara Dubow, "'Not a Virtuous Woman Among Them': Political Culture, Antislavery Politics, and the Repeal of the Marriage Ban in Ante Bellum Massachusetts" (seminar paper, Univ. of Massachusetts Amherst, 1995), esp. pp. 9–12.

[89] Dubow, "'Not a Virtuous Woman,'" pp. 15–16.

[90] *Lib,* Mar. 15 and May 3, 1839. Also Ruchames, "Race, Marriage, and Abolition," pp. 266–9.

[91] Dubow, "'Not a Virtuous Woman,'" pp. 23–4.

[92] Massachusetts House Documents, Document No. 28, 1839. Also see Levesque, *Black Boston,* pp. 136–49.

[93] See, for example, *Lib,* Feb. 8, 1839; Ruchames, "Race, Marriage, and Abolition," pp. 257–9; and Dubow, "'Not a Virtuous Woman,'" pp. 19–21. Also see Henry Wilson, *Rise and Fall of the Slave Power,* 1: 488–92.

[94] Wilson, *Rise and Fall of the Slave Power,* 1: 491.

[95] Saxton, *Rise and Fall of the White Republic,* pp. 260–2.

[96] The engrossment (final) vote was 174 to 140: 81 to 74 on the Whig side and 93 to 66 on the Democratic side.

[97] BDA, Feb. 6–7, 1843. Quote is on Feb. 6.

"creation of a matrimonial union which inevitably entails upon its off-spring, wretchedness and probably disease and shortness of life?"[98] He answered his own question two weeks later in still another strident piece reiterating the specter of race mixing and mongrelization and ended by accusing legislators of undoing what "God has forbidden."[99] While the tone of the opposition remained unchanged throughout this period, the political winds shifted and blew much stronger into the early 1840s, almost enough in fact to put across repeal. Committee and joint committee reports favoring repeal were approved in 1840 and 1841; in 1842 a bill cleared the Senate (24 to 9) but narrowly went down in the House (136 to 140). The following year, the Senate reaffirmed its previous vote and the House reversed itself (174 to 139 for repeal), ending the decade-long struggle to erase a glaring vestige of slavery from the statute books.[100]

How to explain this remarkable and unexpected reversal? George Bradburn, a Nantucket Whig with abolitionist leanings, traced the victory to the expanded petition drive started in 1839, which produced "great change in the public mind on this subject during the last twelvemonth. A similar change," he said, "has been wrought in the minds of many legislators since the commencement of this session."[101] Actually, the legislators favoring reform expressed three distinct positions on the intermarriage ban. We have already encountered one of these in the form of the abolitionist claim that the marriage ban was racist and an embarrassment to the people of Massachusetts – the kind of proscription favored by hateful Southerners. Opposition to the marriage ban essentially affirmed Northern, and more narrowly Yankee, identity. The second position, popular with libertarian Democrats and possibly some Whigs as well, also found the law outmoded, not because it was racist but because it put government in the questionable position of deciding who could marry whom; the

---

[98] Ibid., Feb. 6, 1843.

[99] Ibid., Feb. 16, 1843.

[100] Ruchames, "Race, Marriage, and Abolition," pp. 270–1. The bill could not have passed without Democratic support, support that was ensured by the bargain made between Democrats and Libertyites following the 1842 election, in which the latter put the former in power in return for support for the civil rights measures passed by the 1843 General Court. See Journal of the House of Representatives, mss., Bill No. 13, 1843, Massachusetts State Archives, Boston. Repeal was the first of several civil rights laws that reached the floor of the House and the only one that enjoyed a roll call vote, possibly because the others were simply too controversial for Democrats whose support would not stand scrutiny in their districts. Also see DuBow, "'Not a Virtuous Woman,'" pp. 25–9 and appendixes A and B.

[101] *Lib*, Apr. 17, 1840.

choice of a marriage partner, said one lawmaker, was a matter of personal "taste" and beyond the purview of law.[102] Still a third stance, even farther removed from the morality and merits of the issue, and perfectly consistent with racism, saw the law as a "dead letter."[103] Most Bay Staters, this argument ran, viewed racial intermarriage with "natural repugnance" and would not consider entering such a union. So there was no danger in repealing a law that no one cared about.[104] For their part, abolitionists believed that their influence was decisive. Garrison certainly thought so. In 1844, a year after repeal, he told the annual meeting of Massachusetts Anti-Slavery Society that "four or five years" of "agitation" had not only changed minds. It had also confirmed his long-time strategy of making use of "existing political parties for the accomplishment of their purposes, rather than to expend their energies upon the establishment of a third."[105] The rupture with political abolitionists four years earlier was never very far from the "great agitator's" mind.

Garrison was unabashedly self-serving. Though his forces had weighed in early and then energetically against the odious laws on intermarriage, the fact is that repeal was put across by politicians, and even more significantly on the insistence of third-party men, not by regulars. This is precisely what Garrison chose to ignore in his postmortem. Most of the credit for repeal belonged to the Libertyites, not to apolitical abolitionists as Garrison liked to believe, or even to the Democrats, as recent historians argue.[106] Democrats (95 to 63) favored the bill more strongly than did the Whigs (81 to 74). But it is unlikely that Democrats would have voted for the bill at all without the deal that their leaders had made with the Libertyites the previous January in which the Democrats agreed to get behind several civil rights measures in return for the Libertyites' giving Democrats the governorship, the speakership of the House, and control of the Senate. Democratic support owed to Libertyite leverage.

The one group conspicuous for its absence in this drama was African Americans. At the last minute, in mid-February 1843, William Cooper Nell forwarded to the legislature resolutions passed at a meeting of African Americans that called the marriage ban unconstitutional and racist and urged repeal in no uncertain terms.[107] Nell and his friends had been

---

[102] For example, *BP*, Feb. 4, 1843.
[103] Wilson, *Rise and Fall of the Slave Power*, 1: 491–2.
[104] *Lib*, Mar. 10, 1839, and *Eman*, Feb. 9, 1843.
[105] MASS, *Twelfth Annual Report* (1844), p. 6.
[106] Dubow, "'Not a Virtuous Woman,'" pp. 28–34.
[107] *Lib*, Feb. 10, 1843.

prudently silent through the debate in the State House. They probably spoke up at the end for fear that their silence might be interpreted as support for the law; in fact, blacks felt strongly indeed about repealing the marriage ban. They felt equally strongly about other measures pending before the legislature, all of them sponsored by Liberty men, and each focused on fighting segregation in public accommodations.

Massachusetts blacks had long endured humiliation and worse on public transportation. Overland and seafaring carriers either maintained separate facilities for African Americans or refused to transport them altogether. This tradition of Jim Crow provisions was carried over to the commuter rail lines started in 1836 that connected Boston with points to its north and with larger cities and towns to its south. Racism on the rails drew the fire of white abolitionists, most notably of Garrison, who routinely reported indignities suffered by black travelers. An episode he found particularly outrageous involved a black clergyman, his wife, and two female friends who seated themselves in the main cabin on a sloop bound from Nantucket to New Bedford. When a white traveler sitting nearby objected, the blacks were ordered to the main deck in a driving winter rain until a steward made room for them in the forecastle.[108] There is no evidence that black rail commuters had to bear inclement weather, but plenty that they were forced into separate cars, which became known as "dirt cars" for their filth and squalor.[109] Douglass described his experiences on "public conveyances" as "extremely rough" and the black response to his complaints as disappointing. Black people, he observed, had adjusted to the "mean, dirty, and uncomfortable" Jim Crow car, as well as to the rudeness of railway conductors. "The colored people," he said, "generally accepted the situation and complained of me as making matters worse rather than better by refusing to submit to this proscription."[110]

Douglass may have been right. Local blacks did not object to the racist regime of the railways, possibly because they had grown accustomed to Jim Crow, knew no other way, and had little or no hope for change. It took an outsider to confront the system. The first major episode in the 1840s involved David Ruggles, a New York abolitionist and legendary Underground Railroad conductor who had met Douglass in New York

---

[108] Ibid., Jan. 15, 1831.
[109] Ibid., Dec. 30, 1831, and Lewis Ruchames, "Jim Crow Railroads in Massachusetts," *AQ* 8 (1955): 62. Also, *Lib*, Dec. 14, 1838.
[110] Douglass, *My Bondage and My Freedom*, in Gates, *Douglass Autobiographies*, p. 669.

shortly after Douglass's escape and recommended that he seek refuge in Massachusetts. In early July 1841, Ruggles prepared to board a passenger car on the New Bedford and Taunton Railroad in southeastern Massachusetts. He barely settled into a seat in the white section when a conductor ordered him into the dirt car. He refused to budge, drawing a crowd of angry railway workmen who tore him out of the seat, ripped his clothing, and pitched him from the train. Ruggles responded by suing for assault and battery. The ensuing trial two weeks later cleared the railway of any wrongdoing on the grounds that it was a private company that had the right to make rules and regulations for its enterprise, and that its personnel had not used excessive force when they evicted Ruggles.[111]

The Ruggles incident was the first in a quick succession of skirmishes between racist railways and black leaders.[112] Douglass had two such run-ins. In one, in September, officials on the Eastern Railway moved him from a seat in the white section to the black car. A few weeks later Douglass was again on the Eastern, this time with a party of white abolitionists, including John A. Collins, headed for Newburyport. A conductor, possibly the same one who had removed him earlier, unwittingly created a scene when he tried to dislodge the feisty abolitionist from his seat. Another traveler, who said that he had no objection to riding with Douglass, slyly recommended the car passengers vote on where the black man would sit. Douglass added that he would go willingly if he heard a "good reason why," which caught the conductor off guard and brought forth still more support from the passengers. "Give him one good reason," demanded another ally, who baited the conductor into saying what everyone knew: "Because you are black." With that, the flustered conductor darted out of the car, returning with reinforcements who threw Douglass from the train and evicted Collins at a later stop.[113]

Such episodes galvanized abolitionists like nothing had since the imposition of gag rule five years earlier. "Old org" and "new org" supporters swung into action around a broad array of activities. Garrisonian and Libertyite newspapers pilloried Jim Crow railways in headline stories and blistering editorials.[114] They told of antislavery societies calling for boycotts of the three major commuter lines in the eastern part of the state. The Worcester North Division Anti-Slavery Society recommended that

[111] MASS, *Tenth Annual Report* (1842), pp. 75–81.
[112] Ibid., pp. 63–85.
[113] *Lib*, Oct. 14, 1841. Douglass, *My Bondage and My Freedom*, in Gates, *Douglass Autobiographies*, pp. 669–70.
[114] Ruchames, "Jim Crow Railroads," pp. 67–8.

travelers to New York or Portland, Maine, "patronize the Boston and Norwich in preference to the Providence and Stonington Railroad, the Boston and Exeter in preference to the Boston and Newburyport Railroad, inasmuch as colored people are by these companies respected and treated as equal human beings."[115] White travelers continued to do their part, standing behind blacks resisting Jim Crow and defending those who ran afoul of the law. In October 1841, several white men who had protested the eviction of a black man from the Eastern were also ejected. One of them, the Boston dentist Dr. Daniel Mann, pressed charges against the railway for assault and battery on the advice of counsel, only to hear the judge in his case echo the judge's ruling in the Ruggles case earlier in the year.[116]

The Mann case exposed a neglected feature of the surging civil rights movement. Mann's lawyer was the Libertyite leader Samuel E. Sewall, whose role underscores the deepening involvement of "new org" abolitionists in the political fight against Jim Crow. Indeed, Libertyite leaders pressured fellow legislators into forming a joint committee in 1842 to look into segregation on the railways. The leading abolitionists Wendell Phillips and Ellis Gray Loring and the black activist Charles Lenox Remond all testified. They stressed the injury and insult inflicted on African Americans by segregation, insisting as well that the practice violated the state constitution's guarantee of equal rights for all. Remond, an ardent integrationist who had just been forced from a whites-only railroad car, made a particularly strong impression on the committee. Having recently returned from a speaking tour of Great Britain, he observed that blacks could expect better treatment in Old Europe than in the first republic of the New World.[117]

This shrewd attempt at shaming, coupled with strong attacks on the railways as arrogant corporations, had a strong impact. The committee drafted a report assailing segregation on the railways and backed it up with a surprisingly tough bill that prohibited separate accommodations "on account of descent, sect, or color." Moreover, the bill prescribed fines and jail terms for railway officials and employees "who shall assault any person for the purpose of depriving him of his right or privilege on any car or other rail-road accommodation, on account of descent, sect, or color."[118] Though this bill was defeated in the Senate, a similar bill was

---

[115] *Lib*, Oct. 29, 1841.
[116] Ibid., Nov. 5, 1841. Also MASS, *Tenth Annual Report* (1842), pp. 71–81.
[117] Ruchames, "Jim Crow Railroads," pp. 71–4. Also, *Lib*, Feb. 18 and 25, and Mar. 4, 1842.
[118] *Lib*, Mar. 4, 1842

filed the following year with the endorsement of Libertyites, abolitionist Whigs, and some radical Democrats. This one passed the Senate, but got stuck in the House, and for good reason. It was one thing for lawmakers to repeal a dated ban on interracial marriage that many believed was a dead letter anyway, but it was quite another to seek to constrain a potent corporate interest. Those legislators in the House who were more responsive to the railroads and no friend of black people further complicated the bill's passage by adding a poisonous amendment desegregating all corporations, not just railways.[119]

Although this ploy sank the bill, all was not lost. In early spring, not long after the final vote, the railroads responded to the pressure on them from the boycotts, the publicity over the legislative debate, and the prospect of fighting yet another desegregation bill the following year by suddenly announcing an end to their policy of racial separation.[120] Some black commuters, it is true, continued to be harassed by racist railway conductors and other employees, but even so outspoken a figure as Charles Remond conceded that things had changed for the better.[121] Frederick Douglass, who had been at the center of the commotion over segregation from the beginning and remained extremely sensitive to racist slights, also testified to the new climate on the carriers. In his second autobiography, published in 1855, Douglass referred to improved accommodations on the railroads.[122]

The crowning Libertyite achievement of 1843 was a personal liberty statute commonly known as the "Latimer Law." The momentum for this landmark measure emerged from the movement to free the fugitive slave George Latimer in early fall 1842. At the mid-November meeting of abolitionists to celebrate Latimer's release, Henry Bowditch called for petitioning to tie the hands of slave catchers by restraining Massachusetts officials who might otherwise collaborate with the Slave Power, as so clearly had happened in the Latimer case. Such collusion particularly galled Bay State abolitionists. At the same October 1842 meeting in which he denounced Latimer's pursuers as a "pack of bloodhounds," the maverick but principled Edmund Quincy assailed their minions in state and local government.

[119] Ruchames, "Jim Crow Railroads," pp. 74–5. See also Wilson, *Rise and Fall of the Slave Power*, 1: 492–4.
[120] MASS, *Twelfth Annual Report* (1844), pp. 6–8.
[121] *Lib*, Apr. 28, 1843. Also, MASS, *Twelfth Annual Report* (1844), p. 7.
[122] Douglass, *My Bondage and My Freedom* in Gates, *Douglass Autobiographies*, pp. 394–8. He was hardly the only observer to comment on the improved racial climate. Also *Lib*, Mar. 11, 1859.

"Your police officers and jailers, under the compulsion of no law," he fumed, "are the voluntary partakers of this hideous case; and your streets and your prisons form the hunting-ground on which this quarry is run down and secured."[123] *Emancipator* editor Joshua Leavitt likewise denounced the "man-hounds" and the "cowardly and mercenary truckling of our Sheriffs, Constables, and Jailers, aye, of our judges," who groveled before the South "at the glance of the eye and the gingle [*sic*] of a purse."[124]

The Latimer petition addressed both dimensions of the problem. It first called for an amendment to the Constitution that would "forever separate the people of Massachusetts from all connexion with slavery," through repeal of the three-fifths clause; it then demanded that the state forbid "all persons who hold office in Massachusetts" from "aiding in or abetting the arrest or detention of any person who may be claimed as a fugitive from slavery," and it prohibited the "use of jails or other public property . . . for the detention of any such person before described."[125]

The petitioning exacerbated tensions between "old org" and "new org" stalwarts. Though both sides organized to collect signatures, they worked separately and seldom in harmony. Garrison correctly sensed that "new org" men exploited the cause. He stopped short of discouraging his followers from signing the petition, but in late December he accused the Libertyites of using Latimer for "partisan gain."[126] The Libertyites had indeed made the Latimer petition a party function. To coordinate the campaign, party activists had formed the Latimer Committee, a statewide organization with representatives in each county and in over two hundred cities and towns.[127] Committee members drummed up support at party rallies and distributed petitions through the party's press and through clergymen known to have Libertyite leanings.[128] They worked quickly and efficiently, collecting some sixty-five thousand and fifty-two thousand signatures on two petitions, one for the General Court and the other for the U.S. Congress, respectively. When it came time to unveil the petition in early February coincident with the start of the legislative session,

[123] Quoted in Wilson, *Rise and Fall of the Slave Power*, 1: 478–9.
[124] *Eman*, Jan. 26, 1843.
[125] Ibid., Mar. 2, 1843.
[126] *Lib*, Dec. 23, 1842.
[127] House of Representatives, "The Joint Special Committee of the Senate and House of Representatives, to whom was referred the Petition of George Latimer," House Doc. No. 41 (1843).
[128] Ibid. Also see Patrick Crim, "'The Ballots Are Our Arms!': The Latimer Fugitive Slave Case and the Liberty Party in Massachusetts" (seminar paper, Univ. of Massachusetts Amherst, 1999).

Henry Bowditch strained to muffle the partisan accent of the campaign. He invited prominent Whigs to a Faneuil Hall meeting and insisted in his opening remarks that the petition represented "no political party."[129] He assured his audience that the committee had worked with clerics and with town meetings, neither of which bore the taint of partisanship, and had the support of adult women as well as men. Nonetheless, there was no mistaking the partisan cast of a campaign that was, after all, the brainchild of Libertyite leadership and the field project of the party, with the cooperation of Charles Francis Adams and a few other Conscience Whigs in the making. Nor was there any doubt about the party's capacity for political theater when it came time to deliver their documents to General Court. Bowditch and his helpers ceremoniously rolled into the State House a great coil of paper two feet wide and nearly a half mile in length pasted with two hundred thirty petitions.[130]

The personal liberty bill drafted by Charles Francis Adams languished in legislative committee until the end of the term. Its month-long rest on the shelf provided more than enough time for the opposition to organize. Those who expected a reprise of the heated debate over repeal of the intermarriage ban, however, were disappointed. The bill sailed through both houses of the legislature with hardly a dissenting vote. The *Emancipator* gloated that the "action of the legislature has been prompt, firm, thorough, and unanimous. No distinction of parties was recognized here." The Democracy, which in some states were "the natural allies of slavery, eagerly jumped at the opportunity of signalizing their first year's rule." Leavitt, in a reference to the civil rights measures approved by the 1843 legislature, added that "it was an edifying and encouraging sight," to see the various bills pass without opposition and "without debate – as a matter of course, precisely like the pay roll or an order notice in regard to the change in town lines –. The Latimer Committee got all they asked."[131] The committee actually got more, for the legislature repealed the "anti-Christian" marriage ban and warned the railways to "behave better" or face "no mercy next year."[132]

That was as close as anyone came to saying that the Latimer Law was the second installment of the debt the Democrats owed to the Libertyites. Leading Democratic sheets hardly mentioned the civil rights legislation of 1843; their Whig counterparts were more concerned with the Democrats'

[129] *BC*, Feb. 7, 1843.
[130] Ibid., Mar. 9, 1843. Also see Mayer, *All on Fire*, pp. 316–20.
[131] *Eman*, Mar. 30, 1843.
[132] Ibid.

failure to reduce the poll tax or reform state finances. The Whigs mentioned the Latimer Law obliquely, in a reference to the "indecent haste" that propelled through several bills that "ought never to have" been proposed at all.[133] For its part, black Boston was jubilant. Their white allies had cleared the books of the last vestige of the state's slavery legacy, dealt a death blow to Jim Crow on the railways, and helped thwart the slave catchers. The hundreds of fugitive slaves in the city could breathe a bit easier.

But could African Americans attend public schools with whites? Not in most cities and towns, and certainly not in the Commonwealth's capital, which had established a separate school system for African American children in the opening decade of the century. Boston maintained several black-only schools – the Abiel Smith School, founded in 1815, as well as two more established in 1820 and 1831.[134] Abolitionists of both races protested in futility against white control of black schools. Their petitions fell on deaf ears through the 1830s, as the various school committees simply refused to respond. Protest picked up in 1840, however, because of the work of William Cooper Nell and other blacks activists and white sympathizers.[135]

For many black Bostonians, school integration was the most important objective of the civil rights movement. Nell and his colleagues resumed their campaign in 1840–1 by drawing attention to the Abiel Smith School, first calling for dismissal of its headmaster, who was suspected of being a racist and of abusing the children, and then demanding that the school be closed.[136] Nell's project picked up momentum in 1843 from the mass action and politicking over the intermarriage ban and railway segregation, and from the first black boycotts of public schools in the name of integration. Boycotts in Salem and Nantucket in 1843 achieved their goals, and some form of direct action, not necessarily a boycott, ended segregation in Lowell as well.[137] Not long afterward, in June 1844, a meeting of the Boston leadership and concerned parents at the First

---

[133] *BA*, Apr. 13, 1843.
[134] Horton and Horton, *Black Bostonians*, pp. 70–1, and Levesque, *Black Boston*, pp. 167–9.
[135] Mark Santow, "These Little Republican Temples: Race, Ethnicity and Public Schooling in Antebellum Massachusetts" (seminar paper, University of Massachusetts Amherst, 1992), pp. 5–9.
[136] Ibid. Also see *Report to the Primary School Committee, and the Petition of Sundry Colored Persons for the Abolition of the Schools for Colored Children, June 15, 1846* (Boston: J. H. Eastburn, 1847).
[137] Santow, "Little Republican Temples," p. 4, and Wilson, *Rise and Fall of the Slave Power*, 1: 495–8.

Independent Baptist Church passed resolutions again demanding closure of Boston's black-only schools and lighting into the Boston School Committee for its inaction. The meeting called the committee's posture "erroneous & unsatisfactory" and expressed "surpriz and regret" for its defense of the Smith School headmaster. The resolutions closed on an audacious note by recommending that black parents "withdraw their children from the exclusive schools established in contravention of that equality of privileges which is the vital principal [*sic*] of the school system of Massachusetts."[138]

Nell caught the attention of white abolitionists as the boycott got under way and shifted its focus from the School Committee to the Primary School Committee, which had much wider jurisdiction. Nell worked closely with Henry Bowditch, the Libertyite operative whose budding friendship with Frederick Douglass and leadership in the Latimer affair had enhanced his reputation among black Bostonians. Indeed, the public health physician threw the full weight of his party behind the cause. In early 1845 the Liberty Party demanded that the legislature prohibit levying taxes or fees to support separate schools and that it end the exclusion of any student from public school on the basis of race. The party also called for fining school officials who upheld separate schools.[139] Their memorial became the basis for a measure passed later in the year permitting blacks to sue school officials for barring their children from public classrooms.[140] Bowditch, now a member of the Boston School Committee, was an important ally and a rare voice of enlightenment on the racist board.[141] In 1846, for instance, the committee made short work of another petition, signed by nearly ninety blacks, which argued that separate schools were unequal and hindered the development of black youths. The committee overwhelmingly endorsed a report asserting that palpable differences in color as well as in "physical, mental and moral natures," which set the races apart, were established by the "All Powerful Creator" and not amenable to legislative meddling. Separate schools were not arbitrary or capricious, but were creatures of the law of God – and the law of the city. Besides, added the report, most black families had not even signed the petition, which meant that most of them preferred their own schools.

---

[138] C. Peter Ripley, ed., *The Black Abolitionist Papers*, 5 vols. (Chapel Hill: Univ. of North Carolina Press, 1991), 3: 446–7. Quotations are on p. 447.

[139] *Eman*, Jan. 19, 1845.

[140] Ibid., Mar. 19 and 26, 1845. Also see Levesque, *Black Boston*, pp. 186–8.

[141] Bowditch, *Life and Correspondence of Henry I. Bowditch*, 1: 133–5.

The petition was the work of mischievous white abolitionists looking to stir up trouble.[142]

A minority report, written by Bowditch and the abolitionist Edmund Jackson, envisioned public education as an inclusive institution in the republican tradition. Common schools promoted social equality and republican habits of mind, and reflected the will of the Commonwealth; separate schools violated public policy and set a pernicious example that could easily justify the exclusion of any group – the poor, for instance. Separate institutions also abetted racism by keeping blacks apart from whites and socially subordinate to them, as well as by condemning blacks to inferior schooling, leaving them illiterate, ignorant, and easy targets for "the most inveterate hater of the[ir] race."[143] The report recommended the bold step of phasing out the Smith School by gradually allowing blacks to disperse among schools of their choice, an early version of school choice and one that did not sit well with the white supremacists on the Boston School Committee. Committee conservatives voted down any consideration of redress for the petitioners and, in another rebuke, flatly refused to publish the minority report.[144]

Nonetheless, this initial assault on the ramparts of school segregation in Boston and in the country was by no means a total failure. It produced results in some towns and generally strengthened abolitionist support for integrated public education.[145] It also laid the groundwork for the next stage of the struggle in the mid-1850s, which brought together a wider circle of white politicians and black activists, one that would have more success in state politics.

Looking back in 1844 on the achievements of the Liberty Party, John Greenleaf Whittier told its followers that their party was "no longer an experiment.... It is a vigorous reality."[146] Yet only a few years before, the Amesbury poet had seen it quite differently. His usual buoyant optimism in 1840 changed into deep despair as he thought about the state of antislavery. He had to wonder if the Libertyites had raced blindly onto

[142] *Report to the Primary School.* Quote is on p. 7.
[143] *Report of the Minority of the Committee of the Primary School Board on the Caste Schools of the City of Boston with Some Remarks on the City Solitor's Opinion.* Doc. 23½. *Boston City Documents* (Boston: J. H. Eastburn, 1846). Quote is on p. 10.
[144] Santow, "Little Republican Temples," pp. 7–9.
[145] Ibid., pp. 6–13.
[146] JGW to the Liberty Voters of District No. 3, Jan. 1, 1844, in Pickard, *Letters of John Greenleaf Whittier*, 1: 623–5. Quote is on p. 624.

hostile ground that they did not fully understand. "In the present mad whirlwind of party excitement," he mused, addressing a party colleague, "its voice, I fear, will be scarcely heard, or its influence felt."[147] Henry Wilson painted an equally gloomy picture of abolitionism in his account of antislavery politics. The "baptism of fire and blood . . . mobs and martyrdom" marking the early years of the movement had given way in the early 1840s to "general apathy." Antislavery had lost much of its "zest and potency," meetings were poorly attended as well as "less frequent," and organizations "began to die out."[148]

Garrisonianism *had* reached a crisis. Its rate of growth, measured by the number of societies and members, fell by about 25 percent from 1834/5 to 1838/9. The movement's torrid early days, which had seen a growth rate of 125 percent in the mid-1830s, were over. Historians have offered two explanations for this decline. Some scholars emphasize the precipitous drop in fundraising due to the seven-year depression following the panic of 1837, along with the bolt by large state organizations from the national organization. Other scholars, closely following Whittier's position, trace the decline to the schism in the late 1830s.[149] But as the historian Gilbert Hobbs Barnes argued in the 1930s, abolitionism did not decline in the 1840s; it "broadened" as a result of a new political "impulse," an observation that is borne out in the Bay State.[150] In Massachusetts, as we have seen, the Liberty Party reached a plateau of ten thousand votes by the middle of the decade (rivaling the male membership in the affiliates of the Massachusetts Anti-Slavery Society).[151] Political abolitionism, or at least antislavery, was even stronger if we factor in antislavery Whigs, a significant if quantitatively elusive group and the one that Barnes had in mind when he offered his thesis. Garrisonianism and political abolitionism, with or without Whiggery, were headed in different directions by the middle of the 1840s, with the former in decline and the latter on the rise.

Politics gave antislavery activists a new and different forum that Garrisonians rejected but that great numbers of men and some women in

[147] JGW to Colistus Burleigh, Sept. 24, 1840, in ibid., p. 445.
[148] Wilson, *Rise and Fall of the Slave Power*, 1: 504–5.
[149] Richards, "*Gentlemen of Property and Standing*," pp. 156–65. Gilbert Hobbs Barnes, *The Antislavery Impulse, 1830–1844* (1933; New York: Harcourt, Brace and World, 1964), pp. 161–97, was the first modern historian to point out the decline of the AASS at the turn of the 1830s.
[150] Barnes, *Antislavery Impulse*, pp. 161–97.
[151] Computed from the MASS, *Annual Reports, 1836–1838*.

antebellum America embraced, despite the recent claim to the contrary by Glenn C. Altschuler and Stuart M. Blumin.[152] Politics was a pervasive and absorbing activity. No other realm of antebellum life, with the possible exception of organized Protestantism, saw participants donate more money or volunteer more time; nor did any realm, again with the notable exception of religion, reach more people on a regular basis. Politics was one of the most effective channels of communication and persuasion in the nation. It does not really matter that political activity was promoted and orchestrated by a minority of party elites; political organization is by its nature "elitist" if only because there are the few that lead and the many that follow. What matters is the response of the many to the few. In this case, the few successfully evoked support for civil rights laws, one of the most controversial issues of the period. It is difficult to believe that the General Court would have acted as it did on civil rights without the spur of political agitation. Politics, and more particularly insurgent politics, made a difference.

To say that politics promoted antislavery and civil rights is to question the received wisdom on political abolitionism, or to be more accurate, wisdoms, for there are two interpretations of political abolitionism. One view has it that abolitionism lost its conscience and moral fervor when it entered politics;[153] the other is that the Liberty Party got bogged down in the mire of the moral absolutism it inherited from the evangelical church and refused to let go of "one ideaism" for fear of slipping into unprincipled pragmatism that was the sine qua non of electoral politics.[154] There is some validity to each position. No doubt some Libertyites took a more pragmatic approach to slavery than did the Garrisonians, settling generally for stopping the expansion of slavery, ending the interstate traffic in slaves, and halting the addition of more slave states to the Union rather than insisting on outright abolition (despite the dubiousness of Garrison's solutions of either preaching to planters or seceding from the Union and making the North a huge safe house for fugitive slaves). The other position also has merit, for the single-issue men at the party helm rejected the appeals of eclectic abolitionists to broaden the party's platform. That

[152] Glenn C. Altschuler and Stuart M. Blumin, *Rude Republic: Americans and Their Politics in the Nineteenth Century* (Princeton, N.J.: Princeton Univ. Press, 2000).

[153] See esp. Mayer, *All on Fire*, pp. 261–84, and Stewart, *Holy Warriors*, pp. 97–123.

[154] Alan M. Kraut, "Partisanhip and Principles: The Liberty Party in Antebellum Political Culture," in Kraut, ed., *Crusaders and Compromisers: Essays on the Relationship of the Antislavery Struggle to the Antebellum Party System* (Westport, Conn.: Greenwood Press, 1983), pp. 85–6.

said, it is also clear that politics and conscience were not antithetical in the 1840s or the 1850s. Abolitionists like Henry Bowditch did not leave their morality at the door when they voted for the Liberty Party or when they were elected to public office.

Nor did political engagement blunt the racial toleration of Libertyites like Bowditch and Elizur Wright. They used the political arena to advance the cause of civil rights for African Americans. Garrisonians, of course, worked in parallel if not in concert with them. The "great agitator" was the leading voice for the civil rights of African Americans in the Commonwealth. He was far ahead of anyone else in calling for repeal of the intermarriage ban, for an end to slave catching, and for opposition to Jim Crow accommodations on public carriers. He was without equal when it came to raising awareness of racial injustice and reminding the nation of its egalitarian heritage. Few Americans were better at laying the ground for social change. Fewer, however, were more disappointing when it came to following through on the promise of equality, because it was not a matter of conscience over the law, or indeed of having to choose between them. There was simply no way to change the consciences of enough Americans to bring about even the compromised racial justice Garrison had in mind; the law would have to be changed, as it was for intermarriage, or written anew, as with the Latimer Law. It was the Libertyites, not the Garrisonians, who grasped this point and who brought pressure on political regulars. That is why it is hard to accept the characterization of the Liberty Party as a hapless "spoiler" that "eschewed the pursuit of power" for any purpose except "slavery's abolition."[155] In the context of state politics with competitive elections, in which the Libertyites sometimes held the balance of power as they did after the 1842 election, the Liberty men in the Bay State were power brokers.

---

[155] Ibid., p. 85 and 89.

4

"To Favor the Poorest and Weakest"

Libertyism and Labor Reform

If the single-issue abolitionism shared by the Garrisonians and the Leavitt faction of the Liberty Party had been the only version of antislavery, labor activists would have been as isolated and friendless in the 1840s as they had been a decade earlier. After all, Garrison had made no secret of his antipathy to organized labor in the 1830s, an antipathy he reaffirmed in the 1840s. Leavitt was only slightly more forgiving in the opening years of the new decade, expressing some feeling for the plight of workers while keeping his distance from their organizations and largely ignoring their demands.[1] His caution, however, was not shared by the faction of the Liberty Party headed by Elizur Wright and other labor advocates in the Commonwealth's industrial towns and villages eager for broader political support. They were elated when in the early 1840s workers in the Commonwealth regrouped to resume the struggle for a shorter workday.

The ten-hour movement of the 1840s was actually two movements, one in the old handicrafts and one in the new factory system, which sometimes overlapped but usually operated separately. The craftsmen's movement would have been stillborn if a group of flexible petty proprietors had had its way. Employers like Joseph Buckingham argued that

---

[1] The most recent work in this long debate is Herbert Shapiro, "Labor and Antislavery: Reflections on the Literature," *NST* 2(1989): 471–90, and Jonathan A. Glickstein, "'Poverty is not slavery': American Abolitionists and the Competitive Labor Market," in Lewis Perry and Michael Perman, eds., *Antislavery Reconsidered: New Perspectives on the Abolitionists* (Baton Rouge: Louisiana State Univ. Press, 1979), pp. 195–218. See also Timothy Messer-Kruse, *The Yankee International, 1848–1876: Marxism and the American Reform Tradition* (Chapel Hill: Univ. of North Carolina Press, 1998), esp. pp. 6–44.

eleven- and twelve-hour workdays made brutes of the otherwise sturdy and upstanding men in their employ and worse. It fomented class strife that disrupted the harmony of the workshop and drove angry journeymen to unionism and under the regrettable influence of firebrands. Better to meet the men halfway, the bosses believed in private, than risk a break-down in labor relations. Their position suddenly got a public airing in Boston in fall 1835 following the failure of the third general strike in ten years for a ten-hour workday.[2] The unrest was the talk of the city months after the dust settled. The *Boston Mechanic and Journal of the Useful Arts,* the leading voice of master craftsmen, came out meekly for a shorter work-day on the grounds that there "seems ample reason for limiting the hours of labor among mechanics, to ten."[3] Time off the job would strengthen tired bodies, restore weary minds, and usher in social peace after years of class warfare. Later that year the journal reiterated its stand, reprinting a piece written by the popular writer George W. Light for *New England Magazine,* a middle-brow journal founded by Buckingham several years before. In it, Light reiterated labor's reform catechism, adding the more parochial point that continued resistance to a reform adopted in New York and Philadelphia made the "Athens of America" look bad – rather more like Sparta. Light went on to scold labor agitators and antilabor conserva-tives alike, and then to appeal to master mechanics to do the right thing.[4]

Such polemics were timed to influence a meeting of the city's mas-ter craftsmen scheduled for December. An earlier gathering in November changed the dinner hour to noon from 1:00 P.M., rejecting a stronger proposal to make an unspecified "change in the hours of labor for the coming season." It was a trivial concession, said liberal proprietors, who

[2] See Charles E. Persons, "The Early History of Factory Legislation in Massachusetts (from 1825 to the Passage of the Ten-Hour Law in 1874)," in Susan M. Kingsbury, ed., *Labor Laws and Their Enforcement with Special Reference to Massachusetts* (1911; New York: Arno Press, 1971), pp. 3–129; John R. Commons et al., *History of Labour in the United States,* 4 vols. (New York: Macmillan, 1918–35), 1: 158–62, 298–301, and 306–25; David R. Roediger and Philip S. Foner, *Our Own Time: A History of American Labor and the Working Day* (Westport, Conn.: Greenwood Press, 1989), pp. 1–79; and Teresa Anne Murphy, *Ten Hours' Labor: Religion, Reform, and Gender in Early New England* (Ithaca, N.Y.: Cornell Univ. Press, 1992), pp. 32–56.

[3] *BMJA* (1835), pp. 143–4.

[4] Ibid. For Light's original piece, see *New England Magazine* (1835), pp. 429–33. For more opinions in this spirit, see the *Boston Journal,* Nov. 30, 1835; Gary J. Kornblith, "From Artisans to Businessmen: Master Mechanics in New England, 1790–1850" (Ph.D. diss., Princeton Univ., 1979), pp. 514–29; and Murphy, *Ten Hours' Labor,* pp. 148 and 157–8. On *New England Magazine,* see Jean Houstra and Trudy Heath, comps., *American Peri-odicals, 1741–1900* (Ann Arbor, Mich.: Univ. Microfilms, 1979), p. 155.

demanded reconsideration at another meeting in December. The second meeting, one of the largest of its kind with over one hundred masters from fifty different trades, reaffirmed the earlier decision to change the dinner hour. Workers who broke at noon, it was said, were less likely to drink their way through lunch.[5] Thus Boston journeymen, along with their country colleagues, entered the 1840s smarting from their inability to cut the length of their workday and badly in need of new and more effective allies. Eclectic abolitionists took notice.

Meanwhile, the gentle paternalism that was the hallmark of the region's textile mills began to break down. Managers in 1842 tightened discipline and increased workloads to catch the winds of recovery from the 1837 panic. A critic who looked back to the end of the depression noted that when the tariff of 1842 went into effect "new mills were started. How? By doubling the number of operatives? No. By doubling the work of those already employed." Loom speed was stepped up to 480 strokes a minute from 280; "pieces," or "cuts," were lengthened to 32 yards from 28; the rate of pay per piece was slashed to 11 cents from 15. This pattern of paying less money for more work continued through the next six years, so that by 1848, says one modern historian, the increase in productivity (70 percent) far outstripped the increase in earnings (20 percent).[6] In addition, owners used better lighting to stretch the workday into early evening.[7] Many more employers resorted to tougher management, sacking traditional supervisors for stricter and more rigid managers unencumbered by the reciprocity of the old paternalism. At Lowell workers began to complain of harsh and arbitrary treatment from frontline managers. Thus "Snooks" wrote of a hard-boiled overseer who systematically cleansed his department of dissidents.[8]

Renewed ten-hour élan in the 1840s spread north and west from textile villages in Bristol County. Labor reform groups, variously known as

[5] BP, Dec. 22, 1835.

[6] VI, Feb. 11, 1848. Also, ibid., Apr. 24, and Oct. 23, 1846. The rates are estimated by Thomas Dublin, Women at Work: The Transformation of Work and Community in Lowell, Massachusetts, 1826–1860 (New York: Columbia Univ. Press, 1979), pp. 108–11. Also see David Zonderman, Aspirations and Anxieties: New England Workers and the Mechanized Factory System, 1815–1860 (New York: Oxford Univ. Press, 1992), p. 33, and Roediger and Foner, Our Own Time, pp. 51–2.

[7] Rev. William Scoresby, American Factories and Their Female Operatives; With an Appeal on Behalf of the British Factory Population, and Suggestions for Improvement of Their Condition (1845; New York: Burt Franklin, 1968), pp. 63–4. Also see VI, Oct. 23, 1846.

[8] VP, Nov. 3, 1842. Also, VI, May 15, 1846.

Mechanics' Associations, Republican Associations, and so on, appeared first in Attleborough and Mansfield in 1842–3, and then in Fall River, the leading maker of thread and cloth in the southeast. The Fall River Mechanics' Association in 1844 hired an organizer, the Universalist minister and Fourierist Simon Hewitt, to drum up support for the ten-hour cause elsewhere in the state.[9] With Hewitt's help and without it, a rash of ten-hour organizations emerged, most notably in Lowell, which became the center of the movement. There in 1844 male workers, already organized on their own as the Lowell Association, invited women textile hands to join them. Several meetings later the sides parted ways amicably, with the women forming the Lowell Female Labor Reform Association (LFLRA) in December.[10] Two months earlier, the Lowell groups had come together with ten-hour associations and other labor reformers in Boston under the New England Workingmen's Association (NEWA), a coordinating council that in 1846 would become the New England Labor Reform League. The ten-hour movement was reborn.[11]

Historians have long described the work of the NEWA.[12] We now know that it represented a coalition of middle-class radicals, closely identified with such causes as land reform and various forms of cooperation, and working-class advocates of both genders who were involved in the ten-hour movement and active as well in abolitionism, women's rights, and temperance. The NEWA was the first labor reform group to encourage women's unionism and include women in its leadership. The Lowellite Sarah G. Bagley, a founder and then president of the LFLRA, rose to corresponding secretary in 1845 and a year later was chief editor of the *Voice of Industry*, its official organ.[13] Huldah Stone worked closely with

---

[9] On Hewitt, see Carl J. Guarani, *The Utopian Alternative: Fourierism in Nineteenth-Century America* (Ithaca, N.Y.: Cornell Univ. Press, 1991), pp. 295 and 297–8.

[10] Dublin, *Women at Work*, pp. 116–20, and Murphy, *Ten Hours' Labor*, pp. 146–7.

[11] Any number of historians have charted this organizational configuration since Commons, *History of Labour*, 1: 536–47, and Norman Ware, *The Industrial Worker, 1840–1860* (1924; Chicago: Quadrangle, 1964), pp. 124–48. Two of the clearer modern accounts are Murphy, *Ten Hours' Labor*, pp. 131–63, and Zonderman, *Aspirations and Anxieties*, pp. 217–33.

[12] George McNeill, ed., *The Labor Movement: The Problem of To-Day* (1887; New York: Augustus Kelley, 1971), pp. 104–8. Also see Persons, "Early History of Factory Legislation," pp. 23–54. A fine account is Dublin, *Women at Work*, pp. 116–20.

[13] On Bagley, see Edward T. James, ed., *Notable American Women, 1607–1950: A Biographical Dictionary*, 3 vols. (Cambridge: Harvard Univ. Press, 1971), 1: 81–2; Philip S. Foner, *Women and the American Labor Movement from Colonial Times to the Eve of World War* (New York: Free Press, 1979), pp. 60–7 and 75–6; and Dublin, *Women at Work*, pp. 114–25 passim.

Bagley on the *Voice* and served at least a term as recording secretary of the NEWA.[14] Their great achievement in the mid-1840s was petitioning for a legal ten-hour workday, building upon and then dwarfing previous efforts. Whereas the petitions in the early 1840s bore a few thousand names, petitions circulated by the NEWA and its local affiliates boasted several times that number, reaching nearly ten thousand in 1846, about half of them from Lowell.[15]

Not all workers thought highly of petitioning. In Fall River the Mechanics' Association in November 1844 expressed doubt that it was up to the task. It proposed to canvass candidates for state office and to throw its support behind those who agreed to vote for a ten-hour bill. A subsequent meeting recommended that eligible voters mark their ballots for candidates "who will sign the petition that has been presented to this meeting, and who will pledge themselves, if elected, to do all in their power to have such a law passed as is prayed for in the petition."[16] Whether they knew it or not, the mechanics were copying tactics used by Henry Stanton and other political abolitionists in the late 1830s. They seem to have been no more successful than Stanton and his friends, if we can judge from the posture of local abolitionists and textile proprietors, who were sometimes one and the same. The textile manufacturer Nathaniel Borden told the Whig press earlier in the year that a long workday was the true test of manhood and self-worth, and not the abomination some believed it to be. The "best men" in his employ were so "industrious" that they had no objection at all to fourteen-hour workdays.[17] His distant relative, Colonel Richard B. Borden, who traced his abolitionist pedigree to the founding of the city's antislavery movement in the 1830s, was Fall River's wealthiest industrialist in the 1840s, with holdings that included several textile mills, the Bay State Steamboat Company, and the Fall River Iron Works, one of the largest firms in the state. When confronted at the end of the decade by ten-hour activists about to go on strike, Borden is said to have responded, "I saw this mill built stone by stone; I saw the pickers, the carding machines, the spinning machines put into it, one after the other,

---

[14] On Stone, see Zonderman, *Aspirations and Anxieties*, pp. 113, 159, 220–1, 228, and 264.

[15] Dublin, *Women at Work*, pp. 113–14, and Murphy, *Ten Hours' Labor*, pp. 131–63.

[16] Quoted in Murphy, *Ten Hours' Labor*, p. 158. Also see M, Nov. 16, 1844.

[17] Murphy, *Ten Hours' Labor*, p. 166; FRM, Apr. 27, 1844, and Edward Magdol, *The Antislavery Rank and File: A Social Profile of the Abolitionists' Constituency* (Westport, Conn.: Greenwood Press, 1986), p. 9. This Borden was not Nathaniel B., the "Quaker Hatter," and a founder of Fall River abolitionism in the 1830s.

and I would see every machine and stone crumble and fall to the floor again before I would accede to your wishes."[18]

The ten-hour movement in the textile centers of the state in the 1840s presented an irresistible opportunity for Elizur Wright's faction in the Liberty Party to reach out in a more definitive way to the Commonwealth's labor movement. In some cases, as in Fall River, Liberty men worked hand-in-glove with labor groups on committees to distribute propaganda and petitions. In summer 1844 the party founder, the Reverend Asa Bronson, encouraged the Mechanics' Association to open up to "all that are friendly to the *Ten Hour System*," women in particular; the militant Baptist simultaneously skewered the Bordens in the local press for their "idolatry," a rhetorical jab that cost him his job and had little if any impact on the local labor movement.[19] In Lowell in 1846, Bagley and her friends in the Labor Reform Association followed the political strategy recommended two years earlier by the Fall River Mechanics' Association, quizzing office seekers on ten-hour legislation.[20] They endorsed the Libertyite Chauncey Knapp for Congress in 1846, and a year later, labor groups in other industrial towns in the country came out for Samuel E. Sewall, Henry I. Bowditch, and indeed Wright himself.[21]

The political mobilization in 1845 and 1846 had little impact in the state. Whigs were too close to the manufacturers and Democrats too wedded to small government. Neither could see beyond the doctrine of freedom of contract, which viewed workers not as economic subordinates but as free agents with the capacity to negotiate their own terms and conditions of employment – even though most such workers were women. The House Committee on Manufacturing did not issue a minority report or draft a bill in 1845, and only grudgingly agreed to take testimony on conditions in the factories. William Schouler of Lowell, a rising Whig star and proprietor of the *Lowell Courier*, chaired the hearing. Cautiously antislavery but uncompromising in his opposition to ten-hour legislation,

---

[18] Magdol, "Window on the Abolitionist Constituency," in Allen M. Kraut, ed., *Crusaders and Compromisers: Essays on the Relationship of the Antislavery Struggle to the Antebellum Party System* (Westport, Conn.: Greenwood Press, 1983), pp. 49–50 and 58–9. Also Murphy, *Ten Hours' Labor*, pp. 16–17. Quote is from McNeill, *Labor Movement*, p. 215. See also Gustavus Myers, *History of Great American Fortunes* (1907; New York: Modern Library, 1936), pp. 328–9.

[19] Murphy, *Ten Hours' Labor*, pp. 149–50 and 169–73.

[20] *DC*, Oct. 27 and Nov. 4, 1846.

[21] Ibid., Nov. 2, 1847.

Schouler nonetheless initially appeared to be accommodating, scheduling hearings that featured workers – the first time they made such an appearance – and then escorting his colleagues on a tour of the mills. Sarah Bagley and her co-workers described industrialism's demoralizing conditions and exhausting regime, pleading for the relief of a ten-hour law. Their pleas were in vain. Schouler's final report recommended against legislation on the grounds that the law would have to apply to mechanics' shops as well as to factories, that cutting the workday would require a corresponding adjustment in wages, and that the "parties themselves" and not lawmakers ought to resolve their differences.[22] Schouler also referred the petitions to the ensuing General Court, handing the Senate a chance to speak up. The Senate's 1846 report elaborated the hands-off policy implied in Schouler's report by recommending greater faith in the free market. It predicted that "flourishing competition" will necessarily enhance "demand" for labor so that "those disposed to work will . . . be well paid. But impose restrictions, you injure business, and the . . . laborer is sure to be the sufferer."[23]

Historians treat this phase of the ten-hour movement as a failure.[24] It did fail to achieve its goal, but it did not go away empty-handed, at least not in Lowell or other corporate outposts of the Boston Associates, where the midday dinner break was extended by fifteen minutes for eight months and by thirty minutes for four months.[25] Some operatives made light of this concession, and not a few would later – and justifiably assail managers for resorting to a speedup in compensation for the change.[26] Nonetheless, middle-class critics of the factory system and some workers saw it differently. Operatives had for years complained of indigestion caused by gorging down their meals because of the brief dinner breaks.[27] "I object to the constant hurrying of every thing. We cannot have time to eat, drink or sleep" went a typical complaint, not in the labor press, it turned out, but in the *Lowell Offering*, the house organ for the more compliant

[22] Dublin, *Women at Work*, pp. 114–15.

[23] Quoted in Persons, "Early History of Factory Legislation," p. 51.

[24] See, for instance, Ware, *Industrial Worker*, pp. 125–53, and Foner, *Women and the American Labor Movement*, pp. 55–79.

[25] Roediger and Foner, *Our Own Time*, pp. 61–2, and Zonderman, *Aspirations and Anxieties*, pp. 248–9.

[26] See, for instance, Philip S. Foner, ed., *The Factory Girls: A Collection of the Writings on Life and Struggles in the New England Factories of the 1840s* (Urbana: Univ. of Illinois Press, 1977), pp. 88–9, and Zonderman, *Aspirations and Anxieties*, pp. 248–9.

[27] Zonderman, *Aspirations and Anxieties*, pp. 238–41.

hands.[28] The operatives predictably expressed stronger protests in their own organs. One operative explained that co-workers in her department had a half hour in which to run down "three flights of stairs," dash a "fourth of a mile" to the dining hall in their boardinghouse, gulp down lunch (the largest meal of the day), and race back to work. It was getting even worse in recent years because agents shaved time from both ends the lunch break, leaving the operatives with four to six fewer minutes.[29] Such complaints made sense to John Greenleaf Whittier, who lived part-time in Lowell in the middle of the decade. The Quaker poet observed that the imposition of "brief intermissions for two hasty meals" took advantage of the Yankee New England's "proverbial facility in dispatching their dinners in the least possible time." Factory owner and cotton operative alike, he concluded, "would in the end be greatly benefitted by the general adoption of the ten hour system."[30] If no one confused the reform of 1847 for a ten-hour day, neither did most operatives belittle the concessions. It was something of a moral victory and morale booster that whetted appetites for more.

The winds of change blew harder through the male-dominated handicrafts. Here, as we have seen, petty proprietors in Boston had found themselves constrained by outsiders – merchant capitalists and industrialists – who brooked no opposition on the hours question. A similar pattern prevailed in some provincial towns. In Fall River, textile elites with interests in housing and urban development resisted ten-hour men as resolutely as their Boston counterparts, fighting off reform in the building trades as well as in their own factories. Nathaniel Borden spoke for local employers when he asserted, in summer 1844, that it was impossible to contain ten-hour sentiment to the building trades because the fervor would inevitably "penetrate the factory walls."[31] Such implacable resistance brought the master craftsmen to heel, leaving their journeymen alternately disappointed and angry. One of them observed that local tradesmen had trusted "petty boss carpenters," who stood to benefit equally from a

---

[28] "The Spirit of Discontent," *Lowell Offering* 1 (July 1841): 111–14. Quote is on p. 112. Rptd. in Benita Eisler, ed., *The Lowell Offering: Writings by New England Mill Women, 1840–1845* (Philadelphia: Lippincott, 1977), pp. 160–2. Quote is on p. 161.

[29] VI, Jan. 1, 1847. Also, ibid., Oct. 23, 1846, Feb. 27, 1846, and Jan. 9, 1847. Also Zonderman, *Aspirations and Anxieties*, p. 249 and passim 234–60.

[30] John Greenleaf Whittier, *The Stranger in Lowell* (Boston: Waite, Pierce, 1845), p. 115.

[31] *FRM*, June 29, 1844

new work regime, only to suffer betrayal. *"[S]lave-like,"* he fretted, "they kiss the hand that smites them."[32]

A significant bloc of small employers, however, came through on the hours question. This tendency emerged in towns with diversified economies dominated by small shops, and where textile elites were either absentee or weak. Master craftsmen in such places eluded the heavy-handed intervention of textile bosses that proved so decisive in Boston and Fall River. They held fast to the ethic of reciprocity embedded in the community-of-interest ideal that had regulated the social relations of craft work longer than anyone could remember. The mutualism in the crafts, to be sure, went into eclipse in the sweated trades, but it endured in the more respectable callings. It was reinforced in country towns, if not in cities, by the easy sociability of everyday life and by the economic parochialism and town pride that were so much a part of Timothy Dwight's "village manner." Dwight's villagers were atavistic people who took comfort in the togetherness and stability of their towns and cast suspicious glances at the acquisitiveness of the age. If they did not adjust easily to the new individualism, neither did they accept one of its more troubling manifestations, namely, a freer flow of population that accelerated both the departure of their sons and daughters and the inflow of strangers from other parts of New England and from Europe.[33] Such disruptive change strengthened localistic cultures, forcing villagers back on what they knew. The durability of village culture helps explain why the Boston Associates elected to build their industrial towns anew, from the ground up, rather than superimpose them on preexisting villages. It is also why the mills and factories erected in the towns by local entrepreneurs resembled contemporaneous versions of colonial churches, blending almost imperceptibly into the built environment.[34] Men of the country with entrepreneurial ambitions either adapted their managerial policies to local customs or went elsewhere.

The central Massachusetts town of Worcester was the home of exemplary proprietors in the spirit of the village. To Richard Henry Dana,

[32] Ibid., June 8, 1844.

[33] See, for instance, Robert Doherty, *Society and Power in Five New England Towns* (Amherst: Univ. of Massachusetts Press, 1977); Jonathan Prude, *The Coming of Industrial Order: Town and Factory Life in Rural Massachusetts, 1810–1860* (New York: Cambridge Univ. Press, 1983), pp. 183–216; and Mark Voss-Hubbard, "Slavery, Capitalism, and the Middling Sorts: The Rank and File of Political Abolitionism," *ANCH* 4 (Summer 2003): 53–76.

[34] See, for instance, John R. Stilgoe, *Common Landscape of America, 1580–1845* (New Haven, Conn.: Yale Univ. Press, 1982), esp. pp. 324–6.

Jr., Worcester was a world apart from the textile satellites of the Boston Associates. "Wealth and industry," he said, were in "individual and not corporate hands." Except for banks and insurance companies, there were few corporations amid the myriad workshops run by "a large class of active, independent proprietors instead of the various grades of servants of great corporations, as at Lowell and Lawrence."[35] The city's mechanics, fiercely independent and wary of finance capitalism, organized associations within and across trades to police the market behavior of individual firms and pursue interests in common. In 1851 one of their meetings complained that exorbitant rents charged by downtown landlords gave competitors in larger cities an unfair advantage. "Capital," they argued, "'like a huge sponge,' absorb[s] the profits of toil, and leave[s] the hardworking artizan and enterprizing manufacturer to struggle...in the market." They proposed to build their own quarters on the edge of town, a sort of multipurpose mechanics' mall.[36] We do not know if the mechanics went ahead with their project or if the local landlords cut rental rates. We do know that the mechanics were in the main a highly ethical group of employers whose principled behavior won the admiration of those in their employ. In the controversial Mexican War, the carriage makers Tolman and Russell turned down government contracts to make wagons because they believed the conflict "unjust, and did not wish to profit from the injuries of such injustice."[37] This firm and others like it had earlier reached the conclusion that excessive toil was also bad for business. In 1844, as ten-hour agitation surged, the city's master mechanics concluded that the growing unrest on their shop floors was fueled by overwork and erratic work schedules. Regular hours, they reasoned, would make production runs more predictable, and shorter workdays would improve the health and morals of all. As a result, they "unanimously" adopted an "*eleven hour system*."[38]

---

[35] Robert F. Lucid, ed., *The Journal of Richard Henry Dana, Jr.*, 3 vols. (Cambridge: Harvard Univ. Press, 1968), 2: 676. Also see George F. Hoar, *Autobiography of Seventy Years*, 2 vols. (New York: Charles Scribner's Sons, 1903), 1: 158–9, and John Brooke, *The Heart of the Commonwealth: Society and Political Culture in Worcester County Massachusetts, 1713–1861* (New York: Cambridge Univ. Press, 1989). pp. 269–309.

[36] *MS*, May 29, 1851.

[37] Ibid., May 9, 1851. For more on the carriage-making trade, see Mark Voss-Hubbard, "The Amesbury-Salisbury Strike and the Social Origins of Political Nativism in Antebellum Massachusetts," *JSH* 29 (Spring 1996): 576–7.

[38] *SSWR*, Apr. 19, 1844. Although the employers reserved the right to increase the working day, there is no evidence of their doing so in the 1850s; on the contrary, they cut the workday to ten hours.

The reach of Worcester-style management is still unclear. Evidence suggests that it stretched beyond the "heart of the Commonwealth" to other cities and towns in the provinces, far enough, it would seem, to have cut a pattern of its own.[39] Only additional research can disclose how far and deep it ran. For the moment it is enough to see flexible management in the old handicrafts and in pockets of newer pursuits as an alternative to the tough-minded managerialism prevalent in the corporate sector of Bay State industry.[40]

The agitation over workday hours in Worcester and Lowell in the 1840s took place in a new political context. A decade before, labor reformers and rank-and-file workers had stood alone against hostile Whigs, indifferent Democrats, and skeptical abolitionists, including Garrison and even Wright. No longer. The involvement of Libertyite partisans like Wright gave labor reform a useful political partner, raising its profile in public and strengthening its hand in party politics even though it remained a minority tendency within the party. The single-issue men continued to keep the labor movement at arm's length but showed greater awareness of its interests. Joshua Leavitt modified his thesis on the economic costs imposed by the Slave Power, as if to take account of the importance of labor in politics.[41] It was bad enough, Leavitt argued, as he had before, that the South dampened the economy as a whole, dragging down the earnings of the North. He was now convinced that the Slave Power would not rest until it had knocked white workers in the North down to the same level as black slaves in the South.[42]

This laborist twist to the Slave Power thesis, Eric Foner tells us, had passed into popular rhetoric by the mid-1840s.[43] It did not take much to convince mainstream abolitionists like Leavitt of its essential validity; as for Wright and his fellows, it was an article of faith early on but did not quite explain the common thralldom of Southern blacks and

---

[39] Voss-Hubbard, "Amesbury-Salisbury Strike."

[40] Labor historians have long discussed this tendency. For one of its more vivid renditions in Fall River, one of the ruder and more gritty industrial cities in the region, see Mary Blewett, *Constant Turmoil: The Politics of Industrial Life in Nineteenth-Century New England* (Amherst: Univ. of Massachusetts Press, 2000).

[41] *Eman*, Apr. 15, 1846. Also ibid., Apr. 14, 1844 and Apr. 21, 1847.

[42] See, for instance, *SSWR*, Apr. 15, 1846

[43] Eric Foner, *Free Soil, Free Labor, Free Men: The Ideology of the Republican Party before the Civil War* (New York: Oxford Univ. Press, 1970). Also see Jonathan A. Glickstein, *Concepts of Free Labor in Antebellum America* (New Haven, Conn.: Yale Univ. Press, 1991), and Bruce C. Levine, *Half Slave and Half Free: The Roots of the Civil War* (New York: Hill and Wang, 1993).

Northern workers. They found an answer in the "lords of lash and the lords of the loom" thesis developed a decade earlier by labor radicals. Although Wright may have considered this idea before his formative tour in England in 1844, there is no question that he was on board after his return later that year. With impressions of industrial England fresh in mind, he doubted that American operatives had slid into the industrial abyss of their British comrades, but he felt certain that the "relation between Labor and Capital" under modern industrialism approximated relations "between master and slave."[44] His fellow Libertyite William West likewise drew on this metaphor. He found it hard to understand why the "many . . . victims" of "wage slavery" mistook free labor for "freedom." There was a thin line, if any, between employers of labor and owners of slaves; for all practical purposes employers and owners were equivalent, distinguished only by the incidental fact that employers did not have to "perform the duties of 'ownership.'"[45]

Wright and West, of course, were recent converts to labor reform but not to abolitionism. They had grown up with antislavery and were well known in abolitionist circles in Massachusetts and beyond. Their tiny circle expanded in the 1840s as new leaders appeared in the Bay State, one of whom was Chauncey Langdon Knapp. Knapp followed the same life path trod by Joseph T. Buckingham, Elizur Wright, Jr., and many other sons of village New England who trained as printers and became political activists. Born in central Vermont in 1809 to a family of small farmers, Knapp served a printer's apprenticeship in Montpelier and then worked as a journeyman before becoming coeditor of the (Montpelier) *State Journal* in the middle of the decade and editor of the *Voice of Freedom* at decade's end. He was an evangelical Congregationalist involved in temperance and antislavery and, by turns, an avid Anti-Mason and a Whig. His Whiggish faith was shaken in 1840, however, when the party nominated William Henry Harrison for president. Discouraged with his party but doubtful of Libertyism, Knapp sat out the presidential election in 1840. Such independence angered party officials, who nursed their antipathy for a year, when they purged him following his (lukewarm) endorsement of the Vermont Libertyites, who organized in 1841 in the Green Mountain State. Knapp served as secretary of the Liberty Party and editor of its organ for

---

[44] See, for instance, *SSWR*, Apr. 15, 1846

[45] *DC*, Apr. 21, 1847. Also see "W. W." in ibid., May 1, 1847. For more on West, see Timothy Messer-Kruse, *The Yankee International*, pp. 76–9, 86–8, and 160–6.

FIGURE 16. Chauncey Langdon Knapp. (Courtesy of the Center for Lowell History. Lowell, Mass.)

several more years before settling in Lowell in 1844, a pivotal move in his political development.[46]

Knapp was drawn more deeply into labor reform by his political ambitions and by the ten-hour ferment in his adoptive city. Lowell's labor reformers in 1845 and 1846, who planned to contend for state and national offices on the Workingmen's ticket, adopted the old abolitionist policy of questioning the candidates.[47] The field included Whig

[46] On his early years, see Andrew Barker, "Chauncey Langdon Wright and Political Abolitionism in Vermont, 1833–1841" (seminar paper, Univ. of Massachusetts Amherst, 1999). Also see Henry Wilson, *History of the Rise and Fall of the Slave Power in America*, 3 vols. (Boston: James R. Osgood, 1872–7), 1: 291 and 2: 306 and 348, and JGW to the *Beacon of Liberty*, Oct. n.d., 1848, in John B. Pickard, ed., *The Letters of John Greenleaf Whittier*, 3 vols. (Cambridge: Harvard Univ. Press, 1975), 2: 118.

[47] *VI*, Sept. 23 and Oct. 9, 1846.

nominee Joseph Tinker Buckingham, who revealed his growing conservatism and caution by asserting that it "always appeared to me the hours as well as the *price* of labor should be settled by agreement between the employer and the employed." As if this were not enough to disqualify him, the erstwhile ten-hour advocate added that it was the "duty" of government to clear away obstacles that "restrain individual freedom ... paralyze competition ... or ... any honest effort to secure pecuniary independence."[48] Nor did the Liberty candidate, Ebenezer Hunt, help himself. Hunt replied that all issues, including the ten-hour day, were of "minor importance" when compared to "human liberty and equal rights for all, without distinction of color." Fully in step with his party's one-idea orthodoxy and then some, Hunt said he could "pledge myself to nothing until Slavery is overthrown."[49]

For his part, Knapp at once established himself as the friend of slaves and workers. Confident that the "slave population of this country is destined to be free," he looked forward to the "transition from chafing chains to chartered rights." He transferred the paternalist role from the individual to the state, envisioning an "epoch when the fostering care of the government will be specifically claimed by them to secure the blessings of liberty." The budding labor advocate, clearly influenced by the land reform program of the National Reformers, could think of no more important federal program than to "set apart the public domain" for freed people "in common with all 'other persons.'"[50] Knapp's intent here can be read two ways. Was his plan for settling former slaves on the national domain an instrument for inclusive paternalism or punitive exclusionism? His reference to the term "in common" with other people would suggest the former, but we simply cannot be sure. We do not know enough about the racial views of this intriguing but still obscure figure. Knapp later joined the Free Soilers, becoming clerk of the House of Representatives in 1851; in 1856 he was elected to Congress on the Republican ticket. He did not leave much to the imagination, however, on the question of a shorter workday. He openly embraced eclectic abolitionism, using his own interpretation of the Bill of Rights to berate political regulars. He could well understand why the "republican tyrants" of the South trampled human rights under foot; in the North, however, such politics was

---

[48] *DC*, Nov. 11, 1846. Also see Voss-Hubbard, "Slavery, Capitalism, and the Middling Sorts."

[49] *DC*, Nov. 11, 1846.

[50] Ibid., Nov. 4, 1846

inexcusable. Government had to "favor the poorest and weakest members of the body politic. They that are strong should bear the infirmities of the weak," most especially in the industrial districts, where hands asked no more than "common and statute law have accorded to dumb animals." In Knapp's view it made no sense to say, as Buckingham did, that "the laborer is a voluntary party to a contract. Intrinsic wrong can never be made right by consent of the parties, or any degree of voluntariness in its perpetration."[51]

This abolitionist perspective on the consonant interests of slave and free labor was not restricted to Libertyite leaders like Wright and Knapp. It also began to permeate the ranks of workers and plebeians in and around the labor movement and affiliated with the Liberty Party. A delegation of Worcester workers preparing to go to Boston for the convention that would establish the New England Workingmen's Association complained in the temperance press that the "hours of labor required by the employer in this country, are by far more than are necessary, or proper." As a result, laborers are "near[ly] reduced to that, which in another portion of this country is known under the title of *Domestic Servitude*.... [I]f nothing is done to arrest the progress of capitalists in the reduction of the prices of labor, the working man will, virtually, be reduced to a state of servitude and dependence, scarcely to be preferred to that of the Old World, or that of *actual slavery*."[52] "An operative – a Workingman," puzzled by the refusal of a local Libertyite editor to acknowledge the importance of the ten-hour movement, expressed his belief that government was empowered to define the workday and ought to act. If there was ample precedent in law to bridle and restrain "brutes," the rule of law could also be extended to "protect and defend human beings." Factory rules, he went on, were not legitimate simply because operatives had to submit to them, as the editor had said. "Does not the slave submit to the regulations of the master, when he knows that it is ... useless to resist?" he asked, declaring it ludicrous to insist, as the editor had, that workers were not abused by overwork. His fellow operatives were distressed by conditions in the mills and not only worthy of state protection but in need of it because of the obvious imbalance of power. "Workingman" was baffled by the editor's myopia but guessed it had to do with the editor's preoccupation with

[51] Ibid.
[52] *WRTW*, Oct. 8, 1844. For more on this laborist faction of the temperance movement, see Ian Tyrell, *Sobering Up: From Temperance to Prohibition in Antebellum America* (Westport, Conn.: Greenwood Press, 1979), pp. 207–9.

abolitionism, with the one-issue politics of the Liberty Party's leadership. If so, the editor ought to say so. As for his own perspective, he concluded:

I, sir, am not behind that gentleman in the desire to see the Æthiopian free. But while I contend for the colored man, I contend also for my brother operative, and he has my strongest sympathy. For I know that his fate and mine, and those of like condition who come after me, are involved in the same cause; and we *do* invoke the authority of the Legislature, and more – We offer up prayers to our heavenly Father, for a change and relief from our burthens.[53]

Thus it was possible for some ordinary men and women to be aware of the injustice of the mill and of the plantation – to support one another and to sympathize with slaves. Such a perspective reflected Wright's strain of abolitionism, which was no longer the pipe dream of a small but vocal stratum of middling abolitionists; it had penetrated the ranks of labor, however thinly. This is not to say that working-class abolitionism burst suddenly on the scene, for as we have already seen, plenty of abolitionists resided in places like Lowell in the 1830s. The point is that, in the 1830s, working-class abolitionism was tied largely to evangelical Protestantism; a decade later, it was also tied to labor reform.

Liberty stalwarts like the Bostonian Elizur Wright, the transplanted Vermonter Chauncey Knapp, and the Fall Riverian Asa Bronson – and perhaps presumed rank-and-filers like "Workingman" – represented one side of the relationship between abolitionism and labor. They were political abolitionists turned labor advocates in the 1840s. This relationship also had another side – labor activists who became abolitionists or at least antislavery supporters. In one sense, this side of the dynamic was not new, for as we have already seen, several leaders of the New England Association of Farmers, Mechanics, and Other Working Men spoke the language of antislavery by the middle of the 1830s. A decade later, however, working-class abolitionists were not so exceptional; they were common in the labor movement of the Commonwealth's industrial centers where the term "permanent wage earner" was not as anachronistic as it had been a decade earlier. More and more such workers were surrendering the bi-employment of the past, losing ties to the refuge of land and remaining wage earners for longer and longer stretches.[54] Not all, of

[53] *SSWR*, Mar. 28, 1845.
[54] The best treatment of this discrete but still incomplete transition is Prude, *Coming of Industrial Order*, pp. 217–37. Also see Christopher Clark, *The Roots of Rural Capitalism: Western Massachusetts, 1780–1860* (Amherst: Univ. of Massachusetts Press, 1990), pp. 252–61.

course, were landless men. A good number were women who still had access to the family farm; many of them were in Lowell, and none stood taller than Sarah Bagley.

Born around 1820 to a farm family in the lakeside village of Meredith in New Hampshire, Bagley left home in 1836 for a job at the Hamilton Manufacturing Company in Lowell. She worked at loom and spindle for a decade, leaving the mills in 1846 for a brief stint as a telegrapher before a rusticating return to the place of her birth.[55] Bagley's early years at work were unexceptional and even pleasurable; indeed, she may well have been "S.B.," the contented operative correspondent we met earlier who contributed several pieces in 1840 to Harriet Farley's *Lowell Offering*. In her tellingly titled "Pleasures of Factory Life," Lowell was a "pleasant place for contemplation," where young women were "enabled to assist aged parents who have become too infirm to provide for themselves; or perhaps to educate some orphan brother or sister." But the city was not simply a setting for a domestic form of missionary work. It was also an exciting place for young women to discover what it meant to be on one's own – to forge new social bonds and experience the heady intellectual stimulation offered by Lowell's many attractions. "And last, though not least, is the pleasure of being associated with the institutions of religion ... Bible Class, Sabbath School, and all other means of religious instruction," wrote the young operative in obvious appreciation of the religious dimensions of the burgeoning city's undeniable blandishments.[56] Though she was a precocious feminist at this stage of her life, she was also a dutiful worker involved in the church.

Bagley's labor activism coincided with the revived ten-hour movement in the winter of 1844/5. Bagley got very little rest for the next two years, working tirelessly for the Lowell Female Labor Reform Association and the New England Workingmen's Association, as well as leading the ten-hour movement. In 1845 she joined the editorial board of the *Voice of Industry* when it was moved to Lowell and later became the voice of the Fourierist movement and the Workingmen's Protective Union, a cooperationist group formed in 1845.[57] A year later, in 1846, Bagley started the "Female Department" in the *Voice*, a column dedicated to "the females of our country and through which they shall be heard." She ran pieces

[55] James, *Notable American Women*, 1: 81–2, and Foner, *Women and the American Labor Movement*, pp. 60–1, 66–7, and 75–6.
[56] Quoted in Benita Eisler, ed., *The Lowell Offering*, pp. 63 and 65. Also see pp. 66–73.
[57] VI, May 15, 1846.

by regional writers, including Whittier, but favored her own musings on feminism and radical evangelicalism. She told her readers that the "department devoted to woman's thoughts will also defend woman's rights, and while it contends for physical improvement, it will not forget that she is a social, moral and religious being."[58]

Bagley took an expansive view of moral reform. She assembled an informal group of volunteers to help unlettered women in town negotiate the demands of home and work. She wrote letters for illiterate operatives to family and loved ones, and helped "some few girls in my *sleeping apartment*" in "the simplest branches of education," teaching them "how to write."[59] Possibly, this daughter of hardscrabble New England was also behind a women's group seeking to elevate the moral tone of Lowell, singling out surly and impudent boys and young men who staggered about town and bunched on street corners "in a cloud of moral stupor."[60] The women recommended honest and productive employment instead of speculative ventures, or the "Profanity, obscenity and swaggering, [and] unblushing rowdyism" of the street.[61] Yet Bagley and her associates were far from finger-wagging prudes or Aunt Pollys in a righteous stupor of their own. One of them urged wayward youths to "Be industrious, but do not fail to speak against this system of servitude, that the beautiful land of your forefathers bled and died for, may not be converted to a field of misery and oppression."[62]

Bagley herself took this advice to heart. The resistance she encountered from men in the course of the ten-hour movement strengthened her own feminism. In summer 1845, still smarting from the legislature's spring rebuff, she told a gathering of the NEWA in Boston:

For the last half a century, it has been deemed a violation of woman's sphere to appear before the public as a speaker; but when our rights are trampled upon and we appeal in vain to legislators, what shall we do but appeal to the people. Shall not our voice be heard; and our rights acknowledged here, shall it be said again to the daughters of New England, that they have no political rights and are not subject to legislative action?[63]

---

[58] Ibid.
[59] Ibid., Jan. 9, 1846.
[60] Ibid., May 28, 1847. Also ibid., Nov. 7, 1845, and May 29, 1846.
[61] Ibid., Feb. 13, 1846. Also ibid., Feb. 27, 1846.
[62] Ibid., Feb. 27, 1846.
[63] Ibid., June 5, 1845.

As a leading women's historian has observed, for women like Bagley labor activism was another, if overlooked, portal to feminism.[64]

Bagley – labor activist and abolitionist – was fully conversant with the language of "wage slavery." She drew liberally on its rich vocabulary to talk about the factory. In one of her earliest pieces for the *Voice*, she scorned the popular view that women "have come to the mills voluntarily and . . . can leave . . . [at] will," asserting that a "slave too goes voluntarily to his task but his will is in some manner quickened by the whip of the overseer. The whip which brings us to Lowell is NECESSITY."[65] Factory operatives, she had earlier told a summer gathering of the NEWA, were "doomed to eternal slavery in consequence of their ignorance."[66] Huldah Stone and other leaders of the LFLRA similarly likened the factory regime to the plantation and factory workers to slaves.[67] "The long hour system of labor," intoned Stone, was part of a "grand scheme" to hold the operative in "servitude and ignorance."[68] "Juliana" assailed Lowell's "Cotton Lords" who had been "waxing fat" on the "blood and sinews" of beleaguered factory hands whose prospects were no better than those of field hands.[69] "Olivia" compared the intimidation that muffled dissent in Lowell to a "state of servitude more servile than slavery itself. . . . A man who in addition to being a servant *physically* will be one mentally."[70] "Mary" put her abolitionist thoughts in a five-stanza verse that ended

> Remember, too, that wrong is here,
> And give the north one pitying tear;
> Oh! let the fruits of love go forth,
> To free the South, and bless the North![71]

Such evocative language from women who did industrial work raises several points about how abolitionists are perceived in current academic circles. One point has to do with the question of social class. How do we define "Mary" and her friends in social terms? Were they part of the broad middle class, as nearly every study of abolitionism, including recent ones,

[64] See Mary P. Ryan, *Womanhood in America from Colonial Times to the Present* (New York: New Viewpoints, 1975), pp. 80–5 and 115–17.

[65] *VI*, Sept. 18, 1845.

[66] Ibid., July 10, 1845.

[67] Ibid., Mar. 6 and May 22, 1846.

[68] Ibid., May 22, 1846.

[69] Ibid., May 7, 1847, and Foner, *Factory Girls*, pp. 275–83.

[70] *VI*, Aug. 14, 1845.

[71] Ibid., Feb. 13, 1846.

chooses to describe them?[72] Answering this question depends on how one defines class and whether one thinks class identity derives from an individual's own social status or from that of his or her family of origin. Without getting into a discussion of class taxonomy, it is enough to say here that we simply do not know enough about Mary's family to say anything about her social inheritance, though it is likely that she was the offspring of a farm family like so many of her co-workers in places like Lowell.[73] We do not know if her family carried on the tradition of bi-employment, if her family's farm allowed her to leave the mill when she felt the need to restore her strength or simply get away. We do know that women like Mary who left farm for city were less and less inclined to return home to settle down and raise a family. As one observer perceptively put it, as taxing as factory work may have been, it compared favorably with farm work as far as women were concerned. The daughters of farm families who did a tour in Lowell's mills favored careers in teaching among other nonfarm pursuits and preferred to marry urban men over farm boys because they realized that wedding "a farmer is serious business. They remember their worn-out mothers."[74] The factory was a stop on the road from country to city for women who either no longer had the option of returning to the family farm or refused to do so, and who more often than not chose to marry urban mechanics and working men. They were in flight to a working class that was taking firmer and firmer shape, a class that looked rather more appealing to them than the social world they left behind. Thus their own careers in the mills, however abbreviated, and their choice of husbands argue strongly for considering such women working class. Their great numbers in the larger industrial districts of the Commonwealth indicate, moreover, that such women formed an important part of the larger abolitionist constituency.

What about their motivation? The language of Sarah Bagley and her sisters reflected the ongoing influence of the evangelical church, for they continued to think of slavery as "sin," just as they had a decade before. The difference in the 1840s was that more of them drew on the idiom of slavery to describe their own conditions. Factories became plantations,

---

[72] See, for instance, Julie Roy Jeffrey, *The Great Silent Army of Abolitionism: Ordinary Women in the Antislavery Movement* (Chapel Hill: Univ. of North Carolina Press, 1998), esp. pp. 6–7.

[73] Dublin, *Women at Work*, esp. pp. 14–57.

[74] "Farming Life in New England," *Atlantic Monthly* (August 1858), p. 341, and Dublin, *Women at Work*, pp. 54–7.

overseers "lords," and workers "slaves" – and not simply in letters to newspaper editors. Such language also suffused the discourse of reform groups. The constitution of the LFLRA asserted that the reason the factory hands could not "hold that place in the social, moral and intellectual world, which a bountiful Creator designed ... [them] to occupy ... is obvious. He is a slave to a false and debasing state of society." But now duty called on workers to break the "shackles" that held them in "ignorance and servitude."[75] The dependence of their employers on Southern cotton made it easy to associate the "lords of the lash and the lords of the loom," as the equation went. This kind of thinking also owed something to personal experience in the fights against slavery and against long hours. Women – and men, for that matter – who fought against the "Slave Power" and the "Money Power" developed a vocabulary in one arena that they applied to the other. This language casts doubt on the argument advanced by historians of whiteness that working people in the North were simply too racist to speak of "wage slavery," with its parallels between the factory and the plantation.[76] Such workers took exception if outsiders, and Southerners especially, compared them to slaves, but they had come to expect as much in the banter of the Lowells and Fall Rivers of the state.

This cross-fertilization of abolitionism and labor reform was encouraged by sectional strife in national politics over the expansion of slavery. No event of the period proved to be more polarizing than the Mexican War, which shook the Second Party System to its foundation, as we shall see in the next chapter. The prospect of war for slave territory also aroused antislavery activists at the local level, and labor reformers especially. In January 1846, as the Polk administration girded for its spring invasion of Mexico, the NEWA gathered at Lynn. A war for slavery was on everyone's mind. A resolution on the "question of slavery," penned by a group of antiwar women, stated that because "three millions of our brethren and sisters groaning in chains on the Southern plantations ... we wish, not only to be consistent but to secure to all others those rights and privileges for which we are contending ourselves." It affirmed that "[we] will never be guilty of the glaring inconsistency of taking up arms to shoot and to stab those who use the same means to accomplish the same objects" and

---

[75] *VI*, Feb. 27, 1846.
[76] See David R. Roediger, *The Wages of Whiteness: Race and the Making of the American Working Class* (1991; New York: Verso, 1999), esp. pp. 71–4.

will not "take up arms to sustain the southern slave holder in robbing one fifth of our countrymen of their liberty." The resolution concluded:

we recommend our brethren to speak out in thunder tones, both as associations and as individuals, and to let it no longer be said that Northern laborers, while they are endeavoring to gain their own rights, are ... a standing army, that keeps three millions of their brethren and sisters in bondage at the point of the bayonet.[77]

This was a signal moment in the history of the antebellum labor movement, one that marked the first time a major labor organization came out against slavery. But it was scarcely the last time. Two years later, following the collapse of the ten-hour movement and the withering away of the NEWA, Faneuil Hall in Boston was the scene of an overflow meeting of workers and their supporters called to celebrate the revolutions of 1848 in Europe and assess the state of "reform" in the United States. All of the officers were men and some – Albert J. Wright, Elizur Wright, and John Orvis among them – were veterans of the ten-hour movement or popular abolitionism or both, but most were newcomers, an indication perhaps that the torch had been passed. Only the resolutions survive from the meetings, and they are of a piece with the NEWA's historic declaration, if put more directly and with greater rhetorical force. The resolutions congratulated the French for overthrowing their oppressive monarchy, because "despotism and slavery *are not* the necessary and natural condition of the people." They also encouraged the economic reforms announced by the provisional government and expressed solidarity with the Chartists and with republican revolutionaries on the Continent. Having taken care of half the agenda, the delegates moved on to consider the domestic scene. They deplored in their midst the "despotick attitude of the *Slave Power* at the *South*," and the "domineering ascendancy of a *monied oligarchy* in the North," as equally hostile to "*Labor*, and incompatible with the preservation of popular rights." They summoned the "manly resistance" of honest labor against the Bay State's "*shabby genteel* aristocracy," before listing demands headed by "a reduction in the hours of labor" and including the "destruction of all White and Black Slavery," and the provision of a "just and adequate reward" for "female labor."[78]

Not all abolitionists welcomed support from the labor movement. Since the inception of the *Voice of Industry* in 1845, the paper's editors had heard from Garrisonians who objected strongly to combining labor

---

[77] *VI*, Jan. 23, 1846.
[78] *DC*, May 11, 1848

reform with antislavery and to drawing what they thought to be specious comparisons between the factory and the plantation. *Voice* editor William Field Young had a brisk exchange with one "H.W." over the question. It was not "our wish to measure the comparative difference between Lowell and southern slavery. It is enough for us to know," Young averred, "that there is slavery *both* in Lowell, and the South, and he who professes to be an abolitionist, and at the same time fosters the manufacturing slavery of the north disgraces the name. A true abolitionist is ready to oppose all kinds of slavery, wherever it exists."[79] This festering dispute came to a head a year later in May 1846 when Garrison himself came to Lowell for a meeting of the Middlesex County Anti-Slavery Society. The state's first abolitionist predictably laid into local labor activists for their "criticism of us," which diluted and distracted the cause. Young was in no position to reply. Hobbled by failing health and in need of rest, he turned to his coeditor Bagley, who vehemently denied that labor reformers thwarted the antislavery crusade. She agreed that fellow activists pursued several reforms simultaneously, none more aggressively than "the reduction of the hours of labor," but she argued that their pursuit was not "to the *exclusion* of others." If anyone was "partial" it was the Garrisonians. "Have we given them no evidence of the broad ground upon which we stand, by selecting one of their own number to lecture before us? – Have we not sought to bring all the different reforms before the people during the course of lectures just finished? and still, we are charged with 'partial reform.' Well, let it be so; we shall not retaliate, although we might do so." Then Bagley turned the tables by asking if Garrisonians ever discuss "the merits of the Labor question? the Peace question? or the abolition of capital punishment" since labor reformers consider "all of these and Slavery, South and North." Who was "more liberal," she asked rhetorically, "friend Garrison?" She concluded on a more congenial note, observing, "Affinities find each other, say you, and we shall understand each other in due time. Till then let us exercise charity for each other, and not claim for ourselves more of the genuine spirit of reform, than we are willing to award others, who are laboring as sincerely as ourselves."[80] Another critic put it less delicately, dismissing Garrison as the "Pope of Anti-Slavery," an epithet that soon took on a life of its own among "new org" abolitionists.[81]

---

[79] *VI*, July 3, 1845.
[80] Ibid., May 8, 1846.
[81] *DC*, Sept. 11, 1846.

This nearly decade-long feud between the antislavery camps resurfaced in May 1847, for the third consecutive spring. Perhaps because it was so central to their outlooks neither side could let the dispute die. Its latest – and for all practical purposes last – iteration, in the 1840s, may be attributed to a Garrison editorial in the *Liberator* lambasting National Reformers as misguided zealots. In response, the *Voice* editors feigned "surprise," not at the accusation but at Garrison's having "stoop[ed]" to using the same epithets that proslavery critics had used against him. They did not appreciate being called "fools, knaves, or madmen" simply for speaking the truth that "there is any other slavery but that which exists in the South." The editors said, as they had in the past, that although chattel slavery was "the worst" form of bondage, it was not "the only one." "Wages slavery" was the other, and it "cause[d] as much physical and mental suffering" as its Southern cousin. It was "degrading, impoverishing and enslaving [to] so large a portion of our race" merely because of the "Monopoly of the Soil and the instrumentalities of life, only by the enjoyment of which a man can really become free, and without which he becomes a slave; selling himself in the market to the highest bidder."[82]

More was at stake for labor reformers than winning polemical skirmishes against Garrisonians – or against the single-issue men in their own party. They were, after all, political actors out for votes. What difference did it make if they won the argument but could not deliver at the polls? One noteworthy political venture of the period took place in Lowell. Few modern histories of the ten-hour movement in Massachusetts fail to mention the political fallout in the Spindle City from the women's campaign for a ten-hour day. Representative William Schouler in 1845, who chaired the committee hearings on factory reform and wrote its report recommending against legislative action, aroused such opposition in his district following the release of the report that Bagley and her friends vowed to get even in the fall election.[83] Calling Schouler a "corporate... tool," the LFLRA vowed to "use our best endeavors to keep him in the city of spindles" after the next election.[84] Though the women probably mounted the petition canvass against Schouler – the details are sketchy – the result is well known. Schouler was defeated in November, and at the end of the month the LFLRA published a sarcastic resolution congratulating

---

[82] *VI*, May 7, 1847.
[83] Dublin, *Women at Work*, pp. 114–15.
[84] Quoted in ibid., p. 115.

the voters for "consigning Wm. Schouler, to the obscurity he so justly deserves."[85]

A closer look at the 1845 election and two successive ones, however, yields a more complicated story bearing directly on the relationship between the Liberty Party factions. The LFLRA strongly influenced Lowell voters, who did as they were asked by singling out Schouler for electoral embarrassment. The hated Whig ran dead last among the Whig slate for the State House, polling 600 votes fewer than his party's frontrunners. The political field, however, was wider than the Lowellites had ever known or than historians have acknowledged. In addition to Whigs and Democrats, there were nativists and pro-railroad candidates as well as Workingmen and Libertyites. The Workingmen's candidates gathered between 332 and 460 votes, and the Liberty Party's candidates gathered between 127 and 131 votes.[86] Thus Workingmen mustered two to three times the number of Liberty votes. For all the rhetoric from labor reformers about the symmetry between chattel and wage slavery, abolitionism and labor reform continued to be sharply divided at the political level.

Lowell's labor activists with abolitionist leanings looked ahead to the next election with some enthusiasm. Daniel H. Jacques, the outspoken Fourierist about to succeed Bagley at the *Voice*, optimistically surveyed prospects for reform in spring 1846. Separate meetings of antislavery activists, labor reformers, and cooperationists did not dampen his optimism. They were merely "divisions" in the "great Army of Reform" about to charge into battle as one under the colors of "HUMANITY FIRST OF ALL."[87] Jacques's brow furrowed, however, when a unity meeting scheduled for Anti-Slavery Hall did not pan out. Factionalism plagued labor reform once again. Workingmen in the the local Industrial Reform Association committee questioned candidates on ten-hour legislation and land reform. Their endorsements included the abolitionist Chauncey L. Knapp, a choice that signaled some political convergence between labor reformers and antislavery advocates but not enough to make much of a difference.[88]

The political breakthrough of the decade in Lowell came a year later following a shift in the organizational landscape. Nativists and pro-railroad forces folded, probably merging back into the Whigs. The

[85] VI, Nov. 28, 1845.
[86] Ibid., Nov. 7, 14, 21, and 28, 1845.
[87] Ibid., May 15, 1846.
[88] Ibid., Nov. 6 and 13, 1846.

women's labor movement suffered badly with the demise of the LFLRA in winter 1846/7, along with the departure from Lowell of several of its leaders. Huldah Stone left for a tour of eastern cities and factory towns to hawk the *Voice*, before leaving for parts unknown.[89] Sarah Bagley returned to her family's farmstead in rural New Hampshire, ending her career in the labor movement.[90] Lesser figures seem to have departed as well. Little is known, for instance, of Maria L. Varney, a radical women's rights advocate who may have spent time in Bagley's Lowell. Fluent in the idiom of "wage slavery," Varney objected strongly to the idea of separate spheres for men and women and its corollary of separate and unequal pay scales. But her strong and unambiguous voice for equality was lost when she left Massachusetts, presumably in the late 1840s, for Connecticut.[91] Such a diaspora deprived Lowell and the NEWA of its founding mothers, those founders also of the city's labor movement who did more than anyone to bridge the organizational divide between abolitionism and labor reform. Their "surviving children" went in a more moderate direction, transforming the LFLRA into the Lowell Female Industrial Reform and Mutual Aid Society, a self-described group that limped along for a time and then expired.[92] Others bent their energies toward consumer cooperatives as members of the Workingmen's Protective Union.

On the political front, the labor reform and Fourierists groups that had formed the Workingmen's Party in 1845 and 1846 thought better of still another campaign. Their Industrial Congress rejected another slate on the grounds that a "party" would be, in the words of William Field Young, "looked upon as a political combination for mere party purposes." Young's argument for following the former policy of "questioning the candidates of the other parties" and then nominating individuals regardless of their partisan affiliation carried the day.[93]

The Liberty Party, durable enough to weather the organizational shakeup, had troubles of its own. Its eclectic wing, led by Gerrit Smith and William Goodell in New York and Elizur Wright in Massachusetts, finally

---

[89] Ibid., July 2 and Nov. 2, 1847. On Stone, see Dublin, *Women at Work*, pp. 120–8 passim.

[90] Dublin, *Women at Work*, pp. 114–28.

[91] *DC*, Mar. 3, 1846. For Varney's activism in the early 1850s see //:www. assumption. edu/whw/old/On-line%Archive.html.

[92] Frances H. Early, "A Reappraisal of the New England Labor Reform Movement in the 1840s: The Lowell Female Labor Reform Association and the New England Workingmen's Association," *HSSH* 13 (May 1980): 33–55.

[93] *VI*, June 15, 1847. On Young, see Jama Lazerow, "Religion and Reform in Antebellum America: The World of William Field Young," *AQ* 38 (1986): 265–86.

lost patience with the single-issue men in control of the national apparatus. They gathered in summer 1847 at Macedon Lock, New York, to form the Liberty League on a platform combining economic reform with antislavery.[94] Though the Liberty Leaguers were a minority of the party in the region, they were its voice in such industrial centers as Lowell. There, in fall 1847, the remnants of the Workingmen came together for the first time with political abolitionists under the same tent. The precedent was not lost on the *Voice of Industry*, which alerted local voters to the Liberty ticket, calling on the "friends of Labor Reform" to take "notice [of] the names of several zealous advocates of the movement, on the above ticket," including Chauncey Knapp. Printing the Liberty slate for the first time – the antebellum equivalent of an endorsement – the editors urged their readers to "Give them your votes."[95]

Lowellites gave the Liberty ticket 6 percent of the vote, some 3 percent less than its average but still encouraging from the perspective of organizational politics.[96] The union of abolitionism and labor reform had not only set a significant precedent in the Commonwealth; it had also provided an example for emulation in the opinion of the *Voice*. In January 1848, not long after the election, the editor reckoned that local agitation on the labor question had a broader effect. He described the antislavery movement as the "beautiful constellation of reforms" in the forefront "against the unrequited toil and chattelizing features of slaveholding." Succeeding years of struggle taught "Abolitionists" that their cause was bound up with numerous other questions which had seemed to bear only "subsidiary and collateral relations to slavery." Abolitionists gradually realized that the "whole theory of labor is involved in the idea of liberty and social equality, of which technical antislavery forms but a branch." Now, "we see a large body of Abolitionists basing their action on the broad grounds of Justice to Labor." The "Anti-Slavery and Labor Reform Movements, which two years since appeared as antagonists, are now seen to have a common basis, and a common representation in Gerrit Smith and his co-adjusters."[97]

---

[94] *DC*, June 19 and July 8, 1847; Lawrence J. Friedman, "The Gerrit Smith Circle: Abolitionism in the Burned-Over District," *CWH* 26 (1980): 19–38; and Lawrence B. Goodheart, *Abolitionist, Actuary, Atheist: Elizur Wright and the Reform Impulse* (Kent, Ohio: Kent State Univ. Press, 1990), pp. 132–3.

[95] *VI*, Nov. 5, 1847.

[96] Carl Siracusa, *A Mechanical People: Perceptions of the Industrial Order in Massachusetts, 1815–1880* (Middletown, Conn.: Wesleyan Univ. Press, 1979), appendix C-2, p. 254.

[97] *VI*, Jan. 7, 1848.

This columnist was too optimistic. He could not see that Smith's Liberty League would not survive to the next election; it would merge in the summer with the newly formed Free Soil Party. What he did see, however, was the common platform that stood on the twin pillars of abolitionism and labor reform. Libertyism had laid the foundation for Free Soilism, a fresh insurgency larger in size and perspective than any before it.

5

"Fifty Thousand Might Have . . . Assembled"

Sources of Free Soilism

Just about a year after Elizur Wright and his fellow abolitionists left the Liberty Party for the Liberty League, antislavery leaders summoned the faithful in the Bay State to Worcester for what was called the "People's Convention." This meeting, in turn, elected delegates to attend a gathering in Buffalo, New York, in early August that gave birth to the Free Soil Party.[1] The new party arose phoenix-like from the ashes of the Liberty Party but seems at first blush to have had a different cast of characters. One historian described its founders who met at Worcester as "a mongrel assortment of disgruntled Conscience Whigs, a few Webster followers, and other disaffected persons" angry with their party for having nominated Zachary Taylor for president over their vociferous objections.[2] It was bad enough, as they saw it, that Taylor was a hero of the Mexican War, a planters' war for slave land; even worse, he was a Southerner and a slaveholder himself, a living symbol of their party's subservience to the Slave Power. Other scholars have likewise depicted the insurgents as renegade Brahmins fed up with Southern domination of their party.[3] It is easy to see why one would reach such a conclusion given the speakers at the

[1] *MS*, June 29, 1848; *NC*, July 1, 1848; and *DC*, June 30, 1848.

[2] David H. Donald, *Charles Sumner and the Coming of the Civil War* (New York: Fawcett Columbine, 1960), p. 116. Also Michael F. Holt, *The Rise and Fall of the American Whig Party: Jacksonian Politics and the Onset of the Civil War* (New York: Oxford Univ. Press, 1999), pp. 331–82.

[3] Frank Otto Gatell, "'Conscience and Judgment': The Bolt of the Massachusetts Conscience Whigs," *The Historian* 21 (Nov. 1958): 18–45, and Richard H. Sewell, *Ballots for Freedom: Antislavery Politics in the United States, 1837–1860* (New York: Oxford Univ. Press, 1976), pp. 139–42.

rostrum of the People's Convention. Henry Wilson, the one-time shoe-maker, former Whig, and now Free Soil wirepuller, was the lone leader of common origins on a card thick with wealthy men of genteel origins. Convention president E. R. Hoar, a lawyer from an old-line Concord family, opened with an extemporaneous roasting of the Whig conven-tion for brushing aside objections to Taylor. Charles Sumner read a letter of support from Harvard College administrator John Gaylord Palfrey. The Ohioan A. D. Campbell dismissed the Whig convention as a "mob," which in the opinion of Stephen Phillips chose an "ignoramus and ruf-fian" for president. Joshua Giddings, another Ohioan and a favorite of antislavery Whigs in Massachusetts, brought the afternoon session to a close with a meandering and lackluster speech that ran into the dinner hour. When the gathering reconvened at 6:00 P.M., the crowd heard from no one but Whigs from the Commonwealth's first families, including Hoar and Charles Francis Adams. Then came a rhythmic chant for Sumner, one of the party's architects, who was rapidly becoming the darling of party followers.[4]

Former Whigs like Sumner and Adams were pushed from Whiggery, not pulled by Free Soilism. Critical of President James Polk in the 1844 presidential election, they joined the opposition in 1845 as the president inexorably drew the Mexicans into war to satisfy his plans for territorial expansion.[5] The popularity of Polk's single-minded pursuit of expansion-ism forced Whiggery's conservative leaders, now known as Cotton Whigs, to reconsider their antiwar stand. When in fall 1845 Adams asked Nathan Appleton to join their anti-Texas movement, the party solon snapped, "I consider the question settled."[6] Appleton then wrote Adams, Palfrey, and Sumner to say that as far as he was concerned, "Texas now virtu-ally composes a part of our Union" – stating the new party line.[7] As the troops marched on Mexico City the following summer and fall, the Conscience men went to the Bay State's Whig convention determined to carry on the fight against slavery now that they had failed to prevent

---

[4] *DC*, June 30, 1848.

[5] Kinley J. Brauer, *Cotton Versus Conscience: Massachusetts Whig Politics and South-western Expansion, 1843–1848* (Lexington: Univ. of Kentucky Press, 1966); Donald, *Charles Sumner*, pp. 143–6; and Martin B. Duberman, *Charles Francis Adams, 1807–1886* (Boston: Houghton Mifflin, 1961), esp. pp. 87–109. Paul W. Foos, *A Short, Offhand Killing Affair: Soldiers and Social Conflict during the Mexican-American War* (Chapel Hill: Univ. of North Carolina Press, 2002), is a stirring account of the war at the battlefront.

[6] Quoted in Donald, *Charles Sumner*, p. 141.

[7] Brauer, *Cotton Versus Conscience*, pp. 134–58. Quote is on p. 124.

war for slave territory. Their resolutions, which condemned slavery outright and declared Whiggery to be an antislavery force, far exceeded the party's official stand against the war and against annexation of additional land. Such audacious language raised the hackles of the conservatives, who loudly condemned and then defeated the resolutions handily.[8] Their press then subjected the Conscience men to unrelenting ridicule. The *Atlas* called them "shallow ... demagogues" in cahoots with the extremism of Garrison who would lead the party to ruin.[9] The *Daily Advertiser* dismissed their resolutions as "suicidal" pronouncements born of "desperation."[10] Even the provincial press, normally sympathetic to antislavery politics, piled on. The *Springfield Republican,* for one, equated Conscience Whiggery with "ultra doctrines" as "injurious" as they were "impractical."[11] Although Adams was by now accustomed to such venomous assaults, he took this editorial onslaught particularly hard. It left him shaken and demoralized, if still loyal. "We do not mean to leave the Whig party," wrote Adams and his fellows in his *Whig,* the leading Conscience Whig organ. "Still less do we propose to sanction the suicidal system of third parties."[12] What looked like suicide in fall 1846, however, became the only realistic alternative a year later when the Whigs gathered for their state convention. Convinced that supporting Taylor was the sine qua non of party unity, the Cotton Whigs closed ranks. They defeated two Conscience resolutions, one that would have prevented the nomination of any candidate and the other, an infamous one proposed by Congressman John G. Palfrey, that would have eliminated all candidates except "those who are known by their deeds or declared opinions to be opposed to the existence of slavery."[13] Adams and his acolytes who left the convention convinced it would be their last as Whigs were essentially right.[14] The denouement came in late spring 1848 at the party's national convention in Philadelphia. When it nominated Taylor, Henry Wilson and some fifteen other Conscience men from several Northern states broke in disgust for a small room to plan a counter-convention in late summer, acting on a plan they had agreed upon in advance. The Bay Staters among them instructed

[8] Ibid., pp. 184–92.
[9] *BA,* Sept. 29, 1846. Also ibid., Oct. 3, 8, and 14, 1846.
[10] *BDA,* Sept. 28 and 29, 1846.
[11] *SR,* Sept. 26, 1846.
[12] Quoted in Brauer, *Cotton Versus Conscience,* p. 204.
[13] Quoted in ibid., p. 217. Also see Gatell, "Conscience and Judgment."
[14] Brauer, *Cotton Versus Conscience,* pp. 217–28. Also see Donald, *Charles Sumner,* pp. 157–9.

friends back home to organize what became the People's Convention in Worcester.[15]

A look from the podium of the People's Convention reveals that the meeting was hardly a rump of disgruntled Whigs. Its scale alone indicates as much. Whig conventions typically brought together about two hundred party activists hailing mostly from Boston and constituting a tiny fraction of the party's base. The People's Convention, by contrast, attracted at least five thousand people from across the state, an unheard-of number for a political gathering. This figure takes on added significance when we consider that Free Soilers averaged around thirty thousand votes statewide over the next few years. What drew such a throng – fully one-fifth of the party vote – to Worcester? Operatives denied that partisan motivation or political machinery was at work, in part because they shared the antiparty animus common to political insurgency.[16] They thought of themselves as "the people," pure and simple, unsullied by the taint of partisanship.[17] Elizur Wright reckoned that if organizers had relied on "the aid of state, county or town committees, coonskins, banners, and hard cider, fifty thousand might have...assembled."[18] John Milton Earle, publisher of the *Massachusetts Spy*, likewise denied that political organization had much to do with the spectacular turnout, insisting that the faithful "came forth without party or party machinery"; they were driven by "irrepressible emotions" about the "slave power." He implied that the name recognition of the speakers helped attendance, a point stressed by Wright in his assessment of the crowd. The "simple call of 'Conscience Whigs' of this [eastern] end of the State," Earle suggested, was enough.[19]

There is no question that the celebrity of the Conscience men not only swelled the ranks of the People's Convention but also helped secure the popular base of Free Soilism. Many of the speakers had the popular touch despite their origins – and wooden bearing away from the podium. On the hustings they readily hewed to the histrionics of the

---

[15] Henry Wilson, *History of the Rise and Fall of the Slave Power in America*, 3 vols. (Boston: James L. Osgood, 1872–7), 2: 106–13 and 123–8.

[16] On the antiparty stance of such movements, see Ronald P. Formisano, *The Birth of Mass Political Parties, Michigan, 1827–1861* (Princeton, N.J.: Princeton Univ. Press, 1971), pp. 56–80, and Formisano, *The Transformation of Political Culture: Massachusetts, 1790s–1840s* (New York: Oxford Univ. Press, 1983), pp. 73–6, 91–2, and 185–7.

[17] See Mark Voss-Hubbard, *Beyond Party: Cultures of Antipartisanship in Northern Politics before the Civil War* (Baltimore: Johns Hopkins Univ. Press, 2002), pp. 9–10 and 44–7.

[18] *DC*, June 30, 1848.

[19] *MS*, June 29, 1848.

FIGURE 17. John Milton Earle. (Hamilton D. Hurd, *History of Worcester County, Massachusetts, with Biographical Sketches of Many of its Pioneers and Prominent Men*, 2 vols. [Philadelphia: J. W. Lewis, 1889], 1: plate following p. 1538.)

Second Party System. Sumner, for one, was rapidly creating his legend as a spellbinding and adored speaker. Scheduled to follow Charles Francis Adams at the evening session of the People's Convention, Summer was figuratively dragged to the podium by the "deafening shouts" that "went forth" for him.[20] Even the stiff and cold Adams had learned how to drop his guard now that the people had embraced him as their own. At the Buffalo convention Adams had became the center of attention for the recent death of his beloved if aloof father. A colleague reported a great outpouring of "feeling" for John Quincy Adams and much admiration for his son. "People crowded about" him, "shook his hands, spoke of their admiration for the 'old man'& seemed...to show him the respect they

[20] *DC*, June 30, 1848.

could not show the father."[21] The younger Adams, who normally rivaled his father's reserve, did nothing to discourage the adoration. He invited it by tucking a piece of black mourning crepe in his white hat as he strutted around the convention grounds.[22] Henry Wilson, of course, needed no such props, for he rarely let anyone forget that he was no arriviste and that he had come up the hard way. A genuine friend of labor and an entertaining orator who had mastered the use of personal inventive and colorful language, Wilson may well have been Free Soilism most popular figure.[23]

Attributing the throng at Worcester to the authority of star-quality personalities or to visceral hatred of the Slave Power and the South, as party journalists were wont to do, would be a mistake. Conscience men had considered a divorce from Whiggery for years, only to pull back each time at the last moment in the hope that *their* party would come to its senses about the designs of the Slave Power. The seemingly constant rehearsal for the final break had an important impact. It prepared the Conscience men for the leap of faith into third partyism and helped them gather a following when the moment of decision arrived, because several of them had been in contact for years with activists in the provinces. Anti-Texas meetings in fall 1845 had brought Adams to the same podium as Garrisonians and Libertyites as well as Conscience Whigs. He soon found himself in charge of the State Texas Committee, which was formed in fall 1845 in suburban Boston and initially led by Samuel Sewall, who used it as a center to lure Whigs to his party. When Adams took over, he resisted overtures from Sewall to make the group permanent and turn it into an instrument with which to influence Whigs. The collapse of the committee coincided with a more earnest dialogue between the citified Conscience Whigs and the provincial Libertyites over their next step.[24] In an 1846 letter to Stanton, Palfrey, Sumner, and others, the irrepressible Whittier despaired over the inability of the Libertyites to erode the base of the Whigs or to pull in Democrats.[25] He continued to ruminate about electoral strategy into 1847 with Conscience men, fellow Libertyites, and independent-minded

[21] Robert F. Lucid, ed., *The Journal of Richard Henry Dana, Jr.*, 3 vols. (Cambridge: Harvard Univ. Press, 1968), 1: 352–3.

[22] Brauer, *Cotton Versus Conscience*, pp. 238–45.

[23] On Wilson, see Richard H. Abbott, *Cobbler in Congress: The Life of Henry Wilson, 1812–1875* (Lexington: Univ. of Kentucky Press, 1972).

[24] Brauer, *Cotton Versus Conscience*, pp. 138–46.

[25] JGW to HBS, Aug. 4, 1846, and to JGP, Sept. 21, 1846, in John B. Pickard, ed., *The Letters of John Greenleaf Whittier*, 3 vols. (Cambridge: Harvard Univ. Press, 1975), 2: 29 and 36–7.

moralists of no particular politics.[26] But when Sumner wrote him just before the People's Convention about the Liberty Party's likely position on a merger, the poet averred that "they are ready and anxious to cooperate with the Conscience Whigs and Independent Democrats"[27]

This exchange between Summer, the former Whig, and Whittier, the Liberty man, carried much deeper meaning. It represented the merger of two antislavery factions that had been divided along partisan lines since the formation of the Liberty Party eight years earlier. Indeed, this antislavery front may well have extended wider, to include Garrisonians who, as we have seen, had shown nothing but contempt for political antislavery. African American leaders who were openly identified as friends of Garrison – including William Cooper Nell and William J. Watkins – joined the Free Soil Party shortly after its formation.[28] How many African Americans followed their leaders into the new party is not clear, though it seems certain that their membership was more welcome in Massachusetts than in New York, where the new party's position on civil rights was too suspect to appeal to African Americans. Indeed, Barnburner Democrats, who loomed much larger in Free Soil leadership in New York than in Massachusetts, had thwarted an initiative at the 1846 constitutional convention to extend the franchise to African Americans.[29] How many white Garrisonians went along is not known either, though several Garrisonians did attend the founding convention of the party. Samuel May left the Syracuse, New York, meeting greatly impressed. Garrison, his longtime comrade, disliked the party's retreat from the qualified abolitionism of the Liberty Party but still found grounds for optimism.[30] With or without Garrison, the Free Soil Party in the Bay State was a signal achievement for antislavery. It was no political "fringe," as Whigs had described the Libertyites, but a potent threat with a solid base and an experienced leadership.

---

[26] Ibid., JGW to Samuel Fessenden and John Parker Hale, July 26 and 30, and Nov. 2, 1846, pp. 93–5.

[27] Ibid., JGW to CS, June 23, 1848, pp. 105–6. Quote is on p. 105.

[28] James Oliver Horton and Lois E. Horton, *Black Bostonians: Family Life and Community Struggle in the Antebellum North* (New York: Holmes and Meier, 1979), p. 87.

[29] Milton C. Sernett, *North Star Country: Upstate New York and the Crusade for African American Freedom* (Syracuse, N.Y.: Syracuse Univ. Press, 2002), pp. 122–8. Racial toleration, though hardly absent, was obviously much weaker in New York. Also see Eric Foner, "Racial Attitudes of the New York Free Soilers," in Foner, *Politics and Ideology in the Age of the Civil War* (New York: Oxford Univ. Press, 1980), pp. 77–93.

[30] *Lib*, Aug. 10 and 25, 1848. Henry Mayer, *All on Fire: William Lloyd Garrison and the Abolition of Slavery* (New York: St. Martin's Press, 1998), pp. 382–3.

Nearly to a man, Free Soil leaders such as Sumner and Whittier had been identified with some aspect of antislavery. This was true for a substantial portion of the party base as well – at least a third, if we can assume that virtually all Libertyites (some ten thousand) voted for the party in 1848 when it collected about thirty thousand votes. Even if the antislavery vote was greater, about half of the electorate probably had not stopped at the halfway house of Libertyism on its way to Free Soil or indeed to the People's Convention in Worcester. The portion of the party from outside the ranks of antislavery consisted of several different and sometimes overlapping groups. Democrats, for one, came from the geographic periphery of the state and largely from the radical wing of their party. Such Locofocos are normally and accurately seen as the source of the economic radicalism that would inform Free Soil policy.[31] Another group consisted of onetime Whigs in the larger industrial cities and towns, places like Lowell, Worcester, and Fall River. Both groups, as well as several others with pet projects, supported what become known as State Reform, that is, a hodge-podge of popular reforms unrelated to slavery. The groups agitated for reforms ranging from prohibition to a legal limit on the length of the workday to the secret ballot to political reapportionment. Their presence greatly complicated the work of the "one idea" faction of the party leadership.

The party became more complex still when it moved from an informal coalition in 1849 into a formal Coalition with the Democrats in 1850. This relationship, which was formalized in fall 1850, had not come easily. It was a substitute for fusion, a controversial step that never quite allayed mutual suspicion and distrust. The elitism and economic conservatism that made it hard for Conscience Whigs to leave their party, made it just as hard for them to cooperate with Democrats. Charles Francis Adams, the self-described "conservative," never did make peace with Democrats or with State Reform.[32] Neither did Richard Henry Dana, the activist lawyer whose work for fugitive slaves in the early 1850s masked an essentially Whiggish sensibility. If former Whigs found the Democrats to be too radical on economic issues, former Libertyites worried about the Democrats' stand on race and slavery. Many doubted that Democrats could be counted on in the struggle for civil rights and against the Slave Power. Whittier nervously followed talk about alliances among Free Soilers and Democrats

---

[31] For instance, Donald, *Charles Sumner*, pp. 192–3 and 223.
[32] William F. Hartford, *Money, Morals, and Politics: Massachusetts in the Age of the Boston Associates* (Boston: Northeastern Univ. Press, 2001), esp. pp. 124, 170, 179, and 189.

in neighboring states. Writing to Lewis Tappen in New York in summer 1849, the activist poet confided that he did not doubt the "good intentions of the great mass" of Free Soilers or the "integrity of the old Liberty men, who may get off track now and then but their instincts will set them right." His fear was that Empire State Free Soilers would get "drawn into some unworthy compromise" with proslavery Democrats.[33] None of that bothered Sumner or Henry Wilson, the more pragmatic – and some would have said the opportunistic – Free Soiler who had relished such an alliance. In fact, Sumner had sought out Democratic higher-ups not long after the 1848 election. He then appealed to their base – and his own as well – by drafting the resolutions at the Free Soil state convention in September 1849 that assailed the Money Power and by laying out the agenda of State Reform.[34]

The Coalition was not, however, imposed from above by scheming operatives in the city. Its formation also benefited measurably from growing discontent in the country over the hegemony of Boston Whiggery, as well as over the power of the South in national politics. This antiurban animus, which had flared into the Regulator rebellion in the 1780s, had been suppressed but never completely wiped out.[35] It lingered in the provinces and rose to the fore in the late 1840s, thanks largely to Henry Gere, who was the editor of the *Northampton Gazette*, and Whiting Griswold, a Greenfield lawyer elected to the House of Representatives on the Democratic ticket in 1848, who articulated the grievances of "the country." Gere was one of several provincial journalists pressing for some sort of union with Democrats in summer 1849.[36] The only question for him was the source of the bond, the glue that would hold the coalition together. He told Free Soil power brokers that antislavery was not enough for a coalition. The country would respond more readily, he supposed, to a program that tapped into its pervasive antiurban feeling.[37] No politician exploited that animus more deftly than did Griswold, who had proposed political reforms in 1849 only to be thwarted by the Whigs he was trying

[33] JGW to LT, July 14, 1849, in Packard, *Letters of John Greenleaf Whittier*, 2: 140–1. Quote is on p. 140.

[34] Donald, *Charles Sumner*, pp. 164–7 and 177–82.

[35] Leonard L. Richards, *Shays's Rebellion: The American Revolution's Final Battle* (Philadelphia: Univ. of Pennsylvania Press, 2002), makes clear that the maldistribution of political power, not rural debt, was the source of discontent. On the Commonwealth's unusual electoral rules, see *BDA*, Nov. 7–9, 1850, and Oct. 31 and ff. 1851.

[36] *NC*, June 12, 1849. Also ibid., July 3, 10, 17, and 24, 1849. Also *MS*, June 25, 1849.

[37] *NC*, June 12, 1849. Also ibid., July 3, 10, 17, and 24, 1849.

FIGURE 18. Martha C. and Henry S. Gere. Daguerreotype. Courtesy of the Forbes
Library, Northampton, Mass.

to contain.[38] Griswold, the Democrat, linked up with Sumner and Wilson
who in summer 1849 widely publicized his program of reapportionment
and the secret ballot, an issue with great appeal in the country and rather
more in the industrial cities.[39] The following October, Free Soilers bought
Griswoldism wholesale, enshrining his reforms in their platform and borrowing his populist rhetoric asserting that the "Money Power" in the

[38] See later in this chapter for more on Griswold.
[39] NC, July 30, 1849, and *Eman*, July 26, 1849. Also see Kevin Sweeney, "Rum, Romanism,
Representation, and Reform: Coalition Politics in Massachusetts, 1847–1853," *CWH* 6
(June 1976): 120

Commonwealth not only had eclipsed the "instinct for Freedom" but had also "joined hands with the Slave Power." The "natural influence" of the "Money Power" was "still further enhanced," read the Address of the State Committee of the Free Soil Party, by corrupt and unfair apportionment, highlighted by rules that allowed general tickets and single districts in large cities but carved the "country" into small towns divided against themselves by party affiliations. As a result, the "large cities, which are the seat of the Money Power, are ... able, though a minority, to control the state."[40]

Though such logic – and its mathematics especially – made Whiggish eyes roll, it was a powerful formulation that at once reflected the antiurban instincts of the country and laid the foundation for the Coalition of Democrats and Free Soilers. The Coalition never quite resolved its own differences. It proved to be a precarious union of temperance advocates, labor reformers, country dissidents, and so on, drawn together under the leadership of antislavery advocates and professional politicians, and united by shared antipathy to the presumed union of the Money Power and the Slave Power – Free Soilism's rhetorical equivalent of the slogan "lords of the lash and lords of the loom" coined by labor activists a decade before. Some of its supporters were members of formal movements; others were simply constituents. Both were out in force at the People's Convention.

One of the movements represented at the People's Convention consisted of workingmen and their political advocates. Workers were immediately conspicuous to Elizur Wright as he debarked from the Boston train that had taken him to Worcester for the convention. Working people and farmers, he wrote, came to Worcester "spontaneously from hill and dale, counter and workshop, plough and loom."[41] They were thicker still in the town center, where he and his traveling companions were met "by a body of 200 workmen from the great plough [-making] establishment of Ruggles, Nourse, & Mason, with a banner and a band ... by which we were escorted through" the main street.[42] The employer of these workers was part of a large complex of innovative machine shops and foundries headed by self-made businessmen drawn to Free Soilism in part for its implicit critique of slavery and finance capital. In addition, such men were

[40] *NC*, Oct. 2, 1849.
[41] *DC*, June 30, 1848.
[42] Ibid. also *MS*, June 29, 1848, and *NC*, July 1, 1848.

fiercely independent, intensely civic-minded, and very critical of the corporately inclined Boston Associates who had become synonymous with Whiggery and also with the rival textile towns of Lowell and Lawrence. Free Soilism reflected their civic capitalism and also the fraternalistic ethic that mediated labor relations in their shops, making Worcester a model of enlightened labor management.[43]

The tough-minded managerialism in the outposts of the Boston Associates and in such places as Fall River not only made the Worcester proprietors somewhat different, it also provided a political opening for Free Soil politicians like Elizur Wright and other refugees from the Liberty League. Wright and his ilk carried on into the 1850s, but they were eclipsed in party affairs by such younger men as James M. Stone from Charlestown and William S. Robinson from Lowell.[44] No one could miss William S. Robinson at the People's Convention. He was on the platform as the meeting's secretary pro tempore and then was officially designated one of several secretaries by the delegates. Robinson's biography closely follows that of Wright, Buckingham, and any number of other antebellum printers from middling families in village New England who gave voice in the late 1840s to the popular disenchantment with conservative Whiggery in the Bay State. Robinson was the youngest son of a Concord hatmaker, whose own father had been a poor shoemaker. The family's "fortune had reached the lowest point in its descent" when he was born in 1818 and

---

[43] See George F. Hoar, *Autobiography of Seventy Years*, 2 vols. (New York: Charles Scribner's Sons, 1903), 1: 159. For more on such firms, see Bruce Laurie, "'We are not afraid to work': Master Mechanics and the Market Economy in the Antebellum North," in Burton J. Bledstein and Robert D. Johnston, eds., *The Middling Sorts: Explorations in the History of the Middle Class* (New York: Routledge, 2001), pp. 50–68. Also see Joshua S. Chasan, "Civilizing Worcester: The Creation of an Institutional and Cultural Order, Worcester, Massachusetts, 1848–1876" (Ph.D. diss., Univ. of Pittsburgh, 1974), and John L. Brooke, *The Heart of the Commonwealth: Society and Political Culture in Worcester County Massachusetts, 1713–1861* (New York: Cambridge Univ. Press, 1989), pp. 269–309.

[44] On Stone, see Charles M. Persons, "The Early History of Factory Legislation in Massachusetts (from 1825 to the Passage of the Ten Hour Law in 1874)," in Susan M. Kingsbury, ed., *Labor Laws and Their Enforcement with Special Reference to Massachusetts* (1911; New York: Arno and the *New York Times,* 1971), pp. 61–2, 85–6, and 102. Also Hartford, *Money, Morals, and Politics,* pp. 174 and 181–2. Though Stone claimed to have been involved in the ten-hour movement as early as 1842, an early historian of the movement finds no evidence of this or of Stone's involvement in the New England Workingmen's Association or other groups associated with the cause. He appears to have been a Democrat during this period and a temperance advocate who edited the Washingtonian *State Sentinel and Worcester Reformer.* See Persons, "Early History of Factory Legislation," pp. 61–2.

FIGURE 19. William S. Robinson. (Mrs. William S. Robinson, comp., *"Warring-ton" Pen-Portraits: A Collection of Personal and Political Reminiscences from 1848 to 1876 . . .* [Boston: Mrs. William S. Robinson, 1877], frontispiece.)

never improved much thereafter.[45] After completing a brief but productive apprenticeship to a country printer in 1837, young Robinson worked by turns as a journeymen and editor in and around Concord and then had the good luck in 1830 to run into William Schouler, the ambitious and gifted journalist making his mark in politics. Schouler took a liking to Robinson and agreed to endorse and help finance the young man's first newspaper, not long, incidentally, after Daniel Webster had helped Joseph T. Buckingham launch his *Boston Courier*. Just as Webster's patronage sealed Buckingham's long-term allegiance, so did Schouler's solicitude solidify Robinson's loyalty. "I thank God," he wrote "that there is one man with whom I have had business. I assure you that I shall always remember this kindness."[46] Though Robinson broke with his patron about the same time that Buckingham parted ways with his, the printer and journalist was a grateful and compliant client, following Schouler into Whiggery

[45] Quoted in Claudia L. Bushman, *"A Good Poor Man's Wife": Being a Chronicle of Harriet Hanson Robinson and Her Family in Nineteenth-Century New England* (Hanover, N.H.: University Press of New England, 1981), p. 64.
[46] WSR to William Schouler, July 26, 1830, WSRP, box 1.

but not necessarily in lockstep. Robinson's *Concord Republican*, after all, was inflected with the nasal twang of the party's rambunctious temperance faction, which had angered the urban faction at the turn of the 1830s over liquor licensing.[47] It would not be the last time the drys made political mischief.

It is not clear if this intraparty battle tainted Robinson's relationship with Schouler. Possibly it did not, for Robinson was no Wright. Unlike the more radical and personally prickly Wright, Robinson was politically cautious at first, studiously shunning Wright's Libertyites and dutifully cultivating his Whiggish garden through the 1840s. He was, in addition, a likeable man with a disarming wit and gift for the arresting quip. He got along well with party men, none of whom was more accommodating than Schouler. In December 1841 Schouler bought Robinson's *Republican,* and then hired him as assistant editor for his *Lowell Journal and Courier.*[48] It was another step up for a striver too destitute before to afford an overcoat to brave the blustery winter. No matter, Robinson wrote to his mother, "I sniff up the east wind, like the jackasses, and grow fat at it."[49] Nor did his marriage do much for the family coffers. In 1848 he married Harriet Hanson, the daughter of a carpenter whose widow went to Lowell to manage a boardinghouse. Harriet worked at the loom but left gainful employment in fall 1848 following her marriage. Theirs was a hand-to-mouth existence until Robinson began a decade-long tenure as Clerk of the Massachusetts House of Representatives, a job that brought a steady if modest income that underwrote the young couple's status among the "middling sort."[50]

Despite his move to Lowell and Whiggish politics, Robinson remained a son of the country. He never completely accepted the policies of his patrons, any more than Buckingham had. Like Buckingham, he began to distance himself from the regulars who seemed all too eager to get along with the South. When he was assistant editor for Schouler's moderate *Lowell Courier,* Robinson was on his best behavior if his boss was nearby. But when Schouler left for a European tour in 1845 before the Mexican War, Robinson seized the opportunity to attack the party establishment in demeaning terms, committing what he later called "my first act of insubordination against the Whig

---

[47] Formisano, *Transformation of Political Culture*, pp. 276–7 and 297–9.
[48] *DC*, May 16, 1846. Also, a clipping dated Dec. 31, 1841, in WSRP, "Warrington," vol. 4.
[49] Quoted in Bushman, "*Good Poor Man's Wife*," p. 77.
[50] Ibid., pp. 81–121.

leaders."[51] Similar hyperbole had helped crystallize his dispute with Schouler over a matter of personal integrity. He had quit his job the year before rather than follow an order to dun the paper's subscribers, declaring it "beneath" him to do so.[52] Although he returned to the paper within a year, he was by this point a vocal Conscience Whig disgusted with his party's romance with its Southern wing. Robinson was no latecomer to political antislavery. He started out as a antislavery moderate in the early 1830s, and at the end of the decade he lined up for Nathan Brooks against William Parmenter in the 1838 congressional race in the Fourth District. A critic of both the Garrisonians and the Libertyites by the mid-1840s, Robinson publicly identified with the Conscience men by 1846. In spring 1848 he finally exploded as the Cotton Whigs lined up behind Zachary Taylor, penning an editorial that proved too strong even for his Conscience friends who had recommended he hold his fire. Robinson refused to back off even when two emissaries of the paper's new owner from the Lowell corporations bluntly told him that he could "keep his position as editor" if he "said nothing of Taylor" and could still be a Whig if he "let the 'conscience' part of it alone."[53] He rejected both conditions, leaving the paper and the party in mid-June.[54]

Robinson's laborist sympathies took shape at the turn of the 1840s. He had conspicuously avoided the rancor of ten-hour politics coursing through Lowell in the middle of the decade, an understandable avoidance for a Whig in the employ of the man who had led the opposition to making ten hours a legal day's work. He was, in addition, Schouler's political correspondent for the *Atlas*, the official voice of the Boston Associates and a leading political organ in the Commonwealth. Schouler was intolerant of deviation from the party line on labor reform and only a bit more accepting of tactful antislavery opinion. That was the rub, for Robinson was a political aspirant in a party dominated by Cotton Whigs and in a city with a fitful but influential labor movement recently at low ebb but about to resurface. Caught between fealty to his boss and party and to potential constituents in the center of the ten-hour movement, Robinson forced Schouler's hand through a series of "caustic" field reports on Cotton Whiggery he wrote as a correspondent for the

[51] Mrs. W. S. Robinson, comp., "*Warrington*" *Pen-Portraits: A Collection of Personal and Political Reminiscences from 1848 and 1876 . . .* (Boston: Mrs. W. S. Robinson, 1877), p. 29, n. 1.
[52] Bushman, "*Good Poor Man's Wife*," pp. 76–7.
[53] Robinson, "*Warrington*" *Pen-Portraits*, p. 36.
[54] Bushman, *Good Poor Man's Wife*, pp. 73–80.

Atlas.[55] Though fired by Schouler, Robinson wrote that he hoped that they could at least retain the "sacred relationship of friends" now that they were political enemies.[56]

This rupture between political patron and journalist client bore more than a casual resemblance to Joseph Buckingham's break with Daniel Webster. The ties that had bound both men to Whiggery were several; indeed, their disaffection was undoubtedly intensified by their common experience of bearing the arrogance of Whig power so intimately. The difference between these apostate Whigs was both generational and ideological. Twenty years older than Robinson, Buckingham was looking forward to retirement and still in step with Whiggery on just about all issues save cooperation with the Slave Power. He represented considerable Free Soil opinion rooted in both regular parties that was more anti-Southern than antislavery; if anything, his conservatism deepened with age. The man who had lambasted Whiggish merchants in 1832 for their antiunionism had since moved on to more cautious ground. For his part, Robinson was not only younger but also driven by political ambition amid a resurgent labor movement that simply could not be ignored. When Robinson threw in with the Free Soilers in summer 1848, he carried the dual colors of antislavery activist and ten-hour advocate. It could not be otherwise in Lowell at the end of the 1840s.

These were new colors for William Robinson. Although he was about to become Free Soilism's leading voice for the ten-hour day, he had long been a warrior against the liquor traffic in Concord and Lowell. Indeed, the temperance crusade in the Commonwealth may well have been one of the largest and most visible factions of the Free Soil coalition in Worcester at the People's Convention. The column that paraded that morning from the train station paused briefly in front of the American Temperance House, the town's chief dry hotel and, as Wright put it, the "headquarters of that bolting army" of cold water combatants.[57] Their conspicuous presence at the People's Convention comes as no surprise given the size of the movement and its stormy relationship with mainstream politics. Temperance men found Free Soilism to be far friendlier than Whiggery.

The temperance crusade in New England diverged from its counterpart in other Northern states, which relied on moral suasion before turning to

[55] See JGW to WSR, June n.d., 1848, in Pickard, *Letters of John Greenleaf Whittier*, 2: 107.
[56] WSR to WS, May 2, 1848, WSRP.
[57] *DC*, June 30, 1848.

government regulation of liquor.[58] In the Bay State the movement smacked of prohibitionism at the local level from its inception, in no small measure because of shared belief both in the importance of personal morality and in the need to yield to the community will. "Every individual who incorporates himself into the mass of civil society necessarily yields up such rights," said the Worcesterite Ian Barton in 1835, "as in their exercise would conflict with the general welfare."[59] By the time Barton uttered such imperiousness, Bay Staters had already decided that drinkers threatened the general welfare. Although some preferred a voluntarist solution that loaded responsibility onto the individual drinker, many more welcomed the use of local government against miscreants. Thus the temperance crusade in Jacksonian Massachusetts included a mass base that looked to criminalize the traffic.[60]

The Commonwealth's system of local licensing rooted in colonial times, in conjunction with the strength of town government, made town government the primary field of battle. Publicans and retailers applied for liquor licenses to town boards of selectmen, which in turn recommended candidates of "good and moral standing" to county commissioners. It was always assumed that the fewer licensees the better, but by the mid-1830s even a few were deemed excessive by an aroused temperance movement, which elected town selectmen or packed town meetings. Before the 1830s drew to a close temperance forces in Massachusetts dried up half the towns in two central counties and virtually all the towns in the southeastern counties.[61] Even that was not enough for movement militants, who objected to loose enforcement in some hamlets and none at all in the cities and larger towns. It was these militants who in 1838 pressured the Whigs into the infamous fifteen-gallon law prohibiting the sale of liquor in quantities under fifteen gallons. It proved a pyrrhic victory that split the party in the 1838 election, delivering the governorship and State House to the Democrats who repealed the law at the ensuing

---

[58] This framework, first identified by John Allen Kraut in *Origins of Prohibition* (New York: Knopf, 1925), continues to inform most scholarly work on the topic. See W. R. Rorabaugh, *The Alcoholic Republic, An American Tradition* (New York: Oxford Univ. Press, 1979), esp. pp. 187–222, and Jed Dannenbaum, *Drink and Disorder: Temperance Reform in Cincinnati from the Washingtonian Revival to the WCTU* (Urbana: Univ. of Illinois Press, 1984), pp. 49–105.

[59] Quoted in Ian Tyrell, *Sobering Up: From Temperance to Prohibition in Antebellum America, 1800–1860* (Westport, Conn.: Greenwood Press, 1979), p. 245.

[60] Ibid., esp. pp. 227–37. Also see Robert L. Hampel, *Temperance and Prohibition in Massachusetts, 1813–1852* (New York: UMI Research Press, 1982).

[61] Tyrell, *Sobering Up*, pp. 230–1.

session.[62] The stinging defeat convinced prohibitionists to redouble their efforts in the 1840s.[63] Fortified by the surging Washingtonian movement, the most popular temperance group in the period, Bay State prohibitionists finished at the local level in the 1840s what they had started a decade earlier, drying up the rest of the state by the end of the decade and broadening the liquor ban from distilled spirits to wine and beer.[64] The old joke that began "where can a man get a drink around here?" had been answered definitively.

Thus Massachusetts drys had a major impact on public policy and party affairs – and on Whiggery in particular. Convinced that temperance politics threw the elections of 1838 and 1842 to the Democrats, party operatives worked hard to divert attention from the liquor question in state politics by encouraging drys to concentrate their efforts in the towns and counties and by running one of their number for governor, a purely symbolic gesture in view of the larger party strategy. This gambit paid off handsomely and for the seeming pittance of making George Nathan Briggs governor. A Baptist and one-time village hatmaker from the Berkshire County hamlet of Lanesboro, Briggs, the prohibitionist, was a far cry from the eastern Brahmins who had traditionally been the party's gubernatorial standard-bearers. He won eight straight elections from 1843 to 1850, partly because of his party's deft handling of the politics of drink.[65]

The resurgence of prohibitionism helped bring the era of Whiggish harmony to an end. It did not take long before the drys were again grumbling over light policing.[66] They grew especially alarmed as the trickle of Irish immigrants in the middle of the decade raced into a raging torrent by its end, flooding the cities with aliens and exciting the factionalism within Whiggery over the related issues of drink and immigrants. Brahmins welcomed the Irish as cheap laborers, if not full-fledged citizens; country Protestants, who did not want the immigrants at all, knew they could not count on their party for much help. Many of them fled to the Free Soilers, a defection that simultaneously weakened a party already reeling from the loss of the Conscience men and strengthened Free Soilism.

African Americans were even more conspicuous in the processions of the People's Convention. This may surprise historians who later depicted

---

[62] Formisano, *Transformation of Political Culture*, pp. 297–9, and Tyrell, *Sobering Up*, pp. 94–5, 237–9.

[63] Tyrell, *Sobering Up*, pp. 238–9.

[64] Ibid., pp. 240–41.

[65] Formisano, *Transformation of Political Culture*, pp. 297–301.

[66] Tyrell, *Sobering Up*, pp. 242–3.

Free Soilers as populist racists working to preserve the territories for whites only – and, in particular, for white workers in flight from the benighted blacks and exploitative capitalists of the city.[67] The advent of whiteness studies has obviously strengthened this pessimistic interpretation, and with some reason. As most historians have argued, some Free Soilers undeniably looked forward to a form of racial cleansing or racial exclusion – to what I have called "exclusionism."[68] That said, it is important to recognize that Free Soilism also reflected the paternalism that had informed both "old org" and "new org" abolitionists. No observer at the People's Convention could have missed the qualified racial inclusionism of the Free Soil Party in the Bay State. Elizur Wright reported that the groups of delegates debarking the train that had taken them from Boston to Worcester for the People's Convention formed a procession four abreast, headed by a marshal and an assistant marshal for each car. "In our car," Wright explained, "we appointed for that office our gentlemanly friend, Robert Morris, Esq., belonging to that race from which Mr. Taylor stocks his plantations."[69] It was also "that race" that was largely responsible for the civil rights movement, started by Garrison in the early 1830s and supported by the Libertyites a decade later. Now men like Morris tried to make sure that the Free Soilers followed through.

[67] See, for instance, Aileen Kraditor, *Means and Ends in American Abolitionism: Garrison and His Critics on Strategy and Tactics, 1834–1850* (New York: Pantheon, 1969), esp. p. 182; James Brewer Stewart, *Holy Warriors: The Abolitionists and American Slavery* (New York: Hill and Wang, 1976), pp. 116–18; and C. Duncan Rice, *The Rise and Fall of Black Slavery* (New York: Macmillan 1975), pp. 348–9. Also see James A. Rawley, *Race and Politics: "Bleeding Kansas" and the Coming of the Civil War* (Philadelphia: Lippincott, 1969). For more balanced interpretations see Eric Foner, "Politics and Prejudice: The Free Soil Party and the Negro, 1847–1852," *JNH* 50 (Oct. 1965): 239–56, and Sewell, *Ballots for Freedom*, pp. 158–65 and 170–201. The whiteness school is obviously more sympathetic to the older scholarship on this issue.

[68] Joanne Pope Melish, *Disowning Slavery: Gradual Emancipation and "Race" in New England, 1780–1860* (Ithaca, N.Y.: Cornell Univ. Press, 1998). Also David R. Roediger, *The Wages of Whiteness: Race and the Making the American Working Class* (1991; New York: Verso, 1999), and Noel Ignatiev, *How the Irish Became White* (New York: Routledge, 1995). It bears repeating here that in other states in the East and Midwest the racist wing of the Free Soil Party was stronger than it was in the Bay State. See, for instance, Sernett, *North Star Country*, pp. 122–8. For the broader pattern of racism in the nation, see Leon Litwack, *North of Slavery: The Negro in the Free States, 1790–1860* (Chicago: Univ. of Chicago Press, 1961); for its midwestern expression see Eugene H. Berwanger, *The Frontier against Slavery: Western Anti-Negro Prejudice and the Slavery Extension Controversy* (Urbana: Univ. of Illinois Press, 1967), esp. pp. 30–59, and Robert Dykstra, *Bright Radical Star: Black Freedom and White Supremacy on the Hawkeye Frontier* (Ames: Iowa State Univ. Press, 1993), pp. 68–170.

[69] *DC*, June 30, 1848.

A combination of intellectual talent, personal ambition, and pure luck propelled Robert Morris to the People's Convention. Born in Salem in 1823, Morris was the grandson of an African-born slave brought to Ipswich before the American Revolution, where he married and began a family. Robert's father, York, who was either born free or liberated by the 1780s court decisions that abolished slavery in the Commonwealth, moved the family to Salem, where he worked as a waiter.[70] He may well have been in the employ of the Remonds, the family that was caterer and grocer to the city's old Federalist elite.[71] York unquestionably intended to pass on his occupation to his young son, who at age thirteen divided his time between waiting tables and doing odd jobs around town. One day, while at work for the wealthy King family, young Morris made a strong impression on Ellis Gray Loring, a guest of the Kings' and a leading attorney in Boston with abolitionist leanings. Loring got permission from the Kings to hire Morris as a servant; when his law clerk did not measure up, Loring agreed to train young Morris in the law. Morris studied hard for several years and in 1847 became the first African American to be admitted to the Massachusetts bar.[72]

The luck of a chance meeting with an enlightened Brahmin only begins to explain the path that opened Morris's way to Free Soilism. He quickly developed a highly visible legal practice that turned on defending the poor and vulnerable of both races. In 1844 he married Catherine Mason, an Irish-born white woman, who bore him a child. Soon after, Morris converted to Catholicism. His marriage and faith account for his Irish clients and why he was known in the city as an "Irish lawyer." His chief clientele, however, was African American. Not long after his admission to the bar Morris defended an African American worker who sued his employer for arrears in pay. Nervous to begin with, the novice lawyer got a searing baptism in his new profession when, in a private meeting, the defense counsel flew into a racist tirade. Morris kept his composure, however, and got a favorable jury verdict – one that he never forgot. Years later he recalled that the trial had become something of a fascination for black

---

[70] James M. Rosenthal, "Free Soil in Berkshire County, 1781," *NEQ* 10 (1937): 781–5.

[71] Sibyl Ventress Brownlee, "Out of the Abundance of the Heart: Sarah Ann Parker Remond's Quest for Freedom" (Ph.D. diss., Univ. of Massachusetts Amherst, 1997), esp. pp. 42–78.

[72] On Morris, see Horton and Horton, *Black Bostonians*, esp. pp. 55–7 and 125–7, and Dan Koprowski, "The Roberts Case: Robert Morris, Charles Sumner, and School Desegregation Efforts in Antebellum Boston" (seminar paper, Univ. of Massachusetts Amherst, 1999).

Bostonians, who "filled" the courtroom to see their legal champion in the making. "I spared no pains to win," he said, and when the jury decided for him his "heart bounded up, and my people in the courtroom acted as if they would shout with joy."[73] Morris was better known for arguing (with Charles Sumner) for the integration of Boston's public schools in *Sarah C. Roberts v. The City of Boston*, in 1848, and for his political leadership in the subsequent fight to integrate the state militia. Morris was sincere when he told Edwin Walker, son of the militant David Walker, "Don't ever try to run away from our people."[74]

Morris's politics before 1848 are still mysterious. We do not know if he was a Whig or a Liberty man or if he had any political affiliation at all. Perhaps he came to Free Soilism through his legal collaborations with Loring and then Sumner, who was his partner in *Roberts*. What is clear is that Free Soil activists in 1848 made him marshal of their train-car delegation and then nominated him for mayor of Boston.[75] Free Soilers also thought enough of Morris's African American friends in Boston to welcome them into their ranks. William J. Watkins, another community activist who worked closely with Morris on militia integration, headed the Colored Citizens of the Free Soil Party, a group of African American party activists formed in the early 1850s. A year later the party nominated Morris's associate William Cooper Nell to run for the State House.[76]

No African American candidate running for office from Boston stood much of a chance, and not simply because of race. Boston was the home of Free Soilism's marquee personalities – Charles Francis Adams, Charles Sumner, and Henry Wilson, among others – who, like Garrison, have generally attracted the lion's share of academic attention. Their base, however, was in the countryside, not on farms but in the quiet rural towns and noisy industrial cities, places that were broadly and metaphorically called "the country" in popular jargon. The party leadership structure also reflected the ethos of the country, by which party spokesmen meant almost anywhere but Boston. Only two of fourteen members appointed by the People's Convention to the state committee – Adams and Henry T. Parker – were Bostonians. The remaining twelve came from towns

---

[73] Quoted in John Daniels, *In Freedom's Birthplace* (Cambridge: Houghton Mifflin, 1914), p. 451.
[74] Quoted in Horton and Horton, *Black Bostonians*, p. 57.
[75] Ibid., p. 87.
[76] Ibid. Also, *DC*, June 30, 1848.

and villages throughout the state – from the county seat of Springfield to the industrial hamlet of Oxford to the rural town of Brookfield.[77] Country representation swelled in 1850 when the party drew together with rural-based Democrats to form the Coalition, giving the Free Soil Coalition a discrete social configuration consisting of two pillars – country villages and industrial towns. Thus, fully 80 percent of the Coalition's delegation to the House of Representatives came from small and middling towns; a stingy 6.3 percent hailed from cities. (By contrast, over forty percent of the Whig delegation came from cities, and only forty-four percent from small and middling towns.)[78] A good portion of the middling towns, it is important to add, were not overgrown villages, but were "large towns" in the language of Free Soilers, that is, they were showcase cities of the First Industrial Revolution such as Lowell, Worcester, Lynn, and Fall River. These manufacturing centers had been reliably (Lowell and Worcester) or weakly (Lynn and Fall River) Whiggish and not particularly supportive of Libertyism, which was much stronger in the proprietary industrial towns of the northeast.[79] Free Soilism built on Libertyism and on Garrisonianism before it, capturing the frontline manufacturing cities, where its vote in 1848 ranged from 57 percent in Worcester to 24 percent in Fall River. Free Soilism then slipped a bit across the state, but it still retained its initial shape of a revolt of the country against the city.

As we have already seen, the voice of the country was expressed in cultural terms – in art, literature, and so on – heavily inflected with Timothy Dwight's image of the bucolic Yankee village.[80] An enhanced notion of Yankeedom took on a life of its own following Dwight's death, as New Englanders formed heritage societies celebrating their English Protestant traditions and remaking their built environment to conform to the new ideal. Lineal settlements, which once dominated the hinterlands, gradually gave way to nucleated villages, themselves artifacts of commercialism

---

[77] *MS*, June 29, 1848.

[78] Sweeney, "Rum, Romanism, Representation, and Reform," pp. 116–37, esp. Table iv, 125.

[79] Carl Siracusa, *A Mechanical People: Perceptions of the Industrial Order in Massachusetts, 1815–1880* (Middletown, Conn.: Wesleyan Univ. Press, 1979), appendix C-1, pp. 252–5.

[80] Stephen Nissenbaum, "New England as a Region and Nation," in Edward L. Ayers et al., eds., *All Over the Map: Rethinking American Regions* (Baltimore: Johns Hopkins Univ. Press, 1996), pp. 38–61. Also see David Jaffee, *People of Wachusset: Greater New England in History and Memory* (Ithaca, N.Y.: Cornell Univ. Press, 1999), and Joseph A. Conforti, *Imagining New England: Explorations of Regional Identity from the Pilgrims to the Mid-Twentieth Century* (Chapel Hill: Univ. of North Carolina Press, 2001), esp. pp. 123–202.

and new forms of trade, as merchants, professionals, and artisans became bunched in village centers. Village greens and town commons were either spruced up or carved out for the first time to accommodate meeting houses and churches, which were remodeled or moved from peripheral areas, painted white, and topped with spires. Winding roads were straightened and paved, and town greens fenced to keep loungers safe from wandering pigs and cows.[81]

Yankeedom, observes a recent historian of New England culture, also found its way into the work of popular artists and regional writers. Harriet Beecher Stowe made the Yankee village the center of her nostalgic *Old-Town Folks* (1869), with its sentimentalized Yankee figures and concession to paternalism in the character Primus King, one of the few African Americans in town and a suitably deferential one. King, a former whaler, is a giant of man, built for manual labor and little else, and always at the ready to help a Yankee in need.[82] The "village manner" also informed "The Village Blacksmith" by the middlebrow poet Henry Wadsworth Longfellow, who, it should be recalled, was a self-described fellow traveler of antislavery. Longfellow's celebration of the sturdy village artisan contributed mightily to the sacralization of the New England village by embedding his iconic tradesman in the history of the town and its defining institutions. His smithy works under the "spreading chestnut tree," a metaphor for rooted strength; he goes to church on the Sabbath; he becomes an object of fascination for schoolchildren (who "Look in the open door; / They love to see the flaming forge, / And the bellows roar"), and weeps over his mother's grave in the nearby burial ground. He is no recent migrant but a longtime resident born in the same place as his parents and certain to be buried next to them. He is not an opportunistic entrepreneur but a stolid village mechanic, as well as a citizen, a father, and a neighbor.

The sacralization of the New England village also crept into political discourse and often without partisan implications, for it was a free-floating resource, widely available to all. One did not have to be a nostalgic Whig or a corn-fed Free Soiler to appreciate a John Barber etching or read Stowe or Longfellow. Everyone in public life, regardless of party, laid claim to small-town origins or expressed reverence for the New England

---

[81] Conforti, *Imagining New England*, pp. 124–44; Joseph Wood, *The New England Village* (Baltimore: Johns Hopkins Univ. Press, 1997); and John Stilgoe, "Town Common and Village Green in New England, 1620–1981," in Ronald L. Fleming and Lauri A. Halderman, eds., *On Common Ground* (Cambridge: Harvard Univ. Press, 1982), pp. 7–36.

[82] Conforti, *Imagining New England*, pp. 144–50.

village, just as modern-day politicians claim to have come up from small beginnings. Such an identity made them seem more virtuous and certainly more endearing to ordinary people. Yankeedom and the country had a wide political compass. Nonetheless, the metaphors of the country had special resonance for Free Soilers and their Democratic allies. The same country politicians who saw Yankee ingenuity as the signature of their region denied that their precious villages had anything to do with entrepreneurship, anticipating the idyllic setting later depicted by Stowe. Amasa Walker could easily have written *Old-Town Folks*. A resident at midcentury of the Worcester County village of West Brookfield, Walker traced his family to the founders of Massachusetts Bay Colony.[83] Unlike their progeny, however, he was a Democrat (turned Coalitionist) and one of the only Jacksonians invited to the podium of the People's Convention. Walker was also a leading voice for the country at the constitutional convention of 1853. A learned man with a Harvard education and an able political economist, Walker nonetheless sounded more like an ordinary Yankee idealist when he spoke of the country. He waxed rhapsodic about the New England town at the constitutional convention, explaining to fellow delegates that election days in the backlands doubled as market days. "We have no change houses no change hours; but at these country town meetings we get together and make trades, the constables collect their taxes, the farmer swap oxen, and the people exchange sentiments upon the various subjects connected with their businesses."[84]

Country idelogues were quick to distinguish the feel and spirit of the town from ethos of the city. Urban places, said the Free Soiler Richard Henry Dana, had their own amenities and even "advantages" precisely because they were created for "pecuniary purposes" and as a result attracted *parvenus* impatient for worldly success.[85] The cities were made by capitalists for capitalism. The Commonwealth's "sacred hamlets," by contrast, moved more slowly and to more civil rhythms suited to "quiet, sober and second thought."[86] They were stable places with like-minded residents not very different from one another and proud of their traditions in common – havens, as it were, from the hurly-burly of the metropole.

This invented image of the Yankee town carried over to conventional holidays and celebrations. Nothing was more "Yankee" than

---

[83] Dumas Malone, ed., *Dictionary of American Biography,* 20 vols. (New York: C. Scribner's Sons, 1928–36), 10: 338–9.
[84] *Constitutional Convention,* 1: 237–44. Quote is on p. 238.
[85] Ibid., 1: 948.
[86] Ibid.

Thanksgiving, the oldest American holiday, traditionally celebrated in early December until changed to late November. This "King and high priest of all festivals," as Harriet Beecher Stowe called it, originating as one of many "days of thanksgiving" ordered by early clergymen, became associated in the eighteenth century with the abundance of the harvest season. Worshippers spent the morning in church for a traditional homily before settling down to the family table. By the early nineteenth century, this familial dimension had been transformed into a homecoming, a time when the sons and daughters of the New England exodus returned to visit aging parents and loved ones.[87] The nature of Thanksgiving also became contested as different groups vied to put their own stamp upon it. Whiggish clergy and journalists used pulpit and column to honor Pilgrim forebears, thank the Lord for his bounty, and celebrate the warmth and comfort of hearth and home.[88] The more socially conscious among them appealed to the wealthy to contribute food and fuel to the needy.[89] Some sounded a more explicitly political note now and again. The Whiggish editor of the *Hampshire Gazette* let slip his anti-Catholic nativism in his Thanksgiving Day message in 1846, lacing into the "devotees of a superstitious faith, and the slaves of a cunning and tyrannical priesthood."[90]

The country's fear of "the other" extended beyond Catholics. It included outsiders in general, who in the most extreme cases were seen as a "dangerous floating population." Samuel Houghton, who represented the Worcester County village of Sterling at the constitutional convention, went into a tirade over the prospect of recent migrants having the right to vote. It "would not be long before [such] a class of people might get control of town affairs into their own hands and undertake to vote away the money of property owners."[91] Foreigners and in-migrants to the village posed an especially strong threat to Houghton, in part because the old remedy of warning out (the practice of expelling nonresidents) had lapsed; for generations it had provided towns with their own immigration

[87] Jack Larkin, *The Reshaping of Everyday Life, 1790–1840* (New York: Harper and Row, 1988), p. 273; Conforti, *Imagining New England*, pp. 49, 75, and 76; and John D. Seelye, *Memory's Nation: The Place of Plymouth Rock* (Chapel Hill: Univ. of North Carolina Press, 1998), pp. 17, 379, 361–2, and 379.

[88] See, for instance, *HG*, Dec. 5, 1821, and Nov. 24, 1846; *NC*, Dec, 1, 1830, Nov. 11, 1846, and Nov. 11, 1847.

[89] *NC*, Dec. 1, 1830, Nov. 27, 1847, and Nov. 28, 1848. Also *GGC*, Nov. 26, 1849.

[90] *HG*, Nov. 24, 1846.

[91] *Constitutional Convention*, 1: 571.

policy and border police, which had given the towns some control over their social compositions, not to mention their economic destinies. After all, the town that limited in-migration also restricted the supply of labor, slowing down economic growth and keeping the village unsullied by the factory and its attendant pathologies. This system, however, had long fallen into disuse by the time Houghton and his fellow delegates gathered in Worcester to fix the state constitution.[92]

Ironically, the country's flinty inhospitality to outsiders did not necessarily carry over to African Americans. In his "Thanksgiving Proclamation" in 1849, for instance, Governor Briggs called for charity to the poor in the hope that "the Lord will hasten the time when, without discord of violence, slavery shall cease to exist within these United States." Lest anyone confuse this sentiment with abolitionism or racial equality, the governor ended with an oblique if unmistakable reference to colonization by expressing his hope for the Christianization of a "disenthralled and regenerated Africa."[93] Such exclusionist rhetoric was common and has lead several recent scholars to argue that for all their bluster about their cultural uniqueness, village New Englanders shared the same racist views as the rest of the nation. David Jaffee observes that the makeover of New England culture evident in town celebrations of the period sometimes carried remorse for the treatment of Native Americans but overlooked African Americans. The radical reformer Ezra Haywood learned as much when, in 1859, he disrupted a commemoration in his native Princeton, Massachusetts, with a fiery intervention that uncovered a local antislavery tradition linking the town to the notorious John Brown. The chroniclers of the event got the last word, however, by appending a note to their coverage that corrected Haywood's revisionism and attacked him for "unwarranted . . . trespass upon the proprieties of the occasion."[94] Joanne Pope Melish pushes this theme of village racism a step farther. In her view, white racism was central to developing a sense of "New England Nationalism," a perspective fully consonant with the program of the colonization movement aimed at effacing the black presence by abolishing slavery and then deporting former slaves. The failure of colonization's

---

[92] Richard B. Morris, *Government and Labor in Early America* (New York: Columbia Univ. Press, 1946), p. 14; William E. Nelson, *Americanization of the Common Law: The Impact of Legal Change on Massachusetts Society, 1760–1830* (Cambridge: Harvard Univ. Press, 1975), pp. 15–17, and 188, n. 24; and Barry Levy, "Poor Children and the Labor Market in Colonial Massachusetts," *PH* 64 (Summer 1997): 287–307.

[93] *GAR*, Nov. 26, 1849.

[94] Jaffee, *People of the Wachusett*, pp. 245–8. Quote is on p. 248.

promise, however, made blacks more vulnerable because they "seemed to be unwelcome survivors of an emancipation process that was supposed to have eliminated them."[95]

It is more helpful to imagine Yankee politics on the spectrum of paternalism and exclusionism, shaped by local and national politics, and not as a single, proscriptive force with a life of its own. Exclusionism and paternalism drew strength from each other as tensions over slavery in national politics excited local passions. Bay State Democrats became more openly and viciously racist once they lost their antislavery faction to the Free Soilers and as sectional tensions waxed and waned. In addition, party stalwarts used race to strengthen their ties with the South damaged by the Mexican War and to project themselves as the racist answer to the racial toleration of Free Soilism. This rightward drift on race by the Democracy allowed the Free Soilers to seize the higher moral ground of racial moderation and to campaign on a platform of equal rights regardless of race. Theirs was not complete egalitarianism, as we shall shortly see, but close enough to provide a firm political alternative. Put another way, Free Soilers in Massachusetts were not another racist force distinguished from the Democracy only by their opposition to the spread of slavery. Both parties had broad groups of segregationists in the middle of the spectrum, which shaded into exclusionism on the Democratic side and into paternalism on the Free Soil side. It was this paternalism that attracted the black civil rights activists William Cooper Nell and William J. Watkins, among others, to the Free Soil Party.

Paternalists tried to infuse popular culture with their idea of civil rights. This was no easy task, for as the historian John Seelye demonstrates, antislavery activists found it hard before 1840 or so to lay claim to the region's commemorative conventions. Thanksgiving had long been in the hands of the most conservative elements in the press, in politics, and especially in the pulpit.[96] But just as the Libertyites and then the Free Soilers challenged established political authority in the 1840s, so did they begin to take aim at the icons of culture. Thomas Wentworth Higginson and other movement luminaries began to deliver their own holiday homilies laced with antislavery élan and its companionate racial paternalism.[97] Ordinary people soon expected clergymen to pay homage to abolitionism in their

---

[95] Melish, *Disowning Slavery*, esp. pp. 164–5. Quote is on p. 164.
[96] Seelye, *Memory's Nation*, pp. 142–3, 201–6, and 221–2.
[97] Tilden Edelstein, *Strange Enthusiasm: A Life of Thomas Wentworth Higginson* (New Haven, Conn.: Yale Univ. Press, 1968), pp. 88–9, and *NC*, Dec. 5, 1848.

sermons.[98] This tendency became more pronounced at the turn of the decade in the space between the end of the Mexican War and the debut of Free Soilism.[99] In his 1848 Thanksgiving Day column, the editor of the *Northampton Courier* asked his readers to remember the "oppressed and enslaved" in the South, as well as the poor and unfortunate in their midst.[100] Three years later, in the aftermath of the turmoil over the capture of the fugitive slaves Shadrach Minkins and Thomas Sims, he thanked "the Almighty" for his own health and prosperity and saluted fellow Free Soilers for "enlisting under the banner of progress" in the name of "the annihilation of slave territory, and the utter absorption of all slavery in the vortex of universal freedom."[101]

For antislavery activists it was a short step from embracing Thanksgiving to counting the holiday's founders as one of their own. They pulled off this unlikely appropriation in the course of celebrating Forefathers' Day. This holiday, which anticipated the rites and rituals of Thanksgiving, was started by a group of Plymouth patriots in the heat of the prerevolutionary ardor of the 1760s to mark the landing of the Pilgrims in 1620. Whiggish celebrants, who revived Forefathers' Day ceremonies in the 1830s following a long fallow period, remade their Pilgrim ancestors into Yankee entrepreneurs.[102] They in turn were challenged in 1849 by a mix of "new org" and "old org" men invited by the Old Colony Anti-Slavery Society for a two-day festival honoring the 229th anniversary of "the landing." The celebration was held in the spacious and graceful church on the Plymouth green – the first house of worship in the nation's hometown. Featured speaker Wendell Phillips rewrote the Puritan past in a few moments of astonishing historical revisionism. Never mind the Puritan legacy of religious intolerance and sectarian persecution. "Whatever may have been the views of the Puritan on particular points, he was emphatically the radical reformer of his day, in favor of the largest liberality and widest toleration of which his age had conceived." For the colonists' complicity with slavery, Phillips gave his audience a lesson in revisionist circularity. He first defined the contemporaneous "Anti-Slavery enterprise" as

---

[98] See letter of "J. C.," *Lib*, Dec. 5, 1845. Also letter by Seth Hunt, *NC*, Nov. 28 and Dec. 5, 1848.

[99] See, for instance, Edelstein, *Strange Enthusiasm*, pp. 88–9; *Lib*, Dec. 5, 1845; and *NC*, Nov. 28, 1848.

[100] *NC*, Nov. 28, 1848.

[101] Ibid., Nov. 25, 1851.

[102] Conforti, *Imagining New England*, p. 188. On Forefathers' Day, see Seelye, *Memory's Nation*, pp. 42–6, 54–9, 61–4, 101–3, and 110–13.

the lineal descendant of New England's Founders – Pilgrims and Puritans alike. And since this was the first Forefathers' Day celebration to recognize that continuity, it was also the "first real celebration" of "the landing." He then backed off a bit by conceding the possibility that "our forefathers brought slavery here." If so, it was the "duty" of their "sons" to "undo their evil work." But the Brahmin rebel quickly returned to his initial premise, declaring that "if those old men were haters of bondage, then also it is the first duty of us, their proud sons, to honor their memory by bearing a constant protest against it and keeping the land pure as they left it to us."[103] So much for New England's legacy of slavery.

If Yankees were so virtuous, why were they not more powerful in their own state? Country politicians and cracker-barrel pundits asked themselves this question again and again in the 1840s and with deepening distress, as the power of the backlands seemed to diminish with every passing year. These men were not necessarily affiliated with a movement in quite the same manner as workers or temperance advocates. Some may well have been recruits in the "Cold Water Army," but few belonged to movements outside of politics to bring about reform. They instead represented an interest – something short of a formal movement – largely regional in scope and political from the start. Its voice was Whiting Griswold, from the shire town of Greenfield in Franklin County. Griswold did not attend the People's Convention in 1848, for he was at the time a Democrat and steadfastly loyal to his party. A year later, however, he single-handedly designed the political reforms in the name of the country that sealed the pact between the Democrats and Free Soilers.

Whiting Griswold was an unlikely Moses leading his people out of the political wilderness. Born in 1814 on a small farm in the remote Franklin County hill town of Buckland, he graduated from Amherst College in 1838, and then taught school and edited a local paper before opening a law practice in Greenfield. A fellow lawyer described him as an "ardent politician" who achieved no particular distinction before 1848, when he served the first of his five terms in the State House.[104] Five years and several legislative terms later he still sounded very much the backlander

---

[103] *Lib*, Dec. 28, 1849. Also see Seelye, *Memory's Nation*, pp. 148–50 and 220–5.

[104] Francis M. Thompson, *History of Greenfield, Shire Town of Franklin County, Massachusetts*, 4 vols. (Greenfield, Mass.: T. Morey and Son, 1904), 2: 806–7 and 1199. Also see Paul Jenkins, *The Conservative Rebel: A Social History of Greenfield, Massachusetts* (Greenfield, Mass.: Town of Greenfield, 1982), esp. pp. 100–20 and passim.

FIGURE 20. Whiting Griswold. (*Greenfield Gazette*, centennial edition, Feb. 1, 1902, p. 36.)

cowering before urban sophisticates. The prospect of debating the eminent jurist and Whig potentate Rufus Choate at the constitutional convention appears to have buckled his knees. Nervously rising for his initial speech at the convention, the country lawyer called the omniscient judge the man "we all look (to) for the ripest specimens of learning, eloquence, and power."[105] Such deference, however, may well have been tactical, for Griswold had already formulated a grand program to deliver the country from the thrall of city Whigs like Choate.

---

[105] *Constitutional Convention*, 1: 810.

Griswold's moment of fame came in summer 1849 when he first called for reapportionment. His program got nowhere in the legislature because of implacable opposition from the Whig majority. Undeterred, Griswold soldiered on in the State House over the next few years without much success, then saw a more promising opportunity at the constitutional convention in 1853 where he made his case before a more sympathetic audience. He argued in essence that the current apportionment system was rigged against the country. The town system of representation, which had historically guaranteed that each village, no matter how small, would be represented in the legislature, had been severely compromised. A measure proposed by the Whigs in the mid-1830s, modified by lawmakers, and then approved by the voters in an 1840 referendum produced what Griswold derisively referred to as "partial representation." Under it, towns with 1,200 or more residents qualified for at least one representative each year; smaller towns were entitled to a single representative for as many years as the number 160 divided into their population as a whole. A place with 320 people got two years of representation over a decade, those with 480 people got three years, and so on. Griswold charged that the formula devised to calculate legislative reapportionment based on the decennial federal census was needlessly complicated and even more unfair to the country because it raised the threshold for a single representative and instituted partial representation as well. He also denounced the "general ticket" system in urban elections – or what modern Americans know as at-large, winner-take-all elections – as egregiously tilted toward the Whigs. At-large contests in places like Boston guaranteed that Whigs would win and also that they would grab *all* seats in the yearly race for the House of Representatives. The general ticket rule explained why the Boston delegation of some forty representatives at midcentury consisted exclusively of Whigs.[106]

Griswold struck a blow at Whiggish hegemony with a package of reforms that would enhance the power of the country at the expense of the city. First, it "restored" the town as the basis of representation, so that each town, regardless of size, would get at least one representative in the state assembly year after year. Second, it reconfigured apportionment for urban places. Cities and towns would get an additional representative up to a maximum of thirty for every 5,000 residents. Finally, it substituted "district" voting in cities for the general ticket. While it is impossible to predict the magnitude of the change that district voting would have produced,

---

[106] Ibid., 1: 89–90 and 809–21.

there is no question that Griswold's proposal would have resulted in a massive transfer of political power to the country. Suffolk County, the home of Boston, would lose fifteen representatives, fully a third of its delegation, while Essex and Norfolk counties, which flanked the capital to its north and south, would lose three more. The five westernmost counties, however, would gain thirty-one seats, with the heaviest additions coming in the most remote counties of Franklin (nine) and Berkshire (eight).[107] The country had lashed back.

How did the country faction justify such a breathtaking reform? Griswold and his friends put forth a spirited defense that turned on a few basic themes. As Griswold declared in his opening speech at the constitutional convention, the nub of the problem for the country was "partial representation" adopted by the legislature in the mid-1830s and then ratified by popular referendum. True enough, the people had consented to the handiwork of the politicians on what Griswold called that "fatal day" in 1840 when they approved the referendum on reapportionment. The people voted that way, however, because they "did not understand the proposition submitted to them."[108] They were not simply confused; they had been hoodwinked, tricked by the wily, fast-talking hacks and hucksters from the city. Having charged fraud and deception, Griswold did his part for sanctifying the New England town. He and his friends went beyond earlier writers who had celebrated the village largely as a cultural place with its own spatial arrangements, architectural forms, and institutional patterns. They focused on the political, arguing that village culture underpinned the distinctive practices of republicanism. Griswold insisted that just as the town engendered "a strong natural tendency ... to equality and republicanism," so "town government" reflected "pure democracy" through the agency of its beloved town meeting.[109] This was not necessarily new; it had been implied all along by various writers. Few, however, put it so boldly or searched harder for intellectual confirmation. Country politician though he was, the Greenfielder drew upon no less an authority than Alexis de Tocqueville in what may well have been one of the first references to *Democracy in America*. He freely cited the Frenchman's observations that "local assemblies" of ordinary citizens inculcated feelings of "independence and authority" essential to the "spirit of liberty" and also to public order because the "passions that normally embroil society

---

[107] Computed from Journal of the House of Representatives, List of the Members of the House, 1850 and 1853, mss., Massachusetts State Archives, Boston.

[108] *Constitutional Convention*, 1: 812.

[109] Ibid., 1: 824–5.

change their character when they find a vent so near the domestic hearth and family circle." Local bodies were, in addition, reliable instruments of self-rule because they provided opportunities for homegrown men of political talent who sought office out of duty and not out of a lust for power or status. This "local public spirit" was stronger in the United States than in Europe and strongest in New England. There, Tocqueville said, in an outpouring of sentiment, the "native" was "attached to his township because it is independent and free; his co-operation in its affairs assures his attachment to its interests; the well-being it affords him secures his affection; and its welfare is the aim of his ambitions and of his future exertions; he takes a part in every occurrence ... practices the art of government in the small sphere ... accustoms himself to those forms which can alone secure the steady progress of liberty."[110] Picking up on this theme, Griswold intoned that town government was the guarantor not simply of republicanism but also of democracy, which was why a Whig proposal to substitute population (and political districts) for towns as the basis of representation was so dangerous; towns were the sine qua non of New England culture, offering a unique way of life that now stood endangered for the machinations of urban grandees and satraps.

The New England exodus only enhanced Whiggish power. The population drain of recent years, which sent streams of village youth to the city and the West, necessarily strengthened the city at the expense of the country. As if to underline the deeper implications of this troubling trend, Griswold again turned to Tocqueville, who had said that village "patriotism" sustained a healthy suspicion of the "centralization" of power in America and more particularly in New England where local affinities were older and more deeply felt.[111] He did not know it, but the august Frenchman provided the country lawyer with his battle cry. "Centralization!" became the slogan of the country in its war against the railways and factories that lured its sons and daughters to the insidious centers of political power. Whiggish treachery in politics only made the exodus worse. The Whigs may have deceived the people of the country on the "fatal day" in 1840. No longer.

Elizur Wright was likely mistaken when he estimated that "fifty thousand might have ... assembled" at Worcester for the People's Convention.[112]

---

[110] Ibid., 1: 827–8.
[111] Ibid., 1: 830.
[112] *DC*, June 30, 1848.

But he still had reason to be encouraged by the turnout and what that represented. Ever since he had repudiated the single-issue, moral suasionist program of the Garrisonians in the mid-1830s, Wright had dreamed of an antislavery party supported by the "middle ground." Along with other abolitionists, he had come around to the position that single-issue abolitionism was too parochial, that it would have to be paired with other reforms if the movement was to grow. It would have to be eclectic. His Liberty Party, for all its promise, had come up short. It had attracted some labor activists like himself and possibly a larger number of temperance enthusiasts, but it had remained pretty much a single-cause formation firmly controlled by one-issue men like Joshua Leavitt. The demise of the Liberty Party in 1847, however, did not sink the one-idea ship. The party's Free Soil successor not only took on Leavitt and his allies, it also drew in former Conscience Whigs whose perspective was of a piece with Leavitt's. The difference was that the Free Soilers faced a much greater challenge than Leavitt had met at the helm of the old party. The new party ranged far beyond Libertyism by embracing a patchwork of reform movements and interest groups. Cautious men like Charles Francis Adams recoiled from the local and state issues driven by the laborist politics of places like Lowell or the populist politics of the country. Their gaze was fixed on the politics of slavery at the national level.

Another tendency fused antislavery with civil rights. This tendency was reflected at the state convention of the Free Soil Party in 1849, a year after the party was formed and a year before its coalition with the Democrats was formalized, in a speech by the main speaker, Anson Burlingame of Boston. Burlingame was something of an oddity in Bay State politics because, like Chauncey Langdon Knapp, he was born outside the state – in a small town in upstate New York. His family moved to Ohio when he was a youth and then to Michigan where young Burlingame attended the University of Michigan. He left for Boston in 1843 at age twenty-three to attend Harvard Law School, joining the law firm of George P. Briggs, the son of the popular Whig governor, George N. Briggs, soon after graduation. He would be elected to the Senate in 1852 on the Free Soil ticket, and then serve three consecutive terms in Congress, first as a Know-Nothing and later as a Republican.[113] (In 1868, as minister to China, he would negotiate the treaty bearing his name that opened U.S. trade and

---

[113] On Burlingame, see Dumas Malone, ed., *Dictionary of American Biography*, 20 vols. (New York: C. Scribner's Sons, 1928–36), 2: 289–90.

immigration with China.)[114] An energetic and articulate man, Burlingame was also a spell-binding orator, a favorite of Free Soil voters on the stump. He delivered an electrifying speech at the state convention in 1849.

Burlingame echoed the party's position on civil rights and slavery in an entertaining speech rich in the local color of Yankeedom. He told the crowd that if a "slaveholder" were to visit Lowell, the "New England Manchester," by train and find in "the cars a person with…black skin" and does not "choose" to ride "in the same car with him [,] let him walk to Lowell on foot." He then covered the idea of slavery as an antifamily force, a theme, as we have already seen, developed by women abolitionists in the 1830s. If the slaveholder made it to Lowell, said Burlingame, and asked to be introduced to "wives and daughters" there, say "No! say a man who sells wives and daughters shall not be intrusted with the honor of our home." He also explained how Free Soilers would bring down slavery. We will "study our principles by the light of day, and we will write them down by the midnight lamp…preach them in Conventions – in Lyceums – in short, we will kindle every fireside in the land which invades the sacred ties of domestic life." "Pulpits," too, will "thunder against it." "Our historians," he added, "will write against it." But the historians would be preceded by "Our poets – ay, Our poets – Slavery never had a poet [Enthusiastic applause] – they shall write a loftier strain" because they were "not only with us in sentiment, but with us in organization –. Our Bryant, and Longfellow, and Lowell." Then some in the crowd shouted "Whittier," and Burlingame responded, "[A]y, and Whittier, with his heart of oak and tongue of fire. Whittier is here."[115]

When Burlingame's paean to Yankeedom ended and the cheering stopped, more pragmatic leaders, like Henry Wilson, knew that antislavery and civil rights were not enough. The party would have to broaden its horizon to compromise with the constitutents of political reform. The Free Soilers would try in the General Court to strike a balance between national and local issues. Their balancing strategy was enshrined in the resolutions adopted at the 1849 party meeting immediately after Burlingame sat down. The resolutions railed against slavery in the familiar language of the Slave Power thesis, and maintained that the "laws and Constitution of the United States, know no distinction of color." Toward the end, however, the address drew attention to "Local Matters," in the distinctive

[114] Andrew Eyory, *Closing the gate: Race, Politics, and the Chinese Exclusion Act* (Chapel Hill, N.C.: Univ. of North Carolina Press, 1998); 26–8.
[115] *NC*, Sept. 18, 1849; Also Sept. 25 and Oct. 2, 1849.

language of the country. It took aim at a "large number of Corporations" chartered by the legislature that exerted "influence" over "political affairs, dispensing a patronage exceeding that of the Federal Government." Such economic behemoths were no friends of "*Freedom*," for they "embodied the Money-Power of the Commonwealth. The instinct of property has proved stronger in Massachusetts than the instinct of Freedom." Even worse, the "Money-Power has joined hands with the Slave-Power. Selfish, grasping, subtle, tyrannical like its ally, it will not brook opposition." The "natural influence" of the "Money-Power," asserted the Address in drawing a stronger link between local and national affairs, "is ... further increased" by the corrupt electoral system in the Commonwealth – the general ticket of the cities that returned "compact delegation[s], united in political opinions, while the country, through the divisions into small towns," was fragmented "into districts, and chooses representatives differing in opinions." "The large cities," it concluded, "which are the seat of the Money Power, are thus able, through a minority, to control the State."[116]

Four years before Whiting Griswold addressed the constitutional convention, the Free Soil Party embraced his program. Because of him – and its strength in the country – the party had to be attentive to State Reform. This meant a cluster of populist economic and political policies as well as moral reforms associated with Yankeedom, along with demands raised by workers for shorter workdays and African Americans for protection from slave catchers and for civil rights.[117] This sprawling agenda of State Reform in conjunction with antislavery made Free Soilism a broader "middle ground" and more formidable force than Libertyism. It also made it a more fragile one.

[116] *NC*, Oct. 2, 1849.
[117] Sweeney, "Rum, Romanism, and Reform," p. 116.

6

"Our Own Time"

Free Soilers and Labor Reformers

It was difficult to find more confident political elites in antebellum America than the Boston Associates. Perhaps this confidence came from their great wealth or their strategic marriages entangling families into the most cohesive elite in the North, and possibly in the nation.[1] The weakness of the opposition doubtless helped too. Nonetheless, Bay State Whigs still confronted the same problem as their counterparts everywhere of how to maintain control in a political democracy. Control did not come naturally; instead, it was a project that had to be achieved, often by using underlings and political surrogates. Their men in the State House included Julius Rockwell, a former bobbin boy who made good on Brahmin patronage, so good that he served several terms as speaker.[2] Rockwell gives us a rare glimpse into how Whigs subverted reform. He told the Worcesterite John Davis in 1836 that unexpected turnover in the composition of the House had alarmed "some persons. Apprehensions were expressed . . . that this legislature would assume a character bordering on the revolutionary" if the "advocates of political changes" got their way. Such fears, he coolly assured Davis, were entirely unfounded. "I have never for a moment entertained such an apprehension," wrote the crafty political boss, explaining

---

[1] Robert F. Dalzell, Jr., *Enterprising Elite: The Boston Associates and the World They Made* (Cambridge: Harvard Univ. Press, 1987); Ronald D. Story, *The Forging of an Aristocracy: Harvard and the Boston Upper Class, 1800–1870* (Middletown, Conn.: Wesleyan Univ. Press, 1980); and Thomas H. O'Connor, *Lords of the Loom: The Cotton Whigs and the Coming of the Civil War* (New York: Charles Scribner's Sons, 1968).

[2] On Rockwell, see *MS*, Jan. 14, 1835.

that he had things well in hand by enforcing party unity and by burying unwanted bills in committee.[3]

Such deft floor management, however, did not matter in the early 1850s when the Coalition seized control of the State House. The insurgency not only hurled the regulars from power; it also blew the lid off the political cauldron, releasing pent-up pressure for a broad array of popular reforms long scuttled by Whig satraps. The Coalition of Free Soilers and Democrats, which began as an experiment in several districts in 1849, covered the entire state in the election of 1850 on the strength of a bargain concocted by party leaders. The insurgency extended beyond Democrats to country Whigs who had long nursed grievances over temperance legislation and political representation against their party's dominant urban wing. Thus the apprehensions that Rockwell had dismissed in 1836 were better grounded in 1850. The Coalition controlled the State House for the legislative sessions between 1851 and 1852, the longest period of non-Whig rule since the party was founded and one that would see an outpouring of reform initiatives. The revolt of the "outs," however, was never secure because of the dizzying political instability at the turn of the 1840s. In the 1849 election, when the anti-Whig parties had not yet formally allied, the Democrats and Free Soilers dealt the old party its greatest defeat, gaining commanding majorities in the House and Senate – or about thirty-five votes in the former and about eight in the latter. A year later, following the formalization of the alliance between Democrats and Free Soilers, the Coalition strengthened its hold on both bodies, with about a fifty vote advantage in the House and about a ten vote advantage in the senate. The Coalition slipped a bit in both houses in the 1851 election and then suffered a huge reversal in the 1852 poll, when many Democrats pulled out of the alliance. As a result, the Whigs regained control of both houses for the first time in three years.[4] The lusty rebellion of 1850–1 had been domesticated but not before severely weakening Second Party System.

The Coalition had a hand in its own undoing. The professional politicians at the Free Soil helm in the State House in 1851 nominated Charles

[3] Quoted in Ronald P. Formisano, *The Transformation of Political Culture: Massachusetts Parties, 1790s–1840s* (New York: Oxford Univ. Press, 1983), p. 341.

[4] This was compiled simply by counting the number of seats held by the various parties, 1850–3, as reflected in Journal of the House of Representatives, List of the Members of the House, mss., 1850–1853, Massachusetts State Archives, Boston. Also see Kevin J. Sweeney," Rum, Romanism, Representation, and Reform: Coalition Politics in Massachusetts, 1847–1853," CWH 6 (June 1976): 116–37, Tables II and III, p. 121.

Sumner for the U.S. Senate with the expectation of Democratic support but in violation of the deal limiting the spoils of office to "state" positions only. Pro-Southern Democrats, now led by the imperious Caleb Cushing and never pleased with the Coalition itself, could not bear the thought of voting for such a man as Sumner.[5] Sumner's election over their objections opened a wound that still festered a year later when a highly controversial Maine Law passed the legislature sharply divided between Whigs and Democrats.[6] The Democracy also deftly exploited the politics of race, which were elevated to fever pitch by the commotion in Boston and provincial towns over enforcement of the Fugitive Slave Act and over the Coalition's attempt to strengthen the 1843 Personal Liberty Law. Growing numbers of Democratic candidates for state office in 1852, angered by the Free Soilers' racial liberalism, withdrew from the Coalition to run under their party's banner.[7] If this were not enough, Bay State Whiggery got a sudden lift from George Morey, the avuncular state leader who set out to restore his party in the industrial districts. Responding to his plans, party operatives in Boston and Lowell campaigned as friends of the ten-hour day, a stunning reversal that played very well indeed.[8] This pincer movement of revivified Democracy and surging Whiggery squeezed much of the life out of what remained of the Coalition.

The Coalition both reinforced and reconfigured the Commonwealth's political map. To demonstrate this dual pattern, I divided cities and towns into four categories: Boston, county seats, industrial towns, and country towns. Urban Whigs survived the Free Soil insurgency largely intact not only because of the general ticket rule but also because of their residual hold on voter loyalty. Few Bostonians in 1850 could remember when they were represented by anyone other than a Whig; fewer still could imagine an alternative. Whigs routinely claimed every representative in the House – 35 delegates in 1850 and 45 in 1853. Bostonians were so attached to their party that in 1856, two years after it was said to have been wiped out, some three-fourths of the Boston delegation identified

---

5 William F. Hartford, *Money, Morals, and Politics: Massachusetts in the Age of the Boston Associates* (Boston: Northeastern Univ. Press, 2001), pp. 119–47; Ernest A. McKay, "Henry Wilson and the Coalition of 1851," *NEQ* 36 (Sept. 1963): 338–57; Martin Duberman, "Behind the Scenes as the Massachusetts 'Coalition' of 1851 Divides the Spoils," *EIHC* 99 (April 1963): 152–60; and David Herbert Donald, *Charles Sumner and the Coming of the Civil War* (New York: Fawcett Columbine, 1960), pp. 179–204.
6 See *NC*, Apr. 27, 1852.
7 Hartford, *Money, Morals, and Politics*, pp. 180–90.
8 *LA*, Nov. 6, 1852.

themselves as Whigs![9] The old party proved nearly as impregnable in the Commonwealth's thirteen shire towns, which served as commercial nodes as well as administrative centers, where it lost only a few seats. In 1850, Whigs controlled 21 of the 26 seats in the county seats; in 1853, they controlled 19 of 29. The exception was Worcester, and this is instructive. In the self-styled "heart of the commonwealth" voters returned a solid bloc of Free Soilers in 1850 and, three years later, divided between Free Soilers and Democrats, ending a decade and a half of unbroken Whig rule. Workers and their allies in the leading shoe and textile cities followed suit, giving Free Soilism strong pluralities and a solid base in the industrial core. In 1850 Whigs had 25 seats as against 16 for the Free Soilers and 3 for the Democrats. This slight plurality eroded over the next three years, as the Whigs lost a thumping 16 seats to their rivals in the industrial heartland of the Commonwealth and never rebounded there. Instead, the industrial cities shifted by 1853 from Whiggery to the opposition of Free Soilers and Democrats, who shared 30 seats.[10]

The vote in the country towns showed a different pattern. This region, which had split between Whigs (in the more prosperous places) and Democrats (in the poorer ones), moved to the Free Soilers but not for long. The insurgents' grip on the country was no more secure than Whiggery's hold on the shoe and textile towns. Indeed, insurgency's dominance in the country proved remarkably fleeting, as can be seen by examining the vote in the country towns in the state's five most rural counties: Worcester, Hampshire, Hamden, Franklin, and Berkshire. Free Soilism had pluralities in every one of these counties except Hampshire in 1850. But three years later, the country accounted for the party's most striking defeats. Free Soilism waned in all five counties, shedding over twenty seats in the House by 1853. Democrats gained an equal number of towns in this period, building on its resurgence in the industrial districts. It was the Whigs, however, who sprung the biggest surprise. Even though the party was about to collapse completely in the Know-Nothing landslide of 1854, it rebounded noticeably beforehand, gaining a respectable twelve House seats. Democrats and Whigs had taken back the country at the expense of the Free Soilers, whose base had shrunk to the industrial cities.[11]

[9] Journal of the House of Representatives, List of the members of the House, mss., 1856, Massachusetts State Archives, Boston.
[10] Ibid, 1850 and 1853.
[11] Ibid.

This reconfiguration of the political landscape, then, had three dimensions between 1850 and 1853. First, Free Soilism surged everywhere outside of the cities – Boston and the county seats – but persisted chiefly in industrial towns. It was not a rural movement, as is often assumed, but neither was it an urban one; it was more accurately an urban-industrial phenomenon. Second, the Democracy made headway in cities but also resurged in the country. It would briefly become a contender in state politics partly on the strength of the Famine Generation of Irish immigrants streaming into the cities. Finally, Whigs lost their hegemony in factory towns but retained their grip on the commercial centers – Boston and the county seats; the Whigs also regrouped in the country, where they shared power with the Democrats.[12]

Erstwhile Conscience Whigs in Boston considered the election of Sumner their crowning achievement; indeed, many of them would have been satisfied if the legislature had done nothing else.[13] The fact is, however, that the Coalition left a much wider legacy from its brief reign, one that reflected the populism and laborism of State Reform. It established regulatory commissions to oversee railroads, banks, and insurance companies. It also substantially increased funding for public schools and for the newly formed network of asylums for the blind and "insane." This populist spirit transformed Harvard College, the most exclusive educational institution in the Commonwealth from the perspective of the country. It had been bad enough, in the eyes of the religious sects in the backlands, that Unitarians dominated Harvard's Board of Overseers; worse was that the board elected itself and thereby perpetuated Unitarian control, even though the college was for all practical purposes a public institution supported in part by taxpayers from trinitarian confessions. Much to the delight of the country and the popular sects everywhere, the Coalition "democratized" Harvard by transferring the appointment of its overseers to the legislature, ending what one village journalist called "sectarian and political exclusiveness."[14] As for laborism, the Coalition passed and then strengthened a mechanics' lien law and enacted a homestead exemption statute, two pet projects of workingmen and their middling allies that Whigs had sabotaged for years. The Coalition also tried without much success to reform the ancient doctrine of *feme covert*, which made women

---

[12] Hartford, *Money, Morals, and Politics*, pp. 183–90, and Sweeney, "Rum, Romanism, Representation, and Reform," pp. 129–34.

[13] Henry Wilson, *History of the Rise and Fall of the Slave Power in America*, 3 vols. (Boston: James R. Osgood, 1872–7), 2: 347.

[14] *NC*, Oct. 28, 1851, and Oct. 12, 1852. Also see *Comm*, May 27, 1851.

the legal wards of fathers and husbands, by granting married and single women rudimentary property rights.[15]

Three additional initiatives – the ten-hour workday, the secret ballot, and prohibition – merit extended treatment, the first one in this chapter and the others in the next one. The political battles attending these measures reveal the salience of State Reform and tell us something about the fit between political insurgency and popular social movements and about the contradictory impulses within the Coalition. Partisanship was an important line of division, for Whigs tended to stick together against the Coalition of Democrats and Free Soilers. That basic polarity, however, was complicated by another fissure separating the city from the country and cutting across the parties. It is important to add that State Reform was not the only imperative at work, for it played out within the broader context of tightening sectional tension over slavery. It was the interaction of these levels, not one or the other, that shaped state politics and the Coalition's work in particular. Slavery polarized the Commonwealth like nothing else had. It was the great specter that haunted Boston in the early 1850s, as planters and their agents, accompanied by U.S. marshals and armed with the hated Fugitive Slave Act, descended on the city to round up runaways in a fearsome display of federal power. Antislavery sentiment, in this context, could not help but have a great impact on state politics. Free Soil stalwarts in the Coalition reacted by trying to strengthen the state's Personal Liberty Law and by redoubling their efforts to make Charles Sumner a U.S. Senator. They encountered fierce opposition over Sumner from conservative Democrats and Cotton Whigs, who held the line against the scores of votes that stretched over three months in spring 1851, prevailing by a single one at the end of the legislative session.[16] The Coalition never completely recovered from the bruising fight over Sumner.

The recrudescent ten-hour movement at the turn of the 1840s came in stages. It began in small shops and some factories with negotiations between employee and employer and then moved into the political arena where it centered on factory workers alone. This pattern is easily explained. Craftsmen and industrial tradesmen like machinists vastly preferred working out their own trade agreements with employers over the

---

[15] Glendyne R. Wergland, "Women, Men, Property, and Inheritance: Gendered Testamentary Customs in Western Massachusetts, 1800–1860" (Ph.D. diss., Univ. of Massachusetts Amherst, 2001), pp. 122–26.

[16] Donald, *Charles Sumner and the Coming of the Civil War*, pp. 184–204.

intervention of government. When a master carpenter in 1852 told a meeting of his craft that it would be better to cut the hours of work "voluntarily" than to be "forced into it" by the state, he reflected a popular perspective rooted in trade tradition.[17] Voluntary agreements were also reinforced by village culture. John Greenleaf Whittier, a leading voice of the village, said he "prefer[red]" to see the ten-hour day arrive in local mills by "voluntary action of owners and directors."[18] Whittier and the craftsmen saw the alternative of legislative action as acceptable only for the weak and subordinate and as a last resort for everyone else – fine, that is, for dependent women and children, but not for men independent and strong enough to look out for themselves.

Artisans and craftsmen who pursued the struggle for shorter hours on the job found it to be slow and sticky going. Some benefited from comradely employers like Joseph Buckingham as well as Elizur Wright, who bragged that he not only honored the ten-hour day but also respected the Sabbath by giving his men Sundays off.[19] Affiliates of the New England Workingmen's Association got behind the futile ten-hour movement of women factory hands and had to settle for the compromise of extended dinner breaks. Local groups of mill hands and tradesmen in Salem and Lynn convinced employers to bend a bit, just as employers had in Worcester.[20] Their fellow workers in Boston and in the industrial belt, however, still put in eleven- and twelve-hour days when markets were up.

Two different but related drives, one in the sweated trades and the other in the respectable trades, ended the frustration. In July 1849 journeymen tailors in Boston walked out to increase their wages, but spurred a counterreaction by recalcitrant employers who started to blacklist members of the newly formed Journeymen Tailors' Union.[21] The workers attracted the attention of Elizur Wright, the only journalist in the city to cover their work stoppage. Wright's labor correspondent became the union's adviser, urging the workers to abandon both the strike and wage labor entirely by forming a cooperative.[22] The correspondent got help from Henry Trask,

[17] *BET*, Apr. 23, 1853.
[18] JGW to Harriet Farley, July 8, 1852, in John B. Pickard, ed., *The Letters of John Greenleaf Whittier*, 3 vols. (Cambridge: Harvard Univ. Press, 1975), 2: 192.
[19] *DC*, Nov. 4, 1850.
[20] Charles E. Persons, "The Early History of Factory Legislation in Massachusetts (from 1825 to the Passage of the Ten-Hour Law in 1874)," in Susan Kinsgbury, ed., *Labor Laws and Their Enforcement, with Special Reference to Massachusetts* (1911; New York: Arno Press, 1971), pp. 75–6.
[21] *DC*, July 22 and Aug. 22–24, 1849.
[22] Ibid., Sept. 11, 1849.

a journeyman carriage maker from Cambridgeport who had joined Brook Farm and then set up on his own in 1844 when that Associationist experiment failed.[23] Trask was a central figure in a group of working-class refugees from Fourierism who had given up on utopianism but not on its underlying ethic of cooperationism. In 1845 he figured prominently in a group of cooperationists with abolitionist sympathies who bolted the Boston Mutual Benefit Association to form the Workingmen's Protective Union, a labor reform group that promoted consumer cooperatives and cooperative workshops.[24] The consumer stage of their project caught on, as groceries and general stores sprouted through the region, mainly in industrial centers like Lowell, which supported eight such stores by 1850.[25]

The embattled tailors warmed to the entreaties of Trask and his friends, organizing their own shop by the end of September. The Journeymen Tailors' Clothing Store, and a branch shop opened later, had a full line of clothing for sale as well as an ambitious welfare plan for its members, including a building fund to erect low-cost housing.[26] Its work rules stated that "No member shall work more than *ten hours* a day until the whole members of our trade are brought into the Association. Should work become scarce, the hours of labor must be reduced so that every member . . . shall have an equal share of work."[27] The ten-hour day had come to the needle trades via cooperative production. Over the next few year, it would reach several other crafts, including printing, by the same route.[28]

The respectable crafts trod a more traditional path to a shorter workday. Building tradesmen had sat out the outburst of unionism known as the "Uprising of 1849–1850."[29] Three years later, however, in fall 1853, journeymen carpenters and other construction workmen mobilized for

---

[23] On Trask, see Carl J. Guarani, *The Utopian Alternative: Fourierism in Nineteenth-Century America* (Ithaca, N.Y..: Cornell Univ. Press, 1991), pp. 309–11.

[24] On the WMPU see ibid., pp. 309–20. Also, *DC*, Aug. 16 and 23, Sept. 9, 19–20, and Oct. 26 and 29, 1849, and *PU*, Jan. 12 and Mar. 30, 1850. Also see Edward Bemis, *Cooperation in New England* (Baltimore: Johns Hopkins Univ. Press, 1888).

[25] Brad Paul, "'The Harmonious Whole': Protective Unionism, Producer Cooperatives, and Massachusetts Labor" (seminar paper, Univ. of Massachusetts Amherst, 1995), esp. appendix.

[26] *DC*, Sept. 7 and 10, Oct. 1, and Nov. 2, 1849.

[27] Ibid., Sept. 19, 1849. Also see Guarani, *Utopian Alternative*, pp. 315–16, and Norman B. Ware, *The Industrial Worker, 1840–1860: The Reaction of American Industrial Society to the Advance of the Industrial Revolution* (1924; New York: Quadrangle, 1964), p. 195.

[28] *PU*, Mar. 3, 1850, and Guarani, *Utopian Alternative*, p. 316.

[29] Guarani, *Utopian Alternative*, p. 313.

another try at carving out more of "our own time," as they called it, stirring a broader movement in a number of trades. One tradesman reiterated the traditional arguments in behalf of the cause, declaring that workingmen needed time off from their jobs for relaxation and self-improvement. He added the ideological point that "all men are born free and equal, and consequently the mechanic has his rights as well as the employer [has] his," but the "master, or overseer can enjoy the privileges and comforts of the fireside, and avail himself of social and intellectual resources, while the hard working mechanic cannot."[30] The signs of unrest led the masters to discuss the "ten hour movement now agitating the community." Few of them agreed with Christopher Dupree, who strongly defended the "old system" of starting his crew at seven A.M. and working them "as long as they could see." Most seem to have endorsed the position of a self-described "small fry" who had already cut his crew's hours to ten.[31] The ten-hour day had finally taken hold in the building trades.

"Small fry" did not elaborate. Perhaps he thought of himself as a modernist tired of the old ways defended by Dupree. No doubt he had latitude to act because industrialists and merchant capitalists, who had long controlled the industry from the outside and had laid down the working conditions for masters and journeymen, were nowhere to be seen. They had withdrawn from housing construction, leaving the industry to jobbers and master craftsmen, at least some of whom abandoned the old "sun to sun" regimen. This structural change may well have had larger implications for the political fealties of small employers. In the era of merchant capitalism, small employers were not simply the virtual employees of financiers; they were also their political clients, men who knew that much could be gained from adopting the politics of their patrons. The new era of greater entrepreneurial freedom for small employers brought them more political flexibility and scope for independence. This may help explain why many master mechanics increasingly found Free Soilism more to their liking than Whiggery.

Factory owners in the new metal trades had troubles of their own. Their employees were the most skilled and well-paid workers in the Commonwealth, a sort of "labor aristocracy" whose standard of living set them apart from ordinary mill hands and even from most traditional

[30] *BET*, Mar. 16, 1853.
[31] Ibid., Apr. 23, 1853.

craftsmen.[32] In Worcester machinists, patternmakers, and kindred workers who had been at their trades for a while owned their own homes and boasted savings accounts.[33] Grinding poverty or even minimal comfort was not the lot of the antebellum machinist in the Bay State. He was the model of the respectable workman, who admired his boss and generally shared his employer's Whiggish politics.

Nonetheless, there were parallels between the experiences of textile operatives and of metalworkers. Like the first-generation textile operatives at Lowell and at scattered mill villages, metalworkers labored under flexible management. Their managers were former workmen who tended to stick to their jobs unless they set up on their own. The managers lived close to their workplaces and were tightly integrated into the localistic culture of the village. Sympathetic men who knew each worker personally, they also shared the worker-centered shop culture that the budding industrial engineer Frederick Winslow Taylor came to despise as a young man a generation later in a Pennsylvania steel mill.[34] They cut employees a great deal of slack on the job, allowing those on task work to carry on mostly at their own pace and winking when the workers stretched out morning and afternoon breaks or missed days because of personal business.[35] But just as the paternalism of cotton mills began to fade in the 1840s so did the supple management of the foundry and machine shop.

---

[32] The classic work on the British labor aristocracy is E. J. Hobsbawm, "The Labour Aristocracy in Nineteenth-Century Britain," in Hobsbawm, *Labouring Men: Studies in the History of Labour* (Garden City, N.Y.: Anchor Books, 1964), pp. 321–70. On the incomes of metalworkers in Worcester, see Bruce Laurie, "The 'Fair Field' of the 'Middle Ground': Abolitionism, Labor Reform, and the Making of an Antislavery Bloc in Antebellum Massachusetts," in Eric Arnesen, Julie Greene, and Bruce Laurie, eds., *Labor Histories: Class, Politics, and the Working-Class Experience* (Urbana: Univ. of Illinois Press, 1998), pp. 45–70. Also see David Montgomery, "Workers' Control of Machine Production in the Nineteenth Century," *LH* 17 (Fall 1976): 486–508.

[33] The Worcester leaders had $1,000 to $3,000 in real property at this time. *MS*, Feb. 19, 1852, and Oct. 1, 1853, and U.S. Census Bureau, *Seventh Census, Population Schedule for Worcester* (ms.), 1850.

[34] See Montgomery, "Workers' Control of Machine Production."

[35] On textile flexibility, see Mark Voss-Hubbard, *Beyond Party: Cultures of Antipartisanship in Northern Politics before the Civil War* (Baltimore: Johns Hopkins Univ. Press, 2002), pp. 25–9 and 82–3, and Thomas Dublin, *Women at Work: The Transformation of Work and Community in Lowell, Massachusetts, 1826–1860* (New York: Columbia Univ. Press, 1979), esp. 77–8. On metalworkers in Massachusetts, see Dan Clawson, *Bureaucracy and the Labor Process: The Transformation of U.S. Industry, 1860–1920* (New York: Monthly Review Press, 1980), and Bruce K. Tull, "Springfield Armory or Industrial Policy: Interchangeable Parts and the Precision Corridor" (Ph.D. diss., Univ. of Massachusetts, 2001).

Factory management stiffened with the retirement of the first-generation managers who had given textile paternalism its trademark permissiveness on the job and philanthropic spirit in civic affairs. In Whittier's Amesbury, Joshua Aubin, who put in thirty years as superintendent of the Amesbury Flannel Manufacturing Company, founded the local library and stocked its shelves with seven hundred volumes. His gifts also included Thanksgiving turkeys for workers and townsfolk. In his factory, Aubin followed a limber personnel policy that included allowing workers morning and afternoon breaks from the rigors of machine-paced production.[36] But such perquisites ended in 1852 when Aubin's replacement, Samuel Langley, canceled the breaks. Langley was following the example set two weeks earlier at the mill in nearby Salisbury, disrupting the labor peace that had reigned for a generation. In both places, workingmen and workingwomen reacted by leaving their machines for the picket lines and for job actions that merged into the larger movement for a ten-hour workday.[37]

Industrial paternalism did not go down without a fight, both rhetorical and social. Northerners, and Yankees in particular, grew touchy about being branded as paternalists, especially as Southerners were embracing the mantle to defend their treatment of slaves. Yankees rejected any association with paternalism for the new faith of free labor, the opposite of paternalism. A dispute over this distinction broke out in 1850 during an inquiry on labor conditions in the North conducted by Senator Jeremiah Clemens of Alabama. He was a reverent Southern sectionalist whose views of the North mimicked George Fitzhugh's. Clemens created a furor in the Whiggish press when, during his probe into their conditions, he referred to Northern factory workers as "wage slaves."[38] Clemens aroused the Yankee ire of William Schouler, who took pains to deny any vestige of paternalism in the Commonwealth's mills, arguing that regional workers deferred to no one. They were neither paupers nor slaves, and as a "rule," they earned enough to cover their own health care, provide for aging parents, and support their own retirement; some even earned enough to invest in land and industry. The former Lowellite turned Bostonian also got his "old friend" C. W. Blanchard to weigh in for free labor. A living embodiment of free labor's promise, Blanchard had gone from lugging bobbins to managing labor in a Lowell mill. He served a term or two as a

---

[36] JGW to Harriet Farley, Mar. 8, 1850, in Pickard, *Letters of John Greenleaf Whittier*, 2: 151–2. Also Mark Voss-Hubbard, "The Amesbury-Salisbury Strike and the Social Origins of Political Nativism in Massachusetts," *JSH* 29 (Mar. 1996): 567–8.

[37] Voss-Hubbard, "Amesbury-Salisbury Strike."

[38] *BA*, Feb. 4, 1850.

Whig in the state legislature and then returned to industry to oversee metal shops and textile mills in Manchester and Waltham. Blanchard was confident that his personal occupational biography also described "scores" of ordinary factory hands who would be "more likely to be *independent* of charity when old age or infirmity comes upon them, than any other class in the community." In his estimation, superintendents had nothing in common with Southern overseers, just as free labor differed from slave labor and factories from plantations. Managers came up through the ranks on their own merits and kept their jobs on the strength of their "popularity with the operatives," something that could scarcely be said of Clemens's vaunted paternalists. Managers reflected the best of modern-day "Yankee ingenuity," which stood in bold contrast to the suffocating paternalism of Clemens's backward region.[39]

This eulogy for industrial paternalism was premature. If we think of the paternalist framework as one in which subordinates enjoy social provisions such as housing, health care, and kin hiring in return for deference to superiors, then it is clear that traces of the system persisted well into the 1850s, especially in metal factories. Lowell's journeymen machine makers were given preference over external candidates for promotions. Superintendents and room bosses lived in commodious cottages set apart from the barrack-like tenements for ordinary workers but not far enough to blur the point that the accommodations reproduced the hierarchy of the mills.[40] Such managers were expected to support the dominant party; indeed, nearly all had been Whigs before 1850 and the few who were not switched allegiance following promotion.[41] They were assumed to be on call (on company time and money) for party work, politicking on shop floors and escorting workers to the polls on election day; those who sought public office enjoyed corporation support.[42] For journeymen machinists who never became overseers the stakes were smaller but still significant. The hiring of kin, which most historians of paternalism associate with the dusty mill villages of the antebellum and postbellum South, was also a feature for male machinists in Massachusetts and New Hampshire.[43]

---

[39] Ibid., Feb. 7, 1850. Also see letter of James Johnson in ibid.

[40] Massachusetts House of Representatives, House Doc. 230, "Report of Special Committee on Alleged Election Irregularities in Lowell" (1852), pp. 103–4. Hereafter House Doc. 230. On Lowell, see Dublin, *Women at Work*, pp. 75–85.

[41] House Doc. 230, pp. 68–70 and 120–2.

[42] Ibid., esp. pp. 109–11 and 133–6.

[43] Philip Scranton, "Varieties of Paternalism: Industrial Structures and the Social Relations of Production in American Textiles," *AQ* 36 (1984): 235–57. Also Tamara K. Hareven,

A good number of ordinary workers told government investigators that they had relatives in the same mill or in nearby ones, indicating that their workplaces were webs of fathers and sons, uncles and nephews.[44]

The prospect of Free Soilism in 1848, however, made Lowell anything but a happy family. Talk in bars and on shop floors of insurgency caused great anxiety in boardrooms and countinghouses. Mill agents in Lowell and their superiors in Boston, who had never experienced political insubordination, discarded the velvet glove for the heavy hand on election day, ordering managers to police polling places and either bribe voters or fire them.[45] Mill managers vehemently denied any electoral irregularities, but stepped up intimidation three years later in a runoff that pitted Whigs against Free Soilers. At first, Linus Child, a Whig strongman and an agent of the Hamilton Corporation, took no responsibility for posting a flyer at his factory gate on the eve of the runoff threatening the job of anyone who voted for the "ten-hour" ticket. He denied ordering overseers to "meddle" in the political affairs of the men, claiming that the coercion, if there was any, was unauthorized and contrary to company policy.[46] Child was not being completely disingenuous, at least so far as tradition was concerned, for in the past political coercion had been unnecessary. No one had had to tell the Jacksonian machinist that his bread was buttered by Whiggish protectionism or that political loyalty yielded social reward. But the election of 1851 took place in a completely different context. Company agents, faced with the novelty of political rebellion over the length of the workday, flew into a panic and acted foolishly, ordering supervisors to "draw the line," as one of them put it, if not in the first election, then most assuredly in the runoff.[47]

Child had his managers and overseers canvass the men in their rooms in the run-up to the election.[48] Some of them distributed Whig ballots in the shops, drove supporters to the polls, and conspicuously monitored polling places. When the dissident overseer Jesse E. Farnsworth was elected to the State House on the Free Soil ticket, he was unceremoniously fired, not for partisanship, said corporate agents, but because he had failed to inform the company of his candidacy in advance

---

Family Time and Industrial Time: The Relationship between Family and Work in a New England Industrial Community (New York: Cambridge Univ. Press, 1982).

[44] House Doc. 230, pp. 53–4 and 111.

[45] Hartford, *Money, Morals, and Politics*, pp. 175–6.

[46] House Doc. 230, pp. 36–43. Quote is on p. 41.

[47] Ibid., p. 98.

[48] Ibid., pp. 8–9, 12–13, 122–3, and passim.

and because his new responsibility would conflict with his obligations at work.[49] As if this were not enough to convince a skeptic of untoward political activism in the boardrooms at Lowell, employees of the Lowell Manufacturing Company, "or [those] who reside in houses belonging to said company," formed the Whig Union Association following the runoff because the "the time has arrived when the [W]higs of Massachusetts are called upon for more united, efficient, and persevering action in support of the principles believed by them to be essential to good order and good government."[50]

The canvass explains management's reaction. William N. Carey, a Lawrence Company overseer, told his supervisor that the fourteen likely voters in Carey's room divided evenly between the parties; fellow Lawrence manager Varnum Shed counted "ten voters besides myself," in his room, seven of whom were Coalitionists.[51] So it went, in room after room including the one in which James Patterson worked under the direction of his father. When asked about his resentment, he candidly explained: "It was because my father came to see me in this way about my politics, that aggravated me so."[52] Though young Patterson's pique was undeniably familial, it may well have reflected a more general divide separating younger, independent-minded workers who had not internalized the Whiggery of older workmates. Certainly surging Free Soilism in the industrial districts owed much to the party's stand on a ten-hour law. As the newly elected state representative Jesse Farnsworth observed, the "terms 'ten-hour men' and '[Co]alitionists' were synonymous in Lowell."[53] No single issue carried more resonance on factory floors.

The ten-hour movement in the factories was not political at first. It started in the shops with a group of Boston activists who in spring 1847 circulated a questionnaire asking local metal entrepreneurs "to state whether they would adopt the ten hour system."[54] When only a few owners bothered to respond, the metalworkers retained the respectful tone of their circular, inviting them to discuss the matter at Faneuil Hall in late May. While owners stayed away, enough workers and reformers showed up to make for a a lively day that offered no

[49] Ibid., pp. 99–118 and 125–36.
[50] Ibid., p. 174.
[51] Ibid., pp. 122–4.
[52] Ibid., p. 55.
[53] Ibid., p. 103.
[54] *DC*, May 22, 1847.

dearth of strategies. An advocate of Protective Unionism recommended cooperatives; Henry Trask favored "combination," by which he meant a union; Francis Parkman, the radical clergyman, agreed and recommended raising money for a strike fund. The workers themselves were just as confused. One of them proposed a morning meeting with employers on Boston Common or in their offices; if the owners declined, the men would take up a collection to set up cooperatives. Though this plan had some appeal, one bemused skeptic said that he had never worked more than ten hours and "never would," because he knew that his employer needed him more than he needed his employer. The proposal for "more intercourse" among the trade carried the day, and the meeting ended by tabling the strike motion and appointing a committee to draft a plan for future action.[55]

No such plan emerged. Instead, machinists quietly and gradually organized around different strategies at their workplaces. Inspired perhaps by the recent example of the tailors in 1850, metalworkers in early 1851 around Boston and Worcester outside the orbit of the Boston Associates either conducted strikes or reached ten-hour compacts without much rancor. Machinists at Hinckley and Drury Locomotive Works, one of the largest independent firms near Boston, prevailed following a short strike and brief negotiations; fellow workmen at Wilmarth's Union Works in South Boston won their demand more amicably. So did tradesmen in Worcester, where discussions with metal entrepreneurs produced several ten-hour agreements.[56]

Industrial tradesmen paid for shorter workdays with their traditional "privileges." Employers cracked down in order to pack more work into fewer hours, fining socializing on the job and tardiness as well as trimming rolls of slower workmen.[57] Some workers complained, but no one called for a return to the old regime. In fact, metalworkers thought they had achieved something worthy of celebration. Machinists at two of South Boston's larger shops marked the first anniversary of their ten-hour day with a procession followed by a dinner and then a fireworks display.[58] Worcesterites had a quieter commemoration in keeping with the signature craft fraternalism of their city. The workmen at Ruggles, Nourse, Mason, and Company, a large and innovative maker of farm equipment, presented

55 Ibid. Also *VI*, May 28 and July 2, 1847.
56 *Comm*, Oct. 9, 1851. Also *MS*, Feb. 21, 1852.
57 *Comm*, Oct. 23, 1851.
58 *BA*, Oct. 4 and 6, 1852.

their employer with a rosewood clock made by local artisans that featured
a large pendulum with the inscription:[59]

TEN HOURS
Presented to Messrs. Ruggles, Nourse, Mason, & Co.
By the Workmen in the their Employ
Oct. 16, 1851[60]

Liberal-minded employers like Ruggles and Company were not confined to Worcester. They formed part of a new provincial elite that thought
of itself as a class apart from the Boston Associates. They were self-made
men who had followed the traditional route of upward mobility within
the crafts unlike the Bostonians who entered manufacturing from the outside on capital earned in trade and commerce. Living embodiments of the
ideology of free labor, they looked upon workmen as younger versions
of themselves, that is, as ambitious upstarts capable of standing on their
own two feet and moving up the social ladder, not as wards cowering for
a paternal hand.[61] They had no use for dependence and paternalism – or
slavery and Whiggery – and took more easily to the free laborism of the
Free Soil Party. Some, like Ruggles and Company, welcomed the ten-hour
day; indeed, party stalwarts had a name for such employers, branding
their workplaces "Coalition Shops."[62]

If most metalworkers were not so fortunate, neither were they isolated.
They were befriended by several groups allied with a revitalized ten-hour
movement rather more muscular than its antecedent. One group consisted
of labor reformers typified by Henry Trask. Fresh from his involvement in
the journeymen tailors' strike, Trask and his erstwhile Fourierist friends,
together with delegates from producers' cooperatives – notably tailors and
cabinetmakers – and Protective Unionists, organized the New England Industrial League (NEIL) in spring 1850 to spread the gospel of cooperation.
Members paid dues for a strike fund and also an "emancipation fund"
to liberate labor from "wage slavery."[63] Groups like the NEIL claimed

---

[59] George F. Hoar, *Autobiography of Seventy Years*, 2 vols. (New York: Charles Scribner's Sons, 1903), 1: 158–9.

[60] *MS*, Feb. 21, 1852.

[61] They were similar in many respects to the "civic capitalists" described by John Cumbler, *A Social History of Economic Decline: Business, Politics, and Work in Trenton* (New Brunswick, N.J.: Rutgers Univ. Press, 1989).

[62] *LA*, Mar. 3, 1853. Also Persons, "Early History of Factory Legislation in Massachusetts," pp. 75–6.

[63] On the NEIL, see Ware, *Industrial Worker*, pp. 163–84, and Guarani, *Utopian Alterna-tive*, pp. 318–19.

to be above party politics, but the advent of Free Soilism made it difficult for them to resist the entreaties of party emissaries.[64] The NEIL soon aroused influential Free Soilers, namely William Robinson, the Lowell editor and now party leader who would be elected to the State House in 1851. Robinson's first lieutenant was James M. Stone, another veteran of the temperance movement attached to the laborist wing of the Washingtonians in Worcester. Stone was a Polk-style, expansionist Democrat influential enough to have landed a patronage job in the Boston Customs House. He nonetheless joined the Coalition, possibly as a Democrat and probably around 1850, when he served two consecutive terms in the House, chiefly as a labor advocate. Perhaps he and Robinson appreciated the political potential of a ten-hour movement in the aftermath of the "Uprising."[65] It is clear that by fall 1850 Stone and Robinson had joined the NEIL, which within a year gave rise to the Ten-Hour State Convention. A virtual adjunct of the Free Soil Party, the Ten-Hour Convention scuttled the radical reforms that had animated the NEIL for the more immediate project of making ten hours a legal day's work.[66] As an observer correctly put it, Coalition candidates in mill towns made sure that elections "regularly turned on this question" from 1851 onward, making local races ten-hour referendums.[67] In fact, their handiwork prepared the political powder keg that Linus Child ignited that fall in Lowell when he tried to bully the men in his employ. Child's reaction is a measure of the relative strength of this phase of labor reform. It was one thing, after all, to face the earlier movement of women who could not vote, had no political support outside of a few Libertyites, and were placated by a modest extension of the dinner hour. It was quite another to face down a force of male workers well organized and linked to a potent insurgency.

Coalitionists made the most of their alliance with labor. For three years, from 1851 to 1853, Ten-Hour Convention activists campaigned hard on several fronts. They staged three major meetings – in January and

---

[64] The best analysis of this nonpartisan-partisan dynamic is Voss-Hubbard, *Beyond Party*, esp. pp. 38–49,

[65] On Stone, see Laurie, "'Fair Field' of the 'Middle Ground,'" pp. 56–7, and Persons, "Early History of Factory Legislation in Massachusetts," pp. 60–3.

[66] Persons, "Early History of Factory Legislation in Massachusetts," pp. 61–3, and David R. Roediger and Philip S. Foner, *Our Own Time: A History of Labor and the Working Day* (Westport, Conn.: Greenwood Press, 1989), pp. 76–7.

[67] Persons, "Early History of Factory Legislation in Massachusetts," p. 70. Also see Voss-Hubbard, *Beyond Party*, pp. 83–5.

September 1852 and October 1853 – encouraged ten-hour committees at the local level or linked up with groups already on the ground, and sponsored massive petition drives, which peaked in 1853 with some ten thousand signatures (double the number collected a year before).[68] Robinson and Stone orchestrated broad social representation at their gatherings, recruiting clergymen and labor reformers for local committees along with working-class activists and Coalition politicians.[69] They also enlisted the Free Soil press in Boston and especially in the industrial centers of Lowell and Worcester, and they worked closely with local groups to identify supportive politicians by canvassing office seekers on the question of ten-hour legislation.[70] The insurgents-turned-labor reformers left very little to chance in what proved to be the broadest and most aggressive labor reform campaign to date.

The Ten-Hour Convention's chief piece of propaganda was the pamphlet *The Hours of Labor*, published in early 1852 but written by Stone two years before as a minority report on ten-hour legislation.[71] Its 1852 iteration laid out arguments that would be repeated for the next few years on the hustings and at ten-hour rallies. It defended a legal solution because "reform has been carried as far as it can go by voluntary adoption."[72] Former voluntarists heartily agreed. Even Whittier conceded that the legislature had to act because of the intransigence of the corporations and because many beneficiaries of reform were women with nowhere else to turn.[73] The report went on that a shorter workday would improve the health and habits of workingmen and workingwomen, just as it had in England. It demonized opponents as the "Money power," too wrapped up in raking in profit to care about morality. The Free Soil backbencher George W. Benchley put it as well as anyone, charging that when the

[68] Persons, "Early History of Factory Legislation in Massachusetts," pp. 63–68, and Laurie, "'Fair Field' of the 'Middle Ground,'" pp. 57–9. See also Voss-Hubbard, *Beyond Party*, pp. 81–5.

[69] See, for instance, *Comm*, Oct. 1, 1852; *MS*, Feb. 19, 1852, and Oct. 1, 1853; *LA* Mar. 5, 1853; and *BC*, Oct. 1, 1822.

[70] See *MS*, Feb. 14, 1853, and *LA*, Mar. 15, 1853. Also see Voss-Hubbard, *Beyond Party*, pp. 84–5.

[71] Massachusetts House of Representatives, House Doc. 153, "Report of the Special Committee on Limiting the Hours of Labor" (1850). Hereafter House Doc. 153.

[72] *The Hours of Labor. Address of the Ten Hours State Convention, held in Boston, Sept. 30, 1852, to the People of the Commonwealth of Masssachusetts; together with a Report and Bill* ... (Boston: N.p., 1852). Quote is on p. 3.

[73] JGW to Ophelia Underwood, July 8, 1852, in Pickard, *Letters of John Greenleaf Whittier*, 2: 192.

question "presented to a Cottoncrat, concerns men versus money, money is certain to obtain his suffrage."[74]

Much of that was old hat; the originality in *The Hours of Labor* was in its economic message. For years defenders of the traditional workday had disarmed critics not only by invoking paternal provisions that buffered effects of such toil but also by promising wage cuts commensurate with the reduction of hours, no small consideration for workers at the lower end of the pay scale and especially for the women among them out to maximize earnings because of their abbreviated careers in the workforce. The pamphlet turned the received wisdom on its head. It asserted that reducing the hours of work in factories that used machinery would initially reduce production, which would amount to a cut in the labor force. But since workers would be needed to regear production to demand, wages would rise as more employers competed to hire labor. Thus competition in labor markets caused by cutting the hours of work would raise wages – not cut them. Higher earnings in turn would trigger what modern economists call a multiplier effect by leading to more consumption, which would require more production and thus higher employment. The ten-hour day would ripple through the entire economy, elevating the general standard of living.[75]

Though Free Soil politicos and worker-activists thought they had covered all possibilities, they stumbled in the General Court in 1850 and 1851. House committees appointed to look into the matter flatly refused to act.[76] The 1850 committee, which was stacked against the Free Soilers (with four Whigs and three Free Soilers), signaled trouble early on, for Solon Carter, a country Free Soiler from Leominister, voted with the Whigs.[77] Two years later, a similar committee divided three ways, with a majority discouraging any action. Another group consisting of the Holyoke Whig George Ewing and the Fall River Free Soiler Nathan Dean proposed a bill with a provision enabling individuals to make their own contracts. William Robinson was a minority of one for a ten-hour law.[78] The Lowellite and party leader compromised to gather support, drafting a bill that would have phased in a shorter workday over several years, but his bill got only

---

74 *MS*, Nov. 1, 1854. See also Laurie, " 'Fair Field' of the 'Middle Ground,' " p. 58.
75 *Hours of Labor*. Also see *Comm*, Jan. 2, 1852; *MS*, Sept. 5, 1853, and Persons, "Early History of Factory Legislation in Massachusetts," pp. 79–80.
76 House Doc. 153 (1850).
77 Ibid.
78 Massachusetts House of Representatives, House Doc. 185, "Report of the Special Committee" (1852), pp. 1–21. Hereafter House Doc. 185.

forty-eight votes, just three more than the one proposed by Ewing and Dean.[79]

Discouraged but determined to carry on, Robinson and his associates redoubled their efforts for the following session in 1853, stepping up the petition drive, holding more rallies, and putting out *The Hours of Labor*. Their work paid off as a new bill sailed through the House with a vote of 137 to 95, only to run into trouble in the Senate, where opponents appended a clause (the so-called Stevenson Amendment) permitting workers to set their own hours through individual arrangements with employers, effectively negating the goal of a uniform workday. The clause so angered Robinson and his lieutenants that they made good on a promise to reject the bill. Its defeat closed the Coalition's political bid for a ten-hour workday.[80]

What had gone wrong? Robinson's quip that "Ignorance as great as the Egyptian darkness pervades the minds of the great mass of the people" was the outburst of a disappointed man.[81] An observer who charged corporate interests with bribery may have been closer to the mark, but probably not close enough.[82] The convergence of hostile interests offers a better explanation. One was the division within what was left of the Coalition between its industrial and rural factions. In 1853 the Coalition voted strongly (107 to 30) for Robinson's ten-hour bill.[83] The rebels consisted of populistic Democrats from the country and a few Free Soilers united around the doctrine of freedom of contract, which saw state intervention as a violation of the right of an individual to bargain over working conditions without prior constraints.[84] This doctrine proved even stronger in the Senate, which an observer accurately described as too conservative to approve the Coalition's bill.[85] Indeed, the margin of victory in the House was supplied not by the Free Soilers, but by fourteen Whigs,

---

[79] Persons, "Early History of Factory Legislation in Massachusetts, pp. 74–5 and pp. 86–7.

[80] Ibid., pp. 87–8. Also see *LA*, Apr. 12 and May 25, 1853; *MS*, May 17, 1853; and *Comm*, May 18 and 24, 1853. Also, see esp. Appendix 2.

[81] Persons, "Early History of Factory Legislation in Massachusetts," p. 87.

[82] Charles Cowley, *Illustrated History of Lowell* (Boston: Lea and Shepard, 1868), p. 149.

[83] House of Representatives, List of the Members of the House of Representatives . . . 1853, appendix no. 104, mss. Also, see Appendix 1. The number of votes in the appendixes do not correspond to the votes in the State House because the votes of the cities and towns in the appendixes do not cover all such places.

[84] On the Democrats, see Hoar, *Autobiography of Seventy Years*, 1: 163–4; on Free Soilers, see *LA*, Apr. 12 and May 25, 1853. On both groups, see House Doc. 153 (1850), and House Doc. 185 (1852), which split three ways.

[85] See *LA*, Apr. 12, 1853, and *Comm*, Apr. 27, 1853. Also see Appendix 1.

almost all of whom were first timers.[86] Even Lowell, the longtime bastion of industrial conservatism, yielded to political necessity. On the eve of the 1852 election the Whig city committee came out for a ten-hour law, and the voters elected a delegation of reform Whigs to the State House.[87] No one reflected old Whiggery's makeover better than the party's gubernatorial candidate, John Clifford, the darling of moderates eager to reclaim the party's working-class base. They could not have found a more suitable candidate. A resident of New Bedford, Clifford probably knew local ten-hour advocates by name; he quickly got acquainted with their South Boston cousins in the 1852 campaign, showing up at their dinner on the anniversary of the ten-hour day. In a gesture that was simply unthinkable to the old guard, Clifford raised a fraternal glass to "The Machinists – first and foremost in the ranks of reform; sure indications that they are inspired by the spirit of our forefathers."[88] Even an urbanite like Clifford could not resist the metaphors of Yankeedom.

The problem was not insufficient political support for the ten-hour movement in South Boston or Lowell. Support had been strong enough in the industrial districts since 1850 to command political respect, so much so that even the Whigs, the sworn enemies of the movement, had to come around, as Clifford's toast to the South Boston men demonstrates. The problem was that the cause never had much support elsewhere, except for Free Soilers in the industrial villages who went along for partisan reasons. It had even less support following the disastrous 1852 elections, which reduced the party's base to the industrial cities and scattered country communities.

A closer look at the 1853 vote in the context of our four political regions reveals the complications posed by the Coalition's shifting base and, in particular, by the Democratic resurgence in the country. The Whig strongholds of Boston and the shire towns (excluding Springfield and Worcester) soundly rejected the ten-hour bill, voting 1 to 20 and 1 to 12, respectively; the industrial towns voted 17 to 0 for the bill, failing to offset Whiggery's opposition and forcing the Free Soilers to make up ground elsewhere.[89] The Free Soil men and their urban Democratic allies filled the vacuum left by the collapse of the Whigs in the industrial

---

[86] The vote was 102 to 88; in the industrial towns it was 28 to 1. House of Representatives, List of the Members of the House of Representatives . . . 1853, appendix no. 103.

[87] *LA*, Nov. 6, 1852.

[88] Quoted in Hartford, *Money, Morals, and Politics*, p. 187. Also see *BA*, Oct. 4 and 6, 1852, and *BC*, Sept. 9, 1852.

[89] See Appendix 1.

belt, gaining some sixteen seats (most of them Democratic) between 1850 and 1853. The problem arose in the country, where Free Soilism slipped and then all but vanished in these three years, losing over twenty seats in the five westernmost counties – and over thirty if we include Middlesex. The larger implications of this political reversal soon became clear. Outraged by the Stevenson Amendment, Robinson drew together enough Coalitionists – Free Soilers and Democrats from the larger towns – to defeat the measure by 12 votes. But he failed to bring along the country because the Whigs had rebounded there and many Coalitionists failed to vote, ending any chance of a stronger bill.[90] The betrayal surprised some observers but not George F. Hoar, then a young Free Soil lawmaker from Worcester, who recalled that his speech for the ten-hour bill evoked "derision" from rural lawmakers in the normally courtly House. No one wanted to hear him out, least of all a country Democrat who twanged, "Isn't the young man from Worcester going to let me get up in the morning and milk my caows," meaning that Hoar was keeping him from his chores or about to regulate his hours on the farm.[91] Either way, the message was clear: there would be no ten-hour law as long as the country had its way.

In addition, the stench of nativism wafted through the Coalition, an odor picked up early on by James Stone in his 1850 report on the ten-hour workday. In it, Stone responded to anti-Irish lawmakers by telling them that the ten-hour law was not misspent charity; it was a salutary instrument to improve the "moral character" of the Irish immigrants.[92] Thus, the coming of the Irish had an ambiguous impact on insurgent politics. On the one hand, the fact that such vulnerable immigrants were easy prey for the factories of "Cottoncrats" strengthened the case for remedial action, just as Stone had argued.[93] On the other hand, the newcomers managed to arouse opposition, both at work and in the community, and in the country as well as in the city. Irish immigrants made no friends in Amesbury or Salisbury when they were used to break the 1852 strikes.[94] Their arrival in large numbers aroused fears of what a country journalist called the "greatest of all curses which can visit a manufacturing community, a

---

[90] Ibid. Also Appendix 2.
[91] Hoar, *Autobiography of Seventy Years*, 1: 163–4. Quote is on p. 164. Also see Carl Siracusa, *A Mechanical People: Perceptions of the Industrial Order in Massachusetts, 1815–1880* (Middletown, Conn.: Wesleyan Univ. Press, 1979), pp. 133–6.
[92] House Doc. 153, p. 19. Also ibid., p. 28.
[93] See Persons, "Early History of Factory Legislation in Massachusetts," p. 56.
[94] George McNeill, ed., *The Labor Movement: The Problem of To-Day* (1887; New York: Augustus Kelley, 1971), p. 120, and Voss-Hubbard, "Amesbury-Salisbury Strike."

permanent class of factory operatives."[95] Such a dangerous class deserved derision – not protective legislation. This nativist sensibility, which was a strong undercurrent in the insurgency, proved enough to turn some Free Soil lawmakers against what they construed to be relief for an undeserving population.

An expected outburst of managerial pragmatism further confounded the ten-hour project. The agitation in mill towns, which had been associated with the "factory girls," shook the "lords of the loom."[96] Sponsored by political insurgents, the ten-hour movement not only mobilized men as well as women; it also coordinated shop floor and polling booth, a feat never before accomplished. It humiliated Whig manufacturers at the polls in their own towns and made them look like tyrants in Lowell. The insurgency even infiltrated the front line of management absolutely essential to control of the shop floor. The defection of Jesse Farnsworth, the Lowell overseer elected to the legislature as a Free Soiler, was a straw in the wind, an ominous sign of the loss of control. It helped persuade the Boston Associates to compromise. Thus in fall 1852 they agreed to prune the workday by one hour to eleven hours in their machine shops, and a year later they extended the new policy to their textile factories.[97] The about-face complicated the response of employees already divided several ways. According to a reliable observer in Lowell, one group, composed largely of Yankee women, continued to believe that a shorter workday meant a shorter pay stub. Such workers preferred the old system even if they did not necessarily fight against the new one.[98] Another group, which took the lead in the early 1850s and may well have been the plurality, continued to favor a ten-hour day enshrined in law. These workers pressed on into the middle of the decade, largely on their own if with some support from the newly arrived Irish.[99] In between stood pragmatists who had always looked forward to compromise and welcomed the

---

[95] Quoted in Voss-Hubbard, "Amesbury-Salisbury Strike," p. 580.

[96] See Hartford, *Money, Morals, and Politics*, pp. 173–8.

[97] See McNeill, *Labor Movement*, pp. 120–1; Persons, "Early History of Factory Legislation in Massachusetts," pp. 87–8; and David R. Roediger and Philips S. Foner, *Our Own Time: A History of American Labor and the Working Day* (Westport, Conn.: Greenwood Press, 1989), pp. 78–9.

[98] For this dialogue among the workers themselves in the various textile centers see *BB*, Feb. 16, Mar. 15, and 27–29, and Apr. 4 and 11, 1855. See also David Zonderman, *Aspirations and Anxieties: New England Workers and the Mechanized Factory, 1815–1850* (New York: Oxford Univ. Press, 1992), pp. 258–9, and Dublin, *Women at Work*, pp. 145–64.

[99] Dublin, *Women at Work*, 198–207.

one proposed by management in 1852. This faction, which would be heard from more clearly in 1855, pressed for accepting the settlement of 1853, and it prevailed over more militant workers thwarted by the combination of the compromise and the drubbing suffered by their party in the 1852 elections.[100]

Compromise worked from management's perspective. It blunted the thrust of the ten-hour movement, which went into eclipse in the fall. The movement would revive briefly in 1855 but then peter out just as quickly. Labor reformers had fallen short of their primary objective but had come close enough to satisfy a sufficiently large constituency of the operatives in the Commonwealth. No one else had beaten the Boston Associates; no one could because the past had been wholly different. Before the advent of the Free Soil Coalition, workers had organized exclusively at the economic level, through the agency of unions or in ad hoc ten-hours groups, and without much political help. They were in political limbo between conservative Whigs responsive to the class interests of the Boston Associates and populistic Democrats critical of elitism but also of active government. Free Soilers filled the void by providing a political force responsive to labor's self-organization, a force that linked the political with the economic but only incompletely. The party's industrial wing got the cooperation of some Democrats in 1850 and again in 1851, when the Coalition went into effect; village Coalitionists, however, refused to go along. Two years later, in 1853, the lack of cohesion was only part of the problem, as floor leaders counterbalanced recalcitrant villagers with the support of progressive Whigs. Such Whigs, however, were far fewer in number than their fellows in the country who gained strength in the election of 1852. Country lawmakers, and Whigs in particular, not only scuttled the Coalition's industrial policy. As we are about to see, they also featured in Whiggery's assault on the the secret ballot, a central plank in the platform of Free Soilers from the cities.

---

[100] Laurie, "'Fair Field' of the 'Middle Ground,'" pp. 60–2.

7

"As Easy as Lying"

Complications of Political Reform

Political life would have been easier for erstwhile Conscience Whigs in the Free Soil camp if their alliance with Democrats had turned on the simple matter of divvying up state offices. They were too conservative and much too focused on the national question of slavery to be bothered by the seeming trivia of State Reform. To be certain, such battle-hardened lieutenants as Henry Wilson had been around too long to believe that all would go smoothly; the "Natick Cobbler" himself lost some sleep over labor reform. No one, however, anticipated the tumult over political reapportionment and the secret ballot – or the furor over the liquor question. Such highly emotive issues, redolent of class resentment and religious fervor, tested the Coalition even harder than had labor reform.

Bay State citizens voted by voice or by ballot before the Civil War but never in private. In local elections, voters gathered at meetinghouses, town halls, or schools and either stood up to be counted or collected together into rival groups behind their candidates. In state and national elections, voters cast paper ballots designed by the party leaders, hand-copied by groups of women and schoolchildren, and distributed by campaign workers.[1] Paper ballots allowed for some secrecy but not much, and not for

---

[1] Several delegates to the 1853 Constitutional Convention reviewed the history of voting and various rules and regulations. See *Constitutional Convention*, 3: 594–6. Also see *Comm*, Aug. 29, 1851; *MS*, Nov. 4, 1851; and *BDA*, Nov. 7–9, 1853. For modern work on these matters, see Ronald P. Formisano, *The Transformation of Political Culture: Massachusetts Parties, 1790s–1840s* (New York: Oxford Univ. Press, 1983), pp. 24–54, and Alexander Keyssar, *The Right to Vote: The Contested History of Democracy in the United States* (New York: Basic Books, 2000), pp. 29–69.

long because in 1829 the fledgling Democratic Party, concerned about surveillance and intimidation at the polls, won a court decision legalizing printed ballots. The ruling had the unintended consequence of collapsing the distinction between voice and ballot voting, since both parties started printing their own ballots coded by color, by symbol, or both.[2] It also led to a game of cat and mouse, as voters who valued secrecy tried to outsmart the politicians, folding ballots or slipping them into envelopes. Whigs reacted in 1839 with a law requiring ballots to be "open and unfolded" when stuffed into the ballot box. They said it fought corruption and fraud; Democrats said it eased monitoring and oversight, and vowed to fight for real secrecy.[3] Several bills of theirs in the 1840s got some support but not enough to pass.[4]

This is where legislative matters stood in 1851 when the Coalition came to power. Though such conservatives as Dana and Adams considered State Reform a diversion from antislavery, Wilson knew they could scarcely duck the secret ballot issue or temporize, for it was a political necessity not simply a question of principle. Rank and filers in the shadows of mill and factory clamored for protection from meddlesome managers; they considered their voting rights as important as shortening their workday. The issue offered Coalition men the opportunity to simultaneously firm up their base and strike a blow at the Money Power.[5]

Voter intimidation was a tradition in the Bay State. At least as early as the 1820s, popular movements that spoke for the "middling sort" of shopkeepers and tradesmen complained about intrusive employers as well as merchants who refused to do business with mechanics out of step with their politics. The *Bostonian and Mechanics' Journal*, the official voice of the populist Middling Interest, warned mechanics who did not support the Federalist establishment in the upcoming elections that they risked the "loss of customers.... Look at your contracts," the article continued, implying this was nothing new, ending with a rhetorical flourish that anticipated the Coalition's discourse on slavery: "*Farewell freedom of opinion – farewell liberty of suffrage. Hail! Slavery of the*

[2] *Comm*, July 29, 1851, and *Constitutional Convention*, 1: 144–5 and 594–5.

[3] Formisano, *Transformation of Political Culture*, pp. 145–8. Also see *Constitutional Convention*, 1: 594–5, and *MS*, Nov. 4, 1851.

[4] Michel Brunet, "The Secret Ballot Issue in Massachusetts Politics from 1851 to 1853," *NEQ*, 25 (Sept. 1952): 254–62, and Carl Siracusa, *A Mechanical People: Perceptions of the Industrial Order in Massachusetts, 1815–1880* (Middletown, Conn.: Wesleyan Univ. Press, 1979), pp. 182–7. Also see *Comm*, Aug. 29, 1851, and *BC* Mar. 18 and 24, 1843.

[5] See esp., *Constitutional Convention*, 1: 189–90, 549–84, and 657–8.

North."[6] A decade later, leaders of the New England Workingmen's Association voiced similar grievances. Some said that the problem extended beyond countinghouses and shop floors to pulpits, that influence peddling was pervasive and stretched from the factory to the village.[7]

Party operatives of all colors tried to sway voters one way or another. Some activists were simply more subtle and possibly more effective than others, though no one ever charged Whigs with subtlety. By the late forties Whig industrialists were singled out as particularly blatant offenders. Critics charged in the run-up to the 1848 election that party bosses in Boston ordered proprietors to take election day off in order to police polling places. In Lowell, factory agents reportedly lingered at boxes in order to "see what kinds of ballots each and every man deposited."[8] Such surveillance only hinted at the more concerted and openly coercive measures in the 1851 election, which Coalitionists deftly exploited in legislative hearings that made factory agents in Lowell look like martinets and lesser managers like pawns.[9] Lowell was a chapter in a tome written by Free Soil and Democratic propagandists posturing as labor's sentinels.[10] Whigs only strengthened the Coalitionists' case when in fall 1850 party chairman George Morey distributed a letter urging employers to persuade employees to "go and vote on our side of the Commonwealth at the present crisis."[11]

The zeal with which Coalitionists pursued electoral reform in 1851 was exceeded only by their effort to elect Charles Sumner to the U.S. Senate. Their bill sailed through the House without a single dissenter on their side (and a stingy 3 Whig votes out of 180 cast).[12] A ringing victory for the Coalition, the law required that all ballots be placed in "self-sealing

---

[6] *BMJ*, Apr. 5 and 12, 1823. On the middling interest, see Matthew H. Crocker, *The Magic of the Many: Josiah Quincy and the Rise of Mass Politics in Boston, 1800–1830* (Amherst: Univ. of Massachusetts Press, 1999), pp. 70–98, 101–22, and 128–30, and Formisano, *Transformation of Political Culture*, pp. 181–7.

[7] *NEA*, Feb. 2, 1832, and Seth Luther, *An Address to the Working-Men of New England, on the State of Education. . . . .* (Boston: By the Author, 1832), p. 28, and Luther (1833), p. 24. See also Formisano, *Transformation of Political Culture*, pp. 238–44.

[8] Quoted in William F. Hartford, *Money, Morals, and Politics: Massachusetts in the Age of the Boston Associates* (Boston: Northeastern Univ. Press, 2001). Quote is on p. 175.

[9] *MS*, Nov. 22, 1853, and *Comm*, May 10 and Nov. 22, 1851, and Feb. 22, 1853.

[10] Massachusetts House of Representatives, House Doc. 230, "Report of the Special Committee on Alleged Election Irregularities in Lowell" (1852); Formisano, *Transformation of Political Culture*, pp. 335–8; and Siracusa, *Mechanical People*, pp. 182–7.

[11] *MS*, Sept. 23, 1854. Quote is in Hartford, *Money, Morals and Politics*, p. 176.

[12] House of Representatives, Journal of the House, 1851, Appendix, No. 48, ms. Massachusetts State Archives, Boston. See also Appendix 3.

envelopes" of "uniform appearance," which were to be distributed by the secretary of state to local election officials by October 1 of each year. It punished fraud and dereliction of duty by public officials with fines ranging from one hundred to one thousand dollars;[13] it was strengthened a bit the next year when voters continued to complain of intimidation.[14] Coalitionists were elated. Editorialists considered ballot reform a major victory, the key to Coalition success in places like Lowell.[15] Even Whigs agreed. "Where would the Coalition be today," asked a dejected journalist, "without the manufacturing city of Lowell and the town of Fall River?"[16] Whigs obviously invested the secret ballot with the same importance the Coalition did, biding their time for a counteroffensive to roll back the objectionable reform. They had to wait no longer than the next election and ensuing legislative session. When the Whigs retook the General Court in November elections, they made secret ballot law their primary issue. Aware that repeal was unlikely, they settled for making the use of envelopes optional, effectively ending secrecy.[17] Coalitionists regrouped shortly after the vote, pushing through the legislature a provision for a constitutional convention, scheduled for the summer, in an effort to regain what they had just lost. Armed with a solid majority at the convention, the Coalition wrote an even stronger secret ballot clause, only to see it go down when the voters rejected the constitution the following fall.[18] The ballot was no longer secret and would remain so until 1888.[19]

This shocking defeat could be traced directly to the Whig resurgence in the election of 1852. The old party's brief but important resuscitation shredded the Coalition for good, effectively dooming the secret ballot along with a host of reforms taken up by the constitutional convention. Whigs, after all, had never accepted the legitimacy of secrecy, and the defeats they suffered in the elections of the early 1850s only intensified their animus. They simmered in 1851 as giddy Coalitionists celebrated the

---

[13] *Acts and Resolves of the Commonwealth of Massachusetts* (Boston: Dutton, 1851), ch. 226, pp. 694–5. Also *MS*, June 2 and Oct. 6, 1851.

[14] Brunet, "Secret Ballot Issue in Massachusetts Politics," p. 359.

[15] *Comm*, May 27, 1851, and *MS*, May 2 and Oct. 6, 1851.

[16] *BA*, Nov. 27, 1851.

[17] Brunet, "Secret Ballot Issue in Massachusetts." See also Appendix 4.

[18] See *Constitutional Convention*, 3: 694–7, for the final text.

[19] Bruce Laurie, " 'The Penitent's Bench': Toward a Social History of the Ballot in Nineteenth-Century Massachusetts," *HC* 16 (1998): 67–88. Originally entitled " 'The Stool or Repentence': Toward a Social History of the Ballot" (paper prepared for the conference on the Generation of '98, Madrid, Spain, 1997).

impressive vote (174 to 132) for their secret ballot bill. However, Whigs ran a successful campaign in 1852 by reversing themselves on the ten-hour workday in the industrial belt and by running hard against secret voting in the country. Their 1853 bill making the secret ballot voluntary drummed up just enough in the party's urban and country wings (145 to 136) to undo the Coalition's handiwork of 1851.[20]

Bay Staters were deeply divided on the issue of the secret ballot by midcentury. One view, and for all practical purposes the plurality position, saw male suffrage as a fundamental right, and not a privilege. This position, shared by most Democrats and virtually all Free Soilers, aimed to expand the white male electorate by stripping away or paring down residency requirements and property qualifications in addition to insuring the secret ballot. Coalitionists asserted that secrecy was essential. They believed that open voting strengthened the opposition by enfranchising men unduly influenced by their betters and employers in particular. Such a specter went back to the Jeffersonian Republicans. It had come up at the constitutional convention in 1821 when political leaders first considered easing restrictions on male suffrage, a prospect that alarmed country delegates and some urban sympathizers. Samuel Hoar of Concord, father of the Free Soiler and ten-hour champion George F. Hoar, worried that a "rich man in a populous town might command the votes of men without property," in an obvious reference to the authority of village elites.[21] Josiah Quincy, the mercurial Federalist with populist leanings who was about to become mayor of Boston, amplified Hoar's point. Dropping the property qualification spelled doom in the long run for the "landowners and yeomanry" because the flow of history was on the side of the "establishment of a great manufacturing interest.... The whole body of every manufacturing establishment," he intoned, "are dead votes, counted by the head, by the employer." Farmers could soon expect a day when "every county of the Commonwealth" would have "one, two, or three manufacturing establishments, each sending... from one to eight hundred votes to the polls depending on the will of one employer, one great capitalist. In such a case, would they deem such a provision as this of no consequence?"[22] Coalition men

---

[20] See Appendixes 3 and 4.
[21] *Journal of Debates and Proceedings in the Massachusetts Constitutional Convention, 1820–1821* (Boston: *Boston Daily Advertiser*, 1853), p. 248.
[22] Ibid., pp. 251–2.

answered that it was secrecy that made greater democracy possible. The secret ballot strengthened Coalition leaders, bringing Henry Wilson together with Marcus Morton.[23] Backbenchers repeatedly hammered at this point on the floor of the constitutional convention. Henry Williams summed it up as well as anyone when he rose to defend the meaning of the secret ballot in an age of advancing industrialism. The "open ballot" was a regrettable relic of the past and a dangerous one because it made the "elector more dependent upon those around him, brings him more immediately under the control of pecuniary and business relations, and thus forces him to abdicate his own opinion to give place and supremacy to that of others." The Taunton Democrat referred to the more nuanced intimidation of the "espionage and supervision of the public" that abetted the "intimidator and the tyrant" in their insidious project to exert "control." He ended by invoking the "duty" of State Reform to put government on the side of the people in order "to protect the weak against the strong...."[24]

Whigs were having none of this. A larger electorate, they believed, was bad enough; one that voted in secrecy was troubling on its face and likely to be disastrous in the context of insurgent Free Soilism. Secrecy had defeated them in the industrial districts, as the election of 1851 showed, and would be their undoing, unless it was reversed. They denied that anything was remiss in the Lowells of the Commonwealth. Otis P. Lord of Salem, one of the party's most respected solons, had "no faith" in complaints of employer intimidation of workers at election time. "I do not believe a word of it," he averred, echoing colleagues on the convention floor refuting charges of improprieties.[25] Lord dismissed such talk as hyperbole, asserting that a fine line separated reasoning with a worker "to vote in a certain way" and forcing the worker to do so. Most employers stood safely on the near side of the line, merely exercising their right to freedom of speech and their powers of persuasion. A troubling double standard marked such discourse, he added, in a shrewd bit of reasoning. In the hoopla of political campaigns – the "transparencies...illuminations...parades, and *'noise and confusion.'* ... This poor, weak-minded brother can be made to vote at the sound of a horn as you choose, but if you influence him by reason you are committing a great crime."[26]

---

[23] *Constitutional Convention*, 1: 189–90, 581–2, and passim. For Morton's views see ibid., 1: 653–6 and 2: 494–6 and 505–7.
[24] Ibid., 1: 547–51. Quote is on pp. 549–50.
[25] Ibid., 1: 576. Also see ibid., p. 640 ff.
[26] Ibid., 1: 577.

Whigs went well beyond denying the need for remedial legislation. They stood firmly on two fundamental points, one of which, implied in Lord's reference to the submissive male, was gender. One party orator after another associated open voting and manliness. Real men did not need secrecy or any other crutch of big government. Real men stated their position openly and boldly for all to see and hear without fear of coercion. Secrecy was not simply superfluous; it was an insult to Yankee manhood and intrepid independence. The Boston cleric and leading Whig warhorse Samuel K. Lothrop certainly thought so. He took his "stand on ... [the] manhood and independence of character" of open voting instead of whining about intimidation; secrecy only lowered "the tone of manly, moral and independent sentiment."[27] As far as the Boston Whig Thomas Hopkinson was concerned, there was something "immoral" and sleazy about voting in private. "If you would raise a man to a feeling of independence, you must ask him to begin by acting and taking the first step of independence, and not allow him to begin by sneaking first. ... If a man goes up to the polls and deposits a secret ballot very slyly because he wants secrecy, he goes away prepared to [do] the next sly and mean thing." But if he takes a "manly step and does a manly act, and vindicates his independence in the first place, he is prepared to do it again."[28] Thus the secret ballot, according to Whigs, weakened manhood, dissolved personal independence, and shredded the moral fibers that bound men to men in a community of mutual trust and respect. No one captured this moral calamity better than the brazen Lawrence manufacturer Henry K. Oliver, who gloated that he "pinned my vote upon ... my frock," for all to see, for he belonged to "that class of the community that had been held up to public indignation and censure as dictating for those in his employ."[29] He ended:

I should infinitely more respect the manliness and courage, and plain dealing of the laborer or operative who works with me, if he should come to the polls on the day of election, and there boldly and freely deposit his own ballot, even in opposition to my candidate ... than he should vote with me ... against his own convictions, and by any such fawning or cringing hypocrisy, seek to win my favor.

If such a voter was "too cowardly to vote the open ballot in accordance with his convictions ... what assurance have I that he will not show both cowardice and duplicity in other matters?"[30]

[27] Ibid., 1: 751.
[28] Ibid., 1: 752–3.
[29] Ibid., 1: 624.
[30] Ibid., 1: 625.

The distrust of change implied in such a construction of manliness emerged more plainly in the Whigs' appeal to tradition, and particularly to Yankee history, as they understood it. Whigs considered open voting part of the Yankee spirit that made New Englanders what they were. The indefatigable Lord said it best during an 1852 State House speech on behalf of rolling back the secret ballot. Repealing or modifying the law would "restore . . . the rights which . . . [Yankee] fathers had exercised for centuries."[31] Lord, of course, was hardly the only politician to summon the past. Free Soilers and Democrats were also quick to use such an idiom and quicker still when provoked by outsiders who questioned the integrity of their regional customs and traditions, as Southerners were wont to do. When a Democrat noted in a debate about voting regulations that many states, including Virginia, had adopted plurality rule, Henry Wilson snapped that the Bay State was patently more democratic than the Old Dominion. "Well, sir, is she not, so?" he asked, comparing the democratic practices of the "sons of Puritans" to the "sons of Cavaliers" who make "merchandize of more than one-fourth [of] her sons." The Free Soil leader was confident that he did not "need to travel outside of New England to learn about democracy."[32] Such an appeal to Yankee heritage went down especially well in the towns of the country. One cannot read through the constitutional convention debates without getting the impression that the Whigs were playing explicitly to Yankeedom, perhaps more so than were the Free Soilers. George Morey, the new state leader, proved particularly adept at this gambit, flaunting his own origins as a son of the village.[33] Others followed in this spirit because lawmakers in the legislature and delegates to the constitutional convention correctly identified the country as an important bloc and, in some instances, as the swing bloc.

As for the country itself, its rural Coalition men in the legislatures of 1851/2 and at the ensuing constitutional convention in 1853 inexorably invested more political capital in changing the system of political apportionment than in protecting the privacy of the ballot. Whiting Griswold and his village allies had pressed for revising the state constitution chiefly to change the urban-heavy system of apportionment. They attacked the general ticket system of elections under which candidates ran at large on a winner-take-all basis and which necessarily favored

---

[31] Quoted in Brunet, "Secret Ballot Issue in Massachusetts Politics," p. 357.
[32] *Constitutional Convention*, 1: 311.
[33] Ibid., 1: 560–2 and 693–5, vol. 3: 102–5.

Whigs in places like Boston. They charged, perhaps correctly, that the general ticket explained Whiggery's hegemony in the Hub – why it sent uniform delegations of some forty Whigs year after year to the House. They also continued to assail "partial representation" for small towns, which severely compromised the traditional town basis of apportionment that had guaranteed each incorporated place – regardless of size – at least one representative each year in the Massachusetts assembly.[34] As we have already seen, Griswold's proposal would have strengthened the country at the expense of the city by substituting district-based elections for winner-take-all ballots in the city, restoring the town basis of representation, and capping at thirty the number of representatives for any single place, a thumb in the eye of Boston Whiggery.[35]

Nonetheless, the Greenfield Democrat's program made Free Soil captains uneasy. Wilson and his friends not only sought to protect the secrecy of the voting booth but also worked to expand the male electorate by easing traditional voting qualifications, notably residency requirements. In addition, they had a stake in majority rule, which, as Libertyite and Free Soilers knew so well, armed third parties with leverage, sometimes giving them the balance of power in races for the State House in small towns. The "townies" themselves were of mixed minds on majority rule. On the one hand, it burdened local budgets because of the run-off elections that invariably ensued; on the other hand, it gave townsfolk the final say because they could always refuse to hold an additional election if they feared the result.[36]

Diminished political influence was the obsession of country politicians. The more perceptive among them understood that quite apart from the mythology of the "fatal day," they were bound to lose influence because the New England exodus drained the towns of their youth, weakening local economies and reducing political representation. None of that mattered to Griswold and his friends, who pointed accusing fingers at the "centralizing" conspiracy of the "Money Power." They saw themselves as the only counterweight to the city, the direct descendants of the Pilgrim Fathers.[37] The New England town, so this argument went,

---

[34] *BDA*, Nov. 7–9, 1850, and Oct. 31 and Nov. 3–10, passim, 1851. Also see Samuel Shapiro, "The Conservative Dilemma: The Massachusetts Constitutional Convention of 1853," *AQ* 33 (June 1960): 207–24.

[35] *Constitutional Convention*, 1: 809–10 and 814–15, and *NC*, Sept. 24, 1850.

[36] For the debate on majority versus plurality election rules, see ibid., 1: 235–71, 274–316, and 385–436; 3: 86–99, 136–8, 101–18, 131–66, and 771.

[37] Ibid., 1: 237–41 and 820–7.

had been appointed by Providence to defend a heritage corrupted by the money changers in the temples of the city. This righteous appeal enjoyed such currency that it was shared by the more conservative Free Soilers. Thus the former Conscience Whig Richard Henry Dana evoked Timothy Dwight's "village manner," in rhapsodizing the slower, more civil pace of life in the "scattered hamlets of the country." Such bucolic peace, Dana added, in passing, was threatened only by a "floating population."[38]

Dana left it to his fellow conventioneers to flesh out the menace he had in mind. They willingly obliged in an outpouring of atavistic fear laced with xenophobia that starkly revealed the intensifying parochialism of the village, its fear of outsiders and of "the other." The "other" appeared in many garbs. They could be college students, as in the mind of Samuel Duncan, a Williamstown Democrat and lawyer who described an early version of a town-gown set-to in which student pranksters burned an effigy of a selectman who had interfered with their right to vote. A waggish delegate chortled that the students seem to have committed no greater an offense than "voting wrong."[39] The gales of derisive laughter that followed this remark provided a rare moment of levity in a debate that was sinking deeper and deeper into the darkness of small-town suspicion. When the Norfolk Democrat Daniel Churchill accused "outsiders" and townward migrants of harboring "no friendly motives," the Whig farmer Samuel Houghton explained why. He conjured up "a class of people ... [that] might get the control of town affairs into their own hands and undertake to vote away the money of the property owners."[40]

Free Soilers representing manufacturing districts had no such delusions. Having come out forcefully for the protection and expansion of voting rights, they condemned any and all constraints on male suffrage. Henry Williams, a radical Democrat and Coalition lieutenant from the industrial hamlet of Taunton, gave one of the more spirited and revealing retorts to country devotees like Churchill and Houghton. "Independence," he thundered, was the essential condition for every voter in the Commonwealth but especially for those in the towns where open voting "makes the elector more dependent upon those around him ... and forces him to

---

[38] Ibid., 1: 947–8. Also Joseph A. Conforti, *Imagining New England: Explorations of Regional Identity from the Pilgrims to the Mid-Twentieth Century* (Chapel Hill: Univ. of North Carolina Press, 2001), pp. 123–202, and Stephen Nissenbaum, "New England as Region and Nation," in Edward L. Ayers et al., eds., *All Over the Map: Rethinking American Regions* (Baltimore: Johns Hopkins Univ. Press, 1996), pp. 38–61.

[39] *Constitutional Convention*, 2: 117 and 492. Also ibid., 2: 511.

[40] Ibid., 1: 571.

abdicate his opinion." Who and what did Williams have in mind? He meant "pecuniary and business relations," the economic pressures long identified by secret ballot advocates. But Williams also looked beyond the tyrannies of mill and countinghouse to the very fabric of village culture, or what he tellingly called "the espionage and supervision of the public."[41] No one could doubt that this was nothing less than a veiled attack on the communalism celebrated by New England nationalists and recent village politicians alike. It disclosed an underlying tension between the advocates of individual rights and the proponents of communal responsibilities, a tension that confounded the Free Soilers' bid to retain the secret ballot.

Free Soil politicians did not help their case for ballot reform. The same House Committee on Elections in the 1852 session, which investigated the fiasco in Lowell the previous fall, also looked into nearly a dozen cases of election irregularities – virtually all of which arose in such places as Bolton, Sunderland, and Hopkinton, that is, in the heart of the country. The committee easily disposed of specious charges by partisans and party hacks seeking to reverse elections on technicalities as well as of more serious violations born of mendacity or sheer ineptitude.[42] It tossed out charges from the losing sides in North Chelsea and Danvers that ballots submitted in open, unsealed envelopes were illegal, invoking the doctrine of "voter intent."[43] The Whig minority joined the Coalition majority in both cases, probably because the Whigs had opposed any electoral regulations and because they expected to gain from relaxed standards. They unquestionably expected consistency, only to see the Coalitionists fall far short again and again. In a blatant about-face, Coalition committee members repudiated the doctrine of voter intent by rejecting votes in unsealed envelopes in a Hopkinton case and then accepted ballots that mysteriously turned up in a store and a private home after the vote count in Bolton – throwing both elections to their side.[44] They also voided a Sunderland poll in which a Whig narrowly prevailed by ruling that the selectmen had done no harm by counting two deciding votes found after the initial count.[45] Understandably outraged, Whig committee member William Schouler wrote a withering minority report that put his party on the side of procedural propriety, bashing Free Soilers with their own weapon. Electoral procedures, he wrote, "keep pure the fountain-head

---

[41] Ibid., 1: 549–50. Quote is on p. 549.
[42] Massachusetts House of Representatives, House Documents, Document No. 52 (1852).
[43] Ibid., Doc. Nos. 59 and 86; also, Doc. No. 96.
[44] Ibid., Doc. Nos. 95 and 96.
[45] Ibid., Doc. Nos. 97 and 102.

of political power," preventing "all sorts of abominations, cheating and corruption on our elections."[46]

Whiggish critics could not have invented a better brief against the secret ballot than the Free Soilers' inconsistency and weakness for treachery. Party spokesmen did not hesitate to proclaim that they had been right all along – reform made things worse, not better. Schouler wrote that as "long as the secret ballot law remains a living, active agent in our elections, the principle involved in this case will never cease to be felt. Cheating would become, as Shakespeare says, 'as easy as lying.'"[47] He was joined by party journalists who attacked ballot reform in language contrived for the country.[48] Otis Lord, the graybeard from Salem and a trenchant critic of secrecy, held forth in that spirit as well, promising that his party would "restore [to] them the rights which their fathers had exercised for centuries."[49] He had every incentive to try. Publicity over the Lowell election had given Whiggery a black eye; party infighting over liquor licensing opened the breach between city and country that had been so costly in the past. Lowell and liquor left men like Lord badly in need of a galvanic issue to unite the party. They were given such an issue by the opposition's ham-handedness on the secret ballot, which gave the Whigs on the House Committee on Elections a tocsin to arouse the people of the towns. Their party's astonishing rebound in the 1852 state elections was fueled in part by the give-and-take of the politics of ballot reform. The Whigs had regained some of the country by repealing the secret ballot; the Democrats would reclaim the rest through other means.

The Whigs' righteous assault on the secret ballot in 1852 set the stage for one of the more raucous legislative sessions of the era. Party leaders had to act quickly and decisively in February a year later so that voters would vote openly when they went to the polls on March 7 to choose delegates to a state constitutional convention, which was expected to revisit the ballot question. The leadership made "evisceration" of the secret ballot law its top priority, drafting a repeal bill within the first week of the term. Pandemonium broke out when debate began in the Senate. Free Soilers fought back, both figuratively and literally, first using parliamentary measures to delay the vote and then threatening a fistfight.[50] Whigs then settled for a bill making secrecy voluntary, a step short of outright repeal but its

[46] Ibid., Doc. No. 102, p. 3.
[47] Ibid., p. 4.
[48] *BA*, Dec. 27, 1852, and Brunet, "Secret Ballot Issue in Massachusetts Politics," pp. 356-7.
[49] *Constitutional Convention*, 1: 175.
[50] Brunet, "Secret Ballot Issue in Massachusetts Politics," p. 358. Also see *Comm*, Feb. 26 and Mar. 5, 1853, and *BP*, Feb. 21 and 28, 1853.

functional equivalent, and rushed it through both chambers in time for the governor's signature a few days before the March election.[51] Free Soilers were dazed. Cocky and confident party leaders thought they could shrug off the embarrassment in the Senate but talk of defections changed their mood. William Robinson and his two lieutenants signed an open letter opposing any tampering with the law, an extraordinary measure intended to firm up discipline.[52] The letter bore 136 signatures, precisely the number of votes party bosses claimed to have in hand in an early vote against the revised bill. That still left them 10 votes short of a majority, votes that they never came close to rounding up in subsequent polls.[53] Robinson could not move some Coalitionists, who were more enthusiastic about prohibitionism or Griswoldism than about the secret ballot. Nor could he reverse the damage done to his party in the fall elections. Free Soilers in the country cast twelve fewer votes for the secret ballot in 1853 than they had cast for it in 1851, reflecting both the 1852 election and perhaps the doubt over secret voting in their ranks. Whig lawmakers (in our four areas) cast twenty more votes against secret voting in 1853 than they had cast against it in 1851. The party's country faction accounted for the bulk of the change – and for ending the Commonwealth's brief experience with voting in secret.[54]

The battle did not end there. In March, the Coalition elected a majority of the delegates to the constitutional convention, who then wrote a secret ballot clause into the draft. They also penned a reapportionment provision inspired by Griswoldism, which aroused something close to the impossible – an opposition of urban Whigs and Democrats.[55] That unlikely alliance, bolstered by some Coalitionists, defeated the draft constitution at the polls in November, insuring that Bay Staters would vote openly for the next forty years.[56]

Political savants were confident that for all their high-minded moralizing country lawmakers and constitutional convention delegates were as

---

[51] *LA*, Feb. 28, 1853, and Brunet, "Secret Ballot Issue in Massachusetts Politics," pp. 358–9.

[52] *LA*, Feb. 28, 1853, and *Comm*, Mar. 1, 1853.

[53] See House Journal, 1853, Appendixes Nos. 56, 59, and 60.

[54] House Journal, 1853, Appendix No. 61. Also see Shapiro, "Conservative Dilemma." On the chronic chicanery attendant in part on open voting, see U.S. Congress, Senate Select Committee to Enquire into Alleged Election Fraud in Massachusetts, Report No. 497, "Intimidation and Fraud in Massachusetts," 46th Cong., 2d sess. (Washington, D.C.: U.S. Government Printing Office, 1880), pp. 5–6, 196–7, and 241ff. Also Richard Henry Dana, "The Practical Working of the Australian Ballot System in Massachusetts," *AAAPSS* 72 (May 1892): 733–50. Also see Appendixes 3 and 4.

[55] Kevin Sweeney, "Rum, Romanism, Representation, and Reform: Coalition Politics in Massachusetts, 1847–1853," *CWH* 6 (June 1976): 116–37.

[56] Laurie, " 'Penitent's Bench.' "

susceptible to horse trading as the political regulars they held in such contempt. Some said that country Free Soilers sacrificed the secret ballot for for Whig support for the Bay State's Maine Law, a sweeping prohibition statute passed in 1852.[57] Not that there was much wet ground left. By the time the law took effect in summer, nearly every county in the Commonwealth was dry; the glaring exception was Suffolk County, the home of Boston. And from the perspective of Yankeedom, that was a problem, an acute one given the country's visceral hostility to the city. The other problem was the seeming apathy of the drys. The popular passion that had fueled the Washingtonian uprising at the turn of the 1830s and its successor Sons of Temperance had cooled. Local lodges slipped into inaction, bringing down vigilance committees that had brought charges against violators of county licensing laws. Then they suddenly sprung back to life at the turn of the 1840s, partly in response to the opportunity posed by the rise of Free Soilism but mostly in a reaction to the influx of the Irish.[58] Press and pulpit reacted to the newcomers with alarm, rallying the troops of the "Cold Water Army" with demonstrations centering in the country. In winter 1849, coincident with the beginnings of the Coalition in eastern counties, the revivified Massachusetts State Temperance Society called the first of several conventions in Boston over the next few years, confronting the putative enemy on its own turf. Local regulation had failed; it was time for a statewide ban.[59]

Bay State prohibitionists drew energy in 1851 from fellow drys in nearby Maine who put the nation's first statewide licensing law on the books. Encouraged by the Maine Law, they "went about their work with fervor not seen since the heyday of Washingtonianism at the start of the decade," as one observer put it.[60] Countywide temperance societies, based in the country and coordinated by the State Temperance Society, followed a two-pronged strategy. They quizzed office seekers in 1851 on their support for a Maine Law and collected signatures on petitions demanding such a measure. The petitions were a huge success, dwarfing similar campaigns against gag rule or, more recently, in favor of a ten-hour day. Prohibitionists gathered over one hundred thirty thousand

[57] *Comm*, May 25, 1852.
[58] Robert L. Hampel, *Temperance and Prohibition in Massachusetts* (Ann Arbor, Mich.: UMI Research Press, 1982), esp. pp. 129–43.
[59] Mark Voss-Hubbard, *Beyond Party: Cultures of Antipartisanship in Northern Politics before the Civil War* (Baltimore: Johns Hopkins Univ. Press, 2002), pp. 71 and 78–81.
[60] *NC*, Oct. 8, 1850. Also Karen V. Hansen, *A Very Social Time: Crafting Community in Antebellum New England* (Berkeley and Los Angeles: Univ. of California Press, 1994), pp. 162–3.

signatures on their 1852 petition, over a dozen times more than would be on the ten-hour petitions submitted the following year at the height of labor reform. About half the signers of the temperance petitions were women.[61]

Prohibition differed from other reform movements as well. It originated in the civil sphere with a network of independent organizations, sometimes affiliated with churches or sponsored by the ministry. Such a provenance distinguished temperance from political reform, which reflected popular grievances, to be sure, but never rose to the status of a movement outside of party politics. Instead, the secret ballot was a hobbyhorse of politicians, first Democrats, then Free Soilers, and finally both. The ten-hour movement also had its own structure but proved more narrowly partisan and somewhat more fitful – rising, falling, and usually having to start anew. Temperance likewise effervesced, but it showed more durability over time, cropping up in different organizational guises in pursuit of similar goals.[62] It predated ten-hour sentiment by at least a decade and had a much wider geographic distribution and a broader social compass. Temperance organizations reached from city to country and, over time, strengthened in the latter without losing the urban base. Ten-hour groups, in contrast, were confined perforce to cities and industrial towns and resonated with a relatively small segment of the population consisting of workers and their middling allies; it cut across class lines, uniting a segment of the emergent working class with the middling sort and, in some instances, with elements of the local elite.[63] Both movements clearly had aspects in common. Labor reform had a populist sensibility, prohibition a class dimension, but each also had an essence. The suppression of drink was to the politics of populism what the ten-hour movement was to the politics of class.

Temperance in part reflected the invasive populist spirit of the country. As local elites in Concord found out in the 1830s when the movement was in its second incarnation, temperance was like a crusade. Self-appointed liquor police in the birthplace of the American Revolution visited every family in town to solicit petition signatures, making a point of exposing first families that "imbibed prejudices against *binding*

[61] Voss-Hubbard, *Beyond Party*, pp. 78–81.

[62] Hampel, *Temperance and Prohibition in Massachusetts*; George Faber Clark, *History of the Temperance Reform in Massachusetts, 1813–1883* (Boston: Clark and Carruth, 1888); and Ian Tyrell, *Sobering Up: From Temperance to Prohibition in Antebellum America, 1800–1860* (Westport, Conn.: Greeenwood Press, 1979).

[63] Hampel, *Temperance of Prohibition in Massachusetts*, pp. 31–5, and Tyrrell, *Sobering Up*, pp. 92–113.

themselves."[64] Such pressure from below persisted into the late 1830s, propelling the town committees prowling for violators of the license laws.[65] The easing of vigilance at the end of the decade set the stage for another outburst of antiliquor zealotry, this time accompanied by a change in tactics. Temperance advocates came out for a statewide ban on the sale and distribution of spirits, that is, for prohibition.[66]

Where to turn for support? Bay State prohibitionists did not have much choice. Urban Whigs, still smarting from the ruinous divisiveness over the infamous fifteen-gallon law, were as stony as New England granite. For their part, conservative Democrats could tolerate the voluntarism of temperance but not the legal coercion of prohibition, and not because of their libertarian outlook alone. The liquor question also complicated their Irish strategy. The Coalition of Free Soilers and radical Democrats, whose leadership ranks just happened to overlap with that of the prohibition movement was the only option. William S. Robinson and Francis Bird, to cite only the most prominent Coalitionists, cut their political teeth on the temperance movement.[67]

Such support made the 1852 Maine Law all but inevitable. The complicated give-and-take that produced this landmark measure is best left for another forum. It is enough to observe here that the vote in the House somewhat qualifies the conventional wisdom of a division between city and country. Free Soilers, who retained their urban-industrial base through 1852, voted overwhelmingly for prohibition (70 to 8).[68] This is not wholly surprising in light of the party's popularity among the Yankee workers with better-paying jobs in the metal industry in places like Lowell. Such workers were drawn to temperance and then to prohibition by their religious heritage and by their tendency to associate abstinence with social respectability.[69] Their growing nativism was an additional motivator.

---

[64] Quoted in Hampel, *Temperance and Prohibition in Massachusetts*, p. 29.

[65] Ibid., pp. 61–78.

[66] Ibid., pp. 147–63.

[67] Claudia L. Bushman, *"A Good Poor Man's Wife": Being a Chronicle of Harriet Hansen Robinson and Her Family in Nineteenth-Century New England* (Hanover, N.H.: Univ. Press of New England, 1981), pp. 71–2, and Donald B. Marti, "Francis William Bird: A Radical's Progress through the Republican Party," *HJM* 11 (June 1983): 82–93.

[68] See *NC*, June 1 and 7, 1852. Also see Hampel, *Temperance and Prohibition in Massachusetts*, pp. 147–51.

[69] See, for instance, Jama Lazerow, *Religion and the Working Class in Jacksonian America* (Washington, D.C.: Smithsonian Institution Press, 1995), and William R. Sutton, *Journeymen for Jesus: Evangelical Artisans Confront Capitalism in Baltimore* (University Park: Pennsylvania State Univ. Press, 1998).

At the same time, Free Soilism also had support in the country, especially in the villages of the northeast and southeast, which voted nearly unanimously for prohibition. Prohibition was strongest in the five western counties. Lawmakers in the state as a whole supported the law by 2 to 1; those in the five western counties supported it by 3 to 1.[70]

The Bay State's Maine Law was one of the more sweeping measures approved by the General Court in the early 1850s. It criminalized the manufacture, sale, and distribution of liquor except for "medicinal, chemical and mechanical purposes." Those seeking an exemption had to apply to county or local officials who could approve sales "in quantities not less than thirty gallons." Violators faced substantial fines of ten dollars and twenty dollars for first and second offenses, respectively, plus jail terms for third missteps. More important still, the law authorized committees composed of three voters to file complaints with local justices of the peace or police courts if "they have reason to believe that spiritous or intoxicating liquors are kept or deposited, and intended for sale, by any person not authorized . . . in any store, shop, warehouse . . . or any building."[71] The measure reflected the dual tendency of local control and citizen surveillance associated with temperance militancy and village communalism.

The Maine Law unleashed a liquor panic that flared into ugly vigilanteeism. This neglected aspect of the measure reached its most extreme expression in the country, where militant clergy and fire-breathing journalists joined hands to take advantage of the provision for citizen enforcement of the draconian law. The ink was barely dry on the measure when, in summer 1852, Congregational ministers in Hampshire County called a meeting in Northampton to get up a vigilance committee to coordinate small groups of volunteer police in twenty-two of the county's twenty-three towns. Local groups of temerance enthusiasts, working with town authorities, began to enforce the law before the Northampton meeting. It was reported at the meeting that the "enemy has not dared to show" itself.[72] Only three search warrants were issued in a month, two of which were found to be groundless. In one instance, the owner of a gallon of liquor that had been discovered in an attic could not be identified; in another, an alleged offender implicated his supplier, who promptly fled.[73]

[70] NC, Apr. 27, 1852.
[71] Ibid., June 8 and July 27, 1852.
[72] Ibid., June 15, 1852.
[73] Ibid., Aug. 3 and 10, 1852.

The identities of the suspects in the country remain unclear in some cases. In others, village zealots clearly used the law to go after undesirables. North Adams officials rifled through the homes and stores of persons suspected of harboring contraband. Tipped off by the town's vigilance committee, they dug out the foundation of a house to reveal a keg buried just below the surface and reachable from the inside of the cellar by removing a loose brick. The suspects, a hapless Irish couple thought to be chronic offenders, were dragged before the authorities, who fined them and clapped them in jail for violating the law and resisting arrest.[74] In the Worcester County village of West Boylston, militants went after the two African American proprietors of a small restaurant. The partners were arrested and hauled before a judge in Clinton. The judge came down hard on them, imposing a fine of thirty dollars for two offenses, and a term of ninety days in jail for a third. Before being carted off, they had to post a one thousand dollar bond under which they could not sell liquor for a year.[75] Enforcement sometimes made for sport and farce at once, as it did in the textile hamlet of Cabotville. Local agents there ceremoniously poured two kegs of confiscated spirits into the street in front of a cheering crowd. A "mischievous boy" struck a match that ignited the alcohol into a blaze, which spread to a wooden sewer, bringing out the volunteer firemen. Fighting crime was complicated business in the village.[76]

Only a timely ruling by a state judge, troubled by the excesses of the drys in and out of government, ended the searches and break-ins of summer 1852. The larger part of the Maine Law, however, remained on the books, the one Coalition measure reviewed here that stuck after getting through the General Court. The ten-hour law was scuttled in the legislature, despite having the backing of a relatively strong movement. The secret ballot, which had some movement support, had made it through the process but could not withstand the backlash from Whigs and their village allies. Thus, in the Bay State, cultural populism trumped laborism.

[74] Ibid.
[75] Ibid., Aug. 17, 1852.
[76] Ibid., Aug. 10, 1852.

8

"Prejudices against Us"

The Limits of Paternalism

Free Soilers dealt with State Reform because they had to, not because they wanted to. It was the political price of coalition with the Democrats, the undeniable wellspring of political reapportionment, labor reform, and the secret ballot, if not the more volatile question of prohibition. The politics of race, however, was another matter. Henry Wilson and his fellows were pressed hard by black activists in Massachusetts, and harder by the mounting storm over slavery in Washington, to respond to the questions of slavery in the territories and institutional racism at home. They did respond to such pressures but had very little to show for their efforts in the legislature under the Free Soil banner, as we shall see in this chapter. Ironically, Wilson and his comrades compiled a more impressive record in the legislature on antislavery and civil rights after 1854 when many of them joined the newly formed Know-Nothing Party, as we shall see in the next chapter.

In April 1850, Joseph Tinker Buckingham, now a Free Soiler from Cambridge, rose on the floor of the state Senate to denounce his old friend and benefactor Daniel Webster for defending the Fugitive Slave Act. Though Webster had actually called for softening the law, no one listened, least of all Buckingham. He explained that Webster for "thirty years was my *beau ideal* of a statesman," and "political mentor." But this "happy intercourse" was "at an end" now that the great orator had disgraced himself by licking the boots of the Slave Power, all but inviting slave catchers to the free soil of the Commonwealth.[1] Buckingham's ostentatious break with Webster and Whiggery was not quite as

[1] *MS*, Apr. 23, 1850. Also see ibid., May 9, 1850.

precipitous as it appeared, however. It had been building for years but stemmed most recently from the feisty's journalist's decision in 1846 to publish Charles Sumner's withering attack on the conservative Congressman Robert Winthrop. Buckingham thereby brought down on himself the wrath of Winthrop's Cotton Whig friends who got an apology from the contrite editor. It was a rare retreat for a man who had held his ground in the ten-hour strike of 1832, stubbornly refusing to appease angry Whig critics by repudiating his support for workingmen. Now tempers were shorter, stakes higher, and compromise more elusive. There was no going back for Buckingham in spring 1848 when his party nominated the Louisiana planter Zachary Taylor for president. The nomination was an egregious act, he wrote in his *Courier,* one that violated his own "notions of honor and independence" and forced him to give up his paper and leave the party.[2] Thus the mounting controversy over slavery proved especially expensive for Buckingham, costing him the paper he had founded twenty-five years earlier, the party he had served for nearly two decades, and the friendship of the man who had launched his career.

Buckingham's departure from Whiggery became the talk of the Hub's journalists. The caustic Elizur Wright, who was about to become Buckingham's brother in the Free Soil fraternity, was especially pleased. In a backhanded tribute to the aging editor who was by now the dean of the city's newspapermen, Wright called Buckingham "the [Whiggiest] of the [W]higs" on the tariff yet a man of principle who would "never be the slave of... party" but who had had the misfortune to serve rich but stingy masters. "If the 'cottonites,' had any decency," he wrote, they would raise money for "[Buckingham's] retirement" as a sort of "acknowledgement" of his work on behalf of "their pockets."[3] Few other observers, with a better appreciation for the larger political context, took such a sarcastic view of Buckingham's dramatic break with his past. The editor's bolt from Whiggery was symptomatic of a grave political crisis not over local issues, as some modern-day historians have argued, but over slavery and its local ramifications – more particularly, over the Fugitive Slave Act. The law that had caused so much controversy in distant Washington, also shook the rocky ground of old Massachusetts, once again erasing the distinction between national and local and packing enough wallop to destroy friendships and snap partisan affiliations.

The toxic force in this personal and political drama, the Fugitive Slave Act of 1850, was something of an anomaly in an age of weak national

---

[2] Gary J. Kornblith, "From Artisans to Businessmen: Master Mechanics in New England, 1790–1850" (Ph.D. diss., Princeton Univ., 1983), pp. 196–7.

[3] *DC,* June 26, 1848.

government.[4] The law stands out for substantially strengthening federal power. Its 1793 predecessor was a spare measure requiring slave owners in search of fugitives to secure warrants from federal judges, who at the time were few in number and too powerless to be of much help beyond issuing hunting licenses.[5] The 1850 update put federal muscle on the side of slave owners by authorizing circuit courts to appoint federal commissioners who, in turn, could muster posses of special officers to track down runaways. Marshals who failed to respond to court orders faced stiff fines; commissioners who ruled in favor of slave owners were rewarded with a ten dollar bounty for each fugitive who was remanded (five dollars if not), a powerful symbol of federal intent. For their part, slave owners or their agents could either get a warrant from a federal judge or commissioner or simply seize a fugitive and bring the runaway before the appropriate authorities. Obstructionists risked fines of one thousand dollars, six months in jail, or both. Fugitives hauled before the tribunals had no legal protections whatever – no habeas corpus, no trial by jury, no right to testify.[6] It was a breathtaking assertion of federal authority.

The controversial law rattled Yankees like nothing else had – not the election of Andrew Jackson, not nullification, not gag rule. It plunged Boston into constant turmoil starting in fall 1850 when black abolitionists rushed to protect the fugitive slaves William and Ellen Craft from federal agents and sent the couple to a safe exile in England.[7] The couple's African

---

4 See Stanley W. Campbell, *The Slave Catchers: Enforcement of the Fugitive Slave Law, 1850–1860* (Chapel Hill: Univ. of North Carolina Press, 1968), and Thomas D. Morris, *Free Men All: The Personal Liberty Laws of the North, 1780–1861* (Baltimore: Johns Hopkins Univ. Press, 1974), esp. pp. 130–47. Also see Don E. Fehrenbacher, *The Slaveholding Republic: An Account of the United States Government's Relationship with Slavery* (New York: Oxford Univ. Press, 2001), esp. pp. 205–51, and James Oliver Horton and Lois E. Horton, "A Federal Assault: African Americans and the Fugitive Slave Act," in Paul Finkelman, ed., *Slavery and the Law* (Madison, Wisc.: Madison House, 1997), pp. 143–60.
5 Campbell, *Slave Catchers*, pp. 8–9.
6 Ibid., pp. 24–5. Also see Richard H. Sewell, *Ballots for Freedom: Antislavery Politics in the United States, 1837–1860* (New York: Oxford Univ. Press, 1976), pp. 326–39, and Leonard L. Richards, *The Slave Power: The Free North and Southern Domination, 1780–1860* (Baton Rouge: Louisiana State Univ. Press, 2000), pp. 71 and 181–3.
7 R. J. M. Blackett, ed., *Running a Thousand Miles for Freedom: The Escape of William and Ellen Craft from Slavery* (1860; Baton Rouge: Louisiana State Univ. Press, 1999). See also Henry Wilson, *History of the Rise and Fall of the Slave Power in America*, 3 vols. (Boston: James R. Osgood, 1872–7), 2: 325–36; James Oliver Horton and Lois E. Horton, *Black Bostonians: Family Life and Community Struggle in the Antebellum North* (New York: Holmes and Meier, 1979), pp. 103–5; and Tilden G. Edelstein, *Strange Enthusiasm: A Life of Thomas Wentworth Higginson* (New Haven, Conn.: Yale Univ. Press, 1968), pp. 105–6. Also see *DC*, Oct. 29–30 and Dec. 2, 1850.

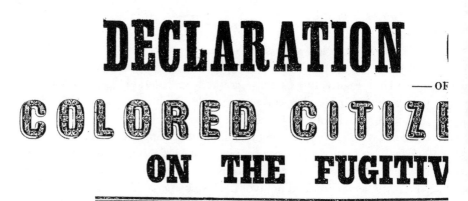

DECLARATION

—— OF

COLORED CITIZ[ENS]

ON THE FUGITIV[E]

Per adjournment, the Friends of Freedom rallied at Belknap Street Church, on Friday Evening, October 5th, 1850, a vast concourse, including Fugitives and their Friends were in attendance,—the organization was completed as follows :—

LEWIS HAYDEN, *President.*

JOHN T. HILTON,
WILLIAM CRAFTS, } *Vice Presidents.*
HENRY WATSON,

WILLIAM C. NELL, } *Secretaries.*
ISAAC H. SNOWDEN,

Th[e] . . . present was . . . adjourned n . . . Monday, and trusted the Vigilant . . . . . . come prepared for definite action on the Fugitive Slave Bill. Though the people were Seventeen Million Strong, he trusted to influences, such as might emanate from these meetings for its Nullification,—the party were now augmenting who knew their rights, and knowing, dare maintain them.

ROBERT MORRIS, Esq., called for the Report of the Committee, which was submitted by William C. Nell, as follows:

The Fugitive Slave Bill, (exhibited in its hideous deformity at our previous meeting,) has already in hot haste commenced its bloody crusade o'er the land, and the liability of ourselves and families becoming its victims at the caprice of Southern men-stealers, imperatively demands an expression, whether we will tamely submit to chains and slavery, or whether we will, at all and every hazard, LIVE and DIE freemen.

The system of American slavery, the vilest that ever saw the sun, is a violation of every sentiment of Christianity and the antipodes of every dictate of humanity.—The slaveholder's pretensions to a claim on human property, are of no more weight than those of the midnight assassin or the pirate on the high seas. "God made all men FREE,—free as the birds that cleave the air or sing on the branches, — free as the sunshine that gladdens the earth,—free as the winds that sweep over sea and land, —free at his birth,—free during his whole life,—free to-day,—this hour —this moment."

The Massachusetts Bill of Rights declares that ALL MEN are born free and equal, and have certain natural, essential and inalienable rights, among which may be reckoned the right of enjoying and defending their liberties.

The example of the Revolutionary Fathers in resisting British oppression, throwing the tea overboard in Boston Harbor, rather than submit to a three-penny tax, is a most significant one to us, when MAN is likely to be deprived of his God-given liberty.

Among the incidents of that seven years' struggle for liberty, and to which the page of impartial history bears record, is the fact that the first Martyr in the attack on residents was a colored man. Crispus Attucks by name, who fell in State Street on the 5th of March, 1770. In that

Whereas, Thousands in the land from every class and profession in life, without exception, are eagerly registering their vows to oppose this infamous enactment, at whatever cost of money, reputation or life.

Whereas, Sustained as we are, by examples of Mosaic and Christian practice, and from the history of civil society from the earliest ages; encouraged by the voices of our brethren from the East and the West, from the North, and even the tyrant's domain, the bloody South (where many true hearts beat for freedom). But above all, and independent of any suggestions, counsels or examples, guided by our own promptings for the freedom of ourselves and families, (by which we mean, of course, all those in any way exposed to danger from the slave power) and believing that Resistance to tyrants is obedience to God, we are now

Resolved, To organise a League of Freedom, composed of all those who are ready to resist this law, rescue and protect the slave, at every hazard, and who remember that

"Whether on the scaffold high,
Or in the battle's van,
The fittest place where MAN can DIE,
Is where he dies for MAN."

Resolved, That in view of the imminent danger, present and looked for, we caution every colored man, woman and child, to be careful in their walks through the highways and byways of the city by day, and doubly so, if out at night, as to WHERE they go—HOW they go—and WHO they go with; to be guarded on side, off side and all sides; as watchful as Argus with his hundred eyes, and as executive as was Briereus, with as many hands; if seized by any one, to make the air resound with the signal-word, and as they would rid themselves of any wild beast, be prompt in their hour of peril.

Resolved, That any Commissioner who would deliver up a fugitive slave to a Southern highwayman, under this infamous and unconstitutional law, would have delivered up Jesus Christ to his persecutors for one-third of the price that Judas Iscariot did.

Resolved, That in the event of any Commissioner of Massachusetts being applied to for remanding a fugitive, we trust he will emulate the example of Judge Harrington, of Vermont, and "be satisfied with nothing short of a bill of sale from the Almighty."

Resolved, That though we learn that bribes have already been offered to our Judiciary to forestall their influence against the panting fugitive, we would not attempt any other offset, than to remind said officers that

"Man is more than Constitutions—
He'd better rot beneath the sod,
Than be true to Church and State
And doubly false to GOD;"

that should he, in the emergency obey God rather than the devil, by letting the oppressed go free, he will have done his part in wiping out from the escutcheon of Massachusetts the foul stain inflicted by Daniel Webster in promoting, and Samuel A. Eliot in voting for this Heaven-defying law.

Resolved, That though we gratefully acknowledge that the mane of the British Lion affords a nestling place for our brethren in danger from the claws of the American Eagle, we would, nevertheless, counsel against their leaving the soil of their birth, consecrated by their tears, toils and perils, but yet to be rendered truly, the "land of the free and the home of the brave." The ties of consanguinity, bid ALL remain who would lend a helping hand to the millions now in bonds. But at all events, if the soil of Bunker Hill, Concord and Lexington is the last bulwark of liberty, we can nowhere fill more honorable graves.

Resolved, That we do earnestly express the hope that the citizens of Boston will rally in Faneuil Hall, and send forth in the ear of all christendom their opinion of the infamous Fugitive Slave Bill, and of their intention to DISOBEY its decrees; their voice, uttered in the Cradle of Liberty, will assure us as nothing else can, whether they are to be reckoned on the side of liberty or slavery—whether they will vouchsafe to us their aid, or will assist the manthief in hurling us and our little ones into interminable bondage.

Resolved, That this meeting would invite the clergymen in this city and vicinity to dedicate a day or part thereof, in presenting to their people by prayer and sermon, their Christian duty to the flying fugitive, and also in acceding to requisitions of this atrocious Bill.

FIGURE 21. Broadside covering a meeting of African Americans in Boston on October 5, 1850, condemning the Fugitive Slave Act. (Courtesy of the American Antiquarian Society, Worcester, Mass.)

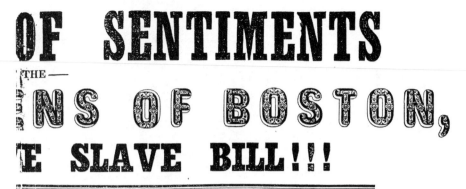

not buy one otherwise to sell his coat for that purpose. As for himself, and he thus exhorted others, he should be kind and courteous to all, even the slave dealer, until the moment of an attack upon his liberty. He should not be taken ALIVE, but upon the slave catcher's head be the consequences. When he could not live here in Boston a FREEMAN, in the language of Socrates, *"He had lived long enough."* Mr. Smith in conclusion made a demonstration of one mode of defence, which those who best know him say would be exemplified to the hilt.

ROBERT JOHNSON proclaimed that the meeting was largely composed of ACTORS, and not speakers merely, they were men of over-alls—men of the wharf—those who could do heavy work in the hour of difficulty. He administered a timely caution to the women, who, in pursuit of washing and other work, visited the hotels and boarding houses, that they should be on the constant look-out for the Southern slave catcher or the *Northern accessory*, and as they valued their liberty be prepared for any emergency. [This word to the *wise* women and others, was greeted with lively demonstrations; some remarking that the spirit exhibited by the women some years since, in a slave rescue from the Supreme Court, was yet alive and ready for action.] He would have it a well understood point in our creed of vigilance, in no case to be ourselves the aggressors; in this it was all important to be cautious; we will not go to the depots or elsewhere after the slave hunter, but when he rushes upon our buckler—*kill him.*

DR. DAN'L MANN spoke of the present state of affairs as affecting us all, white men as well as colored, and detailed many liabilities to which the Fugitive Slave Bill exposed both. He was opposed to war and the spirit of war, but the existing crisis was one that superceded the ordinary scruples:

> "Though space and law the STAG we lend
> Ere hound we slip or bow we bend,
> Who cares HOW, WHERE or WHEN
> The prowling Fox is trapped or slain!"

R. B. ROGERS—would have the Fugitive and his friends remember that it was with the United States Government they were to contend, and that their position in resisting this obnoxious law was that of *Rebels,*— a game however which he did not consider to his credit of

JEFFERSON, and all Martyrs of Liberty. He concurred with Mr. Garrison and others in a reliance upon moral power, but the meeting well understood that in a crisis for *Liberty or Death*, the speaker would not be quietly led like a lamb to the slaughter.

CHARLES LIST, Esq.,—was glad that the fugitives were prepared to defend themselves, and that they solicited a Faneuil Hall meeting of Boston citizens, where they may learn whether their lives and liberties can be secured in the land of the Pilgrim Fathers, or whether men catchers may make hunting grounds of the streets of Boston, driving them at the approach of ◄══════ season to seek in a foreign land, that safety and refuge from oppression which they cannot find here at home.

WM. G. ALLEN being called upon declined in favor of C. C. BRIGGS, of Vermont, the fugitives' friend, Mr. Briggs responded in thoughts that breathed and words that burned for Liberty; testifying to his pride in being a son of the Green Mountain State, where the sentiments of the people had rendered unnecessary any law relative to slavery. He would yield to no man in efforts to befriend and protect the victim of this inhuman law; and though he would caution all against any injudicious movements by way of resistance, yet he could not but express the opinion that those who would not defend, to the death, their Wives, Sisters and Families from the slave hunter were totally unworthy of a position in civil society.

REV. ELIJAH GRISSON urged calling upon the Mayor, and police authorities of Boston for defence. [This was generally opposed, knowing that the city officers were not required by the law to arrest the fugitive, and believing that the police force were not at all ambitious of hunting slaves, the appeal was negatived by an overwhelming vote.]

CHARLES LENOX REMOND—having received word of the meeting at his home in Salem left in express haste to be present and though at a late hour, in obedience to a hearty call, gave vent to one of his best efforts; his zeal to reach the meeting, and his liberty inspiring eloquence was loudly and gratefully appreciated. He alluded to the fact that the infamous provisions of the Slave Bill made all colored persons fugitives, imposing on them the necessity of unceasing vigilance. Numbers are nothing in a good cause;

FIGURE 21. *(continued)*

liberties.

The example of the Revolutionary Fathers in resisting British oppression, throwing the tea overboard in Boston Harbor, rather than submit to a three-penny tax, is a most significant one to us, when MAN is likely to be deprived of his God-given liberty.

Among the incidents of that seven years' struggle for liberty, and to which the page of impartial history bears record, is the fact that the first Martyr in the attack on residents was a colored man. Crispus Attucks by name, who fell in State Street on the 5th of March, 1770. In that conflict, as also in the war of 1812, colored Americans were devoted and gallant worshippers at Freedom's shrine; and pre-eminently at New Orleans, they were warranted in believing that when the victory was achieved, they, as all who fought shoulder to shoulder, would be invited to the banquet. But lo! the white man's banquet has been held, and loud peals to liberty have reached the sky above; but the colored American's share has been to stand outside and wait for the crumbs that fell from Liberty's festive board. And to cap the climax at this advanced hour of the nation's prosperity, and the spread over all Christendom of a sentiment of liberty, fraternity and equality, the colored man, woman and child, bond and nominally free, are hunted like partridges on the mountain, if their hearts aspire for freedom.

The American people glory in the struggle of 1776, and laud the names of those who made the bloody resistance to tyranny. The battle cry of Patrick Henry of Virginia—"GIVE ME LIBERTY, OR GIVE ME DEATH,"—and that of General Warren, "MY SONS SCORN TO BE SLAVES," are immortalized, and we are proud in not being a exception to that inspiration. It warms our hearts, and will nerve our right arms, to do all, and suffer all for Liberty.

The laudation and assistance volunteered by the United States to the Poles and Greeks, and South Americans in their struggles for freedom,— the recent manifestations of sympathy with the Blouses of Paris,—the oppressed of Italy, and with Kossuth and his band of noble Hungarians, are so many incentives to the victims of Republican American despotism, to manfully assert their independence, and martyr-like, DIE freemen, rather than LIVE slaves; confirming also, our pre-determined resolution to abide the issue made with us by the slave power—counting our lives not worth preserving at the expense of our liberties.

In connection with what has been previously adopted, the committee would submit the following preamble and resolutions:

Whereas, the Fugitive Slave Bill is unconstitutional, and in direct conflict with the higher law enjoined by our Saviour, "whatsoever ye would that men should do unto you, do you even so to them."

Whereas, from time immemorial, unrighteous enactments have been nullified by all who feared God rather than man; by Moses the deliverer of Israel, against wicked Pharaoh, and Daniel who welcomed incarceration in a den of Lions, rather than perjure his own soul in obedience to the tyrant's mandate.

Whereas, St. Paul expressly declares that he who will not provide for his own household, is an infidel, having denied the faith.

Whereas, the history of nations attest numerous instances where the gallows stake a████████████comed when security of life and limb might h█████████████to inhuman statutes.

Resolved, That we do earnestly express the hope that the citizens of Boston will rally in Faneuil Hall, and send forth in the ear of all christendom their opinion of the infamous Fugitive Slave Bill, and of their intention to DISOBEY its decrees; their voice, uttered in the Cradle of Liberty, will assure us as nothing else can, whether they are to be reckoned on the side of liberty or slavery—whether they will vouchsafe to us their aid, or will assist the manthief in hurling us and our little ones into interminable bondage.

Resolved, That this meeting would invite the clergymen in this city and vicinity to dedicate a day or part thereof, in presenting to their people by prayer and sermon, their Christian duty to the flying fugitive, and also in acceding to requisitions of this atrocious Bill.

Resolved, That as in union is strength, and in this crisis a combination of power is all-important, this meeting recommend the calling of a New England Convention of the friends of Liberty to operate against the Fugitive Law, and to devise ways and means for consolidating their resources here on the soil.

Resolved, That the doings of this and preceding meeting be published for wide circulation.

The report was accepted, and the resolutions adopted by a unanimous vote.

JOHN T. HILTON, in an eloquent and earnest speech advocated the resolutions—remarking that twenty-five years ago he eulogized, as the greatest talent in the country, Daniel Webster for his efforts on Plymouth Rock on the slavery question, and he regretted exceedingly that that talent should have been used in favor of the odious bill. He was no longer to be trusted by the friends of liberty, for he had done more evil, and committed more sin than a thousand such men as the late Professor Webster ever did. This speaker concluded his remarks which were listened to with marked attention, by saying that when his services should be wanted in defence of their rights, he would desire no greater office than to lead them on to battle and to victory.

JOSHUA B. SMITH, hoped no one in that meeting would preach *Peace*, for as Patrick Henry said, "*There is no Peace.*" He narrated with much feeling the increased consternation of his much loved friend—a Fugitive Slave. Since the passage of this infernal bill a near relative of his claimant having been repeatedly seen skulking around his place of business, evidently anticipating the hour of successful seizure; but that he had done his utmost to dispel the agitation of his friend, bidding him at the outset show himself a man,—*If Liberty is not worth fighting for it is not worth having.* He advised every fugitive to arm himself with a revolver—if he could

Address to the Cler

WE, the trembling, prescribed and hunted fugitives from chattel slavery, now scattered through the various towns and villages of Massachusetts, and momentarily liable to be seized by the strong arm of government, and hurried back to stripes, tortures and a bondage, "one hour of which is fraught with more misery than ages of that which your fathers rose in rebellion to oppose,"— most humbly, importunately, and by the mercies of Christ, implore you at this distressing crisis, to "lift up your voices like a trumpet" against the Fugitive Slave Bill, recently adopted by Congress, and designed for our sure and immediate re-enslavement.

You claim, in a special sense, to be witnesses for God — the ambassadors of Him who came to bind up the broken-hearted, to proclaim liberty to the captives, and the opening of the prison to them that are bound. As you would be clear of the blood of all men, it is for you to give to the down-trodden and the oppressed your deepest sympathies, and to hold up to reprobation those who "frame mischief by a law." It is for you to declare the supremacy of the eternal law of God over all human enactments, whether men will hear or forbear.

After years of unrequited labor, of enforced degradation, of unutterable and inconceivable misery, we have succeeded in making our escape from the southern house of bondage, and in

FIGURE 21. *(continued)*

Ere hound we slip or bow we bend,
Who cares HOW, WHERE or WHEN
The prowling Fox is trapped or slain?"

R. B. ROGERS—would have the Fugitive and his friends remember that it was with the United States Government they were to contend, and that their position in resisting this obnoxious law was that of *Rebels*,—a name however which he did not hesitate to accept, if loyalty to the constitution made him false to humanity. He urged the colored people to strive in securing the moral strength of the community in their favor as a potent lever for their enlargement; but would nevertheless assure them that in the event being forced upon them of a personal contest for Liberty, *God was their helper.*

MR. GARRISON—Though a non-resistant himself and determined with the help of God to live and die such, would yet call upon all to be consistent with their own principles, reminding them that WILLIAM TELL, and GEORGE WASHINGTON were among the glorious names in the world's annals of patriotic devotion to the shrine of Liberty; but after all, the fugitives in this city and elsewhere would be more indebted to the moral power of public sentiment than by any display of physical resistance. In appreciation of their resolution, invoking the religious sentiment in behalf of the poor fugitive, he would submit an address to the clergy;—its reading was called for and produced a marked sensation upon the meeting, and on motion was unanimously incorporated with the minutes. Mr. Garrison also read an extract from Rev. Henry Ward Beecher's late tribute for the fugitive, pledging himself in a characteristic manner to succor and defend him at every conceivable sacrifice. The applause which this demonstration received would have abundantly convinced its noble hearted author that his proffered aid had not fallen upon ungrateful soil;—many prayers ascended to the fugitives' God, for blessings upon him who would thus commit himself unreservedly for the victims of American Slavery.

FATHER HANSON—would tell our oppressors that in condemning resistance on the part of the colored people, they were denouncing the examples of WASHINGTON and

be present and though at a late hour, in obedience to a hearty call, gave vent to one of his best efforts; his zeal to reach the meeting, and his liberty inspiring eloquence was loudly and gratefully appreciated. He alluded to the fact that the infamous provisions of the Slave Bill made all colored persons fugitives, imposing on them the necessity of unceasing vigilance. Numbers are nothing in a good cause;

"Thrice armed is he who hath his quarrel just."

The idea of leaving our homes and firesides was in every sense a mistaken one; the Old Bay State should be our Canada. Boston is the Thermopylæ of the anti-slavery cause. Let us be ready in the trial hour to insure its analogy with that classic spot rendered so illustrious by Leonidas and his Spartan Band, or like the more modern but not less significant—Bunker Hill. The history of our country's struggles for Liberty had never been disgraced by a *colored* Arnold; if then we have not proved traitors to the white man, in God's name shall we not prove true to ourselves? He believed that the Fugitive Slave Law had been enacted in great part at the instance of the hand maid of slavery, the Colonization Society in the wicked hope that the fear of being recaptured into bondage would move the colored man to emigrate to Liberia. But this feature only made the whole more damnable, and was to be opposed at all and every point. After rebuking the colored people for lack of anti-slavery character, he declared that he would not yield to any institution or individual that would abridge his liberties or his efforts for the fugitive, and was happy in believing that the colored citizens of Boston would do their whole duty and defend themselves.

Dr. BOWDITCH moved a general circulation among the masses of the address to the clergy.

The meeting was further addressed by Messrs. SPEAR, PIERCE, PICKETT, and others.

On motion the Address to the Clergy was adopted by acclamation and ordered to be published.

After a hymn of Liberty the gathering separated mutually pledging, as did Hannibal, "*Eternal Hostility to Slavery!*"

LEWIS HAYDEN, *President.*
WILLIAM C. NELL, *Secretary.*

gy of Massachusetts.

Now, therefore, by the solemn injunction of a Christian apostle, " Remember them that are in bonds as bound with them," we implore you, from your pulpits to denounce that iniquitous law!

By the command of Christ, " Whatsoever ye would that men should do to you, do ye even so to them," denounce the law!

By all the horrors and iniquities compressed into that system of slavery, which Wesley has justly styled "the sum of all villainies," denounce the law!

By the cherished memories of Pilgrim Fathers and Revolutionary Sires, denounce the law!

By your warm approval of your country's Declaration of Independence, denounce the law!

By your belief in the scriptural affirmation, that by one God are we all created, and that he "hath made of one blood all nations of men to dwell on all the face of the earth," denounce the law!

By all the woes and warnings pronounced by the prophets against those who refuse to hide the outcast, and bewray him that wandereth—who decree unrighteous decrees, and write grievousness which they have prescribed, to turn aside the needy from judgment—denounce the law!

FIGURE 21. *(continued)*

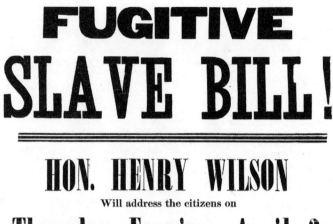

FUGITIVE
SLAVE BILL!

HON. HENRY WILSON
Will address the citizens on
Thursday Evening, April 3,
At the

At 7 o'clock, on the all-engrossing topics of the day—the FUGI-
TIVE SLAVE BILL, the pro-slavery action of the National Government and the general aspect of the Slavery question.

Let every man and woman, without distinction of sect or party,
attend the meeting and bear a testimony against the system which
fills the prisons of a free republic with men whose only crime is a
love of freedom—which strikes down the habeas corpus and trial by
jury, and converts the free soil of Massachusetts into hunting ground
for the Southern kidnappers.

Ashby, March 29, 1851.

White & Potter's Steam Press....4000 Impressions per hour....Spring Lane, Boston.

FIGURE 22. Broadside distributed by the Free Soil Party calling a rally on April 3,
1851, to denounce enforcement of the Fugitive Slave Act. (Courtesy of the
American Antiquarian Society, Worcester, Mass.)

American allies pulled off an even bolder rescue the following February by
snatching the fugitive slave Shadrach Minkins from a courtroom literally
in front of the judge and sending Minkins on his way to freedom in
Canada.[8] The friends of runaway slaves in Boston would never again
manage to thwart the slave catchers, but as the case of Anthony Burns
demonstrates, it was not because they did not try.

[8] Gary Collison, *Shadrach Minkins: From Fugitive Slave to Citizen* (Cambridge: Harvard
Univ. Press, 1997), is the only recent account of this episode. For contemporaneous coverage from a Free Soil perspective, see *Comm*, Feb.– June 1851 passim; for a Democratic
perspective, see *BP*, Feb.–June 1851 passim.

Though the details of his escape from Richmond remain in dispute, Anthony Burns probably stowed away on a ship that landed in Boston in mid-February 1854.[9] Integrating himself within a few weeks into the city's small but supportive African American community, he was befriended by William Jones, a black casual worker and labor contractor wise in the ways of the street. Jones arranged several jobs for the young fugitive eager to begin life anew. But Burns's plans came undone within three months when a letter he had written to his brother wound up in the hands of his master, Charles F. Suttle. Suttle promptly left for Boston with his agent, William Brent, to reclaim his property on the strength of a warrant issued on May 24 by Judge Edward G. Loring. The next day, U.S. Commissioner Asa Butman, a Boston police officer who had tangled with local militants in the arrest and abduction of Thomas Sims in 1851, apprehended Burns on a trumped-up charge of jewelry theft as Burns was leaving his job at Coffin Pitts's second-hand clothing store, located in the black district on the slope of Beacon Hill. Butman took Burns before Judge Loring, who ordered him held under the Fugitive Slave Act. At an uneventful hearing Burns was identified as Suttle's slave, and the court ordered that he be returned to his master on June 2.

Burns's rendition supplied the spectacle conspicuously absent from his trial. Mayor Jerome V. C. Smith placed the city under martial law. He ordered the police to close all businesses along Court Street to Commercial Street and to seal off all intersecting avenues in order to clear a path to the wharf where a ship was waiting in the harbor. At 2:00 P.M. armed police took Burns from his cell and placed him in the middle of a hollow square formed by a marshal's guard with their pistols and cutlasses in hand. Next came a company of U.S. Marines, followed by a horse-drawn field piece and a contingent of the Fourth Artillery Regiment. Just ahead was another Marine company and a force of U.S. infantry. The city's own Northern Lancers led the procession, emblematic of the cooperation between local and federal authority. The Democratic politician Benjamin Hallett, Jr., immediately wired President Franklin Pierce that Burns was about to be removed, adding, in the understatement of the day, "Ample military and

---

[9] The best modern narrative of this episode is Albert Von Frank, *The Trials of Anthony Burns: Freedom and Slavery in Emerson's Boston* (Cambridge: Harvard Univ. Press, 1998). Also see Jean H. Pease and William H. Pease, *The Fugitive Slave Law and Anthony Burns: A Problem in Law Enforcement* (Philadelphia: Lippincott, 1975), and Charles M. Stevens, *Anthony Burns: A History* (Williamstown, Mass.: Corner House, 1973).

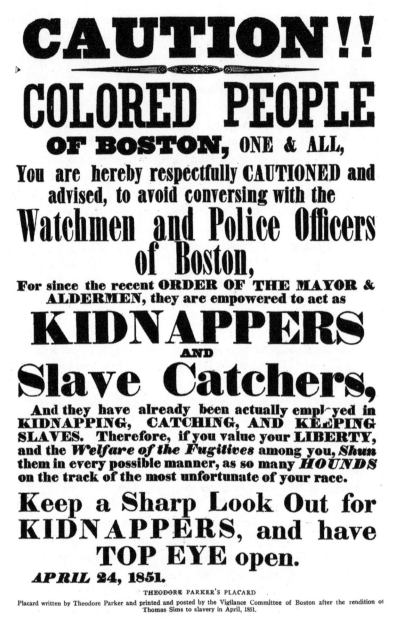

FIGURE 23. Broadside distributed by the Boston Vigilance Committee on April 24, 1851, in the excitement over the abduction of the Fugitive Slave Thomas Sims. (Courtesy of the American Antiquarian Society, Worcester, Mass.)

police force to effect it peacefully."[10] The noise and disorder of the streets contrasted sharply with the spit-and-polish precision of the military. Some fifty thousand people, about a third of the Hub's population, bunched along the figurative gangplank of the streets connecting Court House Square with the harbor. They were taking part in a kind of street theater replete with props but only partially scripted. Merchants and shopkeepers along the route draped their doors and windows in mourning cloth. The publishers of the *Commonwealth*, organ of the Free Soil Party, hung six American flags edged in black from the roof of their headquarters; several stories below, a wire strung across the street bore a black coffin with "Liberty" chalked in white.[11]

What filled the streets on that day? One should not dismiss sheer curiosity. Burns's arrest, after all, had aroused all Bostonians, not only his friends, and abolitionists made sure that anyone who did not know about the event soon would, writing torrid editorials and organizing rallies and demonstrations.[12] It was next to impossible not to be intrigued. The networks of Garrisonians and Free Soilers of both races set aside the old grudge to sound the same notes in a loud if sonorous clarion that called forth the faithful. Two aspects of their propaganda merit extended treatment – the audience and its spirit – to appreciate the fit between the street and the State House.

Ever attentive to their audience in the country, antislavery advocates immediately summoned Yankeedom to the city. Indeed, the *Commonwealth* started plying the backlands on May 26, the day after Burns's arrest, with a blast at the "Slave Power," followed by an appeal to farmers and country tradesmen to "leave any occupation, duty or pleasure, and swarm to Boston."[13] Even the serene Whittier got excited over the potential of the moment for propaganda. Writing to Henry Bowditch on the same day as the *Commonwealth*'s missive, the Amesbury poet declared "That man must not be sent out of Boston as a slave. Anything but that!" The "people must be called out," he advised, and "the country must precipitate itself upon the city." But there was so little time and so little direction. "Send out the fiery cross without further delay! Tell us what you want and what we can do!" he exclaimed. Then, in a burst of opportunism he asked, "Is it not possible to keep the matter open until

[10] Von Frank, *Trials of Anthony Burns*, p. 206. Also see *The Boston Slave Riot and Trial of Anthony Burns* (Boston: Fetridge, 1854).

[11] *Lib*, June 9, 1854. Also see Von Frank, *Trials of Anthony Burns*, esp. pp. 204–18.

[12] For instance, *Boston Slave Riot*, Massachusetts House of Representatives, House Documents, Doc. No. 205 (1854), and *Lib*, June 2, 1854.

[13] *Comm*, May 26, 1854. Also see Von Frank, *Trials of Anthony Burns*, pp. 30–1.

next week?" The delay would allow "the anti-Nebraska pulpits" to vent and galvanize the country as nothing else. "If you want the country into Boston, say so at once. If another man is to be sacrificed to Moloch, let the whole people witness it."[14]

Thousands of provincials streamed into the Hub. Some came as individuals, others as random groups drawn by the spectacle or as members of local abolitionist societies.[15] In Worcester, Thomas Wentworth Higginson, marked by wounds sustained in a clash with the authorities over a failed attempt to free Burns in Boston the previous night, exhorted a huge rally in city hall against the minions of the Slave Power. Others proposed that the people "lay aside business, on Monday, and proceed to Boston en masse . . . to meet with other friends of freedom and humanity."[16] The following Monday some four hundred to five hundred men, styled as the Worcester Freedom Club, mustered at the train station for the trip into Boston under the command of a local militant, Dr. Oramel Martin. Debarking at the depot in the Hub, they marched two-by-two around the Court House bearing a flag emblazoned with the Goddess of Liberty floating above the slogan "Warm Hearts and Fearless Souls – True to the Union and the Constitution."[17]

Countrymen farther west, deeper in the heart of Yankeedom, were just as alarmed. They had been seething since the day the hated act was signed into law in September 1850. Not long after it was signed by President Fillmore, Henry S. Gere, editor of the *Northampton Courier*, printed the text in full on his front page with the exhortation, "Read it, and hand the paper to your Whig neighbor." The execrable law, Gere wrote, had caused "tremendous excitement" in villages of the region.[18] A meeting at the Westlean methodist church in South Worthington vowed to "resist" the law.[19] Cummington pronounced it "unworthy of obedience."[20] Several of these gatherings also elected delegates to a regional meeting scheduled for Northampton on October 23.

---

[14] JGW to HIB, May 26, 1854, in John B. Pickard, ed., *The Letters of John Greenleaf Whittier*, 3 vols. (Cambridge: Harvard Univ. Press, 1975) 2: 257–8.

[15] *Comm*, June 2, 1854; *MS*, June 3, 1854, and *Lib*, June 2 and 9, 1854. Also see the flyer, "Murderers, Thieves, and Blacklegs," ms. Massachusetts Historical Society, Boston. Rptd., in *BP*, May 30, 1854.

[16] *MS*, May 5 and June 1, 1854. Also see Wilson, *Rise and Fall of the Slave Power in America*, 2: 305–11 and 435–44, and Von Frank, *Trials of Anthony Burns*, pp. 122 and 138–9.

[17] *Boston Slave Riot*, p. 43. Also see *Comm*, May 30, 1854.

[18] *NC*, Oct. 8, 1850.

[19] Ibid., Oct. 15 and 22, 1850.

[20] Ibid., Nov. 5, 1850.

The Northampton protest against the Fugitive Slave Act was a Free Soil function in all but name. On its podium were such local party luminaries as William Clark, William Tyler, and Seth Hunt, along with the featured speaker, Charles P. Huntington, scion of the Hadley squirarchy and now a Northampton lawyer. Nearly twenty-five years had passed since Huntington delivered his Fourth of July address in 1830 on the necessity of African colonization. But he was now a changed man who had left behind the Whiggery of his parents.[21] He also repudiated the advocacy of colonization of his early years if not the paternalism that was his family heritage. Indeed, no one could mention his name without invoking his paternalism. One eulogist described him as a "grave and dignified looking man," and asked, "Say, *Father* Huntington! Does not your paternal hand itch every day to buffet some of your uncouth progeny?"[22] Another called him a "sincere friend of the oppressed, always high-toned and humane," and a true Christian "so progressive a conservative, and so conservative a progressive."[23] One beneficiary of his paternalism was Seth Pomeroy, a wayward youth who the prestigious lawyer had defended in court and then taken under his wing. Huntington had a friend agree to hire the youth if Pomeroy "will convince your friends that you will not disappoint their expectations" by giving up the hard life for a "*habit* of industry."[24]

Huntington struck the patrician's pose at the Northampton rally against the Fugitive Slave Act. He scolded those who called for resistance to the law, declaring that African Americans were in no greater danger now than they had been under the 1793 law because everyone in Massachusetts enjoyed the "protection of habeas corpus. "Try *that* before you try pistols," he asserted in a reference to rumors that local blacks were arming. Men like Huntington, after all, expected clients to seek their protection, not to strike out on their own. He introduced resolutions denouncing the law and recommending "legitimate" protest, and they passed without opposition but not without arousing dissonant voices.[25] Henry Gere, for one, wanted stronger measures. Resorting to a tried country metaphor, he wrote, "[I]t is wisdom" to fasten "the door *before* the horse is stolen," a point that also occurred to subsequent speakers.[26] The Reverend Rufus

---

[21] For more on Huntington, see his obituaries in *HG* and *NC*, Feb. 4, 1868, in PPHFP, "Clippings," b. 17, f. 20.

[22] Ibid., "Clippings."

[23] Ibid., *Christian Register*, n.d.

[24] CPH to SP, Aug. 15, 1851, PPHFP, b. 17, f. 9.

[25] *NC*, Oct. 29, 1850.

[26] Ibid.

Ellis allowed that no one should lightly violate the law or become "a Law unto himself," but affirmed that egregious law had to "yield" to "Conscience." Principled resistance need not produce disorder or anarchy, as some charged, because "obedience to human promptings" served the "cause of the highest and holiest order...strengthening...absolute Truth and Justice."[27] Ellis's moralistic radicalism may have satisfied Gere, but it did nothing for William Parker, a local Garrisonian who used the occasion to vent his faction's lingering contempt for the clergy.[28] Mounting the podium – presumably as an unscheduled speaker – Parker railed against the church in a tirade that evoked cries of "down!" "down!" A deflated Gere reported that the meeting "dissolved" into "disorder and confusion."[29]

Aroused Northampton was hardly the only center of discord over the Fugitive Slave Act. Boston's white activists were passionately divided as well. A huge meeting of some six thousand at Faneuil Hall in Boston on October 14, which would form the Boston Vigilance Committee, heard rousing speeches from the celebrities of antislavery including Wendell Phillips and Richard Henry Dana, Jr. Frederick Douglass outdid them all when he called for blood, intoning that the only solution was "a half dozen or more dead kidnappers."[30] His inflammatory rhetoric sent shudders of fear through white moderates. The expectation of militancy explains why only one clergyman, the Reverend Charles Lowell of West Church, deigned to attend the meeting. The rest of the clergy, wary of the new combativeness, stayed away. The moderation of Free Soilers evoked a rebuke from Thomas W. Higginson, who ridiculed the Free Soilers for refusing to stand "outside the pale of good citizenship," an astute observation confirmed repeatedly through the early years of the new decade, and not just in Boston.[31]

In New Bedford, talk of a crackdown by federal agents in fall 1850 drew blacks to a meeting that vowed to fight back "even to death." This policy of "forcible resistance," as it came to be known, divided allies into warring

[27] Ibid.
[28] On Parker, see Christopher Clark, *The Utopian Moment: The Radical Challenge of the Northampton Association* (Ithaca, N.Y.: Cornell Univ. Press, 1995), pp. 67 and 190–1.
[29] *NC*, Oct. 29, 1850.
[30] *Lib*, Oct. 18, 1850. For Douglass's speech, see John W. Blassingame, ed., *The Frederick Douglass Papers; Series One; Speeches, Debates, and Interviews*, 5 vols. (New Haven, Conn.: Yale Univ. Press, 1982–92), 2: 243–8.
[31] Thomas Wentworth Higginson, "Cheerful Yesterdays," *Atlantic Monthly* 79 (March 1897): 344–55. Quote is on p. 346.

camps that squabbled through several meetings over the next two weeks. At a gathering on October 9 chaired by the Quaker activists Charles W. Morgan and Thomas A. Greene moderates emphatically distanced themselves from "forcible resistance" and from open "opposition" to any law, "however odious and unjust."[32] Militants responded by packing another meeting that heard the radical abolitionist Rodney French lay into the moderates. The meeting then approved a resolution repudiating the resolutions of the previous one. The reversal drove Greene from the chair and many fellow Quakers from the meeting hall itself. Dismayed by the turmoil, Morgan penned a revealing entry in his diary in which he came down against blacks as hard as Charles P. Huntington had for advocating "loudly and noisily . . . extremist measures – instead of thankfully accepting a sympathy which would have been . . . universal, as to have their best protection." He darkly predicted that "now many will desert them," adding the next day, accurately, that black New Bedford had "lost a great deal of sympathy and support."[33]

This division between white antislavery activists over the Fugitive Slave Act was, of course, rooted in Quaker pacifism and Garrisonian "nonresistance." These distinctive but mutually reinforcing doctrines rejected violence regardless of the cause, clearly delimiting the lines of legitimate activism in the 1850s just as they had fifteen years earlier. The difference in the 1850s was twofold. First, nonresistance in the 1830s was related to race indirectly through slavery; in the 1850s, thanks to the Fugitive Slave Act, race was primary and direct. Second it was blacks, not whites, in Boston, New Bedford, and even in the country who initially seized the initiative against against the 1850 law. They were hesitant to rely exclusively on the good will of whites. Nor, it should be stressed, did they resort to violence. They armed, to be sure, but never fired a shot or came close to doing so; it was their defiant and intrepid posture – not simply the question of armed violence – that opened the breach with white paternalists.

African Americans were concentrated in two relatively large enclaves in Boston and New Bedford and had a scattered presence in Berkshire County. The Boston community, at the foot of Beacon Hill, numbered about twenty-two hundred in 1850. It was a fairly stable population compared to African American communities in New York and Philadelphia,

---

[32] Kathryn Grover, *The Fugitive's Gibraltar: Escaping Slaves and Abolitionism in New Bedford, Massachusetts* (Amherst: Univ. of Massachusetts Press, 2001), pp. 218–19.

[33] Quoted in ibid., p. 220.

both of which declined in the 1840s, largely in response to racial hostility that often erupted into violence. Boston's black population increased by only five hundred in the thirty years after 1830, with most of the growth coming in the decade before the Civil War.[34] New Bedford's blacks, who have been overlooked until recently, reached fifteen hundred in 1860, nearly rivaling Boston's in size and accounting for a much larger proportion of the city as a whole, 7.5 percent as against 1.3 percent.[35] One had to travel far to find as many blacks beyond the Atlantic coast. Worcester County had under three hundred, Hampshire and Franklin counties only four hundred between them. The exception was remote Berkshire, the westernmost county in the Commonwealth and the one with the most surprising demographic profile, with some twelve hundred African Americans composing 2.4 percent of the population, a greater proportion than in Boston and nearly as great as Springfield's, which is normally seen as an African American center.[36] Just about half the county's African Americans resided in four of Berkshire's thirty-one towns – Great Barrington, Sheffield, Lenox, and Pittsfield – where they formed small but well-defined communities that in some cases reached about 6 percent of the population.[37]

These were not recent settlements. They traced back to the eighteenth century when slavery was legal in the Commonwealth; many African Americans stayed following their liberation in the early 1780s, and many more migrated in over the next fifty years. Untold numbers were fugitives from the state of New York, which had adopted a policy of gradual emancipation in 1799 requiring that before being freed slaves born after July 4, 1799, had to serve their mothers' master for twenty-eight years in

[34] For an analysis of African American demography in Massachusetts, see George A. Levesque, *Black Boston: African American Life and Culture in Urban America, 1750–1860* (New York: Garland Publishing, 1994), pp. 21–110. Also see Horton and Horton, *Black Bostonians*, pp. 1–13.

[35] Grover, *Fugitive's Gibraltar*, p. 265, and Horton and Horton, *Black Bostonians*, p. 2, Table I.

[36] Jesse Chickering, *A Statistical View of the Population of Massachusetts, from 1765 to 1840* (Boston: C.C. Little and J. Brown, 1846), pp. 116–18; Francis DeWitt, comp., *Abstract of the Census of the Commonwealth of Massachusetts... 1855* (Boston: W. White, 1857), pp. 4–9 and 23–30; and Francis A. Walker, comp., *Compendium of the Ninth Census of the United States* (Washington, D.C.: U.S. Government Printing Office, 1872), pp. 217–18.

[37] Glendyne Wergland, "Women, Men, Property, and Inheritance: Gendered Testamentary Customs in Western Massachusetts, 1800–1860" (Ph.D. diss., Univ. of Massachusetts Amherst, 2001), pp. 174–218.

the case of men and twenty-three years in the case of women.[38] The more impatient among them fled New York, stealing across the porous border and beating what may well have been well-worn paths through the gentle Berkshire Mountains to the refuge of village Massachusetts. This source of rural African Americans probably slowed by the 1820s as the slave population in New York aged. Another source, smaller but important, was fashioned by the paroxysms of racial violence in the cities of Jacksonian America that drove some African Americans to the safety of the hills, to judge from comparative black demography. Between 1830 and 1850 the black population in Berkshire County grew by about a third, while in virtually every coastal city north of Baltimore the number of blacks either stabilized or declined.[39] Observers of the urban scene in this period report wagonloads of blacks fleeing racial violence for safer, more secure places.[40] Berkshire County, with its preexisting black settlements far from the urban tumult, was a likely refuge.

More is known about urban leaders in African American Massachusetts than about their rural counterparts. Boston's black leadership showed both continuity and change. Men such as William Cooper Nell and the lawyer Robert Morris, who had figured prominently in civil rights activities in the mid-1840s, were still involved in the struggle a decade later. Their ranks were strengthened by several new arrivals, however, one of whom was Lewis Hayden, among the boldest and brashest runaways of his generation. In 1844, Hayden escaped with his wife Harriet from his Kentucky master with help from the New York abolitionist Calvin Fairbank, who was apprehended and convicted for his effort. While Fairbank wasted away in jail, the Haydens made their way to Canada and then to Detroit, where they settled briefly in 1845 and worked with a black Methodist church and with fellow abolitionists. (Allegedly, Lewis Hayden slipped into the South to rescue slaves and foment rebellion in Louisiana; there is, however, no doubt that he did later meet John Brown and raise

---

[38] See Graham Russell Hodges, *Root and Branch: African Americans in New York and East Jersey, 1613–1863* (Chapel Hill: Univ. of North Carolina Press, 1999), pp. 168–71, and Ira Berlin, *Many Thousands Gone: The First Two Hundred Years of Slavery in North America* (Cambridge: Harvard Univ. Press, 1998), pp. 177–94 and 228–55.

[39] See, for instance, Leonard P. Curry, *The Free Black in Urban America, 1800–1850: The Shadow of the Dream* (Chicago: Univ. of Chicago Press, 1981), pp. 1–14, and Hollis R. Lynch, comp., *The Black Urban Condition: A Documentary History* (New York: Crowell, 1973), p. 4.

[40] Bruce Laurie, *Working People of Philadelphia, 1800–1850* (Philadelphia: Temple Univ. Press, 1980), pp. 124–45 and 156–7.

FIGURE 24. Lewis Hayden. (Courtesy of the Bostonian Society/ Old State House, Boston, Mass.)

funds for the 1859 raid on Harpers Ferry.)[41] A year or so after arriving in Detroit, the Haydens stopped in New Bedford and then settled down in Boston. They opened a small clothing store, which doubled as a meeting place for black activists and possibly as a station on the Underground Railroad, on Phillips Street on Beacon Hill. Harriet Beecher Stowe recalled being surrounded by a dozen fugitive slaves on a visit to the Haydens.[42]

Though Hayden evaded arrest for his antislavery work, Leonard A. Grimes was not as lucky. Born in Leesburg, Virginia, to free parents, Grimes grew up in Washington, D.C., where he worked for local shopkeepers and for himself as a hack with several horses and carriages.[43]

[41] On Hayden, see Stanley J. Robboy and Anita W. Robboy, "Lewis Hayden: From Fugitive Slave to Statesman," *NEQ* 46 (Dec. 1973): 591–613; Horton and Horton, *Black Bostonians*, pp. 54–5; and Benjamin Quarles, *Black Abolitionists* (New York: Oxford Univ. Press, 1969), pp. 112, 149–50, and 164–5.

[42] Quarles, *Black Abolitionists*, p. 150.

[43] William Wells Brown, *The Rising Sun; or, The Antecedents and Advancement of the Colored Race* (Boston: A. G. Brown, 1874), p. 534.

FIGURE 25. Leonard A. Grimes. (William J. Simmons, *Men of Mark: Eminent, Progressive and Rising* [1887; New York: Arno Press, 1968], bet. pp. 664 and 665.)

When not ferrying passengers around the city, he spirited slaves out of the South, risky work indeed that soon ran afoul of the authorities. In March 1840 he was convicted of helping a family of six slaves escape to Canada. Released from prison in 1842, he returned to Washington to live with his wife Octavis and their three children and then followed essentially the same trail northward as the Haydens. The Grimeses left in 1844 or so for New Bedford, where they ran a small grocery, and in 1848 moved to Boston, where Leonard Grimes succeeded the Reverend George Black, who had died, as pastor of the Twelfth Baptist Church. It was Grimes who gave the Twelfth its reputation as the "fugitive slave church."[44]

The turn of the 1840s also brought the black abolitionist John Swett Rock to Boston. Born in New Salem, New Jersey, in 1825, probably to

[44] On Grimes, see Grover, *Fugitive's Gibraltar*, pp. 188–9, and Horton and Horton, *Black Bostonians*, pp. 47–8. Also see Levesque, *Black Boston*, pp. 284–9 and 330–1.

FIGURE 26. John Swett Rock. (*Harper's Weekly* 9 [Feb. 15, 1865]: 124.)

free parents, Rock was one of the more acute and professionally accomplished African American leaders in the city. He started out as teacher in Philadelphia and then studied medicine for a time before settling on dentistry. He also wrote about history and became involved in the Quaker City's abolitionist groups as well as in several projects for black uplift, including a night school. In 1852, Rock graduated from the American Medical College, but he never practiced in Philadelphia. Instead, he moved to Boston in 1853, and at the end of the decade he studied law there. In 1861, Rock was admitted to the Massachusetts bar, and in 1865 he became the first African American to argue a case before the U.S. Supreme Court. During his time in the city, he emerged as one of black Boston's most perceptive commentators.[45]

---

[45] Horton and Horton, *Black Bostonians*, pp. 60–1. Also see George A. Levesque, "Boston's Black Brahmin: Dr. John Swett Rock," *CWH* 26 (Dec. 1980): 326–46.

Hayden, Grimes, and to some extent Rock, cut figures rather different from the older and more established African American leaders. They arrived in Boston as outsiders who had not yet solidified the friendship or patronage of a Garrison or other white abolitionists. Hayden and Grimes had witnessed the horrors of slavery firsthand in the South; Rock had spent his formative years in Philadelphia, the most racially violent city in the Northeast. Such experiences, in the context of the commotion over fugitive slaves in Boston, help explain the defiance of Hayden and his adjutants. Doubtless they supported the boycotts and other mass actions inspired by Nell and Morris for school integration and the legal actions brought by the Remonds for black access to public accommodations. They bent more of their energy, however, toward protecting fugitives from the slave catchers, employing nonviolent measures if possible but willing to use violence or the threat of violence, if necessary.

No African American activist practiced "forcible resistance" more boldly than did Lewis Hayden. Not long after he arrived in Boston, Hayden plunged into resistance work with a passion that propelled him to the forefront of every major incident involving fugitive slaves in the first half of the 1850s. His heroics in the attempted abduction of the Crafts defined his activism. Following an extraordinary escape from their Georgia master in the winter of 1848–9, the Crafts settled in Boston hoping to lead a normal life, with William tending to his cabinetmaker's shop and Ellen taking in sewing. The advent of the Fugitive Slave Act, however, struck fear in black Boston. Hundreds of fugitive slaves – roughly one hundred fifty in the two leading black churches alone – bolted for Canada or the Massachusetts countryside; the rest stood their ground and prepared for the worst. At the end of September Hayden was the featured speaker at two meetings within a week of each other to mobilize for self-defense. The second meeting formed the League of Freedom, a resistance group that merged into or worked closely with the larger Boston Vigilance Committee formed at the famous Faneuil Hall gathering on October 14. Within two weeks, Willis Hughes and John Knight, agents of the Crafts' former master, showed up with warrants for the runaways' arrest, triggering resistance that closely followed racial lines. The executive committee of the Boston Vigilance Committee, which consisted exclusively of whites under the leadership of the Reverend Theodore Parker, pursued nonviolent mass action and legal processes to expose and frustrate Hughes and Knight. Its activists plastered the city with flyers alerting Bostonians to the agents' arrival and trailed them, shouting "Slave-hunters!" and other taunts. They also

FIGURE 27. William and Ellen Craft. (William Still, *The Underground Railroad: A Record of Facts*...[Philadelphia: Porter and Coates, 1872], plate following p. 368.)

used legal harassment by having the Georgians arrested three times, once for slander and twice for kidnapping. Parker, for his part, posed as an honest broker and tried to convince the Southerners to leave while it was still possible for them to go safely. The agents eventually did depart, in frustration and defeat, persuaded not only by Parker but also by a menacing crowd that chased their carriage through the streets of Boston and across the Charles River into West Cambridge.[46]

Black activists were emphatically more combative. The Boston Vigilance Committee had arranged to take Ellen Craft from her house on Beacon Hill to the safety of Henry Bowditch's home in Brookline and then to Parker's place nearby. Bowditch recalled that William insisted on staying put in his shop, "at his bench with his plane and saw, and . . . a loaded 'horse pistol' upon the bench with the tools of his trade. He declared that he would shoot any one, law officer or not, who should attempt to lay hold of him and carry him again into slavery." A week later, Bowditch offered to take Craft to see his wife in Brookline, only to be confronted with a proposal that they go armed. "Here was a contingency I had not thought of," wrote the genteel physician in his diary, "but I thanked God that, though not a little shocked at the idea of my possibly killing another human being, I remembered the saying . . . I deemed most fitting in its application to me; viz., 'to do for others what you wish done for yourself'; and feeling that if I were Craft I should glory in slaying anyone who attempted to make me or my wife a slave, I replied instantly, 'Yes, I accept your proposition.'" It must have been quite a sight – Bowditch in the driver's seat with a sure hand on the reins and a jittery one on the grip of a gun, seated beside Craft, at the ready, with a blunderbuss and a pistol. Weeks later Bowditch was still shaken by having borne arms.[47]

It was Hayden who etched the strongest image of the Crafts' drama. Just as local abolitionists had moved Ellen from place to place to insure her safety, so did they transfer William among safe houses. He wound up at the Haydens' home on Beacon Hill, which was turned into a makeshift arsenal, with firearms and kegs of gunpowder.[48] When the authorities showed up for Craft, they found Hayden on the top step of his house next to the gunpowder kegs and with a flaming torch in his hand. He was shouting that he would blow up the place before he would see anyone

---

[46] The two best recent accounts of the Craft episode are Collison, *Shadrach Minkins*, pp. 91–9, and Blackett, *Running a Thousand Miles for Freedom*, pp. 55–102.

[47] Vincent Y. Bowditch, *Life and Correspondence of Henry Ingersoll Bowditch, by his Son*, 2 vols. (Boston: Houghton Mifflin, 1902) 1: 205–9. Quote is on pp. 206–7.

[48] Robboy and Robboy, "Lewis Hayden," pp. 597–8. See also Horton and Horton, *Black Bostonians*, p. 104.

returned to slavery.[49] His brazen defiance convinced the authorities to drop the case against the Crafts; it also became something of a metaphor for black militancy.

Several months later, amid the excitement over the capture of the fugitive slave Shadrach Minkins, Thomas Wentworth Higginson criticized white activists for their refusal to take direct action. Only African Americans, he said at a rally, had the courage to overcome the pacifist "restrictions of non-resistance and politics," adding that the black militants had just demonstrated their resolve in the Crafts' case and "would doubtless do it again." "Of course, they will," nodded Hayden, although he later took Higginson aside to say that he was only bluffing. "We do not wish anyone to know how weak we are," because of the flight of "colored men" after Minkins's arrest.[50] No other white person knew he was bluffing then, just as none knew if he was bluffing several months earlier when he threatened to blow up his house before he would submit to the Slave Power. All that most whites knew was that African Americans were aroused and militant.

The history of country blacks remains to be written, but what we do know suggests a different pattern of race relations than in the cities. The country, as well as most shire towns, had no equivalent of the tough-minded independence embodied by such a figure as Hayden. The smaller and sometimes scattered populations of African Americans meant that black communities lacked the safety and anonymity of population density that their counterparts in Boston and New Bedford enjoyed. It was harder to hide in Great Barrington or even in Northampton. As a result, country blacks believed themselves more exposed, and they were prone to be on the defensive. Longtime residents either had adjusted to the social subordination of prevailing racial etiquette or kept to themselves; later arrivals on the run from masters in nearby New York and elsewhere had even more reason to live quietly.

Scattered evidence from the tumult over the Fugitive Slave Act indicates that African Americans also looked to white liberals or paternalists for support and protection. Free Soilers in Lowell, whose black population numbered under one hundred, called a meeting on October 3 to reassure local African Americans of their safety. "Be calm, cautious, firm, and determined," advised Henry Wilson. Though "man hunters were in

---

[49] Archibald H. Grimke, "Anti-Slavery in Boston," *NEM* (Dec. 1890): 441–59.
[50] Quoted in Robboy and Robboy, "Lewis Hayden," p. 605.

the land," every African American who had a home "however humble, she had a 'castle'" along with the "moral and legal right to defend its sanctity against prowling man stealers."[51] Although such high-minded rhetoric may have reassured some blacks, when it came to concrete action town patricians proved to be forthcoming, at least on an individual basis. In mid-January 1850, several months before the attempted abduction of the Crafts, the village of Colrain in Franklin County, which had sheltered Angeline Palmer a decade earlier, learned that Elijah Freeman had disappeared. The town leaders, fearing that Freeman had been abducted by slave catchers, formed a committee to "make an inquiry into the circumstances attending this strange disappearance." The committee placed ads in the local press, describing Freeman as "rather short in stature, of African American extraction, though perhaps not quite as dark as some," and a man "of good habits – very inoffensive in his disposition and . . . generally respected," precisely the kind of African American to endear himself to white paternalists.[52] No one ever found Freeman, it seems, or solved the mystery of his disappearance.

Such white solicitude was not unusual. About a year later, the freedom of "Mr. Booth," an African American barber in Lowell who had fled Virginia, looked to be in jeopardy. His master wrote to Linus Child, the agent of the Boston Associates who was at loggerheads with labor over the length of the workday, to say that he would take action to reclaim Booth unless the barber's freedom was purchased – for the bargain price of seven hundred dollars, less than half of his actual value. "Squire Child," as he was known, may well have welcomed the opportunity to regain moral stature lost in the labor unrest. Whatever his motivation, the crusty mill agent had his own lawyer draft papers for Booth's redemption and then started a fund drive to raise the price of his freedom. The local press was confident that it would succeed.[53]

African Americans in the country who organized in their own defense in the face of the Fugitive Slave Act were at pains to come off as models of propriety. For instance, the Northampton meeting that heard from Charles P. Huntington in October 1850 originated not with white Free Soilers but with local blacks who were party sympathizers, if not formal members. Their call for the gathering, which Gere happily published in

---

[51] Wilson, *Rise and Fall of the Slave Power*, 2: 306–7.
[52] *GAR*, Feb. 4, 1850.
[53] *MS*, Apr. 16, 1851. On Child, see Formisano, *The Transformation of Political Culture: Massachusetts Parties, 1790s–1840s* (New York: Oxford Univ. Press, 1984), p. 286.

his *Northampton Courier*, was signed by ten black men, self-described respectable villagers who "by our industry and sobriety . . . have . . . accumulated property, and . . . become citizens."[54] A few of them had lived in Northampton or the adjoining village of Florence for a decade or more, and several – notably, Basil Dorsey and Henry Anthony – were escaped slaves.[55] Henry Anthony was something of the signers' elder statesman. Born a slave in the 1780s, he left his Maryland master as a young man and made his way to Northampton around 1830, eventually settling on a small plot in Florence adjacent to the Northampton Association of Education and Industry, a utopian community of abolitionists and religious perfectionists.[56] He worked as a stonemason when not tending his patch, and later in life he earned small sums as a fiddler at public events and private affairs.[57] Basil Dorsey was also a runaway slave. In 1837 he fled Maryland with his two brothers in one of the more daring escapes of the epoch. With help from white and black abolitionists he wound up in the hill town of Charlemont, where he boarded with the brother of Reverend Joshua Leavitt and in 1844 moved to Florence not far from the Anthonys. Both men and their fellows were small property owners who appear to have gained acceptance by Northampton; indeed, in a sense Anthony was part of white Northampton. Described in the press as a "mulatto," he twice married Irish women and was boarding with an Irish family at the time of his death in 1880.[58]

Blacks in the country were trying for a new and delicate balance between accommodation and resistance. Anthony got along famously with local whites, not only because of his complexion but also because of his sunny disposition, which produced what one white admirer called a "cheerful . . . and most cordial greeting for everybody he met."[59] Though Dorsey alone of the signers seems to have been involved in antislavery politics and civil rights work before 1850, one should not assume that Anthony's smile was the mark of an early "Uncle Tom" all too eager to defer to white authority. Anthony and his friends accommodated in this

---

[54] *NC*, Oct. 22 and 29, 1850.

[55] U.S. Bureau of the Census, Population Schedule mss., 1830 and 1840, Washington, D.C. Also see Paul Gaffney, "Coloring Utopia: The African-American Presence in the Northampton Association of Education and Industry" (ms.).

[56] See Christopher Clark, *The Utopian Moment: The Radical Challenge of the Northampton Association* (Ithaca, N.Y.: Cornell Univ. Press, 1995).

[57] *HG*, Sept. 7, 1880.

[58] Gaffney, "Coloring Utopia."

[59] *HG*, Sept. 7, 1880.

instance by calling on Huntington to serve as their voice at the rally; they resisted by embracing in a very public way the equal rights tradition of the Revolution in the letter that announced the meeting. In it, they denied guilt for any "crime" save "love of liberty." Yet they were imperiled by a ruthless law that denied them their "social, political, and religious rights, reducing them to chattelism, and articles of merchandise, mercilessly separating families, and refusing them the *Bible*, and attainment of all knowledge." They had the support of the Reverend J. N. Mars, an African American minister from nearby Springfield, who followed Huntington to the podium and who was just as high-minded as Dorsey and his friends but also more vigilant. Reading the text of the law aloud, he brandished a copy "enclosed in heavy black lines," and shouted, "I would to God [if] I could preach its funeral sermon" ["great cheering"]. The minister explained that although he had been born in Connecticut and had never been a slave, he would "throw out" any slave catcher who came to his door, and he advised local blacks to do the same. Instead of joining the exodus to Canada, they should stay put to fight the Slave Power and its law.[60]

Gere welcomed Mars's bold resistance. He had hoped Northampton would emulate the militancy of the Faneuil Hall meeting. Aroused by Douglass's war cry, the Bostonians resolved "constitution or no constitution, law or no law, we will not allow a fugitive to be taken from Massachusetts," and then got up a "Committee of Vigilance and Safety," resurrecting the Boston Vigilance Committee defunct since 1846.[61] Douglass was very much on Gere's mind when he drafted his piece on Northampton's response to the Fugitive Slave Act. Mars, like Douglass, had upped the ante by elevating the "the feeling of the meeting somewhat above the tone of Mr. Huntington's resolutions" to the spirit at Faneuil Hall. Gere reckoned that Northampton would have supported open resistance were it not for William Parker's reckless intervention.[62] That is doubtful. Local militants were white, not black, and not numerous enough to make a difference. Few African Americans in the country openly agreed with Douglass or joined Gere in attacking Huntington. In public, at least, they favored the safer course of appealing to white patrons.

---

[60] *NC*, Oct. 29, 1850.
[61] On the Faneuil Hall meeting, see Collison, *Shadrach Minkins*, pp. 75–85; Henry Mayer, *All on Fire: William Lloyd Garrison and the Abolition of Slavery* (New York: St. Martin's Press, 1998), pp. 406–7; and Horton and Horton, *Black Bostonians*, pp. 103–4.
[62] *NC*, Oct. 29, 1850.

The racially charged excitement aroused by the Fugitive Slave Act reconfigured Bay State politics. The Democratic Party, which a year earlier
had coalesced with the Free Soil Party, abruptly changed course. Its state
convention in 1851 came out for the Fugitive Slave Act, and two years
later, on the eve of the 1853 election, Caleb Cushing issued his famous
"ukase" prohibiting cooperation with Free Soilers and formally ending
the relationship. Cushing, the Newburyport lawyer and former Whig,
was by then President Pierce's attorney general and titular head of the
Bay State Democracy.[63] A quintessential doughface in the making, eager
to strengthen ties with his party's Southern wing, Cushing could not easily
ignore local issues.[64] He had to be responsive in 1850 to the clamor in the
country agitated by Whiting Griswold for State Reform – in the form of
the secret ballot and the overhaul of the apportionment system. Although
his lieutenants worked assiduously in the State House for both causes,
Cushing simultaneously directed operatives in the country to exploit the
race question in order to rein in the fickle rural districts and perhaps expand the party's base.[65] Not that race-based politics was anything new
for these latter-day Jacksonians. Their party had long used race to appeal to the popular classes, and to workingmen in particular.[66] Now the
Democrats had an excuse to pursue an old policy with renewed vigor.
One gets the impression that if the law had not existed, Cushing would
have invented it.

Cushing anticipated his party's harder line on race fully a year before
he had it endorse the Fugitive Slave Act. He called on country Democrats
in fall 1850, after it became the law of the land, to come out openly and
loudly for it.[67] Berkshire underlings responded by summoning the faithful
to a meeting in Pittsfield on December 23 to reject "opinions obnoxious to
good order, injurious to sound morals, antagonistic to law, destructive to
peace, and subversive of the fundamental principles of government."[68] An

---

[63] William F. Hartford, *Money, Morals, and Politics: Massachusetts in the Age of the Boston
Associates* (Boston: Northeastern Univ. Press, 2001), pp. 180–90.

[64] On Cushing, see Claude M. Fuess, *The Life of Caleb Cushing*, 2 vols. (New York:
Harcourt Brace, 1923).

[65] Hartford, *Money, Morals, and Politics*, pp. 182–3 and 204–5.

[66] See, for instance, Jean H. Baker, *Affairs of Party: The Political Culture of Northern
Democrats in the Mid-Nineteenth Century* (Ithaca, N.Y.: Cornell Univ. Press, 1983),
pp. 212–58, and George M. Fredrickson, *The Black Image in the White Mind: The
Debate on Afro-American Character and Destiny, 1817–1914* (New York: Harper, 1971),
pp. 90–1 and 130–64. Also see Gilbert Osofsky, "Abolitionists, Irish Nationalists, and
the Dilemmas of Romantic Nationalism," *AHR* 80 (Oct. 1975): 889–912.

[67] *NAWT*, Dec. 12 and 26, 1850.

[68] Ibid., Dec. 19, 1850.

audience of over one thousand, one of the largest of its kind in the region, converged on Burbank's Hall to support what *Pittsfield Sun* editor Phineas Allen called the "Preservation of the American Union."[69] Some speakers, in fact, stuck to that theme. Levi Goodrich, for one, maintained that the Fugitive Slave Act was a necessary feature of a larger compromise needed to preserve the Union. The law's authors were patriots and nationalists who deserved the "thanks" of the people; opponents were subversives because they endangered the Union. Several others, however, spoke to the question of race from an exclusionist point of view. E. A. Newton, the first such speaker, set the tone with a frontal attack on "abolitionists" for their racial hypocrisy. "What good," he asked, "had the abolitionists and their successors [read Free Soilers] done for the slave? Nothing, absolutely nothing." They had made "his condition worse. What were they doing here within our own town limits, to improve the condition of our colored inhabitants? The same – nothing." All they did was "talk." Dr. Timothy Childs denied he had any feeling for slavery but found no good at all in the "'malignant philanthropy' of abolitionist agitation...nor in the infidelity of Garrison; nor in the Jesuitism of Theodore Parker." The solution to the race problem lay in "the small but not to be despised beginnings of the Colonization Society" – a point pursued by Reverend Dewey, from Sheffield, a self-described former abolitionist. The preacher implied that the returning of fugitive slaves to the South was a rough equivalent to colonization. For if the North refused to obey the law, the "slave population would be upon us *en masse* – in five years there would be such internecine hostility and bitterness among us as was never before seen or imagined."[70]

Thus the acrimony over the Fugitive Slave Act was a two-way street. The mobilization of blacks, abolitionists, and Free Soilers set off a backlash fueled by the potent charge of Unionism and racism. While pro-Union sentiment and antiblack feeling enjoyed wide popularity in the Commonwealth, they were linked to two related values that magnified their appeal in the country, or "order" and "localism." Tocqueville, like Timothy Dwight before him, had identified the serenity of the New England town as its unique ethos. Such places exuded an atavistic ambience that preserved order as it evoked a comforting past that insulated everyday life from the disruptions of commercialism. Democrats displaced the source of disorder from the market to blacks and their white friends. As for localism, it had long been the prevailing spirit of the village. It was local institutions – the

[69] *PS*, Jan. 2, 1851.
[70] Ibid.

town meeting, the church, the common – that gave meaning to the village. Localism became the signature of Cushing's Democrats, who thought of themselves as part of a national party because of their ties with the South but who also grounded their nationalism in the local. Localism was the basis for their position on popular sovereignty, which defined slavery not as a national institution but as a local one dependent on the will of the people in their communities. It took only a small step for the people of the towns to transfer their localistic outlook to the Democratic Party – at least momentarily.[71]

Race also played out in the State House. The Free Soilers provided the *casus belli* in winter 1851 by standing behind Sumner for one of the vacant seats in the U.S. Senate. The prospect of sending such a man as Sumner to Washington did nearly as much for the Cushingites as the Fugitive Slave Act.[72] It pushed from the Coalition party moderates who initially had gone along with the Coalition, including Charles G. Greene, editor of the influential *Boston Post*. The defection from the Coalition of men like Greene strengthened Cushing's twenty-five or thirty "Indomitables," so named for their refusal to compromise on Sumner.[73] They held out for three long months, leaving Sumner a few votes short of election and creating the longest political stalemate in the history of the General Court. Country Democratic papers followed the next twenty-four votes through February and into April as if it were a modern sporting event, reporting the totals and commenting briefly on any changes.[74] There was little to report, as Sumner's vote varied only slightly, until on April 24, on the 26th ballot, a deal was struck that remains a mystery to this day, changing a few votes and resulting in a majority of one for Sumner.[75]

[71] On the doughface Democrats, see Leonard L. Richards, *The Slave Power: The Free North and Southern Domination, 1780–1860* (Baton Rouge: Louisiana State Univ. Press, 2000), pp. 85–91, 107–33, and 175–6, and Robert W. Johannsen, *The Frontier, the Union, and Stephen A. Douglas* (Urbana: Univ. of Illinois Press, 1989).

[72] *BP*, Jan. 9 and Feb. 7, 1851. Also, see Ernest McKay, "Henry Wilson and the Coalition of 1851," *NEQ* 36 (Sept. 1963): 338–7; Fuess, *The Life of Caleb Cushing*, 2: 102–4; and Paul Foos, *A Short, Offhand, Killing Affair: Soldiers and Social Conflict during the Mexican-American War* (Chapel Hill: Univ. of North Carolina Press, 2002), pp. 62–9, 94–5, and 101–2.

[73] *BP*, Jan. 9 and 14–15, 1851.

[74] See, for instance, *PS*, Feb. 13 and 20, Mar. 6 and 20, and May 1, 1851. Also see *Comm*, Apr. 25, 1851.

[75] David Herbert Donald, *Charles Sumner and the Coming of the Civil War* (New York: Fawcett Columbine, 1960), pp. 201–3, and Anne-Marie Taylor, *Young Charles Sumner* (Amherst: Univ. of Massachusetts Press, 2001), pp. 328–35.

Although the long and wearying battle over Sumner's election was driven by partisanship, political ideology, and the personal ambitions of Cushing, it had a subtext of Unionism and race, mostly of race. Charles Greene said it well when, at the start of the debate, he charged that the "Democratic party in this state is about to become abolitionized," that is, be taken over by the dupes of slaves who would unleash hordes of freed people into the region to take the jobs of white men and disturb the peace of the village.[76] Who were these Democrats? Why did they resort to race baiting? The conventional wisdom, which divides the Democracy into two wings of urban conservatives and rural radicals, has it that the urbanites who agitated the race question were reflecting the racism of working-class voters, and the Irish in particular.[77] Such workers, forced to compete with blacks for jobs at the lower end of the job market, were vulnerable to such appeals. They undoubtedly adopted the dominant views about African Americans. The question is whether they responded politically; the evidence, as seen in the investigation into the investigation into the Lowell election in 1851, is that they did not, for it is not at all clear that many Irish voted at this time in the industrial belt – or even in commercial Boston.[78] It is more accurate to say that the Democratic politicians based in the city used racism to get the Irish to the polling booth – that politicians aroused working-class racism, not the other way around. Gradually, by the Civil War, the urban Irish vote made the Democracy competitive in state politics.[79]

The Democracy's rural wing was several times larger and thus more important than its urban wing. It was also, at the turn of the 1840s, just as vocal on the race question, raising the politics of exclusionism to new levels.[80] Slightly fewer than half of Cushing's Indomitables came from Essex and Middlesex counties near their leader's home in Newburyport, suggesting that they were Cushing's intimates and friends. Just over

[76] BP, editorial rpted. in PS, Jan. 9, 1851.
[77] The most recent iterations of this thesis are David Roediger, The Wages of Whiteness: Race and the Making of the American Working Class (1991; New York: Verso, 1999), pp. 133–56, and Noel Ignatiev, How the Irish Became White (New York: Routledge, 1995).
[78] House Doc. 230. See also Oscar Handlin, Boston's Immigrants, 1790–1880: A Study in Acculturation (1941; Cambridge: Harvard Univ. Press, 1991), pp. 190–3, demonstrates that the Irish vote changed little from 1845 to 1852, after which it climbed owing to the encouragement of politicians and Catholic prelates aroused by political nativism.
[79] See Dale Baum, The Civil War Party System: The Case of Massachusetts, 1848–1876 (Chapel Hill: Univ. of North Carolina Press, 1984), esp. pp. 112–13, 159–60, and 205–9.
[80] Hartford, Money, Morals, and Politics, pp. 185–6.

half, however, came from the country, from four of the five westernmost counties – Worcester, Hamden, Franklin, and Berkshire. Their most
common occupation – in the east and the west – was farmer.[81] Surging
white chauvinism among Bay State Democrats in 1850/1 boiled down to
northeastern politicians' mobilizing their western counterparts.

The immediate backlash over black resistance to the Fugitive Slave
Act, coupled with sustained race-baiting by the Cushingites, simultaneously weakened the Coalition and revitalized the Democracy. Conservative Democrats in Norfolk County left the Coalition in 1851 (the same
time that the state party convention endorsed the Fugitive Slave Act) and
were followed in 1852 by colleagues in Middlesex (one of the strongest
Free Soil counties in the state) and then by their friends in Worcester
and counties farther west.[82] Some went quietly, others in a blaze of racist
invective calculated to make the most of the political moment. Ithamar
W. Beard, a senator from Lowell and a close associate of Cushing, had
worked hard building a reputation as a "hunker" preoccupied with patronage. Though Beard doubtless was an opportunist, he also had political
principles, principles that cut to the core of the Democracy's resurgence.
In an open letter he vowed to fight the Free Soilers in the Coalition "to
the death," not for their stand on the divisive Maine Law, but for their
support for a personal liberty bill. Free Soilers, he fumed, were "vile,"
and worse, they were "black."[83] If Whigs took back part of the country
by campaigning against the secret ballot, Democrats claimed the rest by
crusading against African Americans.

Beard's animus owed much to several civil rights initiatives proposed
by Free Soilers of both races – a resolution condemning slavery, a personal liberty measure, and an effort to integrate the state militia. That
the resolutions failed to pass (the first two by narrow margins) demonstrates the new racial climate in the wake of the Fugitive Slave Act and
the Sumner battle; after all, in 1843 lawmakers repealed the ban on interracial marriage and passed the Latimer Law; in 1851 they were not
so open-minded, as the Free Soilers learned when they tried to put the
General Court on record against slavery. The resolution "affirmed anew"
the Commonwealth's "devotion to the Union," in a nod to Democratic

---

[81] Alexander Laytin, "Racial Underpinnings of the Coalition Government in the General
Court of Massachusetts" (senior honors thesis, Univ. of Massachusetts Amherst, 2002),
esp. pp. 34–6.
[82] See *BC*, Oct. 18 and Nov. 27, 1851. Also see Hartford, *Money, Morals, and Politics*,
pp. 180–90.
[83] Hartford, *Money, Morals, and Politics*, p. 185. Also *NC*, Sept. 28, 1852.

and Whig critics, before calling for the "overthrow of slavery, so far as the same can be constitutionally done."[84] Conservative Democrats, still smarting from their defeat the previous month over the Sumner vote, staged a vigorous campaign against the resolution in the House. A vote to table the bill (which is as close as it came to a roll-call vote) passed by three votes (167 to 164). Only three Free Soilers and ten Whigs broke ranks, suggesting that party discipline was pretty much intact. The industrial towns, which were shared by all parties at this point, voted 17 to 18 to table the resolves, but fully 10 of the yes votes came from Whigs in the Lowell delegation; the Democrats and Free Soilers in the industrial towns voted 16 to 4 against burying the resolution. The Coalition itself, however, continued to unravel, for nearly half the Democrats in our four categories divided evenly (19 to 20). As expected, Cushing led the attack, just as he had the anti-Sumner campaign. He brought along not only his Indomitables in Essex and Middlesex but also his fellows in the country who voted even more strongly than the Democrats as a whole (16 to 14) for tabling the resolution.[85] This was just the beginning of political disappointment for antislavery and civil rights.

Prospects for civil rights legislation were a good deal worse the following year because of the loss of seats suffered by the Free Soilers in the 1851 election. Still, the leadership drafted a bill greatly strengthening the 1843 law by providing for habeas corpus, trial by jury, and the right to testify in court. In addition, the bill required the state to defray the legal costs incurred by fugitives rounded up by federal agents.[86] It failed by a vote of 152 to 173, a greater margin than the antislavery resolution, and with nearly the unanimous support of Democrats and Free Soilers in the industrial centers, who voted 21 to 1 for the bill, roughly approximating their vote on the antislavery resolution.[87] Such striking support from the political voice of workingmen casts doubt on the conventional identification of workers as both the main source of racism in the North and the source of racism in what was essentially a racist party. We shall return to these points later.[88] For the moment, it is enough to know that the personal liberty bill elicited mixed emotions from Democrats; easterners, who were

[84] House of Representatives, appendix no. 187 (1851).
[85] House of Representatives, appendix no. 57 (1851). See Appendix 5.
[86] *Lib*, Apr. 2. 1852.
[87] See Appendix 6.
[88] This pattern of support for antislavery among workers and shopkeepers was also common in England. See Seymour Drescher, "Cart Whip and Billy Roller: Or Antislavery and Reform Symbolism in Industrializing Britain," *JSH* 15 (Fall 1981): 3–24.

increasingly identified as doughfaces, denounced the measure as an insult to the South and a violation of the region's "constitutional rights," as Greene put it in his *Post*.[89] Country Democrats were more supportive, not out of sympathy for the slave, but for fear of federal power sanctioned by the Fugitive Slave Act. Senator John Knowlton of Worcester County, the only member of his party who spoke up for the bill, never even mentioned runaway slaves. He instead argued that the odious Fugitive Slave Act undermined the people's "*right* to their own self government." He also dusted off the hoary doctrine of nullification, intoning that when the "general government assumes undelegated powers," as it did in September 1850 when President Fillmore signed the Fugitive Slave Bill, "its acts are unauthorized, void, and of no force."[90] It was not enough, however, to bring along the country. Some twenty-four Democrats voted against the bill, just about half of whom represented the five westernmost counties. The country had struck back again.[91]

African Americans fared no better the following year when they raised the sensitive issue of their right to bear arms. Boston leaders Charles L. Remond and Robert Morris petitioned the 1853 session of the General Court to allow African American men to march under their own militia colors. This measure, argued by William Cooper Nell and William J. Watkins among others, would help complete the rights of black men, and perhaps open the door to even more, just as military service had done for blacks in arms in previous conflicts.[92] Proponents may also have believed that the law would serve the more immediate purpose of scaring off slave catchers. Although Watkins made an eloquent case to the committee, he was met with derision and then with defeat when the chair refused to grant even the courtesy of submitting a formal report.[93] Watkins and his friends then petitioned the constitutional convention to erase the word "white" from state laws pertaining to the militia. That was the preferred position all along for men like Nell, who opposed in principle separate facilities of any kind and had supported the drive for a separate company

[89] *BP*, May 6, 1852.
[90] *Comm*, Apr. 22, 1852.
[91] House Journal, appendix 31 (1852). See Laytin, "Racial Underpinnings of the Coalition Government," p. 56, appendix B.
[92] See letter of William Cooper Nell in *Lib*, Mar. 11, 1853. William J. Watkins, "Our Rights as Men," (1853), in Dorothy Porter, ed., *Negro Protest Pamphlets* (New York: Arno Press, 1969), pp. 3–21. See also, *Lib*, May 13, 1853.
[93] Harold Goldman, "Black Citizenship and Military Self-Presentation in Antebellum Massachusetts," *HJM* 26 (Summer 1992): 157–83.

as a political expedient to get around the argument that integrating the state militia would place the Commonwealth at odds with the federal law that restricted service to whites.[94] The convention's committee on the militia, following the action of its counterpart in the legislature, recommend against taking action.[95] Wilson and his lieutenants then tried without success to replace its recommendation with a resolution mandating integration of the state militia. Although this measure failed by a surprisingly small margin given its bold implications (74 to 99), it still went down.[96]

At the end of the 1850s John Swett Rock assessed the progress of his race. Speaking at the celebration of Crispus Attucks Day in 1860, the articulate leader might well have asked which had prevailed – paternalism, segregation, or exclusionism? Rock offered a remarkably candid and nuanced look backward that pronounced exclusionism a failure and paternalism a qualified success.[97] African Americans, he began, were "oppressed everywhere in this slave-cursed land" but recently had made some advances in "progressive" Boston and presumably in the rest of the Commonwealth. They were "seldom insulted here by...vulgar passers by. We have the right of suffrage. The free schools are open to our children, and from them have come forth young men who have finished their studies elsewhere." They had access to public transportation and to "some of the eating houses...many of the hotels, and all the theatres but one." Nonetheless, the educated black had to endure the "embittered prejudices of the whites" (as well as the "jealousies of his own race") along with the humiliations of racism in two "places of amusement" whose "sole purpose" was to "perpetuate...existing prejudices against us!"

Rock dwelled on the economic impact of white racism, delineating the outer limits of racial paternalism. Black professionals, he observed, had no "field" in Boston and mechanics found it much harder to get work there than in Charlestown, where "prejudice is supposed to be very bitter against the colored man." Even "menial workers" struggled because the "friends of slavery" were "trying to starve us out by denying us employment. Fifteen or twenty years ago, colored men had more than an equal chance in menial employment, but today we are crowded out of

---

[94] Ibid. Also Watkins, "Our Rights as Men."
[95] *Constitutional Convention*, 2: 71.
[96] Ibid., 2: 75.
[97] *Lib*, Mar. 16, 1860.

almost everything," including the "patronage of . . . friends." Stevedores once drew good incomes because they worked "all along the wharves," but now they were confined to "Central wharf" because of economic racism.[98]

Thus the doctor, lawyer, and historian identified a dualism in the treatment of African Americans that persists to this day – some integration of public accommodations in civic life but very little integration of economic institutions. The relative openness of public facilities stemmed from several forces on both sides of the racial divide. White paternalists – and perhaps many more whites as well – were genuinely troubled by segregated schools and Jim Crow accommodations, partly because of the paternalists' qualified commitment to equal rights, if not to social equality. In addition, in the 1850s, as in the 1830s, they associated separate institutions with the South, the region that more and more of them were coming to despise and which was becoming a negative reference. City and country paternalists alike had come to see public institutions and especially common schools as sources of a common culture that would make Yankees of everyone, blacks as well as the Irish. For their part, black activists and their followers strongly supported integration across the board. The exception was a group of race nationalists in the 1850s who challenged the integrationist program of William Cooper Nell and his friends.[99] The fact is, however, that their numbers were small and their message not particularly popular.[100] Nell, Hayden, and their allies were considerably stronger because their program enjoyed broad support among their people and because they were well organized into the same kind of civil rights movement that had taken shape in the early 1840s.

The economic realm was another matter entirely. Whites were not as forgiving in part because livelihoods were at stake. The more this meant the livelihoods of poor Irish immigrants, the African Americans' chief rival

---

[98] Ibid.

[99] Robert S. Levine, *Martin Delany, Frederick Douglass, and the Politics of Representative Identity* (Chapel Hill: Univ. of North Carolina Press, 1997), pp. 63–9 and 141–3, and Patrick Rael, *Black Identity and Black Protest in the Antebellum North* (Chapel Hill: Univ. of North Carolina Press, 2002), esp. pp. 209–36. Levesque, *Black Boston*, esp. pp. 3–15, 263–313, and 473–7, sees nationalist sentiment in black Boston as pervasive and not specific to the 1850s, as other historians argue. See Horton and Horton, *Black Boston*, pp. 115–28, and Levine, *Martin Delany, Frederick Douglass, and the Politics of Representative Identity*, pp. 58–98.

[100] Despite an unmistakable tendency toward black pride in the mid-1850s, such a perspective did not translate into strong support for separatism. See Levesque, *Black Boston*, pp. 216–18, as against Horton and Horton, *Black Bostonians*, pp. 115–28.

in unskilled labor markets, the greater the tensions between the races and the easier it was to politicize the attendant racial animosity. Democrats deftly exploited competition in labor markets in the 1850s. They assailed paternalistic abolitionists as frauds and hypocrites, and some advocated colonization as the answer to the Commonwealth's race question.[101] It did not matter that no one, least of all the Democrats themselves, followed up with a concrete program to rid the Commonwealth of African Americans. It was enough to mention the code word of "colonization"; the rest took care of itself.

Paternalism largely failed in the economic realm. It never pretended to offer a solution for the many because by its nature paternalism was personal. It could and did build bonds between the races, but these were unequal and limited. Loring's relationship with Roberts, Garrison's with Remond, and Bowditch's with Hayden are just a few examples of the personalism of paternalism. Roberts got a legal education out of it, and Hayden a lifetime job as a menial messenger in the State House. Several others who owed their advancement to white patrons became doctors and lawyers, a thin upper crust just forming in the 1850s. But these were the fortunate few, a tiny elite that did not even amount to DuBois's famous "talented tenth." White resistance saw to that, as Martin Robison Delany learned at a tender age. Talented, ambitious, and determined to find a suitable outlet for his prodigious gifts, Delany settled on the study of medicine with a view to becoming a physician. He was rejected by several schools, but his strong letters of recommendation impressed no less a man than Oliver Wendell Holmes, dean of Harvard. Holmes admitted Delany for the 1850/1 winter session, only to be confronted by rebellious white students who signed a letter of protest asserting that "we deem the admission of blacks to the medical Lectures highly detrimental to the interests, and welfare, of the Institution of which we are members, calculated alike to lower its reputation."[102] Holmes caved in, informing Delany and his few fellow African American students that they would have to leave Harvard by the end of the term. No white paternalist had a free hand when the natives got restless.

The question of black social uplift through better jobs was on everyone's mind by the turn of the 1840s. Democrats lost no opportunity

[101] Roediger, *Wages of Whiteness*, esp. pp. 140–4, and Ignatiev, *How the Irish Became White*.

[102] Victor R. Ullman, *Martin R. Delany: The Beginnings of Black Nationalism* (Boston: Beacon Press, 1971), p. 112, and Dorothy Sterling, *The Making of an Afro-American: Martin Robison Delany, 1812–1885* (Garden City, N.Y.: Doubleday, 1996), esp. pp. 130–1.

to chide the putative friends of blacks for their inaction in the economic sphere. At the Burbank Hall rally in Pittsfield in 1850, the opening speaker, E. A. Newton, taunted "abolitionists" for neglecting the economic condition of African Americans. "Why did they not, as they ought to do, take them into their respective establishments and teach them their trades and elevate their condition[?]" Was "money wanted to aid in so doing, they know where it could be had. No, they do nothing but declaim – talk."[103] This was not exactly accurate. A few abolitionists and Free Soilers did what they could to locate blacks in more "honorable" work. Both Garrison and Wright, for instance, took on black apprentices. Such tiny islands of charity, however, did not amount to much in the sea of racism that was the handicrafts. Few employers – entrepreneurs and master craftsmen – stepped forward.

As for their white employees, there is reason to qualify the picture of them as racists so prevalent in the literature. Evangelized workers associated with the Quakers and popular sects, as we have seen, tended to see African Americans as human and as partial citizens, if not as their complete equals, and thus worthy of a paternal hand. Better-paid workmen as well could have this view, in particular those in Lowell and perhaps Lynn who voted Free Soil and whose representatives in the House supported the antislavery resolution in 1851 and the personal liberty bill in 1852. The fugitive slave Anthony Burns seems to have benefited from their sufferance. His counsel, Richard Henry Dana, stated that the authorities had made a terrible mistake. They had the wrong man because William Brent, the agent of Burns's owner Charles F. Suttle, testified he had seen Burns in Richmond in late March. If that were the case, argued Dana, the man in custody could not possibly be Suttle's slave because *this* Anthony Burns had been in Boston since February. Dana called to the stand nine witnesses – three black men and six white men – each of whom testified he had seen Burns earlier in the month in the city or at the Mattapan Iron Works. Little is known of these men or of what got them to the witness stand on that day. The prosecution suspected an abolitionist conspiracy, for as one of the men made his way to the stand Benjamin Hallett, Jr., whispered audibly, "Here comes a witness that [Theodore] Parker has got to perjure himself."[104] Although Dana reacted by getting one of his witnesses to deny any abolitionist ties, Hallett may not have

---

[103] *PS*, Jan. 2, 1851.
[104] Worthington C. Ford, "Trial of Anthony Burns," *PAAS* 44 (Jan. 1911): 322–44. Quote is on p. 332.

been completely mistaken. The Mattapan Iron Works, after all, was a Coalition Shop, and its employees may well have been Free Soilers who did not need much persuading to do their political leaders a favor. That Burns worked at the shop without incident is undeniable, although it doubtless would have been preferable if his white co-workers had agreed to train him for better work inside the shop; it was, after all, the dead of winter when he cleaned the windows. They refrained because they could not imagine a black man as a fellow tradesman in any season; blacks, to them, were not proper tradesmen or even tradesmen-in-the-making but casual workers and servants destined for menial labor. That was their place, a rude and restricted place, to be certain, but one that differed significantly from what the exclusionists had in mind and one that was secure as long as blacks did not question its legitimacy and whites thought that they were entitled to it.

How did blacks see the labor question? The issue of black access to craft work had come up intermittently ever since white abolitionists failed to establish a manual training school for African American youths. Anti-slavery activists as different as David Walker and Lydia Maria Child commented on the seeming impenetrability of the color line in craft work.[105] In Boston, Nell tried to crack it by forming a "Registry for Help" in 1853 to find work for unemployed blacks.[106] The question of suitable work for African Americans had stirred heated debate at every gathering of the National Convention of Colored People from the late 1840s onward. The tone was set at the 1848 session in Cleveland when Martin Delany said that he would sooner see his family fall into disgrace then become "servants of any man."[107] He revisited this theme four years later in his book, *The Condition, Elevation, Emigration, and Destiny of the Colored People of the United States* (1852). Now a vocal black separatist, Delany wrote that African Americans constituted a "nation within a nation" that ought to look to itself instead of to white do-gooders. He again came down hard on casual laborers, this time for allowing their wives and daughters to "do the drudgery and menial offices of other men's wives

---

[105] Levesque, *Black Boston*, pp. 115–16.

[106] Ibid., pp. 116–17. Also see *Lib*, July 13, 1853. For the equivalent of this job registry and apprenticeship program in New York and Philadelphia, which seems to have degenerated into a form of indentured servitude that could shade into quasi-slavery, see Germaine Etienne, "Excellence Is the Highest Form of Resistance: African American Reformers in the Antebellum North" (Ph.D. diss., Univ. of Massachusetts Amherst, 2004), pp. 127–51.

[107] Quoted in Rael, *Black Identity and Black Protest in the Antebellum North*, p. 32.

and daughters." The separatist then assailed blacks as a whole for their presumed passivity in the face of economic privation.[108]

Delany did not go unchallenged. J. D. Patterson took Delany's Cleveland address to be the insult of a man with little practical experience and little understanding of the plight of ordinary black people, the very people Delany pretended to represent. Showing a flash of the class consciousness that would take firmer shape after the Civil War in black Boston, Patterson scolded those in the "editorial chair, and others not in the place of servants" for casting "slurs" on those who had no other choice – who worked as menials because they had to.[109] He was no happier when someone proposed a resolution asserting "domestics and servants" among our people are "degrading to us as a class, and we deem it our bounded duty to discountenance such pursuits, except where necessity compels."[110] Frederick Douglass stepped in to mediate, counseling, "Let us say what is necessary to be done, is honorable – and leave situations in which we are considered degraded, as soon as necessity ceases."[111]

What if necessity did not cease? This question weighed heavily on Douglass over the next few years. He returned to it in his newspaper, proposing in 1853 a manual training school for black youths as a way around the racism that closed them off from apprentice training and the more remunerative world of the trades. Douglass thought he could succeed where others had failed because he had a patron in Harriet Beecher Stowe, whom he had defended against critics of the transparent white paternalism in *Uncle Tom's Cabin*.[112] A visit to Stowe at her Andover home strengthened his faith in the scheme and led to more journalistic pieces in which he laid out his vision of a prosperous and industrious population of free blacks sustained by craft work. Such a class, he reckoned, would bring down slavery because it offered the "best refutation" of black inferiority and the South's "peculiar institution." It had no chance, however, without the training afforded by the institute, an institute that placed blacks in what he approvingly called the "fostering care" of a school

---

[108] Martin R. Delany, *The Condition, Elevation, Emigration, and Destiny of the Colored People of the United States*, ed. Toyin Falola (1852; Amherst, N.Y.: Humanity Books, 2004). Quotes are on pp. 12 and 43.

[109] *NS*, Sept. 29, 1848.

[110] Quoted in Rael, *Black Identity and Black Protest in the Antebellum North*, p. 37.

[111] *NS*, Sept. 29, 1848.

[112] On this phase in Douglass's career, see Levine, *Martin Delany, Douglass, and the Politics of Representative Identity*, pp. 71–90, and William S. McFeely, *Frederick Douglass* (New York: Simon and Schuster, 1991), pp. 163–82.

supported by a white paternalist – and the nation's most prominent one at that.[113] Douglass took his plan to the 1853 meeting of the Colored National Convention in Rochester, New York, putting forth what he called a "Manual Labor School" as a major initiative that enjoyed the support of Mrs. Stowe. But at the start of the new year, coincident with Anthony Burns's arrival in Boston, Douglass announced that Stowe "does not, at present, see fit to stand forth as the patron of the proposed institution."[114] The celebrated novelist had pulled out suddenly for some unknown reason. Paternalists could be fickle as well as weak-kneed.

Not that the agitation of the past twenty years failed to produce anything lasting or significant. The bonds forged between wealthy whites and gifted blacks in the civil rights aspects of abolitionism and political antislavery did open up better jobs and even careers in the law and medicine to African Americans.[115] All blacks, moreover, may have benefited, even if slightly, from the ending of Jim Crow schools and "dirt cars" on commuter trains. Ordinary blacks, however, fared much worse. Their problem was largely economic, and it remained so. No one had a workable solution. Delany's doctrine of self-help defeated itself in his utopian scheme for black emigration to Central and South America. Douglass's faith in free labor proved too optimistic; it offered only limited prospects and none at all without the training institute he envisioned. The black masses soldiered on in menial work out of sheer necessity, just as J. D. Patterson had observed.

[113] Levine, *Martin Delany, Frederick Douglass, and the Politics of Representative Identity*, pp. 77–87.
[114] Ibid., pp. 88–90. Quotes is on p. 88.
[115] Kazuteru Omori, "Burden of Blackmen: Quest of 'Equality' among Black 'Elites' in Late Nineteenth-Century Boston" (Ph.D. diss., Univ. of Massachusetts Amherst, 2001).

9

Epilogue

The unraveling of the Coalition in 1853 was an unpleasant sight. Fraught with recrimination, finger-pointing, and accusation, it resembled the undoing of a vexed and troubled marriage. William S. Robinson blamed the Conscience Whigs Charles Francis Adams and John Gaylord Palfrey for the defeat of the draft constitution. He believed that he and his plebeian friends from the provinces had sacrificed much for Free Soilism compared to the patricians, who had risked next to nothing. Their political lives would go on; his own lay stalled in the ruins of humiliation. More than a year later, the radical Free Soiler Francis Bird was still dismayed. In a candid letter to Sumner, Bird pronounced the alliance with the Democrats a failure, a "terrible mistake," and State Reform nothing but a "humbug."[1]

Bird was getting at a fundamental issue that had divided antislavery activists for over a decade, namely, whether to pursue emancipation alone or in conjunction with other reforms. Historians have since addressed this matter in a different way. They have asked whether the Second Party System fell and the Third Party System rose because of slavery or because of state and local issues, such as nativism and temperance.[2] This academic

---

[1] William F. Hartford, *Money, Morals, and Politics: Massachusetts in the Age of the Boston Associates* (Boston: Northeastern Univ. Press, 2001), pp. 189–90.

[2] The basic works are Eric Foner, *Free Soil, Free Labor, and Free Men: The Ideology of the Republican Party before the Civil War* (New York: Oxford Univ. Press, 1970), and Leonard L. Richards, *The Slave Power: The Free North and Southern Domination, 1780–1860* (Baton Rouge: Louisiana State Univ. Press, 2000), as against Michael F. Holt, *The Political Crisis of the 1850s* (New York: Wiley, 1978), and Holt, *Political Parties and American Political Development: From the Age of Jackson to the Age of Lincoln* (Baton

debate boils down to whether the Republican Party and by extension its immediate antecedents – the Free Soil Party and the American or Know-Nothing Party, as it was popularly known – were in essence antislavery or nativist forces, or both.

The Free Soilers were the children of either the early abolitionist movement, like Elizur Wright, or the sectional controversy over the expansion of slavery, such as former Democrats like Amasa Walker or erstwhile Whigs like Charles Francis Adams. Free Soilism might never have taken shape at all had it not been for the hardening of sectional loyalties attendant on the fights over gag rule and then the Mexican War, a war driven by the expansionist nostrums of Southern planters and their Northern sympathizers. Without those events, and the war in particular, the refugees from the regular parties may well have returned to their political homes, collapsing the Liberty Party and strengthening the two-party system. As it turned out, the conflict with Mexico weakened the Second Party System, even if it did not destroy it.[3] Except for some Conscience Whigs and many former Libertyites, a good many Free Soilers came to the new party with additional political baggage. Even Francis Bird, the self-styled one-issue antislavery stalwart, divided his time between antislavery and temperance. His willingness to blame the demise of the Coalition on the distractions of the political reforms demanded by the country Democrats was more than a little disingenuous.

Although Free Soil operatives like Henry Wilson endorsed Griswold-ism in the State House and at the constitutional convention, their party reflected nativist sentiment far more deeply than historians have acknowledged.[4] The Maine Law of 1852 was their project, and it was not an isolated example. The same instinct also propelled several laws passed between 1851 and 1853 to deal with the dependent poor of both American birth and foreign origins. To be fair, this was not a knee-jerk reaction to an abstract threat posed by "the other" from abroad. The number of immigrants to Boston, which rarely exceeded four thousand a year

Rouge: Louisiana State Univ. Press, 1992). Also see William E. Gienapp, *The Origins of the Republican Party, 1852–1856* (New York: Oxford Univ. Press, 1987).

[3] Richard L. McCormick, "Ethnocultural Interpretations of Nineteenth-Century Voting Behavior," and "The Social Analysis of American Political History – after Twenty Years," in McCormick, *The Party Period and Public Policy: American Politics from the Age of Jackson to the Progressive Era* (New York: Oxford Univ. Press, 1986), pp. 29–63 and 89–140. See also Tyler Anbinder, *Nativism and Slavery: The Northern Know-Nothings and the Politics of the 1850s* (New York: Oxford Univ. Press, 1992), pp. 97–8.

[4] A notable exception is John R. Mulkern, *The Know-Nothing Party in Massachusetts: The Rise and Fall of a People's Movement* (Boston: Northeastern Univ. Press, 1990).

before 1840, swelled to nearly thirty thousand in 1849 because of the Irish famine. Six years later, Boston was home to over fifty thousand Irish immigrants, who made up nearly a third of the city.[5] This massive influx of needy people greatly strained social services and flooded the lower end of the job market; it also presented a political threat once the Irish began to vote in greater numbers after 1852.[6] The Free Soilers responded in 1851 with a measure establishing the office of Superintendent of Alien Passengers for the City of Boston to identify foreigners arriving in cities "other than by water" and deport any of them likely "to become public charges."[7] It was followed in 1852 by a law setting up a network of almshouses for "state paupers" – poor people without legal settlement in cities or towns.[8] Finally, an 1853 initiative established the Board of Commissioners of Alien Passengers and State Paupers, liberally staffed with a member of the Governor's Council, the State Auditor, and the Superintendent of Alien Passengers for the City of Boston, with sweeping powers of enforcement.[9] The absence of roll-call votes precludes assessing the extent of Free Soil support for these acts, but the relative weakness of the party in 1852 and 1853 means it had accomplices, presumably the same ones who helped pass the Maine Law.

The fact remains, however, that the "poor laws" and "pauper removal acts" of 1851–3 were Free Soil projects. The party laid the legal and administrative groundwork for a crackdown on the poor and foreign born. In 1855, A. G. Goodwin, the superintendent of alien passengers, and his agents – one ironically named John G. Locke – visited some nine hundred ships in Boston harbor and the state's almshouses and asylums to identify illegal immigrants and inmates without proper settlement. A good number of "able-bodied" native-born poor and inmates were returned to the northern New England states where they had legal residence or were

---

[5] Oscar Handlin, *Boston's Immigrants, 1790–1880: A Study in Acculturation* (1941; rev. ed. New York: Atheneum, 1991), pp. 51–2, 190–3, and Table VIII, p. 244. Also see Kerby A. Miller, *Emigrants and Exiles: Ireland and the Irish Exodus to North America* (New York: Oxford Univ. Press, 1985), pp. 280–344.

[6] Handlin, *Boston's Immigrants*, pp. 206–5, Tables XXI, XXII, and XXV. Handlin observes that the Irish vote in Boston did not increase by much until the middle of the decade.

[7] Documents of the House of Representatives, "Annual Report of the Superintendent of Alien Passengers for the Port of Boston," Doc. No. 17 (1856). Also see *Acts and Resolves Passed by the General Court Massachusetts in the Year 1851* (Boston: Dutton and Whitworth, 1851), Chapter 342, pp. 847ff.

[8] *Acts and Resolves ... 1852*, Chapter 275, pp. 190–3. Also *BP*, Feb. 26, 1852.

[9] House Doc. No. 41 (1856).

sent to inland towns in Massachusetts where they were expected to go to work for local employers. But the law was clearly aimed at the Irish. The commissioners figured that the state risked a deluge of the "refuse and scum of a foreign population" and stiff taxation "for their support" unless something were done.[10] Agent Locke reported that many Irish immigrants in the almshouses were either badly in need of "fresh air" or simply "home sick," because they had, "for a long time, expressed a desire to go home to their friends in Ireland." He thought a "sea voyage would be conducive to their health, and a visit to home and friends would do more for a *perfect* restoration than any other means."[11] His commission deported hundreds.[12]

Free Soilers and country populists were also behind the reforms passed by the 1851 and 1852 sessions, including the "democratization" of the Harvard Corporation, the regulatory commissions, and so on. The Coalition broke down, however, when it came to regulating the workday and the ballot. Many Free Soilers supported shortening the industrial workday and protecting the secrecy of the ballot, but enough of them demurred to scuttle both measures despite the support for the measures in the industrial districts. The Free Soilers were blameless on the antislavery resolves and personal liberty bill, which lost because of the opposition of Whigs and Democrats. The record demonstrates that Free Soilism was an eclectic political force, not a single-issue party in the mold of Libertyism. The Free Soil Party stood for a blend of economic populism, nativism, and antislavery. But insofar as its performance is concerned, it had more success pushing through measures in the spirit of populism and nativism than antislavery or labor reform.

Nonetheless, the Know-Nothing rebellion in the 1854 election caught everyone by surprise. "What a political overturn!" exclaimed Edward Everett in disbelief, reflecting the shock of the political establishment. Garrison could not understand how such an obscure movement could "absorb the electorate of the state and carry everything before it with the sweep of whirlwind."[13] What had been a shadowy network of fraternal lodges suddenly erupted at the polls, electing the governor, all forty senators, and all but three representatives in the House, with 63 percent of

[10] Ibid., p. 22
[11] Ibid., p. 31.
[12] House Doc. No. 17 (1856).
[13] *Lib*, Nov. 17, 1854.

America against the World!

CITIZENS OF BOSTON! Do you love your country, her liberties and her hallowed institutions? Do you desire, do you ever *pray* that those liberties and those institutions may be preserved and perpetuated? Do you truly hope that your off-spring may inherit the glorious birthright you have received from your patriot sires?

Truthfully and soberly answer ye, before Heaven, and your country's bar; for to your answer, given not in words, but in high and holy and independent *actions*, will coming generations point as the great prolific cause to them of weal or bitter woe.

Our liberties, civil and religious are in imminent danger from foes without and foes within. *Domestic Demagogues* strive to rule, though they ruin us. *Foreign Despots* seek to prostrate and enslave us. *Party Spirit*, seizing on us, makes us the subservient followers of the one, and the unsuspecting prey of the other. Shall this continue longer? Shall the selfish Demagogue chain us to his idol car, that he may ride in power over the prostrate forms of the blinded worshippers of his *party* Juggernaut? Is party paramount to Country? Is a *party* ensign dearer than your *country's* flag? Is a *party* triumph to be gloried in at the expense of your native rights, your *country's* freedom? Is love of *party* to eat out love of *country*, and the *patriot* to give way to the *partizan*?

Answer ye at the Ballot Box, in sight of Bunker Hill, as patriots, and as men!

CITIZENS OF BOSTON! Shall *Americans* govern America? or shall we tamely submit to brutal *foreign* domination? Shall foreign men control our elections? Shall foreign ruffians as guards of honor, stand armed around our ballot boxes to drive the native freemen from a near approach? Shall the *ark of our freedom's covenant*, be open to foreign vagabondism, but shut to native worth and patriotism? Shall foreign emissaries decide upon the qualifications of American voters, and the vomit of a foreign prison house oust the *native* son of a patriot hero from his birthright? Shall the glorious stars and stripes give way to foreign ensigns, or be patched over and defaced by emblems of foreign despotism?

It is for you to answer with your patriotism fired at the thought of foreign agression, and your blood boiling at the arrogant assumption of foreign minions to control us and our institutions.— It is for you to answer at the ballot box while you have the power, before you are quite driven thence by armed bands from abroad, and before you are betrayed by *party* Delilahs into the hands of the Philistines.

DESCENDANTS OF THE PILGRIMS! Shall the enemy that sought to enslave your ancestors, enslave you? Shall the arch fiend that strove to take from them the Bible, take it from your children? Will you prove recreant to the sacred memory of your sires, and quietly yield up at the bidding of party demagogues or wily priests, that for which they braved storm and tempest, sickness and death? Will you suffer foreign hands to dig away the very corner stone of your institutions, and remove at the same time the bread of life to your souls, and the foundation principles of your liberties?

Answer ye at the Ballot Box, with the rich memories of the past and the high hopes of the future gushing in your hearts! Answer under a deep sense of responsibility to freedom, to God and your *Native Land!*

WORKINGMEN OF BOSTON! Are you content that the immense influx of needy foreigners shall remedilessly reduce your wages to the lowest pittance? Are you ready to sink to the degraded level of the laborers of enslaved Europe, and bid against the old world paupers for work? Which is of most consequence to you, the welfare of your own flesh and blood, the comfort of your wives, and the education of your little ones, or the ties of party, and the mad excitement of party strife?

Of what use in Heaven's name a GUERILLA strife for a *lien on the materials subject to your workmanship*. When the trained pauper bands of Europe are depriving you of those very materials, and effectually preventing the exercise of that workmanship? Will you be content with the *shadow* while the foreigners seize and devour the *substance*.

Would you prevent the NATIVE AMERICAN MECHANICS and LABORERS from becoming paupers, and protect the American Laborer as well as Capitalist from Foreign competition?

It is for you to answer at the Ballot Box, with the future as well as present welfare of your wives and little ones, of all you hold dear rising up in your heart, and directing you to duty as a Husband, a Father, a Friend, and a NATIVE SON OF AMERICA.

FIREMEN OF BOSTON! Would you have your rights as FREE Firemen respected? Are you capable of self government, or are you fond of being in leading strings? Must you put on a yoke that you may not take off? Are you so wedded to party that your rights may be infringed, and you not venture to remonstrate? And when your right and privilege as Native born Americans are sought to be restored to you, are you content that any faction, for mere party purposes shall thwart the good intent of those who would assist you? Are you men, or are you the playthings of a foreign faction?

Answer ye at the Ballot Box, and when as *AMERICAN* Laborers, and men, you act for your country's rights against all Foreign influences, act for your own, as Firemen and Freeman against the paltry tyranny of mere party councils.

AMERICANS! As men, as patriots, as philanthropists, as moralists, as christians, carry with you to the Ballot Box your manhood, your *patriotism*, your philanthropy, your morality, your christianity. Vote honestly, truthfully, wisely. Leave all old party prejudices outside! Vote as Patriots not as partizans! Vote independently, not at party dictation! Vote as *AMERICANS* for American rights and an *American* policy; not as foreigners for a foreign policy and for extending foreign influence. Forgetful of old party predilections, as of minor consequence, let your rally cry be—OUR BIRTHRIGHT SHALL BE OUR CHILDRENS. Let your watchword be OUR COUNTRY before *party* against the world. Vote so that your children may bless you, and the latest generations revere your memory as that of independent, staunch, bold, patriotic, unwavering, honest and true-hearted

NATIVE AMERICANS!!

the vote.[14] "Sam," as the party was popularly known, wiped the political slate clean, effectively erasing the Whigs and Free Soilers and blunting a Democratic resurgence.

Recent work on nativism indicates that the Know-Nothings were rather more complicated than the monomaniacal anti-Catholic zealots depicted in past accounts.[15] One revisionist treatment describes Northern nativism as a robust antislavery party, a plausible point we will return to in a moment.[16] Another treats the party as a protean force that went through distinctive stages, beginning with fraternal lodges, built on antipartyism; it proceeded through two later stages, North Americanism and Fillmorism, which blended antiforeignism and antislavery.[17] Still another sees political nativism in the Bay State more broadly, as a people's party galvanized by a bold platform of economic and social reform alloyed with nativism. This interpretation finds little or no continuity with the immediate past, arguing that the Coalition represented parochial backlanders who could not overcome their "moral zeal and agrarian biases" by appealing to "the urban majority with programs aimed at the most serious problems vexing society."[18] The Know-Nothings, by contrast, were the legitimate voice of the truly dispossessed and exploited and, more particularly, of workers in the factories. They failed because they were betrayed by political professionals who seized control of the party machinery

---

[14] George H. Haynes, "The Causes of Know-Nothing Success in Massachusetts," *AHR* 3 (Oct. 1897–July 1898): 67–82; William G. Bean, "Party Transformation in Massachusetts with Special Reference to the Antecedents of Republicanism, 1848–1860" (Ph.D. diss., Harvard Univ., 1922), esp, chs. 8–10; Dale Baum, "Know Nothingism and the Republican Majority in Massachusetts: The Political Realignment of the 1850s," *JAH* 64 (Mar. 1973): 959–86; and Mulkern, *Know-Nothing Party in Massachusetts*, pp. 61–86.

[15] For instance, Ray Allen Billington, *The Protestant Crusade, 1800–1860: A Study of the Origins of American Nativism* (1938; New York: Quadrangle Books, 1964), and John Higham, *Strangers in the Land: Patterns in American Nativism, 1860–1925* (1955; Westport, Conn.: Greenwood Press, 1983).

[16] Anbinder, *Nativism and Slavery*, makes a powerful case for the party's antislavery ethos.

[17] Mark Voss-Hubbard, *Beyond Party: Cultures of Antipartisanship before the Civil War* (Baltimore: Johns Hopkins Univ. Press, 2002), p. 108ff.

[18] Mulkern, *Know-Nothing Party in Masschusetts*, p. 175.

FIGURE 28. (*Figure on facing page*) Broadside of the Know-Nothing Party of Boston appealing to the cultured heritage and economic interests of workingmen (probably in 1855). (Courtesy of the American Antiquarian Society, Worcester, Mass.)

after the 1854 election and then suffocated "Sam's" genuine populist spirit.[19]

There are several problems with this interpretation. The evidence does not show that Know-Nothingism was appreciably stronger in the industrial centers than anywhere else in 1854.[20] In fact, it shows that the party was strong from farm to factory.[21] Because the Coalition effectively broke up the year before, using 1853 as the year of comparision costs into doubt the attempt to demonstrate that nativism ran far ahead of the Coalition in urban areas. The Free Soilers were a spent force, but one that had more support, if less than that of the nativists, in the industrial cities than anywhere else. Most important, the Know-Nothings campaigned for the ten-hour day and the secret ballot. Both initiatives came up in the 1855 session of the General Court, before the professional politicians had the opportunity to consolidate control, but they still went down to defeat.[22]

The Know-Nothing Party's larger strategy was forged a year after its formation in 1855 at a convention in Springfield, Massachusetts, which brought together the party's nativist and antislavery wings, led by A. B. Ely and Henry Wilson, respectively. The leadership put across the compromise Springfield Platform, consisting of both anti-immigrant and antislavery planks. One provision called for preventing immigrants from voting or from holding office until twenty-one years after naturalization; another would have restored the Missouri Compromise.[23] Henry W. Gardner, one of the few Brahmins to join the party and governor of the Commonwealth from 1855 to 1857, rhetorically supported Springfield but never overcame his Whiggish background, moderating on nativism a bit and sacrificing antislavery for Unionism.[24] The party as a whole, however, stuck closely to the Springfield Platform. Its nativist policies, to be sure, were not strong enough for the Elyites, despite the tough-minded enforcement of the pauper laws and wholesale sacking of Irish immigrants on the state payroll. Ely and his faction bristled when succeeding legislative sessions, which were far more Republican in composition, whittled down their proposed

[19] Ibid., pp. 175–85.
[20] Ibid., Figure 3, p. 81. This figure shows that the party drew 62.7 percent of the vote statewide, and between 67.4 and 68.2 percent in fast-growing towns, poor towns, manufacturing towns, and large towns, with more than 3,000 people. A "category" called "remaining towns," which is not defined, drew 55.2 percent. If we assume that the poor towns were rural places, one could argue that nativism was marginally strongest there.
[21] Voss-Hubbard, *Beyond Party*, p. 110, on the party's general strength.
[22] Ibid., pp. 111–12.
[23] Mulkern, *Know-Nothing Party in Massachusetts*, pp. 123–4.
[24] Ibid., esp. pp. 158–62. Also see Baum, *Civil War Party System*, pp. 30–9 and 43–53.

probationary period to two years from twenty-one.[25] No one, however, could dispute the party's nativist resolve.

The fact is, however, that the Know-Nothings outdid the Free Soilers on anti-Southernism and antislavery. Their insurgency not only resolved to restore the Missouri Compromise and repeal the Fugitive Slave Act, it also passed the Personal Liberty Law, in striking contrast to the Coalition's failure in 1852. Much had happened since then, of course, to excite the anti-Southernism of Bay State Yankees and bolster support for strengthening the rights of fugitives slaves, notably the highly controversial Kansas-Nebraska Act and, closer to home, the arrest and rendition of Anthony Burns. Nonetheless, the nativists' approval of the 1855 law was a notable achievement. When, as expected, Governor Gardner vetoed the bill, General Court operatives rushed through a successful override and added two more bills enhancing legal protection for fugitives.[26] The vote to override was not even close; even Boston and the county seats, which had voted heavily against the 1852 bill, approved this one 18 to 10 and 16 to 6, respectively. The industrial towns once again came out unambiguously (26 to 5) for personal liberty; the country also delivered a substantial vote in favor (81 to 9), marked by virtual unanimity in Worcester County (42 to 2).[27] Antislavery feeling in the State House, and presumably among the larger electorate, had intensified since the days of the Coalition. The abolitionist militant Theodore Parker was correct when he called the nativist legislature of 1855 "the strongest antislavery body that had ever assembled in the country."[28]

The racial paternalism implicit in the Personal Liberty Law carried over to the lingering question of school desegregation. "Old" and "new" abolitionists, both black and white, had worked together and separately on racial integration of the schools for well over a decade. Nell and his friends in Boston continued to promote the Smith School boycott, and they joined with white allies to pressure the State Board of Education on the issue, focusing on Board Secretary Horace Mann. Although Mann had condemned separate schools in his annual reports, he was "never there" when it counted, wrote Wendell Phillips in an angry 1853 letter to

[25] Mulkern, *Know-Nothing Party in Massachusetts*, pp. 157–58.
[26] *Acts and Resolves of the General Court* (1855), Chs. 13 and 26–8, pp. 506, 941, and 946–7. Also see Mulkern, *Know-Nothing Party in Massachusetts*, p. 104.
[27] See Appendix 7.
[28] Quoted in Henry Wilson, *History of the Rise and Fall of the Slave Power in America*, 3 vols. (Boston: James R. Osgood, 1872–7), 2: 415.

the *Liberator*.[29] School desegregation, notes one recent student, had by then become a "litmus test of sincerity for white anti-slavery activists."[30]

Advocates of school desegregation, momentarily distracted by the crises precipitated by the Fugitive Slave Act, resumed their campaign in 1853. They came together in defense of Edward Tindall, a light-skinned youth of mixed racial parentage who had been admitted to a neighborhood school but ordered to attend Smith when an official learned of his racial heritage. Abolitionist outrage forced Jerome V. C. Smith, Boston's newly elected nativist mayor, to have a committee of the Common Council investigate. George W. Williams wrote a report that found no legal grounds for excluding black children from neighborhood schools, echoing Robert Morris and Charles Sumner in *Roberts*, and recommended that the city give desegregated schools "a fair trial."[31]

It was the nativist legislature elected the previous year, not the city government, that followed through. Much of the credit belongs to Charles Wesley Slack, a Know-Nothing representative from Boston serving the first of his two terms in the House.[32] Appointed chair of the House Committee on Education in 1855, Slack wrote a report that repeated Williams's finding and pointed out that desegregation had worked in cities and towns outside of Boston. He proposed amending the 1845 law that established the current school system to prohibit "distinctions on account of race, color, or religious opinions."[33] A month later, in April, the Bostonian introduced a bill that reflected the language in his report. This bill, passed overwhelmingly by a voice vote, ended Jim Crow schools in the Commonwealth.[34]

Why did a nativist legislature pass such a groundbreaking law? The measure has been seen as part of an assault on Catholics, reinforcing an earlier law banning the use of public money for sectarian schools. Both laws forced Irish-Catholic children into public classrooms where they would be subjected to a curriculum suffused with Protestantism and

---

[29] *Lib*, Apr. 15, 1853.

[30] Mark Santow, "These Little Republican Temples: Race, Ethnicity, and Public Schooling in Antebellum Massachusetts," (seminar paper, Univ. of Massachusetts, 1992), p. 24.

[31] *Documents of the City of Boston for 1854*, Doc. No. 54, "Report of the Committee on Public Instruction," p. 7.

[32] On Slack, see Charles W. Slack Papers, Department of Special Collections and Archives, Kent State University Library, Kent, Ohio. This collection is described on-line (www. Charles W. Slack Papers) http://speccoll.library. Kent.edu/amerhist/slack.html.

[33] Documents of the House of Representatives, House Doc. No. 167 (1855).

[34] *Lib*, Apr. 6, 1855.

FIGURE 29. Charles Wesley Slack. (Courtesy of Charles Wesley Slack Papers, Kent State Univ. Libraries and Media Services, Dept. of Special Collections and Archives, Kent State University, Kent, Ohio.)

Yankee culture. It could make blacks, as well as Irish, into Yankees. By including the words "religious opinions" in the bill, Slack was not simply playing to the anti-Catholic galleries; he was expressing the nativism that had long commingled with antislavery. At the same time, his law was a tool for racial integration, for while the 1855 legislature was a nativist fraternity, many of its members were abolitionists and antislavery men with nativist sympathies. Henry Wilson was hardly the only Free Soiler to hitch a ride on the Know-Nothing bandwagon. Their numbers included Slack himself, a former Free Soiler and the publisher of a party organ, the *Boston Journal*. Slack went on to become an important Republican journalist and a local leader of the party's radical wing. In 1855 he passed abolitionism's "litmus test" with flying colors. A close friend of black Boston, he worked with William Cooper Nell on school desegregation, advising the boycott leader to gather petitions urging legislative action and then use the pressure as a mandate.[35] James Swift, another former Free Soiler who joined the Know-Nothings, further revealed the union of antislavery and nativism in the debate over school desegregation. He described how the "'dirtiest Irish'" stepped out of their "houses into the nearest school," whereas black children had to "go a long way to the Smith School, passing other schools on the way."[36]

Know-Nothings who had passed through Free Soilism and who were possibly political neophytes had no more respect for the plantation system of the South than they did for the Catholic Church. For them the two were similar, with comparable hierarchies of parasitic planters and prelates living off the labor of others – peasants in Old Europe and poor whites in the South.[37] No one wanted that in the Bay State. The same logic of Yankeedom was at work in 1855 when the schools were integrated as in 1843 when the interracial marriage ban was repealed. When the Salem nativist Moses Kimball called in 1855 for ending school segregation, he said that Jim Crow arose from the same "unfounded and indefensible prejudice" that sustained the Slave Power.[38]

The strength of nativism in the Bay State retarded the development of the Republican Party there. The Republican organization stalled after the hoopla of its founding convention in Worcester in September 1854.[39] The party encountered difficulty at first disassociating itself from the dark lantern politics of the Know-Nothings. Its nominating convention in September 1855 nearly endorsed Gardner for governor; a year later, party leaders, fearing an embarrassing defeat, pulled back and worked

---

[35] Santow, "Little Republican Temples," pp. 33–4.
[36] Quoted in ibid., p. 34.
[37] See, for instance, Mulkern, *Know-Nothing Party in Massachusetts*, p. 156, and Anbinder, *Nativism and Slavery*, pp. 103–26.
[38] *BETT*, Apr. 6, 1855.
[39] Gienapp, *Origins of the Republican Party*, pp. 133–8.

out a quid pro quo with the nativists. They would refrain from running candidates for statewide office in return for nativist support for John C. Frémont, the Republican choice for president. The deal of 1856, which guaranteed another term for Gardner (who won again in 1857), masked both the flagging of nativism and strength of Republicanism.[40] Frémont ran an impressive campaign, polling a plurality of 45 percent against a divided field and giving a drubbing to the Know-Nothing Millard Fillmore as well as quietly but decisively reversing the nativist tide of 1854. The ebbing of nativism actually started at the national level in 1855 when the party convention split into Northern and Southern factions over Section XII in the platform, which committed the party to "abide by and maintain existing laws upon the subject of slavery." Such a concession to slavery angered most Northerners, especially the Bay Staters, who stayed in the party but resolved to repudiate the party's pro-Southern tilt. These self-styled "Know-Somethings," wrote a minority report condemning the party's tacit endorsement of the Kansas-Nebraska Act and demanding restoration of the Missouri Compromise. A year later the Northerners left the Know-Nothings for good over the Southern majority's stand on maintaining the spirit of Section XII.[41] The near split in 1855 harmed Gardner, whose vote plummeted twenty-five points to under forty percent, and his party wound up with a plurality of the House because of (all things) a Whig rebirth in Boston and a solid Republican showing in the country. In 1858 the Republicans received a majority of the gubernatorial vote for the first time, and in 1860 their vote for governor (64 percent) matched the nativist landslide (63 percent) of 1854.[42] The difference was their staying power.

The geopolitical configuration of the House in the second half of the 1850s reveals three trends within the larger context of the Republican eclipse of Know-Nothingism. First, antiforeignism declined sharply in Boston and in the shire towns between the elections of 1855 and 1858, shrinking from thirteen seats to two and from eight to none, respectively. Boston and the county seats started to lean toward the Democracy on the strength of the developing Irish vote. Second, nativism's grip on the country loosened further due to a modest rebound by Democrats and

---

[40] Mulkern, *Know-Nothing Party in Massachusetts*, pp. 127–9, and Gienapp, *Origins of the Republican Party*, pp. 134–7, 214–23, and 388–9.

[41] Gienapp, *Origins of the Republican Party*, pp. 239–303, and Anbinder, *Nativism and Slavery*, pp. 162–93.

[42] Carl Siracusa, *A Mechanical People: Perceptions of the Industrial Order in Massachusetts, 1815–1880* (Middletown, Conn.: Wesleyan Univ. Press, 1979), appendix C-2, p. 254.

a great upsurge by Republicans. By the end of the decade the new party had no fewer than three-fourths of the House seats in the five western-most counties; country Republicanism was so robust that it even evicted Democrats from their longtime home in Berkshire County, a development we will return to later. Finally, and no less noteworthy, nativism died hardest in the industrial belt. In 1856, when American Republicanism was in retreat everywhere else in the Commonwealth, it held its own in the industrial districts, with thirty-one out of forty House seats. It took another two years for Republicans to dislodge nativists in the factory towns. Even then, they had to deal with residual antiforeignism and gathering competition from the Democracy.[43] Their hold on the shoe and textile cities was never complete or secure, a political fact that strongly influenced party policy.

Thus the Republican Party stood on two unequal constituencies at the end of the decade. It controlled the country towns and villages, the places that fired the imaginations of Yankeedom's propagandists and gave Republicanism its durable image as the party of small-town America – of the white picket fence and Fourth of July barbecue. It was weaker but still comparatively strong in the mill and factory towns, perhaps more so in metallurgical centers than in such textile towns as Lowell and Amesbury, which were becoming magnets for Irish immigrants.[44] The problem from the point of view of electoral politics was clear enough. Country towns were shrinking, industrial towns growing. Could the industrial towns be ignored? If not, what were the wire-pullers to do to win them over and hold their loyalty?

Historians who have asked such questions about Republicanism divide into three camps, not two as the conventional wisdom has it.[45] One camp, or the antislavery school, argues that insurgent Republicanism made few concessions to nativism, and that nativism itself was dying in the Republican organization.[46] Another, or the nativist school, sees

---

[43] See Appendix 8.

[44] Ibid. It seems hardly coincidental that Lowell was still sending nativists to the legislature at the end of the decade.

[45] See, for instance, Eric Foner, "The Causes of the American Civil War: Recent Interpretations and New Directions," *CWH* 20 (Sept. 1974): 197–214; Don E. Fehrenbacker, "The New Political History and the Coming of the Civil War," *PHR* 54 (May 1985): 1117–42; William E. Gienapp, "Nativism and the Creation of the Republican Majority in the North before the Civil War," *JAH* 72 (Dec. 1985): 529–59; and Michael F. Holt, "The New Political History and the Civil War Era," *RAH* 13 (1985): 60–9.

[46] The most important sustained argument on this idea is Foner, *Free Soil, Free Labor, Free Men*. Also see Dale Baum, *The Civil War Party System: The Case of Massachusetts,*

varieties of antiforeignism as an initial *and enduring* source of Republican strength, discounting the role of antislavery in the party's formation if not in its consolidation of power.[47] A third interpretation, normally associated with the antislavery school, can be read as a kind of third camp. It emphasizes the antislavery ethos of political nativism but argues that nativism influenced party policy well into the closing years of the 1850s. Thus the historian Tyler Anbinder follows the antislavery school by drawing attention to the antislaveryism of nativism and by arguing that nativism "had greatly diminished by 1859" in the Republican Party. He qualifies this point, however, by observing that proscriptive legislation passed by Republicans in the late 1850s "attests to nativism's continuing influence within the Massachusetts Republican organization."[48]

The nativist perspective was anticipated by William G. Bean, who in the 1920s and 1930s said that Republicanism absorbed the Know-Nothings en masse, which made the new party a nativist one with a reformist spirit rooted in the region's hoary Protestantism.[49] A recent critic from the antislavery school counters that his own findings "do not support the conclusion that the Massachusetts Know-Nothings were completely absorbed into the Republican Party after their national organization dissolved over the slavery issue in 1856."[50] The difficulty here is twofold. First, Bean overstated the case when he wrote that the Republican Party drew in Know-Nothings wholesale; his critic repeats this mistake by invoking the same impossibly high standard of absorption. It is doubtful if any insurgency or dominant party ever digested its opposition whole. It is just as doubtful that Republicanism needed to take in *all* former nativists. A small percentage would have sufficed given the new party's obvious need to ensure its own survival in a period of great political fluidity. Everyone knew that two third parties – the Libertyites and Free Soilers – had collapsed and that some sort of compromise with antiforeignism was necessary.

Second, the historical record suggests that some scholars of the antislavery school of Republicanism have been too quick to dismiss the party's

1848–1876 (Chapel Hill: Univ. of North Carolina Press, 1984); Richard H. Sewell, *Ballots for Freedom: Antislavery Politics in the United States, 1837–1860* (New York: Oxford Univ. Press, 1976); Bruce Levine, *Half Slave and Half Free: The Roots of the Civil War* (New York: Hill and Wang, 1992); and Richards, *Slave Power.*

47 Holt, *Political Crisis of the 1850s.* Also see Gienapp, *Origins of the Republican Party,* and Gienapp, "Nativism and the Creation of the Republican Majority."

48 Anbinder, *Nativism and Slavery,* p. 252.

49 Bean, "Party Transformation in Massachusetts," and Bean, "Puritan Versus Celt, 1850–1860," *NEQ* 7 (Mar. 1934): 70–89.

50 Baum, *Civil War Party System,* pp. 53–4.

nativism, just as Anbinder maintains. Two pieces of legislation, approved
in the transition from Know-Nothingism to Republicanism, reveal flagging if significant nativist influence. The so-called two-year amendment,
which required immigrants to wait two years after naturalization to vote
or hold office, started out as a much more drastic proposal sponsored
in 1855 by the most extreme faction of Know-Nothings. Designed initially to prohibit immigrants from voting or holding office in perpetuity,
the amendment was watered down over the next few years by Know-
Nothings and Republicans, who debated waiting periods of twenty-one
and fourteen years before submitting the compromise of a two-year probationary period to the voters, who approved it in 1859.[51] The so-called
reading and writing amendment, required voters to pass a literacy test on
the assumption that it would affect the Irish negatively. It is ironic that
the device used in the South forty years later to strip African Americans
of the right to vote originated in the most liberal state in the North. The
literacy test passed two consecutive sessions of the legislature in 1855 and
1856, and sailed into the statute books with two-thirds of the popular
vote in a referendum in 1857.[52]

A scholar from the antislavery school of the Republican Party argues
forcefully that both amendments passed because of Know-Nothings, not
Republicans. He observes that Republican voters opposed both measures
by strong majorities and that "Republican radicals" in the legislature
in 1857 defeated several constitutional amendments with lengthy probationary periods for foreigners, including the nativists' fourteen-year
proposal.[53] Both points, the second in particular, are well taken. The
question is, however, why such measures, and the more drastic "literacy
test" especially, came up at all? Why did Republican floor managers not
simply bury the amendments, just as Julius Rockwell, the party's early
standard-bearer for governor, had done time and again when he ran the
House of Representatives in the late 1830s? Republican operatives elsewhere had no compunctions about thwarting such proscriptive laws. New
York Republicans, who had consistently kept the nativists at arm's length,
approved in 1857 what one modern historian calls a "feeble" voter reg-
istration law; their fellows in Ohio, concerned about holding the German
vote, acted similarly and went a step further by scolding the Bay Staters

[51] Ibid., pp. 43–8 and 52–3. Also see Foner, *Free Soil, Free Labor, Free Men*, pp. 250–1, and
Mulkern, *Know-Nothing Party in Massachusetts*, pp. 271–4 and 294–5.
[52] Baum, *Civil War Party System*, pp. 45–7.
[53] Ibid., pp. 43–7.

for approving the waiting-period law.[54] The fact is, however, that Republicans in Massachuetts in the second half of the 1850s could afford to moderate nativist sentiment lurking among their followers but could not afford to ignore it, either. They needed all the votes they could get and could not garner support in the factory towns without the blandishments of the constitutional amendments of 1857 and 1859.

This is not to say the Republican Party was a nativist party or that it was too preoccupied with slavery to be anything but an antislavery operation. We need not choose between characterizing Republicanism as one or the other, as an antislavery party or an anti-immigrant party. It was both, at least, at first. And even though it became more antislavery and less nativist, it did not, in the 1850s, sound only a single note. Antislavery became the party's dominate note, but was by no means its only note.

The debate among historians over the nature of the Republican Party roughly approximates the debate among abolitionists over tactics and strategy. The great question that haunted abolitionists was whether to fight only for emancipation or for emancipation in conjunction with other reforms. The factions traded places over time. Garrison, after all, started out as a single-issue man, only to become in the 1830s an energetic advocate of world peace and women's rights; his turn toward eclecticism aroused the ire of single-issue men like Elizur Wright. By the middle of the next decade, however, Garrison sounded more like a single-issue advocate again even though he remained a supporter of women's rights. Wright was by then a leading voice for eclecticism. His position proved far more popular and effective than single-issue abolition regardless of whether it was allied with Garrisonian moral suasion or with political action. By the 1840s Garrison's camp was dwarfed by political antislavery and was probably smaller still a decade later; single-issue abolitionists in politics were only slightly more popular by the 1850s, as the experience of Francis Bird suggests. The East Walpole paper manufacturer and temperance champion came as close as any Bay State politico to being a fully formed racial egalitarian; Bird was also an earnest abolition-first advocate, who loathed antiforeignism on the ground that religious bigotry made racial bigotry easier and more acceptable.[55] He was outraged when in the mid-1850s his old Free Soil associates and fellow founders of the Republican Party cooperated with the Know-Nothings or joined their

---

[54] Anbinder, *Nativism and Slavery*, pp. 256–60.
[55] Ibid., pp. 44–8, and Hartford, *Money, Morals, and Politics*, pp. 189–90.

party and then in 1856 worked out the deal that ceded the state's executive offices to them. Bird responded by putting together separate tickets for the governorship in 1856 and again in 1857, with demoralizing results. His "Honest Man's" candidate in 1856 got a paltry 3 percent of the vote and its successor candidate in 1857 only a few hundred votes.[56] Although Bird's was a protest campaign, it nonetheless illustrates the limitations of single-issue abolitionism.

The bearing of the Liberty Party provides an even stronger example of the problems confronted by single-issue antislavery in politics. The Libertyites established the significant precedent in 1840 of demonstrating the potential of political abolitionism. They then found out that progress was highly contingent. It hinged on the larger political context, on the willingness of leaders to embrace reforms other than abolitionism, and on the strength of likely allies in the larger reform community. Libertyism's signal achievement of the civil rights laws in 1843 traced partly to its alliance with civil rights and mostly to the political leverage it gained by exploiting the Latimer affair. The Libertyites found it impossible to improve upon the ten thousand vote plateau they reached at mid-decade in part because of Whiggery, which continued to provide a home for political abolitionists wary of third partyism. When the Whigs did begin to crack at the end of the Mexican War, it was too late to do the Liberyites much good. The party leadership at the state level gestured toward embracing reform groups and movements because of the dominant voice of Joshua Leavitt and his fellows.

Such alliances were difficult. Abolitionists and labor reformers joined forces in Lowell in the late 1840s, as we have seen, following several years of strained relations. But the labor movement in Lowell and in other industrial towns proved weak, fleeting, and too much of a women's movement to be much help to a party in need of votes. Other movements were as yet thin on the ground.

The eclectic reform of Free Soilism was a mixed blessing, a source of strength and weakness at once. Although the split in Whiggery and demise of the Liberty Party cut loose abolitionists and antislavery activists in need of a new political home, Free Soilism could not count on such allies alone if it wished to become a serious political contender. Antislavery sentiment had by then outgrown its origins in the old antislavery societies and evangelical pulpits, instead emanating from a larger audience with no single organizational base. The party's pragmatists – primary leaders

---

[56] Baum, *Civil War Party System*, pp. 34–7.

Wilson and Sumner as well as secondary ones like Robinson – had always regarded antislavery as fundamental but also faced a very different political landscape than the Libertyites, a landscape laden with opportunities for partnerships with working people and townsfolk as well as with Democrats itching for political power. Their formal union with the Democrats in 1850 strengthened them in the halls of government, setting the stage for the reform legislatures of 1851 and 1852. Although the Coalition passed a long list of reforms, it also disappointed some of its strongest supporters because of tensions from within. The country rebelled against the city, thwarting several ten-hour bills, and then complied with the Whigs' virtual repeal of the secret ballot law. If we can read the struggle over the ten-hour day and the secret ballot as expressions of class politics, it is safe to conclude that country politicians – in alliance with urban nativists – recoiled from the politics of class. They were far more comfortable with the cultural populism of the Pauper Removal Act and the Maine Law.[57]

As for race, most Free Soilers identified with the politics of paternalism rather than with the vicious racism of exclusionism embraced by the most chauvinistic voices in the Democracy. This extended to the party's Yankee workers in the industrial belt, whose representatives voted for antislavery resolutions and a stronger Personal Liberty Law. The forces of racism, it seems, were stronger in country districts with longtime ties to the Democracy. It was in the country, not in the Lowells of the Commonwealth, that racist politics resonated for voters. This is not to say that historians who single out Irish immigrants in the cities as the cutting edge of white chauvinism are mistaken; the point is that there was an important rural expression of racism as well. It also suggests that if the voting patterns in the industrial cities and towns are any guide, Yankee workmen were far more concerned about immigrants than about African Americans. After all, they supported nativist candidates for office long after their country colleagues deserted the Know-Nothing ship. They were, in fact, the bitter-enders of Know-Nothingism, and they seem to have found it easier to live with African Americans, or even to come to their defense when fugitives were threatened by the Slave Power as in the Burns episode.[58]

[57] Ronald P. Formisano, *The Transformation of Political Culture: Massachusetts Parties, 1790s–1840s* (New York: Oxford Univ Press, 1983), pp. 338–9.

[58] One of the only historians to appreciate this point is Jonathan A. Glickstein, *American Exceptionalism, American Anxiety: Wages, Competition, and Degraded Labor in the Antebellum United States* (Charlottesville: Univ. of Virginia Press, 2002), esp. pp. 93–7 and 277–9.

The racial paternalism of Free Soilism carried over to Know-Nothingism. It was the Know-Nothings, after all, who put the finishing touches on social integration by passing the 1855 law that ended Jim Crow in schools and opened public classrooms to African Americans across the Commonwealth – even as they failed to win approval of yet another ten-hour bill or to resurrect the secret ballot. Class politics was no easier under the nativists than under the Free Soilers. It was harder still under the Republicans, and not simply because of the party's aversion to the pursuit of class interests. Labor activism was on the wane by the advent of the Republican Party in the mid-1850s. The ten-hour movement, which had helped sustain Free Soilism in the industrial belt, had dissipated. Scattered strikes and labor actions broke out, but with weak or no organization and few visible leaders pressuring politicians, as there had been earlier in the decade. Supportive politicians were fewer as well, simply because there was no real call for them. In addition, the country was cooler, even placid. Griswoldism was a distant memory and pretty much of a lost cause. Indeed, the first Know-Nothing legislature nailed shut the coffin of the country's political agenda when it approved representation based on population for both legislative houses and election by plurality.[59]

A common thread ran through the experience not only of both third parties but of all parties. Popular movements of working people, temperance advocates, and civil rights workers – to name but a few – provided the momentum for reform. Politicians simply followed along but determined the outcome because they controlled the levers of political power. As the former House speaker Julius Rockwell made clear, left to themselves the politicians would have done very little for the drys, blacks, or working people of the Commonwealth, who had to mobilize on their own to have an impact. All social movements, however, were not equal; they had different political valences, which varied according to each movement's numbers, location, and fit with the agendas of the parties.

How different was Bay State politics? Was it a matter of "Massachusetts exceptionalism," as a reader of this book's manuscript put it? "Exceptionalism" is, of course, a controversial term. The word is laden with chauvinistic implications, as anyone familiar with the debate over American exceptionalism is aware. This debate, set off by the Werner Sombart question

---

[59] Mulkern, *Know-Nothing Party in Massachusetts*, p. 105, and Baum, *Civil War Party System*, pp. 35–7.

"Why is there no socialism in the United States?" is about to reach its centennial.[60] It is probably best to avoid the term or use the word differently to prevent invidious comparison with the Sombart debate, but it would be unwise to duck the question put to me by my referee.

There were undeniable similarities between Massachusetts and other Northern states in the period covered by this book. At first, the competition between the main parties characteristic of other states in the North was absent in the Bay State, with Whigs ruling the roost through the 1830s. The 1840s, however, brought Massachusetts into line with the larger pattern owing to a decline in Whiggery and a mild resurgence of the Democracy. Massachusetts came close to looking like a two-party state, if only momentarily. Massachusetts also reflected the general weakening of partisan ties between 1848 and 1854 that ensued from the Mexican War and the Kansas-Nebraska Act. The nativist rebellion in 1854/5 cut a broad but unequal swath across the North. It was much stronger in the East than in the West, which suggests that Massachusetts was in step with its sister states in the region. Most of nativism's political refugees, moveover, wound up in the same place. A small number dropped out, and some others gravitated to Fillmorism and then to Constitutional Unionism, the conservative movement that stood for accommodation with the South. The vast majority, however, got absorbed into Republicanism. The timing and character of the rise of Republicanism, therefore, varied from state to state. In Ohio, the Republican organization "swallowed" the nativists in 1856 and 1857; in New York, they prevailed without much nativist support; in Pennsylvania, the Republican takeover waited until 1858.[61] The Massachusetts organization came to power between those extremes, that is to say, it was of a piece with the larger pattern.

Massachusetts Republicanism was not unique on the question of policy either. As Mark Voss-Hubbard has persuasively argued, Republican programs differed only slightly in the major northeastern states of Connecticut, Pennsylvania, and Massachusetts. In each state the party added a protectionist plank to its platform, borrowing the Whig policy

[60] I am thinking here of scholarly reaction to Werner Sombart, *Why Is There No Socialism in the United States?* (1906; White Plains, N.Y.: International Arts and Sciences Press, 1976). For a review of the debate, see Bruce Laurie, *Artisans into Workers: Labor in Nineteenth-Century America* (New York: Hill and Wang, 1989), pp. 3–14.

[61] Anbinder, *Nativism and Slavery*; Voss-Hubbard, *Beyond Party*; and Michael J. McManus, *Political Abolitionism in Wisconsin, 1840–1861* (Kent, Ohio: Kent State Univ. Press, 1998).

that had helped sustain the old party in the rising industrial districts and, at the same time, thereby appealing not so subtly to lingering nativist instincts in those places. A Connecticut operative typically said that the tariff would "protect the laborers of this country from the cheap pauper labor of the old world."[62] A labor caucus in the Massachusetts Republican Party, which harked back to Free Soilism, did not appear until the Civil War years.[63] Republicans simultaneously raised the colors of Northern nationalism, appealing to the "plebeian theme" that the "Slave Power threatened republican liberty and white small-producer independence through its domination of the federal government."[64] This discourse enjoyed great popularity through the North and especially in New England, not simply Massachusetts, where it resonated deeply with anti-Southern feeling.[65]

This expression of Northern nationalism and its companion of anti-Sourthernism coincided with a seeming retreat on the race question by Republican organizations across the North.[66] Even Massachusetts, the home of the civil rights movement, appears to have gone along. In 1858 the party softened the provisions of the 1855 Personal Liberty Law, a retreat that angered old-line abolitionists like Garrison and younger Republican radicals like John Andrew, the boyish lawmaker and governor-to-be who had hoped to strengthen the measure only to see the Republican-dominated legislature follow the party line of moderation.[67]

That said, Massachusetts was undeniably different in degree and in kind on the questions of antiforeignism and race. It was more intolerant of immigrants, and Catholics especially, than any other state. Its anti-Catholic animus, which traced back to the state's Protestant origins and which surfaced from time to time in Whiggery, simply erupted in the mid-1850s, overwhelming all before it. The Know-Nothing Party in the Bay State was so potent that it was the only such party in the North to take power on its own; all others – including those in Connecticut and Pennsylvania, which were strong in their own right – were forced

---

[62] Quoted in Voss-Hubbard, *Beyond Party*, p. 209.

[63] David Mongtomery, *Beyond Equality: Labor and the Radical Republicans, 1862–1872* (New York: Knopf, 1967), esp. pp. 230–424, and Timothy Messer-Kruse, *The Yankee International, 1848–1876: Marxism and the American Reform Tradition* (Chapel Hill: Univ. of North Carolina Press, 1998).

[64] Voss-Hubbard, *Beyond Party*, p. 179. Also see Anbinder, *Nativism and Slavery*, pp. 246–68, and Foner, *Free Soil, Free Labor, Free Men*, pp. 88–93, and 96–102.

[65] Ronald P. Formisano, *The Birth of Mass Political Parties: Michigan, 1827–1861* (Princeton, N.J.: Princeton Univ. Press, 1971), pp. 276–81.

[66] Voss-Hubbard, *Beyond Party*, pp. 179–80.

[67] *Lib*, Apr. 2, 1858.

into unions with established parties.[68] Nor will it do, as some have done, to argue that class or antislavery instincts outweighed antiforeignism in Know-Nothing circles.[69] The insurgency in Massachusetts gave no quarter to foreigners, even as it embraced antislavery. No other state passed such sweeping proscriptive legislation aimed at foreigners, from firing Catholics on the public payroll to deporting the paupers among them. Ironically, the exclusionist politics practiced by racist Democrats also gained expression among Know-Nothings; indeed, nativist exclusionism, episodic though it was, proved more powerful than its Democratic version. Racist exclusionists, after all, did little more than rant and rave; nativists actually followed through.

As with nativism, so with race. The Bay State fully deserved its reputation as the most "progressive" state in the union on the question of race, as the African American activist John Swett Rock once put it. Its racial paternalism, as I have preferred to call it, was as deeply rooted as its anti-Catholicism in the state's Puritan past. The tradition of racial paternalism inherited from Yankee slavery and the relatively small size of the black population help explain the more civil tone of racial discourse in the Commonwealth. But we err badly and ignore history if we rely on tradition and demography alone, for the Bay State was also home to the largest and most active antislavery movement in the nation. It boasted the greatest number of abolitionist societies as well as the strongest Liberty and Free Soil organizations. These political groups, along with the Conscience Whigs, invested the Bay State not only with an abolitionist legacy but also with a substantial cadre of leaders – Wright, Wilson, Bird, and others – who carried into Republicanism the racial paternalism that had integrated most public accommodations as well as the schools and put forceful personal liberty laws on the books. The Bay State also had African American leaders who were arguably the most cohesive, talented, and politically savvy in the nation. The white friends of these African Americans, however, often turned out to be summer soldiers. In the middle of the decade, they balked at giving blacks the right to bear arms and, at its end, buckled before Governor Banks's insistence on weakening the Personal Liberty Law. But these were momentary setbacks, not defeats. The 1858 legislative session also condemned both the Dred Scott decision and the Lecompton

---

[68] Anbinder, *Nativism and Slavery*, pp. 127–61; Gienapp, *Origins of the Republican Party*, pp. 103–66; and Voss-Hubbard, *Beyond Party*, pp. 105–77.

[69] On nativism as a class expression, see Mulkern, *Know-Nothing Party in Massachusetts*; on its essential antislaveryism, see Anbinder, *Nativism and Slavery*.

Constitution, and finally removed Judge Edward G. Loring, the state jurist who had ordered the rendition of Anthony Burns.[70] Several years later, as the Civil War raged, Governor Andrew strongly supported the formation of the black regiments – the first ones in the North – that marched off to battle.[71]

Virtually all the other Northern states either clung hard to segregation or lagged behind the Bay State on race relations. Most never integrated their public facilities and failed to pass personal liberty laws, with the notable exceptions of Connecticut, Vermont, Ohio, and Pennsylvania.[72] Some new states, all with tiny black populations, had integrated their public schools.[73] Between 1819 and 1865 every state admitted to the Union limited suffrage to white males. Only in New England, however – with the exception of Connecticut – did black men have the right to vote. Blacks voted in some Pennsylvania counties, where they were few in number, but the Pennsylvania constitution of 1837, which was ratified a year later, formally restricted the franchise to white men.[74] In New York, property qualifications barred the vast majority of blacks from the polls. Black leaders in that state tried in vain to work with sympathetic whites to lift the ban; they then turned to the Libertyites, like their Massachusetts colleagues. The Liberty men proved worthy allies, arguing their case on the floor of the 1846 constitutional convention, where they picked up some Whig support but not enough. The majority Democrats retained the property clause in the draft constitution but agreed to a referendum on universal male suffrage in 1847. The voters rejected it hands down. That blacks had no better luck with the Free Soilers comes as no surprise. The New Yorkers, after all, were dominated by former Van Burenites, who were known to be hostile to African Americans; in fact, Samuel J. Tilden, their gubernatorial candidate in 1848, had vehemently opposed

---

[70] Voss-Hubbard, *Beyond Party*, p. 206. Also see *Lib*, Apr. 2, 1858.

[71] James M. McPherson, *Battle Cry of Freedom: The Civil War* (New York: Oxford Univ. Press, 1988), pp. 490–510 and 564–7; Henry Mayer, *All on Fire: William Lloyd Garrison and the Abolition of Slavery* (New York: St. Martin's Press, 1998), pp. 550–7; and Alfred M. Green, *Letters and Discussion of the Formation of Colored Regiments...*(1862; Philadelphia: Historic Publications, 1969).

[72] Levine, *Half Slave and Half Free*, pp. 169–70, and Thomas D. Morris, *Free Men All: The Personal Liberty Laws in the North, 1780–1861* (Baltimore: Johns Hopkins Univ. Press, 1974).

[73] Wisconsin was one. See McManus, *Political Abolitionism in Wisconsin*, pp. 149–63.

[74] Leon F. Litwack, *North of Slavery, The Negro in the Free States, 1790–1860* (Chicago: Univ. of Chicago Press, 1961), pp. 74–90, and Ira Berlin, *Many Thousands Gone: The First Two Centuries of Slavery in North America* (Cambridge: Harvard Univ. Press, 1998), pp. 211–14, 224–7, and 319–38.

black suffrage at the constitutional convention. An African American proposal went nowhere, in the convention and nowhere in the courts.[75] As the historian Leslie M. Harris concludes, "Only with the passage of the Fifteenth Amendment in 1869 would New York's blacks, along with southern freedmen, gain equal suffrage."[76]

Republican organizations and their nativist forebears tried in other states, without success, to emulate Massachusetts on black suffrage. In neighboring Connecticut in 1854, antislavery forces put through a constitutional amendment, which deleted the constitution's ban on black suffrage, sending the measure on to the nativist legislature for final approval before sending it to the voters. It passed the Senate but came up seventeen votes short of the required two-thirds majority in the House.[77] In Wisconsin, abolitionists and antislavery men had struggled for years to expand the suffrage, beginning with the territorial government. An 1848 proposal failed by a single vote in the territorial legislature, and the new constitution drafted that year with its whites-only clause was approved 2 to 1 by the voters. The next year, however, a suffrage referendum passed easily, but was voided by the court on a technicality. In 1857 a referendum cleared both houses of the Republican-controlled legislature but ran afoul of an energetic campaign mounted by Democratic opponents. Republican lawmakers, now in step with their party's general retreat on race, kept a stony silence even in the face of vicious race baiting by Democrats and watched the referendum go down by a vote of forty-five thousand to thirty-one thousand. Iowans were no more receptive. They defeated a similar measure earlier in the year, as Republicans "kept mute."[78]

The votes in Connecticut and Wisconsin are instructive. In both states the opposition tended to come from Democrats, former Democrats, and one-time Whigs; in other words, opponents were chiefly partisan, with

---

[75] Litwack, *North of Slavery*, pp. 88–90. Also see Eric Foner, "Racial Attitudes of the New York Free Soilers," in Foner, *Politics and Ideology in the Age of the Civil War* (New York: Oxford Univ. Press, 1980), pp. 77–93; Milton C. Sernett, *North Star Country: Upstate New York and the Crusade for African American Freedom* (Syracuse, N.Y.: Syracuse Univ. Press, 2002), pp. 104–28; and Leslie M. Harris, *In the Shadow of Slavery: African Americans in New York City, 1626–1863* (Chicago: Univ of Chicago Press, 2003), pp. 267–70.

[76] Harris, *Shadow of Slavery*, p. 270.

[77] Anbinder, *Nativism and Slavery*, p. 156.

[78] McManus, *Political Abolitionism in Wisconsin*, pp. 19–35 and 149–63. Quote is on p. 161. For a fine treatment of race and Iowa Republicanism, see Robert R. Dykstra, *Bright Radical Star: Black Freedom and White Supremacy on the Hawkeye Frontier* (Ames: Iowa State Univ. Press, 1993), pp. 149–92.

a strong racist accent. Prosuffrage support in Connecticut came from erstwhile Free Soilers;[79] in Wisconsin and Iowa support ran highest not simply among Republicans but among Republicans in counties with large concentrations of New England transplants – Yankees and country people on fresh ground and on rather better soil.[80] It would be naive to assume that all Yankeedom's transplants shared the racial paternalism of villagers back home, for not all villagers did so either. A small faction of Democrats, as we have seen, shared the racism of their party at large. Far more, however, carried with them the cultural baggage of their origins in the New England countryside – respect for education, taste for homegrown literature, and love for Thanksgiving. Racial paternalism was very much a part of that legacy. It was not equality, to be sure, but it was as far as Yankees were prepared to go.

[79] Anbinder, *Nativism and Slavery*, p. 156. See esp. table, "House Opposition to Black Suffrage among Know Nothings".
[80] McManus, *Political Abolitionism in Wisconsin*, pp. 19–35 and 161.

Appendixes

APPENDIX 1. *Ten-Hour Vote, 1853*

Boston	Whig		Democrat		Free Soil	
	Y	N	Y	N	Y	N
	I	30	–	–	–	–
Subtotal	I	30	0	0	0	0
County Seats						
Barnstable	–	–	–	–	–	–
Berkshire	–	2	–	–	–	–
Bristol	–	–	–	–	–	–
Dukes	–	–	–	–	–	–
Essex	–	6	–	–	–	–
Franklin	I	–	–	–	–	–
Hamden[a]	–	–	–	–	–	–
Hampshire	–	–	–	–	–	–
Middlesex	–	2	–	–	–	–
Nantucket	I	–	–	–	–	–
Norfolk	–	2	–	–	–	–
Plymouth	–	–	I	–	I	–
Worcester[a]	–	–	–	–	–	–
Subtotal	2	12	I	0	I	0

(continued)

APPENDIX I. *(continued)*

Boston	Whig		Democrat		Free Soil	
	Y	N	Y	N	Y	N
Industrial Towns						
Amesbury	–	–	1	–	–	–
Charlestown	–	–	–	–	–	–
Fall River	–	–	–	–	–	–
Holyoke	–	–	–	–	–	–
Lawrence	–	–	1	–	2	–
Lowell	–	–	3	–	3	–
Lynn	–	–	–	–	–	–
Oxford	–	–	1	–	–	–
Salisbury	–	–	–	–	–	–
Springfield	–	–	1	–	–	–
Waltham	–	1	–	–	–	–
Webster	–	–	–	–	–	–
Worcester	–	–	2	–	3	–
Subtotal	0	1	9	0	8	0
Country Towns (five western counties)						
Berkshire	3	3	6	–	2	–
Franklin	–	1	2	–	4	–
Hamden	4	1	5	1	–	–
Hampshire	1	6	2	–	–	–
Worcester	–	6	7	–	7	–
Subtotal	8	17	22	0	13	0
Total	10	60	32	1	22	0

[a] The county seats of Hamden (Springfield) and Worcester counties (Worcester) are included with Industrial Towns because of their large number of metalshops and factories.

Source: Journal of the House of Representatives, List of the Members of the House, 1851, appendix no. 104.

APPENDIX 2. *Stevenson Amendment, 1853*

Boston	Whig		Democrat		Free Soil	
	Y	N	Y	N	Y	N
	33	–	–	–	–	–
Subtotal	33	o	o	o	o	o
County Seats						
Barnstable	o	–	–	–	–	1
Berkshire	2	–	–	–	–	–
Bristol	–	–	–	–	–	–
Dukes	–	–	–	–	–	–
Essex	6	–	–	–	–	–
Franklin	–	–	–	–	–	–
Hampshire	–	–	–	–	–	–
Middlesex	3	–	–	–	–	–
Nantucket	1	–	–	–	–	–
Norfolk	4	–	–	–	–	–
Plymouth	o	–	–	1	–	1
Subtotal	16	o	o	1	o	2
Industrial Towns						
Amesbury	–	–	–	1	–	–
Charlestown	–	–	–	–	–	–
Fall River	–	–	–	–	–	–
Holyoke	–	–	–	–	–	–
Lawrence	–	–	–	1	–	2
Lowell	–	–	–	3	–	3
Lynn	–	–	–	–	–	–
Oxford	–	–	1	–	–	–
Salisbury	–	–	–	–	–	–
Springfield	1	–	–	1	–	–
Waltham	1	–	–	–	–	–
Webster	–	–	–	–	–	–
Worcester	–	–	–	2	–	3
Subtotal	2	o	1	8	o	8
Country Towns (five western counties)						
Berkshire	4	3	–	6	–	2
Franklin	2	1	–	3	–	3
Hamden	3	3	–	7	–	–
Hampshire	6	1	–	2	–	1
Worcester	5	1	1	11	–	9
Subtotal	20	9	1	29	o	15
Total	71	9	2	38	o	25

Source: Journal of the House of Representatives, List of the Members of the House, appendix no. 103.

APPENDIX 3. *Secret Ballot Vote, 1851*

Boston	Whig Y	Whig N	Democrat Y	Democrat N	Free Soil Y	Free Soil N
	–	38	–	–	–	–
Subtotal	0	38	0	0	0	0
County Seats						
Barnstable	–	–	–	–	–	–
Berkshire	–	2	–	–	–	–
Bristol	–	2	–	–	–	–
Dukes	–	–	–	–	–	–
Essex	–	4	–	–	–	–
Franklin	–	–	1	–	–	–
Hampshire	–	–	–	–	–	–
Middlesex	–	5	–	–	–	–
Nantucket	–	1	–	–	–	–
Norfolk	–	4	–	–	–	–
Plymouth	–	–	–	–	–	–
Subtotal	0	18	1	0	0	0
Industrial Towns						
Amesbury	–	–	–	–	–	–
Charlestown	–	–	4	–	–	–
Fall River	–	2	–	–	–	–
Holyoke	–	–	1	–	–	–
Lawrence	–	1	–	–	–	–
Lowell	–	9	–	–	–	–
Lynn	–	–	2	–	2	–
Oxford	–	–	–	–	–	–
Salisbury	–	–	–	–	–	1
Springfield	–	–	–	–	1	–
Waltham	–	–	–	–	–	–
Webster	–	–	–	–	1	–
Worcester	–	–	–	–	4	–
Subtotal	0	12	7	0	8	1
Country Towns (five western counties)						
Berkshire	0	8	10	–	1	0
Franklin	1	2	3	–	7	–
Hamden	2	4	4	–	2	–
Hampshire	–	8	–	–	2	1
Worcester	–	5	11	–	23	1
Subtotal	3	27	28	0	35	2
Total	3	95	36	0	43	3

Source: Journal of the House of Representatives, List of the Members of the House, 1851, appendix no. 48.

APPENDIX 4. *Secret Ballot Vote, 1853*

	Whig		Democrat		Free Soil	
Boston	Y	N	Y	N	Y	N
	42	–	–	–	–	–
Subtotal	42	0	0	0	0	0
County Seats						
Barnstable	–	–	–	1	–	–
Berkshire	2	–	–	–	–	–
Bristol	–	–	–	–	–	–
Dukes	1	–	–	–	–	–
Essex	6	–	–	–	–	–
Franklin	1	–	–	–	–	–
Hampshire	–	–	–	1	–	–
Middlesex	5	–	–	–	–	–
Nantucket	1	–	–	–	–	–
Norfolk	3	–	–	–	–	–
Plymouth	–	–	–	1	–	1
Subtotal	19	0	0	3	0	1
Industrial Towns						
Amesbury	–	–	–	1	–	–
Charlestown	–	–	–	–	–	–
Fall River	–	–	–	–	–	–
Holyoke	–	–	–	–	–	–
Lawrence	–	–	–	1	–	2
Lowell	–	–	–	5	–	4
Lynn	–	–	–	–	–	–
Oxford	–	–	–	1	–	–
Salisbury	–	–	–	–	–	–
Springfield	2	–	–	1	–	–
Waltham	1	–	–	–	–	–
Webster	–	–	–	–	–	–
Worcester	0	–	–	2	–	3
Subtotal	3	0	0	10	0	9
Country Towns (five western counties)						
Berkshire	10	–	–	9	–	2
Franklin	6	–	–	3	–	6
Hamden	7	–	–	8	–	–
Hampshire	11	1	–	2	–	2
Worcester	6	–	–	12	–	13
Subtotal	40	1	0	34	0	23
Total	104	1	0	47	0	33

Source: Journal of the House of Representatives, List of the Members of the House, 1853, appendix no. 42.

APPENDIX 5. *Antislavery Resolves, 1851*

Boston	Whig		Democrat		Free Soil	
	Y	N	Y	N	Y	N
	41	–	1	–	–	–
Subtotal	41	1	0	0	0	0
County Seats						
Barnstable	–	–	–	–	–	–
Berkshire	2	–	–	–	–	–
Bristol	3	–	–	–	–	–
Dukes	–	–	–	–	–	–
Essex	6	–	–	–	–	–
Franklin	–	–	–	–	–	–
Hampshire	–	–	–	–	–	–
Middlesex	3	–	–	–	–	–
Nantucket	2	–	–	–	–	–
Norfolk	4	–	–	–	–	–
Plymouth	–	–	–	1	–	–
Subtotal	20	0	0	1	0	0
Industrial Towns						
Amesbury	–	–	–	–	–	–
Charlestown	–	–	3	2	–	–
Fall River	1	2	–	–	–	–
Holyoke	–	–	–	–	–	–
Lawrence	2	–	–	1	–	–
Lowell	10	–	–	–	–	–
Lynn	–	–	–	2	–	2
Oxford	–	–	–	–	–	1
Salisbury	–	–	–	–	–	1
Springfield	–	–	–	–	1	1
Waltham	–	–	–	–	–	–
Webster	–	–	–	–	–	1
Worcester	–	–	–	–	–	5
Subtotal	13	2	3	5	1	11
Country Towns (five western counties)						
Berkshire	6	2	4	4	–	1
Franklin	–	2	2	4	–	9
Hamden	6	–	1	1	1	3
Hampshire	8	1	–	–	–	8
Worcester	2	2	9	5	1	28
Subtotal	22	7	16	14	2	49
Total	96	10	19	20	3	60

Source: Journal of the House of Representatives, List of the Members of the House, 1851, appendix no. 57.

APPENDIX 6. *Personal Liberty Vote, 1852*

	Whig		Democrat		Free Soil	
Boston	Y	N	Y	N	Y	N
	0	43	0	0	0	0
Subtotal	0	43	0	0	0	0
County Seats						
Barnstable	–	–	–	–	–	–
Berkshire	–	1	–	–	–	–
Bristol	–	1	–	–	–	–
Dukes	–	1	–	–	–	–
Essex	–	5	–	–	–	–
Franklin	–	1	–	–	–	–
Hampshire	–	–	–	–	1	–
Middlesex	–	5	–	–	–	–
Norfolk	–	6	–	–	–	–
Plymouth	–	–	–	–	1	–
Subtotal	0	20	0	0	2	0
Industrial Towns						
Amesbury	–	1	–	–	–	–
Charlestown	–	–	–	1	–	–
Fall River	–	–	1	–	2	–
Holyoke	–	–	–	–	–	–
Lawrence	–	3	–	–	–	–
Lowell	–	–	3	–	4	–
Lynn	–	–	2	–	2	–
Oxford	–	–	1	–	–	–
Salisbury	–	–	–	–	–	–
Springfield	–	3	–	–	1	–
Waltham	–	–	–	–	–	–
Webster	–	–	1	–	–	–
Worcester	–	–	1	–	3	–
Subtotal	0	7	9	1	12	0
Country Towns (five western counties)						
Berkshire	2	6	6	7	–	–
Franklin	–	7	8	1	5	–
Hamden	–	6	3	3	–	–
Hampshire	1	5	5	0	3	–
Worcester	2	4	7	1	24	–
Subtotal	5	28	29	12	32	0
Total	5	98	38	12	46	0

Source: Journal of the House of Representatives, List of the Members of the House, 1852, appendix no. 31.

APPENDIX 7. *Override of Governor's*
Veto of Personal Liberty Bill, 1855

Boston	Know-Nothings	
	Y	N
	18	10
Subtotal	18	10
County Seats		
Barnstable	2	–
Berkshire	1	1
Bristol	3	–
Dukes	1	–
Essex	1	3
Franklin	–	–
Hampshire	2	–
Middlesex	3	–
Nantucket	1	–
Norfolk	–	2
Plymouth	2	–
Subtotal	16	6
Industrial Towns		
Amesbury	0	1
Charlestown	2	2
Fall River	2	–
Holyoke	–	–
Lawrence	3	–
Lowell	10	–
Lynn	1	2
Oxford	1	–
Salisbury	–	–
Springfield	1	0
Waltham	–	–
Webster	1	–
Worcester	5	0
Subtotal	26	5
Country Towns (five western counties)		
Berkshire	11	2
Franklin	8	1
Hamden	10	2
Hampshire	10	2
Worcester	42	2
Subtotal	81	9
Total	141	30

Source: Journal of the House of Representatives, List of the Members of the House, 1855,
appendix no. 37.

APPENDIX 8. *Political Composition of the House, 1856 and 1859*

Boston	1856					1859				
	W	D	R	KN	O	W	D	R	KN	O
	30	–	1	13	–	–	8	16	2	–
Subtotal	30	0	1	13	0	0	8	16	2	0
County Seats										
Barnstable	–	1	1	–	–	–	–	1	–	–
Berkshire	–	1	–	1	–	–	–	1	–	1
Bristol	–	–	1	–	–	–	–	2	–	1
Dukes	–	–	–	–	–	–	–	–	–	–
Essex	–	–	–	6	–	–	1	2	–	–
Franklin	–	1	–	–	–	–	–	–	–	–
Hampshire	–	–	1	–	–	–	–	1	–	–
Middlesex	4	–	–	1	–	–	–	3	–	–
Nantucket	–	–	1	–	–	–	–	1	–	–
Norfolk	4	2	–	–	–	–	–	2	–	–
Plymouth	–	–	2	–	–	–	–	2	–	–
Subtotal	8	5	6	8	0	0	1	15	0	2
Industrial Towns										
Amesbury	–	–	–	1	–	–	–	–	1	–
Charlestown	–	–	–	5	–	–	2	1	–	1
Fall River	–	–	–	4	–	–	–	2	–	–
Holyoke	–	–	–	1	–	–	–	–	–	–
Lawrence	–	–	–	3	–	–	1	1	–	–
Lowell	–	–	–	10	–	–	–	4	2	–
Lynn	–	–	–	4	–	–	–	2	–	–
Oxford	–	–	–	1	–	–	–	1	–	–
Salisbury	–	–	–	1	–	–	–	–	–	–
Springfield	–	4	–	–	–	–	1	2	–	–
Waltham	1	–	–	–	–	–	–	–	–	–
Webster	–	–	–	1	–	–	–	1	–	–
Worcester	–	–	5	–	–	–	1	3	–	–
Subtotal	1	4	5	31	0	0	5	17	3	1
Country Towns (five western counties)										
Berkshire	1	4	2	7	–	–	1	7	2	–
Franklin	–	2	3	2	–	–	1	7	–	–
Hamden	–	1	7	1	1	–	4	7	–	–
Hampshire	–	–	6	5	–	–	–	8	–	–
Worcester	6	6	11	21	–	–	2	28	–	–
Subtotal	7	13	29	36	1	0	8	57	2	0
Total	46	22	41	88	1	0	22	105	5	3
Percentage	23	10	20	45	–	–	16	77	4	2

Source: Journal of the House of Representatives, List of the Members of the House, 1856 and 1859. Figures based on roll-call votes.

Bibliography

Primary Sources

Unpublished Materials (arranged by place)

Amherst, Mass.

Porter Phelps Huntington Family Papers. Amherst College Archives and Special Collections. Amherst College.

Boston, Mass.

Manuscript Journals of the Senate and House of Representatives, 1840–1860. Massachusetts State Archives.
Portraits of American Abolitionists.
William S. Robinson Papers, Boston Public Library.
William Schouler Papers. Massachusetts Historical Society.

Kent, Ohio

Charles Wesley Slack Papers. Department of Special Collections and Archives. Kent State Univ. http://specoll.library.Kent.edu/amerhist/slack.html.

Northampton, Mass.

Garrison Family Papers. Sophia Smith Collection. Smith College.

Published Materials

American Anti-Slavery Society. *Annual Reports, 1834–55*. New York: Dorr and Butterfield.
American Colonization Society and Emigration. Edited by John David Smith. New York: Garland Publishers, 1993.
Birney, James G. *The Letters of James Gillespie Birney, 1831–1857*. Edited by Dwight L. Dumond. 2 vols. New York: D. Appleton-Century, 1938.

The Black Abolitionist Papers. Edited by C. Peter Ripley. 5 vols. Chapel Hill: University of North Carolina Press, 1991.

The Boston Slave Riot and Trial of Anthony Burns. Boston: Fetridge, 1854.

Boutwell, George S. *Reminiscences of Sixty Years in Public Affairs.* 2 vols. New York: McClure, Phillips, 1902.

Bowditch, Vincent Y. *Life and Correspondence of Henry Ingersoll Bowditch, by His Son.* Boston: Houghton, Mifflin, 1902.

Bronson, Asa. *An Address on the Anniversary of the Fire....Pursuant to the Request from the Ladies' Mechanic Association.* Fall River, Mass.: N.p., 1844.

Brown, William Wells. *The Rising Sun; or, The Antecedents and Advancement of Colored Race.* Boston: A. G. Brown, 1874.

Buckingham, Joseph Tinker. *Personal Memoirs and Recollections of Editorial Life.* 2 vols. Boston: Ticknor, Reed, and Fields, 1852.

———, comp. *Annals of the Massachusetts Charitable Mechanic Association.* Boston: Crocker and Brewster, 1853.

Butler, Benjamin F. *Butler's Book: Autobiography and Personal Reminiscences of Major-General Benjamin F. Butler.* Boston: M. A. Thayer, 1892.

Chickering, Jesse. *A Statistical View of the Population of Massachusetts, from 1765 to 1840.* Boston: C. C. Little and J. Brown, 1846.

Citizens of the Borough of Norfolk. *Proceedings of the Citizens of Norfolk, on the Boston Outrage, in the Case of the Runaway Slave George Latimer.* Norfolk, Mass.: Broughton and Son, 1843.

Clark, George Faber. *History of Temperance Reform in Massachusetts, 1813–1883.* Boston: Clark and Carruth, 1888.

Commons, John R., David J. Saposs, Helen L. Sumner, E. B. Mittleman, H. E. Hoagland, John B. Andrews, and Selig Perlman, eds. *Documentary History of American Industrial Society.* 10 vols. Cleveland: Arthur H. Clark, 1910–11.

Cowley, Charles. *Illustrated History of Lowell.* Boston: Lea and Shepard, 1868.

Craft, William, and Ellen Craft. *Running a Thousand Miles for Freedom: The Escape of William and Ellen Craft from Slavery.* 1860. Edited by R. J. M. Blackett. Baton Rouge: Louisiana State University Press, 1999.

Dana, Richard Henry, Jr. *The Journal of Richard Henry Dana, Jr.* 3 vols. Edited by Robert F. Lucid. Cambridge: Harvard University Press, 1968.

Delany, Martin Robison. *The Condition, Elevation, Emigration and Destiny of the Colored People of the United States.* Edited by Toyin Falola. 1852. Amherst, New York: Humanity Books, 2004.

Douglass, Frederick. *Douglass Autobiographies.* Edited by Henry Louis Gates. New York: Library of America, 1994.

———. *The Frederick Douglass Papers; Series One: Speeches, Debates, and Interviews.* Edited by John W. Blassingame. 5 vols. New Haven, Conn.: Yale University Press, 1982–92.

Dwight, Timothy. *Travels in New-England and New-York.* 4 vols. London: W. Baynes and Son, 1823.

Eisler, Benita, ed. *The Lowell Offering: Writings by New England Mill Women, 1840–1845.* Philadelphia: J. B. Lippincott, 1977.

Foner, Philip S., ed. *The Factory Girls: A Collection of the Writings on Life and Struggles in the New England Factories of the 1840s.* Urbana: University of Illinois Press, 1977.

Fuhrer, Mary, ed. *Letters from the "Old Home Place": Anxieties and Aspirations in Rural New England, 1836–1843*. Boylston, Mass.: Old Pot Publications, 1997.

Garrison, William L. *The Letters of William Lloyd Garrison*. Edited by Walter M. Merrill and Louis Ruchames. 6 vols. Cambridge: Harvard University Press, 1971–81.

Goodell, William. *The Democracy of Christianity; or, An analysis of the Bible and its doctrines in relation to the principle of democracy*. 2 vols. New York: Cady and Burgess, 1849–52.

———. *Slavery and Anti-Slavery; A History of the Great Struggle in both Hemispheres. . . .* 1852. New York: Negro Universities Press, 1968.

Higginson, Thomas Wentworth. *Cheerful Yesterdays*. Boston: Houghton Mifflin, 1898.

———. *Contemporaries*. Boston: Houghton Mifflin, 1899.

Hoar, George F. *Autobiography of Seventy Years*. 2 vols. New York: Charles Scribner's Sons, 1903.

Holden Anti-Slavery Society. *Report of the Holden Slave Case*. Worcester, Mass.: Colton and Howland, 1839.

The Hours of Labor. Address of the Ten Hours State Convention, Held in Boston, Sept. 20, 1852, to the People of the Commonwealth of Massachusetts; Together with the Report of a Bill. . . . Boston: N.p., 1852.

Larcom, Lucy. *A New England Girlhood*. Boston: Houghton Mifflin, 1889.

Leavitt, Joshua. *The Financial Power of Slavery*. New York: Leavitt, 1841.

———. *Memorial of Joshua Leavitt, praying that, in revision of the tariff laws, the principle of discrimination may be inserted. . . .* Washington, D.C.: Allen, 1842.

Letters and Discussion of the Formation of Colored Regiments. . . . 1862. Edited by Alfred M. Green. Philadelphia: Rhistoric Publications, 1969.

Luther, Seth. *An Address on the Origin and Progress of Avarice, and its Deleterious Effects on Human Happiness*. Boston: By the Author, 1834.

———. *An Address to the Workingmen of New England, on the State of Education, and the Condition of the Producing Classes in Europe and America*. Boston: George Henry Evans, 1833.

Massachusetts (and New England) Anti-Slavery Society. *Annual Reports, 1833–1856*. 24 vols. Westport, Conn.: Greenwood Press, 1970

May, Samuel J. *Some Reflections on our Antislavery Struggle*. Boston: Fields, Osgood, 1869.

Robinson, Frederick. *An Oration Delivered before the Trades' Union of Boston and Vicinity, on Fort Hill, Boston, on the Fiftieth Anniversary of American Independence*. Boston: C. Douglass, 1834.

Robinson, Harriet H. *Loom and Spindle; or, Life among the Factory Girls 1898*. Kailua, Hawaii: Press Pacifica, 1976.

Robinson, Mrs. William S. *"Warrington" Pen-Portraits: A Collection of Personal and Political Reminiscences from 1848 to 1876, from the Writings of William S. Robinson. With Memoir, and Extracts from Diary and Letters Never before Published*. Boston: Mrs. William S. Robinson, 1877.

Scoresby, William. *American Factories and Their Female Operatives; With an Appeal on Behalf of the British Factory Population, and Suggestions for Improvement of Their Condition*. 1845. New York: Burt Franklin, 1968.

Watkins, William J. *Our Rights as Men. An Address Delivered in Boston, before Legislative Committee on the Militia, February 24, 1853.* In *Negro Protest Pamphlets*, edited by Dorothy Porter. New York: Arno Press, 1969.

Weld, Theodore Dwight. *The Letters of Theodore Dwight Weld, Angelina Grimké, Weld, and Sarah Grimké, 1822–1844.* Edited by Gilbert H. Barnes and Dwight L. Dumond. 2 vols. New York: D. Appleton-Century, 1934.

Whittier, John Greenleaf. *The Letters of John Greenleaf Whittier.* Edited by John B. Pickard. 3 vols. Cambridge: Harvard University Press, 1975.

———. *The Stranger in Lowell.* Boston: Waite, Pierce, 1845.

Wilson, Henry. *History of the Rise and Fall of the Slave Power in America.* 3 vols. Boston: James R. Osgood, 1872–7.

Wright, Elizur, Jr. *Myron Holley; And What He Did for Liberty and True Religion.* Boston: Elizur Wright, 1882.

Public Documents

Abstract of the Census of the Commonwealth of Massachusetts... 1855. Compiled by Francis Dewitt. Boston: W. White, 1857.

Acts and Resolves Passed by the General Court of Massachusetts. Boston: By the Secretary of the Commonwealth, 1840–60.

Compendium of the Ninth Census of the United States. Compiled by Francis Walker. Washington, D.C.: U.S. Government Printing Office, 1872.

Documents of the City of Boston for 1854. Boston: City of Boston, 1854.

Documents of the House of Representatives and Senate of The Commonwealth of Massachusetts. Boston: By the Secretary of the Commonwealth, 1843–60.

Journal of the Debates and Proceedings in the Constitutional Convention, 1820–1821. Boston: *Boston Daily Advertiser,* 1853

Official Report of the Debates and Proceedings of the State Convention, Assembled May 4, 1853, to Revise and Amend the Constitution of the Commonwealth of Massachusetts. 3 vols. Boston: White and Potter, 1853.

Report of the Committee on Public Instruction on the Case of a Child Excluded from a Public School in this City. Document No. 54. *Boston City Documents.* Boston: J. H. Eastburn, 1854.

Report of the Minority of the Committee of the Primary School Board on the Caste Schools of the City of Boston. Boston: City of Boston, 1846.

Report of the Primary School Committee on the Caste Schools of the City of Boston with Some Remarks on the City Solicitor's Opinion. Document No. 23 1/2. *Boston City Documents,* 1846. Boston: J. H. Eastburn, 1847.

Report to the Primary School Committee on the Petition of Sundry Colored Persons for the Abolition of the Schools for Colored Children, June 15, 1846. Document No. 23. *Boston City Documents,* 1846. Boston: J. H. Eastburn, 1846.

U.S. Bureau of the Census. *Seventh Census. Population Schedule. Worcester County.* 1850. Mss. Microfilm.

U.S. Congress. Senate. Select Committee to Inquire into Alleged Election Fraud in Massachusetts. Report No. 497. *Intimidation and Fraud in Massachusetts.* 46th Cong., 2d sess. Washington, D.C.: U.S. Government Printing Office, 1880.

Newspapers and Journals (arranged by place)

Amherst, Mass.

Record

Boston, Mass.

Atlas
Bee
Boston Mechanic and Journal of the Useful Arts
Bostonian and Mechanics' Journal
The Chronotype
The Commonwealth
Courier
Daily Advertiser
Daily Mail
Reformer
Emancipator (and Republican)
Evening Transcript
Latimer Journal and North Star
The Liberator
Morning Post
New England Artisan
New England Magazine
Protective Union

Fall River, Mass.

The Mechanic
The Monitor

Greenfield, Mass.

American Republic
Gazette and Courier

Lowell, Mass.

American
Voice of Industry
Voice of the People

North Adams, Mass.

Weekly Transcript

Northampton, Mass.

Courier
Hampshire Gazette
Hampshire Herald

Pittsfield, Mass.

Sun

Rochester, N.Y.

North Star

Springfield, Mass.

Springfield Republican

Worcester, Mass.

Massachusetts Spy
Reformer and True Washington
State Sentinel and Worcester Reformer

Secondary Sources

Books and Articles

Abbott, Richard H. *Cobbler in Congress: The Life of Henry Wilson, 1812–1875.* Lexington: University of Kentucky Press, 1972.
Alonso, Harriet Hyman. *Growing Up Abolitionist: The Story of the Garrison Children.* Amherst: University of Massachusetts Press, 2002.
Altschuler, Glenn C., and Stuart M. Blumin. *Rude Republic: Americans and Their Politics in the Nineteenth Century.* Princeton, N.J.: Princeton University Press, 2002.
Arnesen, Eric. "Whiteness and the Historians' Imagination." *International Labor and Working-Class History* 60 (Fall 2001): 3–42.
Baker, Jean H. *Affairs of Party: The Political Culture of Northern Democrats in the Mid-Nineteenth Century.* Ithaca, N.Y.: Cornell University Press, 1983.
Barnes, Gilbert Hobbs. *The Antislavery Impulse, 1830–1844.* New York: D. Appleton-Century, 1933.
Baum, Dale. *The Civil War Party System: The Case of Massachusetts, 1848–1876.* Chapel Hill: University of North Carolina Press, 1984.
———. "Know-Nothingism and the Republican Majority in Massachusetts: The Political Realignment of the 1850s." *Journal of American History* 64 (March 1973): 959–86.
Bean, William G. "Puritan Versus Celt, 1850–1860." *New England Quarterly* 7 (March 1934): 70–89.
Bemis, Edward. *Cooperation in New England.* Baltimore: Johns Hopkins University Press, 1888.
Benson, Lee. *The Concept of Jacksonian Democracy: New York as a Test Case.* New York: Atheneum, 1965.
Berlin, Ira. *Generations of Captivity: A History of African-American Slaves.* Cambridge: Harvard University Press, 2003.
———. *Many Thousands Gone: The First Two Centuries of Slavery in North America.* Cambridge: Harvard University Press, 1998.

Berwanger, Eugene H. *The Frontier against Slavery: Western Anti-Negro Prejudice and the Slavery Extension Controversy*. Urbana: University of Illinois Press, 1967.

Bethel, Elizabeth Rauh. *The Roots of African-American Identity: Memory and History in Antebellum Free Communities*. New York: St. Martin's Press, 1997.

Billington, Ray Allen. *The Protestant Crusade, 1800–1860: A Study of the Origins of American Nativism*. 1938. New York: Quadrangle Books, 1964.

Blewett, Mary. *Constant Turmoil: The Politics of Industrial Life in Nineteenth-Century New England*. Amherst: University of Massachusetts Press, 2000.

Brauer, Kinley J. *Cotton Versus Conscience: Massachusetts Whig Politics and Southwestern Expansion, 1843–1848*. Lexington: University of Kentucky Press, 1967.

Brodkin, Karen. *How the Jews Became White Folks and What that Says about Race in America*. New Brunswick, N.J.: Rutgers University Press, 1998.

Brody, David. "Charismatic History: Pros and Cons." *International Labor and Working-Class History* 60 (Fall 2001): 43–7.

Brooke, John L. *The Heart of the Commonwealth: Society and Political Culture in Worcester County Massachusetts, 1713–1861*. New York: Cambridge University Press, 1989.

Brunet, Michel. "The Secret Ballot Issue in Massachusetts from 1851 to 1853." *New England Quarterly* 25 (September 1952): 254–62.

Bushman, Claudia L. *"A Good Poor Man's Wife": Being a Chronicle of Harriet Hansen Robinson and Her Family in Nineteenth-Century New England*. Hanover, N.H.: University Press of New England, 1981.

Campbell, Stanley W. *The Slave Catchers: Enforcement of the Fugitive Slave Law, 1850–1860*. Chapel Hill: University of North Carolina Press, 1968.

Chused, Richard H. "Married Women's Property Law, 1800–1850." *Georgetown Law Journal* 71 (June 1983): 1359–425.

Clark, Christopher. *The Roots of Rural Capitalism: Western Massachusetts, 1780–1860*. Ithaca, N.Y.: Cornell University Press, 1990.

———. *The Utopian Moment: The Radical Challenge of the Northampton Association*. Ithaca, N.Y.: Cornell University Press, 1995.

Clawson, Dan. *Bureaucracy and the Labor Process: The Transformation of U.S. Industry, 1860–1920*. New York: Monthly Review Press, 1980.

Collison, Gary. *Shadrach Minkins: From Fugitive Slave to Citizen*. Cambridge: Harvard University Press, 1997.

Commons, John R., Ulrich Bonnell Phillips, Eugene A. Gilmal, Helen S. Sumner, and John B. Andre. *History of Labour in the United States*. 4 vols. New York: Macmillan, 1918–35.

Conforti, Joseph A. *Imagining New England: Explorations of Regional Identity from the Pilgrims to the Mid-Twentieth Century*. Chapel Hill: University of North Carolina Press, 2001.

Crocker, Matthew H. *The Magic of the Many: Josiah Quincy and the Rise of Mass Politics in Boston, 1800–1830*. Amherst: University of Massachusetts Press, 1999.

Cumbler, John. *A Social History of Economic Decline: Business, Politics, and Work in Trenton*. New Brunswick, N.J.: Rutgers University Press, 1989.

Curry, Leonard P. *The Free Black in Urban America, 1800–1850: The Shadow of the Dream.* Chicago: University of Chicago Press, 1981.

Curry, Richard, O., ed. *The American Abolitionists: Reformers or Fanatics?* New York: Holt, Rinehart and Winston, 1965.

———, and Lawrence B. Goodheart. "The Complexities of Factionalism: The Letters of Elizur Wright, Jr., on the Abolitionist Schism, 1837–1840." *Civil War History* 29 (September 1983): 243–59.

Dalzell, Robert F., Jr. *Enterprising Elite: The Boston Associates and the World They Made.* Cambridge: Harvard University Press, 1987.

Dana, Richard Henry, Jr. "The Practical Working of the Australian Ballot System in Massachusetts." *Annals of the American Academy of Political and Social Science* 2 (May 1892): 733–50.

Dannenbaum, Jed. *Drink and Disorder: Temperance Reform in Cincinnati from the Washingtonian Revival to the WCTU.* Urbana: University of Illinois Press. 1984.

Darling, Arthur B. *Political Change in Massachusetts, 1824–1848: A Study of Liberal Movements in Politics.* New Haven, Conn.: Yale University Press, 1925.

Davis, Hugh. *Joshua Leavitt, Evangelical Abolitionist.* Baton Rouge: Louisiana State University Press, 1990.

Dawley, Alan. *Class and Community: The Industrial Revolution in Lynn.* Cambridge: Harvard University Press, 1976.

Degler, Carl N. *Neither Black nor White: Race Relations in Brazil and the United States.* Madison: University of Wisconsin Press, 1971.

Doherty, Robert. *Society and Power in Five New England Towns, 1800–1860.* Amherst: University of Massachusetts Press, 1977.

Donald, David Herbert. *Charles Sumner and the Coming of the Civil War.* New York: Fawcett Columbine, 1960.

———. "Toward a Reconsideration of the Abolitionists." In *Lincoln Reconsidered: Essays on the Civil War Era,* pp. 19–36. New York: Alfred A. Knopf, 1956.

Drescher, Seymour. "Cart Whip and Billy Roller: Or Antislavery and Reform Symbolism in Industrializing Britain." *Journal of Social History* 15 (Fall 1981): 3–24.

Duberman, Martin B., ed. *The Antislavery Vanguard: New Essays on the Abolitionists.* Princeton, N.J.: Princeton University Press, 1965.

———. "Behind the Scenes as the Massachusetts 'Coalition' of 1851 Divides the Spoils." *Essex Institute Historical Collections* 99 (April 1963): 152–60.

———. *Charles Francis Adams, 1807–1886.* Boston: Houghton Mifflin, 1961.

Dublin, Thomas. *Women at Work: The Transformation of Work and Community in Lowell, Massachusetts, 1826–1860.* New York: Columbia University Press, 1979.

Dumond, Dwight L. *Antislavery: The Crusade for Freedom in America.* Ann Arbor: University of Michigan Press, 1961.

Dykstra, Robert R. *Bright Radical Star: Black Freedom and White Supremacy on the Hawkeye Frontier.* Ames: Iowa State University Press, 1993.

Earle, Jonathan. "Marcus Morton and the Dilemma of Antislavery in Jacksonian Massachusetts, 1817–1849." *Massachusetts Historical Review* 2 (2002): 61–88.

Early, Frances H. "A Reappraisal of the New England Labor Reform Movement in the 1840s: The Lowell Female Labor Reform Association and the New England Workingmen's Association." *Histoire Sociale/Social History* 13 (May 1980): 33–55.

Edelstein, Tilden G. *Strange Enthusiasm: A Life of Thomas Wentworth Higginson.* New Haven, Conn.: Yale University Press, 1968.

Elkins, Stanley M. *Slavery: A Problem in American Institutional and Intellectual Life.* 1959. Chicago: University of Chicago Press, 1963.

D'Emilio, John. *The Life and Times of Bayard Rustin.* New York: The Free Press, 2003.

Faler, Paul G. *Mechanics and Manufacturers in the Early Industrial Revolution: Lynn, Massachusetts, 1780–1860.* Albany: State University of New York Press, 1981.

Fehrenbacher, Don E. "The New Political History and the Coming of the Civil War." *Pacific Historical Review* 54 (May 1985): 1117–42.

———. *The Slaveholding Republic: An Account of the United States Government's Relationship with Slavery.* New York: Oxford University Press, 2001.

Feldberg, Michael. *The Philadelphia Riots of 1844: A Study of Ethnic Conflict.* Westport, Conn.: Greenwood Press, 1975.

Finley, M. I. "Slavery." *International Encyclopedia of the Social Sciences* 14 (1968): 307–13.

Fischer, David Hackett. *Paul Revere's Ride.* New York: Oxford University Press, 1994.

———. *The Revolution of American Conservatism: The Federalist Party in the Era of Jeffersonian Democracy.* New York: Harper and Row, 1965.

Foner, Eric. "The Causes of the American Civil War: Recent Interpretations and New Directions." *Civil War History* 20 (September 1974): 197–214.

———. *Free Soil, Free Labor, Free Men: The Ideology of the Republican Party before the Civil War.* New York: Oxford University Press, 1970.

———. *Politics and Ideology in the Age of the Civil War.* New York: Oxford University Press 1980.

Foos, Paul W. *A Short, Offhand Killing Affair: Soldiers and Social Conflict during the Mexican-American War.* Chapel Hill, N.C.: University of North Carolina Press, 2002.

Ford, Worthington C. "Trial of Anthony Burns." *Proceedings of the American Antiquarian Society* 44 (January 1911): 322–44.

Formisano, Ronald. P. *The Birth of Mass Political Parties: Michigan, 1827–1861.* Princeton, N.J.: Princeton University Press, 1971.

———. "The Invention of the Ethnocultural Interpretation." *American Historical Review* 99 (April 1994): 453–77.

———. "The 'Party Period' Revisited." *Journal of American History* 86 (1999): 93–120.

———. *The Transformation of Political Culture: Massachusetts Parties, 1790s–1840s.* New York: Oxford University Press, 1983.

Fredrickson, George M. *The Black Image in the White Mind: The Debate on Afro-American Character and Destiny, 1817–1914.* New York: Harper, 1971.

———. *A Short History of Racism*. Princeton, N.J.: Princeton University Press, 2002.

Freehling, William W. *The Reintegration of American History: Slavery and the Civil War*. New York: Oxford University Press, 1994.

———. *The Road to Disunion: Secessionists at Bay, 1776–1854*. New York: Oxford University Press, 1990.

Friedman, Lawrence J. "The Gerrit Smith Circle: Abolitionism in the Burned-Over District." *Civil War History* 26 (1980): 19–38.

Fuess, Claude M. *The Life of Caleb Cushing*. 2 vols. New York: Harcourt Brace, 1923.

Garnsey, Peter. *Ideas of Slavery from Aristotle to Augustine*. Cambridge, Eng.: Cambridge University Press, 1996.

Gatell, Frank Otto. "'Conscience and Judgment': The Bolt of the Massachusetts Conscience Whigs." *The Historian* 21 (November 1958): 18–45.

Genovese, Eugene D. *Roll, Jordan, Roll: The World the Slaves Made*. New York: Pantheon Books, 1974.

Gerteis, Louis S. *Morality and Utility in American Antislavery Reform*. Chapel Hill: University of North Carolina Press, 1987.

Gienapp, William E. "Nativism and the Creation of the Republican Majority in the North before the Civil War." *Journal of American History* 72 (December 1985): 529–59.

———. *The Origins of the Republican Party, 1852–1856*. New York: Oxford University Press, 1987.

Gitlin, Todd. *The Twilight of Common Dreams: Why America Is Wracked by Culture Wars*. New York: Henry Holt, 1995.

Glickstein, Jonathan A. *American Exceptionalism, American Anxiety: Wages, Competition, and Degraded Labor in the Antebellum United States*. Charlottesville: University of Virginia Press, 2002.

———. *Concepts of Free Labor in Antebellum America*. New Haven, Conn.: Yale University Press, 1991.

———. "'Poverty is not slavery': American Abolitionists and the Competitive Labor Market." In *Antislavery Reconsidered: New Perspectives on the Abolitionists*, edited by Lewis Perry and Michael Perman, pp. 195–218. Baton Rouge: Louisiana State University Press, 1979.

Goldman, Harold. "Black Citizenship and Military Self-Presentation in Antebellum Massachusetts." *Historical Journal of Massachusetts* 26 (Summer 1992): 157–83.

Goodheart, Lawrence B. *Abolitionist, Actuary, Atheist: Elizur Wright and the Reform Impulse*. Kent, Ohio: Kent State University Press, 1990.

Goodman, Paul. *Of One Blood: Abolitionism and the Origins of Racial Equality*. Berkeley and Los Angeles: University of California Press, 1998.

———. "The Politics of Industrialism: Massachusetts, 1830–1870." In *Uprooted Americans: Essays to Honor Oscar Handlin*, edited by Richard Bushman, pp. 161–207. Boston: Little, Brown, 1979.

Goodwyn, Lawrence. *Democratic Promise: The Populist Movement in America*. New York: Oxford University Press, 1976.

Green, L. J. *The Negro in Colonial New England*. New York: Columbia University Press, 1942.

Grimsted, David. *American Mobbing, 1828–1861: Toward Civil War*. New York: Oxford University Press, 1998.

Gross, Laurence F. *The Course of Industrial Decline: The Boott Mills of Lowell, Massachusetts, 1835–1955*. Baltimore: Johns Hopkins University Press, 1993.

Grover, Kathryn. *The Fugitive's Gibraltar: Escaping Slaves and Abolitionism in New Bedford, Massachusetts*. Amherst: University of Massachusetts Press, 2001.

Guarani, Carl J. *The Utopian Alternative: Fourierism in Nineteenth-Century America*. Ithaca, N.Y.: Cornell University Press, 1991.

Gyory, Andrew. *Closing the Gate: Race, Politics, and the Chinese Exclusion Act* Chapel Hill, N.C.: University of North Carolina Press, 1998.

Habegger, Alfred. *My Wars Are Laid Away in Books: The Life of Emily Dickinson*. New York: Modern Library, 2002.

Hampel, Robert L. *Temperance and Prohibition in Massachusetts, 1813–1852*. New York: UMI Research Press, 1982.

Handlin, Oscar. *Boston's Immigrants, 1790–1880: A Study in Acculturation*. 1941. Cambridge: Harvard University Press, 1991.

Hansen, Debra Gold. *Strained Sisterhood: Gender and Class in the Boston Female Anti-slavery Society*. Amherst: University of Massachusetts Press, 1993.

Hansen, Karen V. *A Very Social Time: Crafting Community in Antebellum New England*. Berkeley and Los Angeles: University of California Press, 1994.

Hareven, Tamara K. *Family Time and Industrial Time: The Relationship between Family and Work in a New England Industrial Community*. New York: Cambridge University Press, 1982.

Harlow, Ralph V. *Gerrit Smith, Philanthropist and Reformer*. New York: Holt, 1939.

Harris, Leslie M. *In the Shadow of Slavery: African Americans in New York City, 1626–1863*. Chicago: University of Chicago Press, 2003.

Hartford, William F. *Money, Morals, and Politics: Massachusetts in the Age of the Boston Associates*. Boston: Northeastern University Press, 2001.

Haynes, George H. "The Causes of Know-Nothing Success in Massachusetts." *American Historical Review* 3 (October 1897–July 1898): 67–82.

Hershberg, Theodore. "Free Blacks in Antebellum Philadelphia: A Study of Ex-Slaves, Freeborn, and Socioeconomic Decline." *Journal of Social History* 5 (Winter 1971–2): 183–209.

Hewitt, Nancy. *Women's Activism and Social Change: Rochester, New York, 1822–1872*. Ithaca, N.Y.: Cornell University Press, 1987.

Higham, John. *Strangers in the Land: Patterns of American Nativism, 1860–1925*. 1955. Westport, Conn.: Greenwood Press, 1983.

Hobsbawm, E. J. "The Labour Aristocracy in Nineteenth-Century Britain." In *Labouring Men: Studies in the History of Labour*, pp. 321–70. Garden City, N.Y.: Anchor Books, 1964.

Hodges, Graham Russell. *Root and Branch: African Americans in New York and East Jersey, 1613–1863.* Chapel Hill: University of North Carolina Press, 1999.

Hofstadter, Richard. *The American Political Tradition and the Men Who Made It.* New York: Alfred A. Knopf, 1948.

———. *Anti-intellecutalism in American Life.* New York: Alfred A. Knopf, 1963.

Holt, Michael F. "The New Political History and the Civil War Era." *Reviews in American History* 13 (1985): 60–9.

———. *The Political Crisis of the 1850s.* New York: Wiley, 1978.

———. *Political Parties and American Political Development: From the Age of Jackson to the Age of Lincoln.* Baton Rouge: Louisiana State University Press, 1992.

———. *The Rise and Fall of the American Whig Party: Jacksonian Politics and the Onset of the Civil War.* New York: Oxford University Press, 1999.

Horton, James Oliver, and Lois E. Horton. *Black Bostonians: Family Life and Community Struggle in the Antebellum North.* New York: Holmes and Meier, 1979.

———. "A Federal Assault: African Americans and the Fugitive Slave Act." In *Slavery and the Law,* edited by Paul Finkelman, pp. 143–60. Madison, Wisc.: Madison House Press, 1997.

———. *Free People of Color: Inside the African American Community.* Washington, D.C.: Smithsonian Institution Press, 1993.

———. *In Hope of Liberty: Culture, Community, and Protest among Northern Free Blacks.* New York: Oxford University Press, 1997.

Hounstra, Jean, and Trudy Heath, comps. *American Periodicals, 1741–1900.* Ann Arbor, Mich.: University Microfilms, 1979.

Howe, Daniel Walker. *The Political Culture of the American Whigs.* Chicago: University of Chicago Press, 1979.

Huntington, Arria Sargent. *Under a Colonial Roof-Tree: Fireside Chronicles of Early New England.* Syracuse, N.Y.: Woolcott and West, 1890.

Huston, James. "A Political Response to Industrialism: The Republican Embrace of Protectionist Labor Doctrines." *Journal of American History* 70 (June 1983): 35–57.

Ignatiev, Noel. *How the Irish Became White.* New York: Routledge, 1995.

Jaffee, David. *People of Wachusset: Greater New England in History and Memory.* Ithaca, N.Y.: Cornell University Press, 1999.

James, Edward T., ed. *Notable American Women, 1607–1950: A Biographical Dictionary.* 3 vols. Cambridge: Harvard University Press, 1971.

Jeffrey, Julie Roy. *The Great Silent Army of Abolitionism: Ordinary Women in the Antislavery Movement.* Chapel Hill: University of North Carolina Press, 1998.

Jenkins, Paul. *The Conservative Rebel: A Social History of Greenfield, Massachusetts.* Greenfield, Mass.: Town of Greenfield, 1982.

Jentz, John B. "The Antislavery Constutiency in Jacksonian New York City." *Civil War History* 27 (June 1981): 101–22.

Johannsen, Robert W. *The Frontier, the Union, and Stephen A. Douglas.* Urbana: University of Illinois Press, 1989.

Johnson, Reinhard O. "The Liberty Party in Massachusetts, 1840–1848: Anti-slavery Third Party Politics in the Bay State." *Civil War History* 28 (September 1982): 237–65.

Kerber, Linda. "Abolitimists and Amalgamators: The New York City Race Riots of 1834." *New York History* 48 (1967): 28–39.

Keyssar, Alexander. *The Right to Vote: The Contested History of Democracy in the United States*. New York: Basic Books, 2000.

Kleppner, Paul. *The Third Electoral System: Parties, Voters, and Political Cultures*. Chapel Hill: University of North Carolina Press, 1979.

Knights, Peter R. *Yankee Destinies: The Lives of Ordinary Nineteenth-Century Bostonians*. Chapel Hill: University of North Carolina Press, 1991.

Kolchin, Peter. *Unfree Labor: American Slavery and Russian Serfdom*. Cambridge: Harvard University Press, 1987.

Kornblith, Gary J. "Becoming Joseph T. Buckingham." In *American Artisans: Crafting Social Identity, 1780–1860*, edited by Howard B. Rock, Paul A. Gilje, and Robert Asher, pp. 123–34. Baltimore: Johns Hopkins University Press, 1995.

Kraditor, Aileen S. "The Liberty and Free Soil Parties." In *History of U.S. Political Parties*, edited by Arthur M. Schlesinger, Jr., 4 vols., 1: 741–881. New York Chelsea House, 1973.

———. *Means and Ends in American Abolitionism: Garrison and His Critics on Strategy and Tactics, 1834–1850*. New York: Pantheon Books, 1969.

Kraut, Alan M., ed. *Crusaders and Compromisers: Essays on the Relationship of the Antislavery Struggle to the Antebellum Party System*. Westport, Conn.: Greenwood Press, 1983.

Kraut, John Allen. *Origins of Prohibition*. New York: Alfred A. Knopf, 1925.

Laclau, Ernesto. *Politics and Ideology in Marxist Theory: Capitalism, Fascism, Populism*. London: NLB, 1977.

Larkin, Jack. *The Reshaping of Everyday Life, 1790–1840*. New York: Harper and Row, 1988.

Laurie, Bruce. *Artisans into Workers: Labor in Nineteenth-Century America*. New York: Hill and Wang, 1989.

———. "The 'Fair Field' of the 'Middle Ground': Abolitionism, Labor Reform, and the Making of an Antislavery Bloc in Antebellum Massachusetts." In *Labor Histories: Class, Politics, and the Working-Class Experience*, edited by Eric Arnesen, Julie Greene, and Bruce Laurie, pp. 45–70. Urbana: University of Illinois Press, 1998.

———. "'The Penitent's Bench': Toward a Social History of the Ballot in Nineteenth-Century Massachusetts." *Historia Contemporánea* 16 (1998): 67–88.

———. "'We are not afraid to work': Master Mechanics and the Market Revolution in the Antebellum North." In *The Middling Sorts: Explorations in the History of the Middle Class*, edited by Burton J. Bledstein and Robert D. Johnston, pp. 50–68. New York: Routledge, 2001.

———. *Working People of Philadelphia, 1800–1850*. Philadelphia: Temple University Press, 1980.

Lazerow, Jama. "Religion and Reform in Antebellum America: The World of William Field Young." *American Quarterly* 38 (1986): 265–86.

———. *Religion and the Working Class in Jacksonian America.* Washington, D.C.: Smithsonian Institution Press, 1995.

Lerner, Gerda. *The Grimké Sisters from South Carolina.* New York: Shocken Books, 1971.

Levesque, George, A. *Black Boston: African American Life and Culture in Urban America, 1750–1860.* New York: Garland Publishing, 1994.

———. "Politicians in Petticoats: Interracial Sex and Legislative Politics in Antebellum Massachusetts." *New England Journal of Black Studies* 3 (1983): 40–59.

———. "Boston's Black Brahmin: Dr. John Swett Rock." *Civil War History* 26 (1980): 326–46.

Levine, Bruce. *Half Slave and Half Free: The Roots of the Civil War.* New York: Hill and Wang, 1992.

Levine, Robert S. *Martin Delany, Frederick Douglass, and the Politics of Representative Identity.* Chapel Hill: University of North Carolina Press, 1997.

Levy, Barry. "Poor Children and the Labor Market in Colonial Massachusetts." *Pennsylvania History* 64 (Summer 1997): 287–307.

Litwack, Leon F. *North of Slavery: The Negro in the Free States, 1790–1860.* Chicago: University of Chicago Press, 1961.

Lott, Eric. *Love and Theft: Blackface Minstrelsy and the American Working Class.* New York: Oxford University Press, 1993.

Lynch, Hollis R., comp., *The Black Urban Condition: A Documentary History.* New York: Crowell, 1973.

Magdol, Edward. *The Antislavery Rank and File: A Social Profile of the Abolitionists' Constituency.* Westport, Conn.: Greenwood Press, 1986.

Malone, Dumas, ed. *Dictionary of American Biography.* 20 vols. New York: Charles Scribner's Sons, 1928–36.

Marti, Donald B. "Francis William Bird: A Radical's Progress through the Republican Party." *Historical Journal of Massachusetts* 11 (June 1983): 82–93.

Mayer, Henry. *All on Fire: William Lloyd Garrison and the Abolition of Slavery.* New York: St. Martin's Press., 1998.

McCormick, Richard L. *The Party Period and Public Policy: American Politics from the Age of Jackson to the Progressive Era.* New York: Oxford University Press, 1986.

McFeely, William S. *Frederick Douglass.* New York: Simon and Schuster, 1991.

McKay, Ernest A. "Henry Wilson and the Coalition of 1851." *New England Quarterly* 36 (September 1963): 338–57.

McManus, Michael J. *Political Abolitionism in Wisconsin, 1840–1861.* Kent, Ohio: Kent State University Press, 1998.

McNeill, George, ed. *The Labor Movement: The Problem of To-Day.* 1887. New York: Augustus Kelley, 1971.

McPherson, James M. *Battle Cry of Freedom: The Civil War.* New York: Oxford University Press, 1988.

Melish, Joanne Pope. *Disowning Slavery: Gradual Emancipation and "Race" in New England, 1780–1860.* Ithaca, N.Y.: Cornell University Press, 1998.

Merrill, Walter McIntosh. *Against Wind and Tide: A Biography of William Lloyd Garrison.* Cambridge: Harvard University Press, 1963.

Messer-Kruse, Timothy. *The Yankee International, 1848–1876: Marxism and the American Reform Tradition.* Chapel Hill, N.C.: University of North Carolina Press, 1998.

Micklethwait, John, and Adrian Wooldridge. *The Right Nation: Conservative Power in America.* New York: Penguin Press, 2004.

Montgomery, David. *Beyond Equality: Labor and the Radical Republicans, 1862–1872.* New York: Alfred A. Knopf, 1967.

———. *Citizen Worker: The Experience of Workers in the United States with Democracy and the Free Market during the Nineteenth Century.* New York: Cambridge University Press, 1993.

———. "Workers' Control of Machine Production in the Nineteenth Century." *Labor History* 17 (Fall 1976): 486–508.

Morgan, Edmund S. *American Slavery, American Freedom: The Ordeal of Colonial Virginia.* New York: W.W. Norton, 1975.

Morris, Richard B. *Government and Labor in Early America.* New York: Columbia University Press, 1946.

Morris, Thomas D. *Free Men All: The Personal Liberty Laws of the North, 1780–1861.* Baltimore: Johns Hopkins University Press, 1974.

Mulkern, John R. *The Know-Nothing Party in Massachusetts: The Rise and Fall of a People's Movement.* Boston: Northeastern University Press, 1990.

Murphy, Teresa Anne. *Ten Hours' Labor: Religion, Reform, and Gender in Early New England.* Ithaca, N.Y.: Cornell University Press, 1992.

Nash, Gary B. *Race and Revolution.* Madison, Wisc.: Madison House, 1990.

Nelson, William E. *Americanization of the Common Law: The Impact of Legal Change on Massachusetts Society, 1760–1830.* Cambridge: Harvard University Press, 1975.

Nissenbaum, Stephen W. "The Firing of Nathaniel Hawthorne." *Essex Institute Historical Collections* 114 (1978): 57–86.

———. "New England as a Region and Nation." In *All Over the Map: Rethinking American Regions,* edited by Edward L. Ayers, Patricia Nelson Limerick, Stephen Nissenbaum, and Peter S. Onuf, pp. 38–61. Baltimore: Johns Hopkins University Press, 1996.

O'Connor, Thomas H. *Lords of the Loom: The Cotton Whigs and the Coming of the Civil War.* New York: Charles Scribner's Sons, 1968.

Osofsky, Gilbert. "Abolitionists, Irish Nationalists, and the Dilemma of Romantic Nationalism." *American Historical Review* 80 (October 1975): 889–912.

Pease, Jane H., and William H. Pease. *The Fugitive Slave Law and Anthony Burns: A Problem in Law Enforcement.* Philadelphia: Lippincott, 1975.

———. "The Political Gadfly: Elizur Wright." In *Bound with Them in Chains: A Biographical History of the Antislavery Movement,* pp. 218–44. Westport, Conn.: Greenwood Press, 1972.

Perry, Lewis. *Radical Abolitionism: Anarchy and the Government of God in Antislavery Thought.* Ithaca, N.Y.: Cornell University Press, 1973.

Perry, Mark. *Lift Up Thy Voice: The Grimké Family's Journey from Slaveholders to Civil Rights Leaders.* New York: Viking, 2001.

Persons, Charles E. "The Early History of Factory Legislation in Massachusetts (from 1825 to the Passage of the Ten-Hour Law in 1874)." In *Labor Laws and Their Enforcement, with Special Reference to Massachusetts,* edited by Susan Kingsbury, pp. 3–129. 1911. New York: Arno Press, 1971.

Piersen, William D. *Black Yankees: The Development of an Afro-American Subculture in Eighteenth-Century New England.* Amherst: University of Massachusetts Press, 1988.

Prude, Jonathan. *The Coming of Industrial Order: Town and Factory Life in Rural Massachusetts, 1810–1860.* New York: Cambridge University Press, 1983.

Quarles, Benjamin. *Black Abolitionists.* New York: Oxford University Press, 1969.

Rael, Patrick. *Black Identity and Black Protest in the Antebellum North.* Chapel Hill: University of North Carolina Press, 2002.

Rawley, James A. *Race and Politics: "Bleeding Kansas" and the Coming of the Civil War.* Philadelphia: Lippincott, 1969.

Richards, Leonard L. *"Gentlemen of Property and Standing": Anti-Abolitionist Mobs in Jacksonian America.* New York: Oxford University Press, 1970.

———. *The Life and Times of Congressman John Quincy Adams.* New York: Oxford University Press, 1986.

———. *Shays's Rebellion. The American Revolution's Final Battle.* Philadelphia: University of Pennsylvania Press, 2002.

———. *The Slave Power: The Free North and Southern Domination, 1780–1860.* Baton Rouge: Louisiana State University Press, 2000.

Robboy, Stanley J., and Anita W. Robboy. "Lewis Hayden: From Fugitive Slave to Statesman." *New England Quarterly* 46 (December 1973): 591–613.

Roediger, David R. *Colored White: Transcending the Racial Past.* Berkeley and Los Angeles: University of California Press, 2002.

———. *The Wages of Whiteness: Race and the Making of the American Working Class.* 1991; New York: Verso, 1999.

———, and Philip S. Foner. *Our Own Time: A History of American Labor and the Working Day.* Westport, Conn.: Greenwood Press, 1989.

Rorabaugh, W. R. *The Alcoholic Republic, An American Tradition.* New York: Oxford University Press, 1979.

Rorty, Richard. *Achieving Our Country: Leftist Thought in Twentieth-Century America.* Cambridge: Harvard University Press, 1998.

Rosenthal, James M. "Free Soil in Berkshire County, 1781." *New England Quarterly* 10 (1937): 781–5.

Ruchames, Louis. "Jim Crow Railroads in Massachusetts." *American Quarterly* 8 (1956): 61–75.

———. "Race, Marriage and Abolition in Massachusetts." *Journal of Negro History* 40 (1955): 250–73.

Ryan, Mary. *Womanhood in America from Colonial Times to the Present.* New York: New Viewpoints, 1975.

Salvatore, Nick. *We All Got History. The Memory Books of Amos Webber.* New York: Times Books, 1996.

Saxton, Alexander. *The Rise and Fall of the White Republic: Class Politics and Mass Culture in Nineteenth-Century America.* New York: Verso, 1990.

Scranton, Philip. "Varieties of Paternalism: Industrial Structures and the Social Relations of Production in American Textiles." *American Quarterly* 26 (1984): 235–57.

Seelye, John D. *Memory's Nation: The Place of Plymouth Rock.* Chapel Hill: University of North Carolina Press, 1998.

Sernett, Milton C. *Abolition's Axe: Beriah Green, Oneida Institute, and the Black Freedom Struggle.* Syracuse, N.Y.: Syracuse University Press, 1986.

———. *North Star Country: Upstate New York and the Crusade for African American Freedom.* Syracuse, N.Y.: Syracuse University Press, 2002.

Sewell, Richard H. *Ballots for Freedom: Antislavery Politics in the United States, 1837–1860.* New York: Oxford University Press, 1976.

Shapiro, Herbert. "Labor and Antislavery: Reflections on the Literature." *Nature, Society, and Thought* 2 (1989): 471–90.

Shapiro, Samuel. "The Conservative Dilemma: The Massachusetts Constitutional Convention of 1853." *New England Quarterly* 33 (June 1960): 207–24.

Sheidley, Harlow W. *Sectional Nationalism: Massachusetts Conservative Leaders and the Transformation of America, 1815–1836.* Boston: Northeastern University Press, 1998.

Siracusa, Carl. *A Mechanical People: Perceptions of the Industrial Order in Massachusetts, 1815–1880.* Middletown, Conn.: Wesleyan University Press, 1979.

Smith, James Avery. *The History of the Black Population of Amherst, Massachusetts, 1728–1870.* Boston: New England Historic Genealogical Society, 1999.

Smith, Robert P. "William Cooper Nell: Crusading Abolitionist." *Journal of Negro History* 55 (1970): 182–99.

Sombart, Werner. *Why Is There No Socialism in the United States?* 1906. White Plains, N.Y.: International Arts and Sciences Press, 1976.

Stauffer, John. *The Black Hearts of Men: Racial Abolitionists and the Transformation of Race.* Cambridge: Harvard University Press, 2002.

Sterling, Dorothy. *The Making of an Afro-American: Martin Robison Delany, 1812–1885.* Garden City, N.Y.: Doubleday, 1996.

Stevens, Charles M. *Anthony Burns: A History.* Williamstown, Mass.: Corner House, 1973.

Stewart, James Brewer. *Holy Warriors: The Abolitionists and American Slavery.* New York: Hill and Wang, 1976.

———. *William Lloyd Garrison and the Challenge of Emancipation.* Arlington Heights, Ill.: H. Davidson, 1992.

Stilgoe, John R. *Common Landscapes of America, 1580–1845.* New Haven, Conn.: Yale University Press, 1982.

———. "Town Common and Village Green in New England, 1620–1981" In *On Common Ground: Caring for Shared Land from Town Common to Urban Park,* edited by Ronald L. Fleming and Lauri A. Halderman, pp. 7–36. Cambridge: Harvard University Press, 1982.

Story, Ronald D. *The Forging of an Aristocracy: Harvard and the Boston Upper Class, 1800–1870.* Middletown, Conn.: Wesleyan University Press, 1980.

Sweeney, Kevin. "Rum, Romanism, Representation, and Reform: Coalition Politics in Massachusetts, 1847–1853." *Civil War History* 6 (June 1976): 116–37.

Tager, Jack. *Boston Riots: Three Centuries of Social Violence.* Boston: Northeastern University Press, 2001.

Taylor, Anne-Marie. *Young Charles Sumner.* Amherst: University of Massachusetts Press, 2001.

Thomas, John L. *The Liberator: William Lloyd Garrison.* Boston: Little, Brown, 1963.

Thompson, Francis M. *History of Greenfield, Shire Town of Franklin County, Massachusetts.* 4 vols. Greenfield, Mass.: T. Morey and Son, 1904.

Twombly, R. C., and R. H. Moore. "Black Puritan: The Negro in Seventeenth-Century New England." *William and Mary Quarterly* 24 (1967): 224–42.

Tyrell, Ian. *Sobering Up: From Temperance to Prohibition in Antebellum America, 1800–1860.* Westport, Conn.: Greenwood Press, 1979.

Ullman, Victor R. *Martin R. Delany: The Beginnings of Black Nationalism.* Boston: Beacon Press, 1971.

Van Broekhoven, Debra B. *The Devotion of These Women: Rhode Island Women in the Antislavery Network.* Amherst: University of Massachusetts Press, 2002.

Vickers, Daniel. *Farmers and Fishermen: Two Centuries of Work in Essex County, Massachusetts, 1630–1850.* Chapel Hill: University of North Carolina Press, 1994.

Von Frank, Albert. *The Trials of Anthony Burns: Freedom and Slavery in Emerson's Boston.* Cambridge: Harvard University Press, 1998.

Voss-Hubbard, Mark. "The Amesbury-Salisbury Strike and the Social Origins of Political Nativism in Antebellum Massachusetts." *Journal of Social History* 29 (Spring 1996): 565–90.

———. *Beyond Party: Cultures of Antipartisanship in Northern Politics before the Civil War.* Baltimore: Johns Hopkins University Press, 2002.

———. "Slavery, Capitalism, and the Middling Sorts: The Rank and File of Political Abolitionism." *American Nineteenth Century History* 4 (Summer 2003): 53–76.

Yellin, Jean Fagan, and John Van Horne, eds. *The Abolitionist Sisterhood: Women's Political Culture in Antebellum America.* Ithaca, N.Y.: Cornell University Press. 1994.

Walters, Ronald. *The Antislavery Appeal: American Abolitionism after 1830.* Baltimore: Johns Hopkins University Press, 1976.

Ware, Caroline F. *The Early New England Cotton Textile Manufacture: A Study of Industrial Beginnings.* Boston: Houghton Mifflin, 1931.

Ware, Norman B. *The Industrial Worker, 1840–1860: The Reaction of American Industrial Society to the Advance of the Industrial Revolution.* 1924. New York: Quadrangle, 1964.

Watson, Harry. *Jacksonian Politics and Community Conflict: The Emergence of the Second Party System in Cumberland County, North Carolina.* Baton Rouge: Louisiana State University Press, 1981.

Wellman, Judith. *The Road to Seneca Falls: Elizabeth Cady Stanton and the First Women's Rights Convention.* Urbana: University of Illinois Press, 2004.

Wilson, R. Jackson. *Figures of Speech: The Literary Marketplace, From Benjamin Franklin to Emily Dickinson.* New York: Alfral A. Knopf, 1989.

Wood, Betty. *The Origins of American Slavery: Freedom and Bondage in the English Colonies.* New York: Hill and Wang, 1998.

Wood, Joseph. *New England Village.* Baltimore: Johns Hopkins University Press, 1997.

Wright, Philip G, and Elizabeth Q. Wright. *Elizur Wright: The Father of Life Insurance.* Chicago: University of Chicago Press, 1937.

Zaeske, Susan. *Signatures of Citizenship: Petitioning, Antislavery, and Women's Political Identity.* Chapel Hill: University of North Carolina Press, 2003.

Zonderman, David. *Aspirations and Anxieties: New England Workers and the Mechanized Factory System, 1815–1850.* New York: Oxford University Press, 1992.

Unpublished Works

Barker, Andrew. "Chauncey Langdon Knapp and Political Abolitionism in Vermont, 1833–1841." Seminar paper, University of Massachusetts Amherst, 1999.

Bean, William G. "Party Transformation in Massachusetts with Special Reference to the Antecedents of Republicanism, 1848–1860." Ph.D. diss., Harvard University, 1922.

Chasan, Joshua S. "Civilizing Worcester: The Creation of an Institutional and Cultural Order: Worcester, Massachusetts, 1848–1876." Ph.D. diss., University of Pittsburgh, 1976.

Crim, Patrick. "'The Ballot Boxes Are Our Arms!': The Latimer Fugitive Slave Case and the Liberty Party in Massachusetts." Seminar paper, University of Massachusetts Amherst, 1999.

Dubow, Sara. "'Not a Virtuous Woman Among Them': Political Culture, Antislavery Politics, and the Repeal of the Marriage Ban in Ante-Bellum Massachusetts." Seminar paper, University of Massachusetts Amherst, 1995.

Etienne, Germaine. "Excellence Is the Highest Form of Resistance: African American Reformers in the Antebellum North." Ph.D. diss., University of Massachusetts Amherst, 2004.

Fuhrer, Mary. "'We all have something to do in the cause of freeing the slave': The Abolition Work of Mary White." Paper prepared for the Dublin Seminar, Deerfield, Mass., June 15–17, 2001.

Gaffney, Paul. "Coloring Utopia: The African-American Presence in the Northampton Association of Education and Industry." Manuscript in possession of the author, n.d.

Koprowski, Dan. "The Roberts Case: Roberts Morris, Charles Sumner, and School Desegregation Efforts in Antebellum Boston." Seminar paper, University of Massachusetts Amherst, 1999.

Kornblith, Gary J. "From Artisans to Businessmen: Master Mechanics in New England, 1790–1850." Ph.D. diss., Princeton University, 1983.

Laytin, Alexander. "Racial Underpinnings of the Coalition Government in the General Court of Massachusetts in 1853." Senior honors thesis, University of Massachusetts Amherst, 2002.

Omori, Kazuteru. "Burden of Blackness: Quest of 'Equality' among Black 'Elites' in Late Nineteenth-Century Boston." Ph.D. diss., University of Massachusetts Amherst, 2001.

Rice, Arthur Henry. "Henry Brewster Stanton as a Political Abolitionist." M.A. thesis, Columbia Teachers College, 1968.

Santow, Mark. "These Little Republican Temples: Race, Ethnicity and Public Schooling in Antebellum Massachusetts." Seminar paper, University of Massachusetts Amherst, 1992.

Tull, Bruce. "Springfield Armory as Industrial Policy: Interchangeable Parts and the Precision Corridor." Ph.D. diss., University of Massachusetts Amherst, 2001.

Wergland, Glendyne R. "Women, Men, Property, and Inheritance: Gendered Testamentary Customs in Western Massachusetts, 1800–1860." Ph.D. diss., University of Massachusetts Amherst, 2001.

Whitcomb, Patric. "'A Party of Principle': The Northampton Liberty Party and Antislavery Politics." Seminar paper, University of Massachusetts Amherst, 1999.

Index